Rebel Spirit

Evidence for the continuity of consciousness

By Ian C Baillie, Ph.D.

UPSO

Cover design by Dr Ian C Baillie

A catalogue record of this book is available from the British Library

ISBN: 1-84375-000-7

To order additional copies of this book and visit Ian Baillie's home page please visit: http://www.upso.co.uk/ianbaillie

Published in the UK by:
UPSO (Universal Publishing Solutions Online) Ltd
5 Stirling Road, Castleham Business Park,
St Leonards-on-Sea, East Sussex TN38 9NW United Kingdom
Tel: 01424 853349 Fax: 01424 854084
Email: info@upso.co.uk http://www.upso.co.uk

Dedication

For my daughter Harriet

And in Memory of
Margery Baillie Kell, 'Lil' May' 1867 to 1873

Rebel Spirit

Contents

Part Three: Baillie Returns

Acknowledgements

I would like to thank the many people who have made this project come to fruition, not least my dear long suffering wife Pauline and daughter Harriet. They have had to live with this *forever* and yet they have managed to maintain a sense of humor through out. It is not easy living with a husband and father who is so single minded in the pursuit of knowledge and understanding and I publicly salute my two angels for putting up with me. Next I would like to thank Rosie Lagrue, nee Rose-Mary O'Sullivan, without whom I would still be struggling in the dark as to the real nub of Baillie's problem. She has selflessly given of her valuable time and effort in bringing about the complete accessing of my subconscious memories. Apart from her crucial role as principle witness to the experiment, she has generously contributed part two as a testimony. She has also spent many long hours in editing and proof reading the final draft, managing some how to keep Baillie on the straight and narrow! Incredibly we were to discover quite dramatically, that this is also very much her story, as she has the subconscious memory of Mary Sullivan, Baillie's fiancée from 1870.

The next in line of fire completing the trio of time travelers in this tale, is Dr Norman C Delaney of Corpus Christi, Texas. I owe Norman everything for he found the picture of Baillie and there would be no story at all except for that priceless find. I may now rest easy for the remainder of my days here in the Matrix, because of that one act. Amazingly Norman was to find himself also in the story. For in meeting and shaking hands with him on January 24, 2001, *the Matrix was squared.* Baillie was emotionally reunited with his *soul* brother and the past was healed for all time.

With regard to uncovering the physical details of Baillie's past I would like to thank especially, Ashley Pollette and Tommy Houston for being fountains of knowledge and guardians of the sacred archive. Without their special knowledge and web expertise I would not have been able to piece together so quickly the story of the 5th Georgia Volunteer Cavalry, CSA. For sheer academic rigor I would like to thank Buddy Sullivan, Darien historian *par excellence,* Director of the Sapelo Island National Estuarine Research Reserve and custodian of the mystic isle with its haunting lighthouse. Buddy's book *Early Days on the Georgia Tidewater* proved to be an invaluable source for corroborating my memories and I shall be forever indebted to him. I would also like to thank Ann Davis of Darien for helping in my first days of contact with *home* and for the wonderfully moving exchange of information that took place on this last visit in February 2001, a very special moment. Next is Ian Lekus of the Rare Book, Manuscript, & Special Collections Library, Duke University, Durham, North Carolina - thank you for persevering and sending copies of all the documents asked for in the Kell Papers collection. Also thanks to Myers Brown and Linda Bitley of the Atlanta History Center for their generous help in providing extensive details of the 5th Georgia flag held in the museum.

With regard to our recent research trip I would like to thank Alice and Andrew Blake for discovering Baillie's grave and Rocky Knoll. Also for their love of history, knowledge and generous welcome in making both Roger Lewis and myself at home in Griffin. A special thanks to Sherry K Husak, Superintendent and Carol D Bishop, Administrative Secretary of Oak Hill Cemetery, Griffin, Georgia for helping to gain Baillie a new veteran's headstone, paid for by the Federal Government no less! Also Alice Pounds, President of the James S Boynton Chapter 222, United Daughters of the Confederacy and her husband Ronnie Pounds, of the John McIntosh Kell Camp #107, Sons of Confederate Veterans, for sponsoring and dedicating with fellow members the new headstone. Also Bill Lindsey, his lovely wife Susan and the good folks of Barnesville, Georgia for entering into the spirit of the trip and providing the cannon shoot, a fitting way for Baillie to celebrate being back in Georgia. Thanks to Maggie and Rodney Page for allowing us to use their grounds and for the *stainless banner.* The ambience and sheer elegance was supplied by our hosts Fred and Terry Crane at the Historic Tarleton Oaks Bed and Breakfast, Barnesville for the unforgettable experience of a lifetime; *Gateway to a bygone era…where Southern hospitality is not gone with the wind!* Everette Moriarty for discovering the second photograph of Baillie at Fort King George. And not forgetting Brigadier Truman Boyle of the Georgia State Patrol for his warmth of friendship and kindness.

Finally on this side of the pond I would like to say a very big thank you to my dear friend and colleague Linda Forster, who kindly used her expertise to type up the original manuscript from my verbal notes. Jak P Malmand Showell, my close friend, fellow author, scientist and world authority on German U-Boats - for showing me the way forward in getting published. David Pearman founder and CEO of Universal Publishing Solutions Online, for his enthusiasm and dynamism in bringing this work to print. Also a special thank you to my long-term fellow modeling enthusiast, mentor and co-conspirator in toy soldiering, Major (retired) Roger C H Lewis. Roger kindly acted as photographer and kindred spirit on our recent field trip, January-February 2001. But his influence, enthusiasm for things military and invaluable friendship go way back to my early days at Dover College Preparatory School, Folkestone, Kent; where my research into all this began in earnest. I would also like to thank Maria @ Barnyard Stables, Mystole near Canterbury, for the loan of *Claudia*. Finally and in no way least, Lee Prescott and Jackie Pierce of Warhorse Trading Post, Dover, Kent for supplying such superbly accurate uniforms and equipment. Telephone: +44 (0)1304 823341

Foreword
By Dr Norman C Delaney

When Ian Baillie first contacted me through the Internet, little did I realize the bizarre consequences that would follow. Dr. Baillie is a teacher and a scientist who has an ability to perceive dimensions that most of us are unable to do. He has painstakingly researched the life of a long dead Confederate soldier and in essence has brought him back to *life*. The result is this remarkable book. Dr. Baillie asks only that the reader remain open minded to the possibility of the transference of subconscious memory from one individual to another physical person in another time. If this seems incredible let Dr. Baillie the scientist take you on a compelling journey into both the past and the present. As for myself, I am delighted to be a part of this amazing story.

After our correspondence began, I was able to furnish Dr. Baillie with information from my own research more than thirty years back. During the period 1964 to 1966, I had hand copied a great deal of the correspondence of the Kell family of McIntosh County, Georgia while working on my doctoral dissertation at Duke University in North Carolina. It turned out that I had an abundance of material I never used, but had filed away until contacted by Dr. Baillie. Was it a coincidence that eventually brought us in contact? There are times when I wonder.

My own background is historic New England, Lynn, Massachusetts, where I lived during my early years. Even as a boy I was intrigued with history and was amazed to learn about the events that had taken place in the very area where I lived. History became even more personal when I learned that my great-grandfather had served two enlistments as a Yankee soldier during the Civil War. Although only a private who never fought in any of the great Civil War battles, Lowell Mason became my introduction to the *Tragic Era of American history.* In addition to the pictures I had of him in uniform, I also obtained his enlistment papers and even his U.S. army issued Springfield muzzle-loader. While still in high school, I began collecting Civil War artifacts, which at that time could be obtained at a very low price. At a Marblehead antique shop I purchased two Civil War swords for $5 each, one a decorative staff officer's sword and the other an 1840 model cavalry saber, the so-called 'wrist-breaker'. During the same period, I became a member of the Lynn chapter of the Sons of Union Veterans, the only youth in a group of elderly men, one of whom had served in the Spanish-American War! At our monthly meetings it was awesome to realize that Lowell Mason had once attended his Grand Army of the Republic meetings in the very same hall on Andrew Street and that his picture was included among the scores of other members lining the walls.

After graduating from high school, I spent four years at nearby Salem Teachers College, determined to become a history teacher. But it wasn't until Graduate School at Boston University that I was finally able to take specialized courses in Civil War history. With my MA degree I was able to teach history at the college level, but I looked forward to the time when I could continue studies for a Ph.D. in history. Although BU and other northern universities remained an option, I finally selected Duke University, in Durham, North Carolina. How would the *Civil War* or rather, the *War Between the States,* be taught in the South? It seemed appropriate that I spend the next few years in the South.

By 1964, following two years in India in the Peace Corps, I was once again at Duke, completing most of the required course work. I had not yet selected a dissertation topic, and time was running out. My advisor, Dr. Robert H Woody, who years earlier had produced a major work on *Reconstruction in South Carolina,* was now in his 60's and looking forward to his retirement. He was no longer accepting new students to work with as dissertation advisor. Dr. Woody's initial suggestion for a topic was the South Carolinian writer William Gilmore Simms. But after a half-hearted attempt to get interested in the man, I confessed to Dr. Woody that I would prefer another subject or personality. To my surprise, my advisor suddenly produced a note pad, glanced over it, and responded. 'Delaney, are you familiar with the ALABAMA? Its captain was Raphael Semmes, and John McIntosh Kell was his executive officer. Would you be interested in writing about Kell? We have his papers here at Duke.' To me those were magic words.

YES! I was definitely interested! Later I learned that after Duke had acquired the Kell Papers Dr. Woody had him self considered writing a biography. But with retirement near, he was having second thoughts and was willing to pass along the project to someone else. And there I was. The timing couldn't have been better!

During the following months I became thoroughly immersed in Kell family correspondence. There were so many people to become acquainted with besides Kell himself; his wife Blanche; his widowed mother, Margery, who had to manage a large plantation following the sudden death of her husband; other Kell children: three daughters and a younger brother, Alexander Baillie Kell. The correspondence was so extensive that it covered many decades before, during, and after the war. I was impressed that indeed the Kells were a remarkable family. Central to my study, of course, was John, who served as an officer in the U.S. Navy for twenty years. After the secession of Georgia, he resigned his commission and served his state as a commander before being called upon to serve under Raphael Semmes as executive officer of the commerce raiders *SUMTER* and *ALABAMA.* In order to prepare myself, there was a great deal that I had to learn about the Old Navy. Herman Melville's *WHITE JACKET,* based on the author's own experience aboard a warship was a good starting point, after which came ship's logs and sailor reminiscences. At the same time, for weeks on end I hand copied from family letters and journals, eventually travelling to Georgia for additional research and meetings with two Kell grandchildren whom had additional material that I needed. My dissertation was complete by 1967, the year I received my Ph.D. and later expanded into a book, *JOHN McINTOSH KELL OF THE RAIDER ALABAMA* (University of Alabama Press, 1973).

But, enough said from where I am sitting. What has all of this got to do with an English gentleman who made contact with me only recently in connection with a Kell family member? It is time for Ian Baillie to introduce himself, explain the intricate coincidences of the *Matrix* that is our World and the mystery behind Baillie's memories.

Dr. Norman C. Delaney
Del Mar College, Corpus Christi, Texas.

Part One:

Accessing the Past

Introduction

On World Book Day, March 25, 1999 in a Folkestone bookshop, situated on the South coast of England, I discovered the photograph of a long dead Confederate soldier. The book coincidentally opened at the precise page, the name coincidentally was my name and the face coincidentally was my face, it was all far too much of a coincidence, to be a coincidence!

Gazing into the looking glass of time I spied a familiar reflection, for I recognized the person in the picture. Incredibly he appeared to be me, me as I was 138 years ago in another time and another place. Then over the next two years with research and the use of emotional memory painting, the whole story unfolded in vivid emotional Technicolor. I had always felt that I did not belong in this time or place, a common feeling that many of us often have. This confusion of identity had reigned supreme in my life for forty-four years, but now all that had changed.

With the discovery of the photograph and its associated story nothing in my life would ever be the same again. Suddenly all became clear, I had been right all along, my feelings and emotions had not betrayed me. I realized then, that this odyssey of understanding had begun some thirty-five years ago, when in the playground as a small ten year-old I spied something familiar; the bright pristine images of a long forgotten war that had happened a century ago.

The year was 1964 and the conflict of a hundred years previous was that of the American Civil War. Coincidentally it was exactly 100 years to the day that a Private soldier named Alexander Baillie Kell, was fighting desperately in the ranks of the 5th Georgia Cavalry, as the epic *Battle for Atlanta* was about to reach its horrifying summer climax. The *Civil War* was to redefine the destiny of America and with it shape the major events of World history up until the present day. For we are still living with the reverberating aftershocks of the emotional trauma of that titanic conflagration. Little was I to know then that I myself might be one of those reverberating aftershocks, fall out from the bloodiest war in American history.

The craze that summer of 1964 in the playground was for commemorative centennial bubble gum cards and Confederate money, issued by a company called simply ABC. The bright red three-penny waxed packets held the promise of two or three cards, some Confederate dollar bills and a flat stick of pink sweet scented bubble gum. Most of my contemporaries avidly collected and traded the money, but for me though, it was the cards that were important, those terrible bloody images held a haunting fascination as if rekindling a long lost forgotten memory that dwelt deep in my psyche.

In mute testament to their power I still have those precious icons, all these years later. All in all I collected two and a half sets of the eighty-eight cards. I read and re-read the *Civil War News* on the back of the cards. All the names, events and characters seemed some how very familiar. As 1964 came to a close, interest waned with my contemporaries and I scooped up the surplus dollar bills, often simply swapping them for sweets. I studied and learned the details of the war, the place names, battles and Generals with their many victories and gory defeats.

My attention had been captured, I had gathered my familiar and I had unknowingly found the key to my inner being. Spurred on by a hitherto unknown fervor I hurriedly began saving my pocket money and rushed headlong to the shops each saturday. I bought up little boxes of plastic soldiers, with which to recreate the scenes of long lost carnage. Sundays were spent in the front room playing with my new acquisitions. Old battles where re-contested with vigor and elan, old scores were settled and history re-written. I had discovered the art of War games.

The armies got bigger and the soldiers increased from 20 millimeter to the larger more gratifying 54-millimeter scale, but this was still not enough. War gaming as a lone pursuit was interesting, but far from satisfying, I needed a compatriot in arms. A friend was found, a one Dave Pilcher, a tall lanky red headed lad that looked in lean build every inch a Confederate veteran. He introduced me to the Confederate High Command a newly formed re-enactment group. This was an astonishing discovery, I had found that there were others like me! I was not alone in my passionate feelings for this historical conflict. So at the tender age of twelve I proudly enlisted in the 43rd Battalion Virginia

Cavalry, Mosby's Rangers - the legendary *Gray Ghosts*. Yet coincidentally it was the Confederate cavalry, absolutely perfect! For me it had to be the cavalry, the yellow facings, the gray uniforms and the horses; specifically nothing else would do.

Sergeant Major John Cullis, 43rd Battalion Virginia Cavalry, CSA: John became my guide and mentor as I entered the world of re-enacting at 12 years of age.

Many letters were written, figures painted and artifacts gathered. The collection grew and grew taking over my whole room as it became more than just another hobby. Barry Chalkley, a guy that I knew just from a photo, was the Commander of the romantically titled, *Virginia*

Brigade, made up of the 1st Virginia Cavalry, 43rd Battalion Virginia Cavalry and the Stuart Horse Artillery. And the Sergeant Major of the 43rd was a young solicitor I befriended by the name of John Cullis. I even persuaded my somewhat bemused mother and father to allow him to visit on several occasions. I was in awe of John as he donned his uniform, correct in every detail. The boots were hand made and designed from a pair worn by General George Armstrong Custer from an old photograph. Pride of place however went to his flag, the Confederate *Southern Cross*; it had cost the princely sum of £24, which was an absolute fortune in those days! But I thought it was worth every penny as I saw it fluttering gaily in the breeze. I was so impressed that despite not being able to sew I set about making my own copy of it much to my father's amazement. Fortunately for posterity John left a permanent record of the events for archival evidence, as he owned an expensive color Polaroid camera.

One sunny day 1968, at an Easter Civil War camp in *Dargets Wood,* Chatham, North Kent, I donned his uniform over my home dyed sky blue trousers, and posed for a memorable prophetic picture. A picture that I shall forever treasure during this lifetime: Baillie the Confederate cavalryman breathed again! The smell of the campfire, the sleeping in the open, the camaraderie all seemed so familiar. I went home intoxicated by the experience and started to make my own uniforms and equipment.

With little money I enlisted the help of my school friends and together we tramped the woodlands of Kent, building fortified camps, especially in the area known as Blean woods just north of Canterbury. After a year I managed to persuade my colleagues to help make a Civil War film. For this I built a full size working field gun. I had already completed a working musket, which actually fired, but the cannon would be even more spectacular in the film. It was in my back garden at this time, that I commissioned my Canadian friend Gordon Whyte, as a 2nd Lieutenant in the Confederate Cavalry. Once again all captured on photographs taken at the time, thank goodness. He was the most enthusiastic of my friends and was about to leave for boarding school in Hastings. I wanted him to carry a permanent reminder of our adventures and so I wrote out the commission in cursive script, signed it and then sealed it with bright red sealing wax. The commission was then presented in a formal ceremony; I played the part of the Colonel commanding the regiment and Gordon, became in essence Alexander

Baillie Kell. At the time I had no conscious knowledge that I had just re-enacted and corrected the most crucial single event of Baillie's tragic past. The commission was everything to him and if it had come to pass, all would have been so very different.

Baillie 1968: The Confederate Cavalry live again!

When finally completed the cannon was test fired using a weed killer mixture. Most gratifyingly the barrel belched forth a ten foot long yellow flame towards the unsuspecting neighbors, for some considerable time! In later years my father confided that this moment, was one of his most vivid and favorite memories of me. Whilst reading the paper after a hard morning at work, the whole of the lounge lit up bright yellow. Springing to his feet he looked out of the window to see the cannon in action with his son proudly looking on.

The mixture played a large part in my life, as I diversified into rocketry for my school science project. The space race of the 60's had fired the imagination of the planet's youth and I was an ardent practicing disciple of the technology. It was also at about this time that I found quite by chance that I had a natural affinity for horses. Specifically that I knew exactly how to ride, without ever having had a single lesson. By comparison later, my motorbike although fun seemed cold, tame and soul less compared to the mystic bond between a horse and its rider.

Gradually all these childhood antics faded from memory as *normal* life took over. I graduated, married and became a teacher of Science. Later I gained promotion, had a near brush with death and became deeply interested in Physics. Yet all the while the Confederate cavalryman within hovered, waiting silently in the background, until the glorious moment I stepped into Waterstone's Bookshop, Folkestone, coincidentally on *World Book Day.* My ten year old daughter Harriet was absorbed in looking for an Agatha Christie novel, when somehow in a moment of serendipity I was attracted to a book containing Civil War photographs, *Private Soldiers and Public Heroes.* With an air of casual apprehension I opened the book; there to my incredulous amazement was the name *Baillie.*

I had spent thirty-five years vainly looking in hope of finding some small connection or link to do with my name and the *Civil War.* Yet here was also a photograph! Strangely I had always had a reoccurring premonition that I might one day find myself in an old Civil War photograph, now it had actually come true. But this was far beyond my expectations, a single full-face portrait and a biography. Being prudent and entirely out of character, I shut the book and left the shop not wishing to purchase a whole book for just one photograph. Over the next few days the creeping realization that this was more than just a coincidence drew me back to the shop. I finally purchased the book and then on closer inspection realized just how exactly the physical features of *Baillie* looked like my own, an exact mirror image. It was astonishing, it felt electrifying, as if I had just won the lottery several times over; the chances of finding the photo were incalculable. Yet it was real! I hurried home and not knowing how to break the news to my wife Pauline, I nonchalantly commented whilst watching the six o'clock news, 'Oh by the way, have you seen this?'

My normally dear ever-skeptical wife upon viewing the image exclaimed instantly, 'That's you! Do you think that it is you?'

'No, I'm not really sure?' I replied in a faltering voice, not wishing to upset her. Then as I read and re-read the brief personal history of *Baillie* penned by the article's author Dr Norman C Delaney, I realized that it was a concise outline description of my own personality, character and interests. In a combined moment of euphoric revelation I was acutely aware that all my formulated theories, models and ideas as to how the Universe was constructed had just become very close up and personal.

With that realization the penny finally dropped, I gazed at the face with its mirror like reflection a positive reversal and I welcomed home *Baillie*. The research on my *other* self continued, increased in magnitude and depth, culminating in the triumphal accessing of my subconscious memory through the interaction with a dear colleague and the production of many artworks based on what I now term, *subconscious emotional painting*. Reunited with my past I have accepted the joyous fact that his history is my history and that his life defines my life. As you will soon discover in this epic work, Baillie's life, personality and emotional experiences have subconsciously shaped my entire existence, defining in detail exactly who and what I am.

This book is the product of the search for my inner-self and the understanding of my place in the Universe. It is a unique record of the journey of two lifetimes, which shows that our greatest human anxiety, physical mortality, no longer needs to be feared. It conclusively demonstrates that our journey continues, for it may be argued that if our memories survive then so in essence do we.

It is the purpose of this book therefore to illustrate that we all continue to evolve and progress. For our core being does not dissipate on death. Our character, personality and emotional memory remain intact to continue another earthly journey. Many faiths embrace this idea, but often lack the all-important scientific evidence. I have found that evidence. I am *the* case study and this work, will I hope lead to a do-it-yourself planetary revolution in thought, that for many is long over due.

We stand poised on the brink of a new era of understanding, a revolution of the mind, the discovery of who and what we are. The time is now and the paradigms of dogma are evaporating in the daylight of a new reality. And so I present to you my *magnum opus*: Rebel Spirit...evidence for the continuity of consciousness.

This scientific discovery with its associated emotional story is a complete record of one of the most important experiments ever undertaken.

Dr Ian C Baillie June 4, 2001
Hythe, Kent.
Coincidentally my 47th birthday!

Chapter One
Baillie

'We have shared the incommunicable experience of war. We have felt; we still feel the passion of life to its top. In our youths our hearts were touched with fire.'

Oliver Wendell Holmes

In order to fully understand the complex synchronicity of events that has paralleled my life with that of Baillie's life it will be an advantage to familiarize ourselves with the life and times of Alexander Baillie Kell, known by all simply as *Baillie.*

He was born February 23, 1828 at Laurel Grove, Darien, Georgia. Baillie was the youngest of the six Kell children. His father John Kell, 1784 to 1827, had died on November 10, 1827, just after his conception, so Baillie never knew him. His Mother Margery Spalding Baillie, 1794 to 1870 and his older sisters brought him up at the family home. The six Kell children were as follows:

Mary Jane, born March 12, 1817 to May 11, 1891. Never married.
Sarah Spalding, born September 22, 1818. Died December 15, 1819.
Evelyn West, born August 17, 1820 to August 17, 1891. Married Charles Spalding, January 17, 1808 to February 4, 1887, of Sapelo Island.
John McIntosh, born January 26, 1823 to October 5, 1900. United States Navy Commander and Confederate naval hero married, Julia Blanche Munroe, January 31, 1836 to June 14, 1917.
Hester Margery, born August 14, 1825 to July 7, 1898. Never married.
Alexander Baillie, born February 23, 1828 to September 30, 1912.

John Kell had previously been married to a Barbara McIver in

1808, but she died three years later and there were no children from this union. In 1816 he married Margery Spalding Baillie, daughter of Alexander and Hester Jane *McIntosh* Baillie. John Kell was a successful lawyer and rose to be a Superior Court Judge. He founded and purchased Laurel Grove plantation as the family home in Darien, McIntosh County.

Women surrounded Baillie from the outset; but with his brother the two young boys would have had many Mark Twain adventures among the reeds and sea-islands of the Georgia coast in the halcyon days of youth. News of the Alamo in 1836 would have stirred the latent Scottish values of freedom, honor and duty within the two boys' hearts as William Barrett Travis' immortal words echoed around the world. Yet all too soon his older brother John had left to be a midshipman aboard a navy vessel. He had escaped the petticoat regime of antebellum plantation life by pursuing a successful career with the United States Navy. John became a Naval Lieutenant in his own right and gained some recognition by sailing with Commodore Perry to Japan in 1853. The sea ever present at Darien ran strong in the blood of the Kells and John, his Mother's favorite son, followed his maritime instincts to the full.

Baillie, being the youngest, was brought up in a more polite, sensitive, caring environment and became well educated, attending Princeton, then the College of New Jersey, 1848 to 1851 and the Kentucky Military Institute, 1851 to 1852. This was paid for by his brother John, who was determined that Baillie should have the very best education he could provide. At the time, Baillie did not know that his brother had funded his education, as he was kept unawares by his proud mother and other family members. At Princeton Baillie embarked in 1848 on a three year Civil Engineering course. He enjoyed the student high life to the full and was indeed suspended for, 'throwing fireballs in the entry to North College, October 22, 1849.'

He joined the Clio debating fraternity and engaged in the many diverse activities on offer, it appears that he was not as serious or studious as his elder brother was, neither did he have his responsibilities as eldest son. His room-mate at Princeton is recorded as being a one E B Showell. It is possible that he played football for Clio as Princeton records show that inter-fraternity football was in progress during these years. As Princeton did not offer a degree in Civil Engineering until 1888, Baillie had to complete his degree studies else where, and ended up at the Kentucky Military Institute. The syllabus was demanding and included, Mathematics, Natural Sciences, Modern and Ancient Languages among many other subjects. Baillie graduated with a Bachelor of Arts in 1852, fifth in his class of eight, finding the intense mathematics difficult and not the pursuit of a gentleman. He was now an accomplished young man of twenty-four and documents described him as a, 'high toned honorable gentleman.' He returned to the family estate and took over the running of the plantation from his hard-pressed mother. The Kell's owned eighty Negro slaves at Laurel Grove, planted rice, sea-island variety cotton and corn. The estate was never large or economic and the Negroes were treated more as an extended family. They often took advantage of Baillie's good nature, for they were his childhood friends and Baillie was not a harsh taskmaster.

After the demise of their father in 1851, the two sons of Thomas Spalding of Sapelo, Charles and Randolph began to throw high society balls and other diverse *entertainments* at the Big House, South End, Sapelo Island. Randolph in particular liked to party in the grand style, with Charles his elder more staid brother being ever the more cautious soul, yet both had cut free with from the rigor of their father's rigid puritanical regime. Randolph converted the big house into a palace of splendor and delight; filled with every form of sophistication that civilization could offer. Boat and horse racing were favorite past-times of the Southern elite and races were held often and for large wagers. It was here that Baillie fraternized with free spirited and exotic characters such as William Brailsford. For he had wandered into a magical world of antebellum decadence, which he quickly learned to enjoy to full. Fortuitously his eldest sister Evelyn West Kell had married Charles Spalding and therefore he was naturally invited as family, to attend, despite not having the monetary means of his wealthy peers. So Baillie as a member of polite society with his two unmarried sisters, Mary and Hettie in tow, accompanied by their chaperone and revered mother, were frequent guests to the island festivities.

Travel was by boat and the expectant party would navigate from Kell Landing adjacent the plantation, down the creek past Fort King George and into the mainstream of the mighty Altamaha River. From there they would sail across Doboy sound, towards the distinctive landmark of Sapelo lighthouse, ever blinking in the distance. Baillie at the tiller and the plantation Negroes rowing strongly at the oars, once into the Sound the sail could be unfurled and a favorable wind might waft the party towards the shores of Sapelo, the enchanted isle. Upon nearing, the party would enter the creek leading to the landing at the big house. There to be greeted by servants bearing lighted torches dressed in full regalia, music laughter and revelry tinkling through the air from the open doors of the Big House; this was the majestic civilization of the Old South at its epoch.

It was here and in this atmosphere that Baillie first set eyes on the Princess of Sapelo, Sarah Elizabeth Spalding, 1844 to 1916, oldest and only daughter of Randolph and Mary Bass Spalding. By 1859 *Sallie* as she was known, grew to be every man's dream, blonde, petite, aristocratic, artistic and intelligent; the jewel in the Spalding crown. As she became of age Baillie fell completely and hopelessly in love with her. She was a frequent visitor to the Grove and a constant companion of Baillie's favorite sister Hettie who taught the gentle arts. They loved to paint and draw, play music and engage in girlish pleasures. Baillie attended on them and in time Sallie and Baillie came to have feelings for each other.

Baillie was determined to be his own man and strike out away from the family home to demonstrate that he could support and look after *his princess* in the manner to which she had been accustomed. It was with this in mind that Baillie persuaded his brother and mother to purchase another plantation:

'Baillie ever enthusiastic attempted to build on the family fortune and purchased more land to develop at Rushlands, just to the North of Darien alongside the old Savannah stage road near present day Eulonia. In 1859 his brother John back from the sea found him optimistic over the first crop of sea-island cotton on the new land.' *Taken from John McIntosh Kell of the Raider Alabama by Norman C Delaney.*

This euphoria did not last however, as the specter of secession loomed black on the horizon. Major national events now unfurled and the two lovers were cast upon a turbulent and stormy sea.

Election fever swept the land in 1860 and the South knew that if Abraham Lincoln, the backwoods lawyer from Illinois, was elected they would consider secession from the Union a possibility, as the time for compromise was drawing to a close. Yet in truth they had only to modify their stance by changing to a wage economy in order to avert war on the slavery issue. Despite two thirds of all Southerners not owning slaves, the issue became entrenched as one of maintaining the wealth and opulent life style of an agrarian way of life. For the great plantation family's wealth was bound up inextricably in their work force. States rights became the Southern watchword and with the Nation a divided military camp, the dam had to burst. Just as luck would have it, at the exact time that Baillie's own secret plans for marriage to Sarah Elizabeth *Sallie* Spalding were coming to fruition.

Caught up in the jingoistic military fervor of early 1861, Baillie a land owning gentleman and therefore a natural horseman joined the local McIntosh Light Dragoons, as a 3rd Lieutenant. In a somewhat cavalier and picnic air, the atmosphere increased in tension. Gallant home spun uniforms and high manners were the order of the day as the dashing troops reviewed in front of the town ladies. Those ladies most certainly included the beautiful blonde seventeen year old, Sarah Elizabeth Spalding.

Alexander Baillie Kell 1861: A very special portrait of a confident young man trying to win the favors of his lady. Baillie aged 33 at the time was at the height of his wealth and power. He commissioned this portrait for Sarah Elizabeth Spalding, the object of his undying affections, so that she might remember him whilst he was away.

It was at this time that Baillie sat for the portrait that we see today, proudly displaying his 3rd Lieutenant's Officers bars denoting his class and status for his young lady. Upon studying the eyes and face one can perceive his hopeless devotion and undying love for the object of his affections; the photograph was without doubt especially commissioned for none other than Sarah Elizabeth *Sallie* Spalding, the Princess of Sapelo. It was also in Baillie's mind a very practical gesture, for it would help young *Sallie* to remember her *beau sabeur,* whilst he was away discharging his duty, lest she forget him in the testing time that was to come.

The test came soon enough, the Yankees set too with a will to blockade the Southern coast, thereby putting Darien and the Georgia tidewater squarely in the front line. The vigilant local cavalry militia patrolled the coast and skirmished against the ever-increasing tide of naval raiding parties. After his initial six month enlistment, Baillie was faced with a dilemma; should he try to be an officer in the Infantry or seek some other lesser position in the arm blanche; the Cavalry? Being on patrol, close to *Sallie* and not on some forsaken battlefield far from home seemed to be the better option to the thoughtful Baillie. One can only guess now at the possible outcomes of this fateful decision. His military training at the Kentucky Military Institute meant that he could have been an officer from the outset in the Infantry, but he felt that the glamour and elan of the Cavalry was more suited to his status as a *Southern Gentleman.* In the event, a concern for his properties, the excitement of horses and the real love in his life, *Sallie* made the decision for him. Alexander Campbell Wylly, one of Sallie's many relations became a Lieutenant in the newly reorganized cavalry, which blocked Baillie's possible position among the officer class. Finally decision made he enlisted as a private soldier in May 1862 with another of Sallie's Uncles, Captain William Brailsford's, in the Lamar Rangers at Sutherland Bluff. This was the site of the Brailsford plantation and became the area headquarters for Confederate forces. As the war intensified the *Rangers* later mustered in as Company H, 5th Georgia Volunteer Cavalry, CSA in December 1862. Although it meant being a private soldier, Baillie hoped to gain rapid promotion in the field through his gallant actions, intelligence and social position. Indeed with the charismatic if somewhat hot headed Captain Brailsford life would be far from dull. He had also escaped the command of his less than adventurous, monetary orientated brother-in-law Colonel Charles Spalding, who despite having attended West

Point and a fellow class mate of the Confederate President Jefferson Davis no less, declined to take a more active role in the war. Upon the death by pneumonia, caused by the alcoholism of Sallie's father, Randolph Spalding, in May 1862, Charles decided to resign his commission as Colonel of the 1st Battalion Georgia Cavalry, to concentrate on preserving the family's wealth and power. He decided to act swiftly and assumed over all control of the entire Spalding Negro workforce. He then marched them all to a retreat plantation near Quitman, on the Florida border, well away from the Yankee coastal forces.

Throughout 1862 the Rangers were engaged on the patrol and skirmish front around McIntosh County and up to Savannah often hunting down run away contrabands and returning then to their owners. In one such incident a number of such were killed on Sapelo in a firefight. The Captain later justified this action stating that the Negroes had been found, 'in arms against the white man.' For this a reprisal gunboat attack was launched against Captain Brailsford's plantation on Sutherland Bluff. The Rangers made a determined effort with their carbines at repelling the infantry, but the shelling took its toll on the plantation and the war entered a new and more ugly phase, culminating in the burning of Darien.

The war moved swiftly on and the New Year of 1863 saw the newly formed and reorganized 5th Georgia Volunteer Cavalry headed for Savannah and with them Baillie marched into history.

Whilst on duty near Savannah at camp Davant in August 1863, Baillie was finally recommended for promotion to 2nd Lieutenant by Colonel Robert H Anderson, affectionately known to the men as *Marse Bob.* His qualities as a gentleman and potential officer had finally been recognized, surely with the counter signature of General PGT Beauregard, he would get the long awaited promotion that he desperately required to win Sallie's hand in marriage? However, due to the exceptional caliber of soldier drawn to the cavalry and low mortality rate of the officer class, Baillie's plans went awry. The war had developed to a stage when fancy notions of promotion became meaningless among the massed carnage and destruction being wrought across the land. It would, despite the recommendations of his senior officers never happen. Two small words in the Colonel's letter stood in the way, *Drill Master* (sic), the last thing wanted after the combined loss of Gettysburg and Vicksburg in 1863, was a drill master! Anything

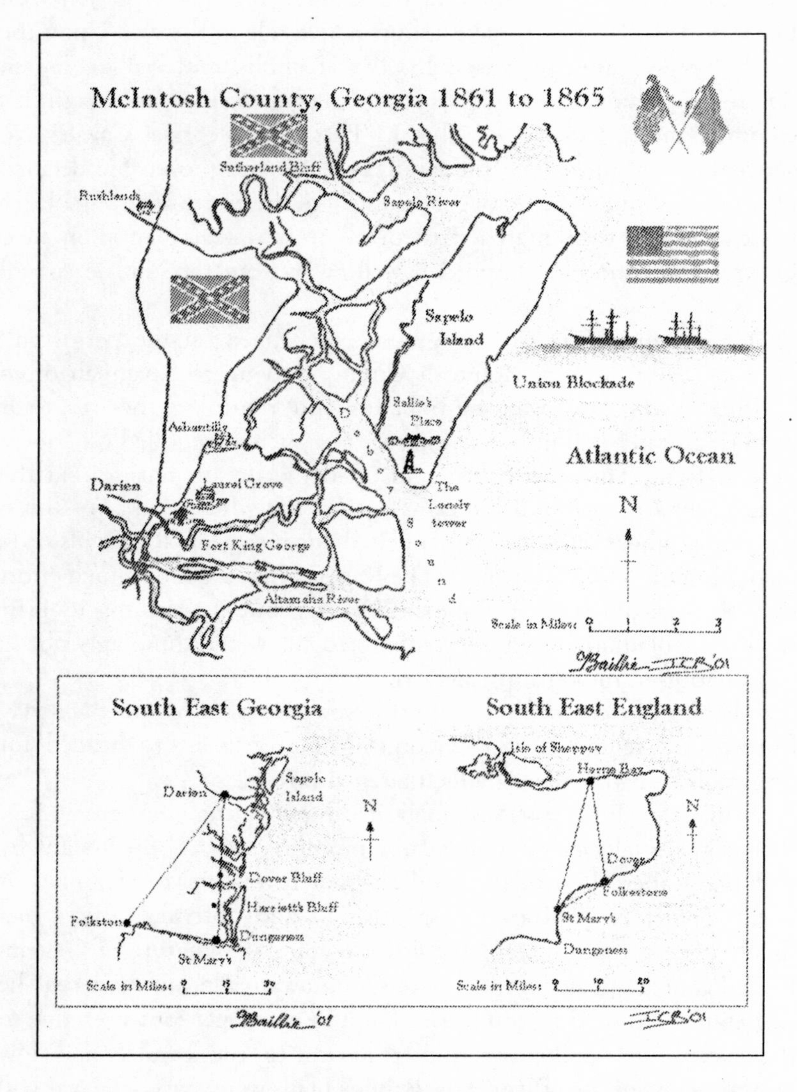

McIntosh County during the Civil War 1861 to 1865: This shows the relative positions of the major places mentioned in this true story. Inset is a fractal map of coincidence, showing the corresponding positions of equivalent places in both Baillie's life and my life, note the mirror like symmetry displayed, mirroring my own likeness to Baillie in the photograph on the back cover.

but those two fateful words, may have secured Baillie his promotion and with it, the fair hand of his blonde Princess, Sarah Elizabeth *Sallie* Spalding.

The Photograph: Baillie gives the picture to Sallie in the hope that she will remember him whilst he is away at the front.

Richmond's refusal dashed all hope for the present time. This for Baillie was the crucial turning point in his fortunes, which in fact mirrored that of the Confederacy itself. For at Gettysburg in Pennsylvania and Vicksburg on the Mississippi, the tide of the war had turned and the sun had begun to set on the fledgling Confederacy. Everything had been decided in the events of that fateful summer and Baillie's fate, would be a fractal image of the Confederacy's.

Come the autumn the 5th Georgia Volunteer Cavalry marched into South Carolina to defend the railroads around Charleston. The campaigns came thick and fast and the fighting grew ever more bloody as the high hopes of 1863 turned into the attrition and waste of 1864, with the epic campaign for Atlanta. In February 1864 the unit was ordered to Florida in time for the Battle of Olustee.

Last Train to Olustee: The regiment entrained and traveled down to Florida for the ensuing campaign, February 1864.

Whilst on its way back to Savannah the regiment was diverted to join the intensifying firestorm of fighting, that was raging in front of and around Atlanta. Baillie wrote several letters to Blanche his sister-in-law at this time. The letters have survived and are reproduced in this volume. She, despite losing two of her dear little children to diphtheria, offered to nurse Baillie in the event of him becoming wounded at Kennesaw Mountain.

Somehow miraculously Baillie managed to avoid injury, death or capture. Mid-summer the cavalry units were detached with *Fightin' Joe Wheeler* for a raid into Tennessee.

Brailsford: Prince William or simply 'Capt' as he was known leads the way into Tennessee.

It was here that Yankee cavalry at Murfreesboro captured Captain William Brailsford in October 1864. The ambush happened as some men from Company H with lame and unshod horses were out with the *Capt* foraging. The detached unit was left behind in Tennessee, whilst waiting for a sympathetic blacksmith to shoe the horses. They were suddenly surprised, *bushwhacked* by the Yankee cavalry and all but a lucky few escaped the trap. Baillie with a sound horse and with the main regimental party had narrowly avoided life in a prison camp. Alexander Campbell Wylly assumed command of the troop and would later with his brother William, become a life long friend of Baillie's. The war dragged relentlessly on and Baillie still thinking of Sallie, had only a tattered picture to remind him of the high times before the war. Despite heroic acts of valor, attrition was setting in. Baillie and the 5th continued to give it their best shot along with the other *boys' in gray*, but the Yankees now, just kept on coming, an endless tide of blue.

The Protectors: Baillie and the 5th strive against the odds to protect the citizens against Sherman. The small blonde child represents Sallie and how Baillie feels towards her, shielding her from the ravages of war.

November 1864, Atlanta had fallen and the 5th Georgia along with the rest of Joe Wheeler's remaining cavalry were ordered at all costs to attempt to halt Sherman's juggernaut of 60,000 men. They had cut loose from their lines in Atlanta and were now headed towards Savannah and the sea. Sherman had vowed, 'to make Georgia howl' and it was up to Wheeler's 3,000 troopers to limit the damage. This they did to some measure, but Savannah fell in time for Sherman to present the city to Lincoln as a Christmas present.

In the New Year, Sherman's jubilant army set out upon their march through the Carolina's. The devastation wrought there was far greater than anything Georgia had experienced. The Union soldiers blamed South Carolina for starting the *whole darn war* and were determined to wreak havoc in revenge. The 5th still fighting to the last round knew it was a hopeless cause, there were just too many Yankees with overwhelming resources. So many in fact, that the boys just couldn't load fast enough to shoot them all!

To the Last Round: The final desperate battles against overwhelming odds herald the end of the war.

Finally Baillie, along with the remnants of the 5th Georgia Volunteer Cavalry surrendered in good order on April 26, 1865 at Hillsboro, North Carolina. A sad and bitter day, all hope for an independent

South was gone and a dejected Baillie, paroled on May 3, 1865, headed home.

Darien had been raised to the ground in June 1863; this infamous act of barbarism was captured in the film *Glory*. Laurel Grove escaped the burning, but was an empty shell. A local white man had run off with all the furniture during the war and all was in total disrepair. Yet Baillie, at this late stage, still fostered hopes of marrying his true love Sallie and after talking with the Yankee soldiers on the Ridge, set too to farm the land again. He hired freedmen and oxen with which to plough the land; he started to rebuild that summer and tried to get a crop in. He also again found himself responsible for the family women folk, his mother and two unmarried sisters. But then came the mortal blow; *Sallie* was to marry another!

How cruel could fate be and destiny an even harsher mistress for poor Baillie? Mary Bass Spalding, Sallie's widowed mother had found another more eligible suitor for her daughter. This had occurred during the war whilst the family were away at Milledgeville, the old State Capital in Baldwin County. Mary deemed a 1st Lieutenant of the 57th Georgia Infantry, Archibald Carlisle McKinley, capable of bringing financial stability to the marriage in these uncertain times. It was a marriage of status and class, wealth and power, but not love.

Poor Baillie, was no longer a suitable match. For he had lost his wealth, *Laurel Grove* and *Rushlands* were in ruins. He was not even now an *Officer* and McKinley was the younger man, being only one year older than *Sallie*. The Kell's land was now relatively worthless in McIntosh County due to Special Order #15 and so his world fell apart. This single blow inflicted more damage than any Yankee bullet or bloody battlefield could ever have done in the entire war. The lone warrior had lost his princess and as he stood and gazed distraught with grief towards Sapelo's now dimmed lighthouse, he reflected on what might have been. In 1866 as he watched his beloved *Sallie* walk down the aisle to be married to another man, he knew that he would never be able to remain in Darien.

His heart broken he had lost the will to survive. He tried renting out *Rushlands* to his former slaves now freedmen, but this did not work. There was a total lack of money in the South, all remained chaos and destitution. General Sherman's Special Field Order #15 giving the coastal land to the former Negro slaves meant that there was no living to be had in Darien. His sister Mary in a letter to John seriously doubted his capacity to run a plantation. Baillie was mentally shattered and so in 1867 he sought refuge with his brother at Sunnyside, near Griffin in Spalding County. Baillie now lived with John and Blanche at Rocky Knoll alongside the old Atlanta road and railroad track. The childless Varner's had given the land to their favorite niece Blanche, in the hope that she would come to live by them as company in their old age.

John contented himself with simple farming and it was here that the Kell's mother Margery, now living with friends died amongst her kinfolk in 1870. Whilst he pondered his next moves now aged forty and just when life seemed to have abandoned him, Baillie fortuitously met an attractive Irish girl.

Mary Sullivan, the eldest daughter of Patrick Sullivan an immigrant farmer lived with the Varner's as a housekeeper in close proximity to the Kell farm at Rocky Knoll. Mary also seemed greatly disturbed by her father's marriage to a younger woman, which occurred upon the death of her mother, Easter. The new stepmother also named Mary caused problems, so Mary Sullivan had taken up the position at the Varner's old place next to Rocky Knoll. Baillie struck up a relationship with her, he on his horse with tales of daring and she the young farm girl turned housekeeper, they fell in love spurred on by the stirring jigs and reels that were the hallmark of Irish Gaelic culture in Georgia. Baillie was in his natural element for he played the guitar, violin and always loved a good singsong. Baillie's fortunes seemed somewhat restored, he was now managing the Varner's farm with woodlands after the death of aged Hendley Varner in 1868 and in 1870, on Mary's eighteenth birthday they became engaged. This however, was not a popular decision with the family. They considered the Sullivan's not their class. So again poor Baillie's relationship was doomed from the start. Fate then stripped Baillie of what little security he had tenuously built. *Childless old aunty* died and left the Varner estate to her favorite niece Julia Blanche Munroe Kell. Mary and Baillie's world then fell apart due to the settlement of the Varner's will, with Blanche gaining the estate. Her sister Hattie was not pleased and contested the will and Mary had to leave as, 'the home was now broken up.' On a bright December morning in 1871, as she boarded the northbound steam locomotive for Atlanta at Griffin station, Baillie and Mary shared an emotional farewell. Baillie without money and Mary without a home the couple had to split up. Mary became a music teacher in the city and

Baillie was once more cast upon his brother's charity, a lonely and increasingly bitter fellow.

This bitterness was further exacerbated by the loss of his favorite niece *Lil' May*, Margery Baillie Kell, aged six in 1873. She had been named after him and Baillie had taken a great interest in watching her grow up after losing the two women that he loved. He desperately tried to rationalize the loss of May without success. Infant mortality through disease caused many deaths at that time and this terrible event made a great impression on Baillie's emotional nature. Death and trauma in battle through choice could be rationalized, but never the taking of such a sweet and innocent child's life by an unseen enemy. Greatly perturbed Baillie began to search for answers and became even more intensely interested in Religion and the Church.

In 1876, Baillie then went to work on the railroad and the Kells continued their struggle to survive. John as a quiet farmer raising a second family, only young *Johnnie* had survived from the first three children that Blanche had been blessed with. He would go to Medical school, qualify as a doctor, but be tragically struck down with tuberculosis aged twenty-four. The disease was rife due to the lack of medicines, poor diet and living conditions. One of Griffin's most infamous sons to die of this condition, was none other than, *Doc Holliday*, the gun-fighting dentist of Wild West fame.

Finally in 1886, John McIntosh Kell, Baillie's brother, having performed great and legendary war service aboard the CSS Alabama, had the good fortune to be asked by General John B Gordon's administration to become State Adjutant General for Georgia. This post in public life gave John the financial stability he needed to bring up his now large family. John held this prestigious office until he passed away in 1900 being buried with full military honors and a special funeral train with escort. Baillie worked for a time on the Rome Carrolton Railroad as a civil engineer, which amalgamated with the Central Railroad of Georgia. Baillie had great respect for its President, E Porter Alexander. This fine gentleman had commanded General Robert E Lee's artillery in the Army of the Northern Virginia and of all things Baillie had a passion for cannons. From his railroad base at Americus, south of Griffin, Baillie struggled to make a living. Ever unsure of which way to turn or what to do, instability ruled his life. All hope of romance having now faded, the only time that he found relief from his condition was when he was diverted by games and music with the young folks in John's ever expanding family. Uncle Baillie was to be his station in life, yet even then all did not run smoothly. He argued and fell out with his brother in 1888 aged sixty, the reason most certainly was over finance, John's success and wanting to move back to Rocky Knoll due to his deteriorating health. In short John had everything Baillie didn't have. But the large family now had no room for him and so he struggled on. He lived to regret this rift with his brother and never made amends before John died.

Supported only by the charity of his friends and without means, in 1899 aged seventy-one, he petitioned for a State disability pension claiming paralyzed feet and rheumatism prevented him from working. He had the support of his long-term *friends* Alexander Campbell and William Cook Wylly despite all that had transpired in Baillie's fortunes, adversity and a common foe made for strong bonds of comradeship. Now receiving a small pension, Blanche took him in and he came to live at Rocky Knoll; Uncle Baillie had returned.

In 1901 he helped to found the John McIntosh Kell Camp #1032 of United Confederate Veterans with sponsorship from the United Daughters of the Confederacy in McIntosh County. Spurred on to honor his brother's memory and perhaps to atone for the argument, he became a major figure in this movement. He attended every event and it is in this role that we see him in the second Baillie photograph (page 323), the story etched into every line of his face. His proud bearing still undefeated, his old adversaries now a distant memory. Ironically frozen in this moment of time are his two old rivals, to the left Archibald Carlisle McKinley, Sallie's husband and to the right Alexander Campbell Wylly, Company H's troop commander, both having played a hand in his unlucky fate. All united by the common experience of having fought in a great and terrible Civil War.

Baillie continued living with Blanche and John's family at Rocky Knoll. And it was in this neat whitewashed one story farmhouse, adjacent to the railroad tracks in Sunnyside, Griffin, Georgia, that he passed peacefully away. The time was 1:00pm, on September 30, 1912, aged eighty-four years, he was *kind and attentive to the end*. The vivid memories of those four unforgettable years with the cavalry and the two beautiful women whose love he had won and then lost were forever burnt into his soul. So much so that the same *vivid memories* would even survive his death and surface in another future generation.

Written coincidentally this day February 23, 2001, about Baillie, by Baillie, on Baillie's 173rd Birthday!

Chapter Two
Norman

I made Dr Norman C Delaney's acquaintance by e-mail in the early part of May 1999. This was due entirely to Ashley Pollette, who had tracked Norman down in order to secure permission to use the scanned photograph of Baillie on the 5th Georgia Cavalry web site. By clicking on the label kindly posted by Ash, I was able to contact Norman directly and correspondence was established. Immediately, I offered my sincere gratitude to the professor for having the foresight to publish the article on Baillie in Civil War Times Illustrated 1988. I was somewhat tentative in my introductions, as I did not know what response I would elicit upon the startling revelation that I had more than a passing connection, with this long lost Civil War soldier. Yet I need not have worried, as we soon struck up a pleasant and most cordial relationship. Norman was in fact most enthusiastic and interested in the story of this eccentric English gentleman with the same face, same name and same memories as Baillie. For both Norman and his dear wife Linda for many years had felt sorry for *poor Baillie* as they had come to regard him; the unsung younger brother of a much more famous older sibling. Coincidentally Norman's interest began to gather momentum in the autumn of that year. But, none of us as yet, knew of the important role that this gentle professor of History would play in the unfolding of Baillie's past. For Norman C Delaney was about to take center stage in providing the crucial evidence, that would confirm the decoding of Baillie's memories and even more incredibly, he was to also find himself, a fellow participant in the story.

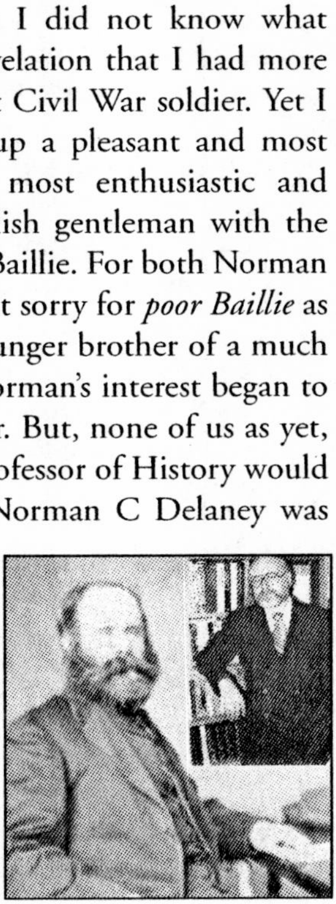

John McIntosh Kell - Dr Norman C Delaney: As one can see Norman bears a striking resemblance to Baillie's brother!

My Intelligent Universe thesis had gained recognition and I was awarded an Honorary Ph.D. on October 6, 1999, which put the work on a higher academic footing. The inkling of the importance of this discovery was now beginning to set in and the possibility of producing a wholly original piece of work was about to become reality. The conversation turned to the model that I had been making during the summer recess at Herne Bay after returning from Georgia.

Date: Tuesday, October 12, 1999:
To: Dr Norman C Delaney
From: Dr Ian C Baillie
Re: CSS Alabama

Hi Norman
I'm at home now... I realized I goofed when I looked at my model re gun layout.
I have attached a quick sketch that I have just scanned in. Can you give it the once over?
Ian
PS I'll send you a picture of me as a safety boatman! To show you that us Baillie's (Kell's) have the sea in our blood. I love this new scanner!
Here's one of me taken in Darien July'99 John's Plaque behind, I was trying to stand still whilst dodging the 'Skeeters' and 'ninja gnats'. How the heck did they live there on that marsh!?
Ian C. Baillie 'Two 11 inch Dahlgren's make a difference!'

Norman wrote back in characteristic fashion expanding the topic:

Date: Friday, October 15, 1999:
To: Dr Ian C Baillie
From: Dr Norman C Delaney
Re: CSS Alabama

Yes, congratulations, Ian, for the recognition you are receiving for your work. When it comes to Science and technology, I realize my utter ignorance. (I'd love to be in one of your classes.) There are courses on using Computers, Internet, etc., but I've been trying to teach myself. So, as to breaking the 'code', I'm going to have to work on that.
I have found a 'paint' under 'accessories', under 'programs', if I can just get it all together.
Interesting to know that you tried to find the USS KEARSARGE model. I've been trying to find one for years, finally wrote to the

company, and learned that it was no longer among their items. Too bad I missed the opportunity some years back.
My ALABAMA model (Revell) is my second. A long time ago when I lived in Newburyport, Massachusetts with my parents, I made the model, then I moved to Texas, because it was too fragile to move. But I knew I'd make another one, which I did. It's right above my desk, along with Semmes' and Sinclair's books. (I never did find Kell's, a rare book indeed.)
I'll keep experimenting with 'paint'.
Best wishes,
Norman

I was enthused as to this new working relationship with Norman in Texas, courtesy of the e-mail. I was struck by the similarity of attention to detail that John McIntosh Kell had given to writing as Norman displayed, whilst checking my article on Baillie.

Date: Monday, October 18, 1999:
To: Dr Ian C Baillie
From: Dr Norman C Delaney
Re: Article on Baillie

Ian
I got it! This has helped to restore my faith in e-mail communication. Whatever method you used it came through perfectly. I like your article and agree with your assessment of poor Baillie. Oh, to be overshadowed by a famous older brother and those doting sisters! (They had acted the same with John, 'Donny', as they called him, until he was able to break away in the navy. The mother, Margery, actually acknowledged that her son John was her favorite child. Imagine what a blow psychologically that would have inflicted on poor Baillie!)
There are several typo errors in the manuscript that I can point out but only if you want me to, i.e. 'succession' instead of 'secession' and a lot of apostrophes where there shouldn't be. Regarding content: on page 2 You state that 'War fever swept the land in 1860...' Idon't think so then. I would state that 'secession fever' swept the states of the Lower South after Lincoln's election in November of 1860. 'War fever' would not have come until after the firing on Fort Sumter on April 12, 1861. Up to that time many in the South believed that they would get away with having left the Union without having a war. On two occasions you refer to 'sea cotton,' whereas that reference should be to 'Sea Island' cotton. One other thing comes to my attention right toward the end. You state that 'John made a name for himself in Atlanta...'

That would not be the case until he was appointed Adjutant General by Governor Gordon in 1886. Good article, Ian, I hope you plan to have it published.
(Have you seen a copy of my Kell book? It has a drawing of Laurel Grove sketched by Hetty Kell.)
Thanks for letting me see your article.
Norman

A drawing of Laurel Grove! Wow, how fantastic a picture of where Baillie was born and raised, drawn by his favorite sister. After a little help from a colleague, Norman sent the picture, the scan appeared miraculously and with it much more new detail.

Hello, again! I'm going to have to admit that I don't know how to send pictures over e-mail, but I'll ask my colleagues tomorrow if they can do it for me. A scanner: Is that something that has to be installed in the computer or is it outside the computer? There's so much I don't know about computer technology! Right about the sea island variety of cotton; it was ideally suited for the coastal areas. Somewhere in my files I have information from the 1860 agricultural census (McIntosh County) that would indicate what other crops and livestock were being grown/raised at the Kell plantation. In fact, Hetty Kell's sketch includes grazing sheep. I'll see what I can do about scanning that picture to you. The more I think about it the better I can understand your bonding with your relative, Baillie Kell. It's great!
Signing off,
Norman

Here is Hetty Kell's picture of Laurel Grove. Let me know if it comes through OK.
Norman

Brilliant the front porch is exactly as I imagined it... amazing!

Ian, a few other things that have come to my attention. Darien was torched by the black soldiers of Col. Robert Gould Shaw's 54th Massachusetts Colored Regiment in 1863, but Laurel Grove was spared until it burned to ground several years later.

Was it not also Montgomery's 2nd South Carolina? Shaw was unfairly blamed and found the whole affair distasteful? I didn't know that? Curiouser and curiouser. I always assumed that it copped it when Darien did, due to its close proximity. Mind you your initial article

mentioned that it was in a 'run down state' upon Baillie's return after the war. I should pay more attention to the detail! I wouldn't make a very good lawyer!

You might mention that although the plantations were initially turned over to the Freedmen by the Yankees, within a short time they were forcibly removed by Federal troops and the lands returned to their original owners.

That's true the Tunis Campbell affair followed by the Spalding's managing to get their 'enemy' to do their bidding! Brilliant... thank you so much for all of your excellent points
Ian

The detail that Norman had accumulated was astounding and he was really warming to the research challenge in true Delaney style. Also there was another new first, Norman had actual letters from the family regarding Baillie's background and situation, this was becoming truly amazing. All this information had survived the ravages of time. Stored so that one day I might find it and piece together my past.

Date: Friday, October 29, 1999:
To: Dr Ian C Baillie
From: Dr Norman C Delaney
Re: Laurel Grove

Ian, I hope you received the picture of Laurel Grove. It took a real team effort here to get it done. It turned out that my Department Chair couldn't do it after all; he had never done it, so we had to find someone who knew how, our Department Whiz Kid. I watched him, but it still seemed fairly complicated and he didn't slow down to explain the procedure. I have something else to tell you that you may find interesting. Laurel Grove belonged to Margery Kell through her Baillie/McIntosh kin. I found a copy of the Marriage Contract between John Kell and Margery Spalding Baillie (1816) which concerns Laurel Grove, containing 240 acres, and the 21 Negro slaves that she brought to the marriage. The burning of Darien, which Colonel Shaw deemed 'distasteful and barbarous,' occurred on June 11, 1863. Although Laurel Grove was not burned, Margery and her daughters were compelled to evacuate. Here is from a letter that Hetty wrote to Blanche Kell soon afterwards: 'Mother says I must tell you, she has given up. She is sick at heart.
She is grieving so over old Darien. She says she has no heart to write

Donny for she has nothing good to tell him. She thinks we shall never live at the Grove again and is really miserable about it.' And when Margery was finally able to write to her daughter in law, she wrote, 'Poor old Darien. I felt as though I had lost my oldest friend - it is linked with my earliest recollections and I feel that we would be so isolated at the Grove without Darien. No church - no friends nearer than over the river. Charles will never go back. The Holmes and Gouldings broke up...'

The 1850 Agricultural Census indicates that 160 acres were under cultivation - cotton, sweet potato, peas, and beans. The estate was valued at $10,000, livestock at $550, and farm implements at $100. Let me know if you need any additional information.
Norman

The information was beginning to trigger my memory. I was able to make sense of many strange feelings that had occurred for no apparent reason in my life. I began to realize that my subconscious had been responding to similar places, events and historical sites that I had physically visited during this lifetime. My phrase, ***emotion is the language of the soul,*** was taking on a concrete reality through personal experience. The thrill of seeing all this come to life before my eyes was electrifying, for I was not merely a spectator, but actually in the plot. This was real life X-files happening to little old me, who would have thought it?

Date: Sunday, November 17, 1999:
To: Dr Norman C Delaney
From: Dr Ian C Baillie
Re: Appomattox Court House

Hi Norman
Just a quickie... I took the boarders swimming at the leisure center in Tenterden this afternoon and had a chance to analyze the picture... so here I go. I think I recognize the view!
In the background to the left is Fort King George across the marshes towards the Altamaha. The sheep are cows lying down... I don't think they had sheep the view is of the back of the house? With the land sloping to the left towards Kell's landing and the marsh. The Wilmer Mclean House at Appomattox Court House was similar in layout... the stairs appeared to be the front, but are actually the back... this surprised me at the time, but it did look familiar in '91 when I visited.

Just a thought! It may be that this was indeed the front of the Kell's house in the picture, which is why the Appomattox Mclean house shocked me, as it seemed to be the wrong way around? Darien would be off to the right at a reasonable distance so the house is at an angle... I'll work out orientation tomorrow on the map and scan it to you. The white fence to the right separates the estate from the other parts of Darien.
Please excuse any mistakes, but this is really exciting and it is late. I will check out my facts tomorrow... mean time
How am I doing?
The picture is brilliant thank you so much for your team effort!
Regards Ian

Norman replied:

Ian,
I'm glad you like Hetty's painting of Laurel Grove. You know, I never considered those beasts any other than sheep, but maybe you're right, I guess they could be cattle after all. I borrowed the painting (the original is rather small size) and others (including Baillie's picture) from Munroe d'Antignac, a grandson of Kell, back in 1966 when I was researching my Kell biography as a graduate student at Duke University. Good thing I did, as I'd never be able to obtain these pictures now. d'Antignac is long dead and he co-operated fully with my research endeavors while alive. I was glad that he lived long enough to see the book on his grandfather published (in 1973) and that he liked it. I still can't get over my actually sending a picture by e-mail! Or, rather, my colleague did it for me, so I can't take full credit. I like your analysis of the picture, Ian, and connecting it with the Kells the way it would have been before the war.
Great!
Till later, then, Norman

The next day I hurried to work out the exact location of the plantation from the picture and orientation points. When completed I scanned it in and sent a copy to Norman, he was pleased with the results and my methods. Praise indeed from the professor!

Ian,
Your map looks good to me. (Wouldn't it be nice to be able to go over the area with a metal detector? I wonder if anyone has done that.) Yesterday I failed to mention your sketch of a cavalryman of the 5th Georgia Regiment. Very nice! Be sure to include it with your Baillie

article. The way you look at history, as a scientist, intrigues me. As I see it, an historian should view his subject from all perspectives the way a scientist/detective conducts an investigation. The way an artist looks at an object as well. Not to mention a psychologist, etc.
A meeting of the minds. Keep up the good work.
Norman

My reply came instantly, coincidences were beginning to flow freely and the information gathering accelerate:

Good idea Norman! But there are a lot of shanty dwellings on the site round about. It could be worth a try on a future trip. We have a channel 4 TV program called 'Time Team', which uses a similar multiple technique of excavation over a two-day period. It would be interesting :) It's definitely different!
We tend to chase down linear corridors of inquiry like academic rottweilers! Sherlock Holmes... elementary my dear Norman! Thank you for your encouragement and your time I appreciate both very much!
Latest Kell picture I just had my driving License photo taken today as I have to change my title from Mr to Dr so I made a composite of it for comparison with Baillie. Note the stunning similarity!!!
Oh yes a colleague of mine said that looking at Baillie's eyes he may have been short sighted... perhaps that is another reason why he might not have won promotion?
Kind regards Ian

Norman advised me of an Internet bookseller that had a copy of his long out of print book *John McIntosh Kell of the Raider Alabama.* Taking advantage of the roll that we were on, I did not hesitate but to immediately purchase it.

Hi Norman
I've managed to secure your book from the shop so it should be on its way... hurrah and many thanks:) as regards History approach, I favor the practical one, reconstructing artifacts and technology. I see history in a technology geography scenario, the side with the high ground and superior tech wins. Back to those Yankees again! Firing my Colt Walker tells you more in two minutes than countless books on the subject about the limitations and advantages of the artifact.
I also like modern geophysical methods, multi-source documents, re-enactment etc. Ken Burns did one hell of a job on the Civil War series which actually took longer than the war to make.

It was always the haunting realism of Civil War photographs that drew me back to the Civil War. I always imagined that I would find myself in a Civil War photograph and it finally came true!
I'm also an ardent war-gamer and have reconstructed many battles and periods since being a lad. I have made Viking armor, English Civil war armor and taken part in living history camps. At school my best subjects were Chemistry (gunpowder!), History, and Art - straight A's. I chose Science, as the job prospects were better and I love rockets and space; back in '69 I wanted to work for NASA, still do. As a scientist we always look for cause and effect. The Civil War has been a massive 'effect' in shaping my life and now I think I've found the cause, old Baillie!
I think also I have discovered the physics to back it up. My thesis is mainly about that. So I am ecstatic that after some 35 years I now have some answers and it is thanks to you and your clarity of mind that all this has been resolved. I am eternally in you debt, good Sir!
Regards Ian

Out of the blue came this message from Norman, his son would soon pay a visit and I would get to see a chip off the old block. The eerie parallels were unfolding, Baillie had been extremely fond of his young nephew Johnnie, the eldest son of John McIntosh Kell. Now Baillie present would get to meet the Matrix equivalent of young Johnnie! I intuitively knew that we would hit it off immediately.

Ian,
I'm not sure I ever mentioned that I have a son, Stephen, teaching in France, in Tours. It's quite an experience for him of course. Last year he was teaching (English, public schools) in Loches, France, which is a much smaller community. He even used a bicycle to get around, whereas this year in Tours he uses the buses to get to the three schools he's assigned. Last year he came home for the Christmas holiday, but it's so expensive that he won't be coming home this year. The pay he's receiving is just enough to get by. I suggested to him that he uses some of the two-week holiday to visit England, and I'm sure he'd enjoy hearing English for a change. Is there a possibility that he might visit you for a few days if that would be no problem? You could advise him as to a place to stay and show him around. (?) This may be the worst time of the year for you to consider such a request, but I thought I'd ask. Steve is a fine boy. There was a time when he considered Physics as a major, but was drawn to his true love: Creative writing (an M.F.A. from Wichita State). He was a Teaching Assistant during that time,

then discovered this wonderful opportunity to teach abroad. He's been using some of his free time to explore Paris and other places, but should really get to see England while he's over there. I've suggested Youth Hostels as inexpensive and a chance to meet interesting people. I know that you'd like Steve and he certainly would love meeting a Renaissance man like yourself. Anyway, hope you don't mind my bringing it up. Hope that all goes well.
Norman

The plans were going well and we were busy at school getting ready for the end of term. I was quite excited at the prospect of meeting Steve and discussing the many aspects of the structure and function of the Universe that I had discovered. I was beginning to know Norman well from the communications and I had built a mental picture of him in my head. The chance to find out more about him with Steve filled me with anticipation. I was already planning what I would show him of Canterbury as the end of the Millennium was drawing near. With the discovery of the photo and the chain of events that had culminated in my Doctorate everything seemed to be climaxing toward the Christmas New Year period, a time of intense novelty.

Ian,
Thank you for your quick response. It would be great if you could find a place for Steve to spend a few days at Canterbury. Even if the YMCA doesn't work out, there should be some other lodging place. He intends to go on to London and stay at a Youth Hostel while there. (Sure wish I could be there with him!) I've sent Steve your e-mail address (hope that's OK) and will send you his.
He's able to get to a computer there in Tours at least a few times a week. The dates of his Christmas break seem to be pretty much the same as yours. He'll need to send you more specific dates when he expects to be in England. Thanks again!
Norman

Affirmative Sir! 5th Cav. all the way... sure we can fix something.
We are now into exam week followed by report writing and the best bit, pre-Christmas frivolities! Oh and by the way 'Happy Thanksgiving on the 25th'. Shame Steve is in France I bet you will miss him? Have you any other family apart from Steve and your brother?
Books coming along OK, I'll have a bash at Christmas to knock it into shape. The Kell memories keep piling up. I now know what

happened to Captain Brailsford and his capture at Murfreesboro, Tenn 1864. Turns out that it was not the whole of Co H that was mostly killed or captured, but only those that had stayed to get their horses shod etc. Baillie must have been with the main party as his horse was probably OK? So he got away with it! This is from a first hand account in the new book 'In the Saddle' Exploits of the 5th Georgia Cavalry in the Civil War by Timothy Daiss. An endearing little book with mostly first hand sources and some photos showing the Uniform detail which is useful. I intend to commission a uniform as accurate as possible after Christmas. I already have several pieces. This will be photographed with me on horse back for the book, sometime in the spring. Claudia the horse is already lined up for the job!
Baillie's possible uniform: not 100% sure, but it's getting there. Note the turning round of the belt to make the cartridge box accessible in skirmishing... you can load your Sharp's a lot quicker that way.
Well better close. Best wishes and thanks for your chat, much appreciated Norman!
Regards Ian

After receiving Hettie's picture of Laurel Grove I was inspired to produce a picture of Baillie returning home on his horse at the end of 1864. The feel of the white clapboard walls and the setting in snow fitted nicely with the image of the lone horseman returning. I often produce a unique Christmas card using my artistic skills and the card usually reflects my current interests and research efforts. Little was I to know the importance of this process that I was about to unleash, for this was about to become the major tool for unlocking the *memes* of Baillie with in my mind. The artistic creative part of the brain allows the subconscious a channel to communicate through, to visibly manifest into the presence of the conscious. In scientific terms I was about to indulge in a spot of *remote viewing*. The uncanny feel and accuracy of the picture was suddenly validated as I read a passage of Norman's book over the holiday period. I had kept the time free to indulge my pleasure of sinking into a good book during the traditional festivities of the Christmas break.

Hi Norman
I have sent an e-mail to Steve and we are looking for places to stay... meanwhile here's a little picture based on Hetty Kell's drawing you sent me. I am going to use it on my Christmas card, it's called

'Almost Home; Winter of '65' and shows old Baillie returned from fightin' in the backyard for a brief look at home.
Hope you like it and thanks once again for your efforts in sending me the drawing. Your book should be well on the way by now so I look forward to reading it over Christmas.

Kind regards, Ian
'We fought to the end and surrendered in good order as Southern Gentlemen should'

Hillsboro, NC April 26, 1865

The Return:
This was the first picture, I produced as a Christmas card in 1999. The scene is based on Hettie's drawing of Laurel Grove, with Baillie returning alone out of the blue to view the property, whilst fighting rearguard in the winter of '65. I was amazed to find in Norman's book, read after I had drawn and colored this, that Baillie had indeed turned up out of the blue on a cold November day to see his brother and sister-in-law, but at Wathourville near Savannah not Laurel Grove.

For as I read the passage on page 188; John and Blanche had set up home in Walthourville near Savannah, on November 21, 1864, in a little rough wood cabin with solid shutters. Then came the magic sentence, **'Baillie also came to see them and was afterward impressed into the defense of Savannah while trying to rejoin his regiment.'** Baillie had made it! Exactly as I had felt the emotion deep within, which had impelled my painting. It was not Laurel Grove as I had painted, but very similar, the lone horseman had arrived to see his brother and dear sister-in-law whilst covering a fighting retreat against General Sherman's mighty legion of 60,000 men. Out of the blue, single-handed, he had turned up. The sentence and the image were one and the same. I was stunned at the accuracy of prediction. Upon returning to school I decided to try to help repay Ashley and Tommy for all their hard work by painting some pictures for the 5th Georgia Cavalry web site. It was just my way of saying thank you to the guys. I have always found art relaxing and not having time in my busy schedule to make toy soldiers as I used to, I set about drawing and depicting scenes from the life of the regiment. A new enterprise was born and one which was to pay handsome dividends in the pursuit of Baillie's memory. On cue in the Matrix the book arrived at just the right time:

Date: Monday, November 29, 1999:
To: Dr Norman C Delaney
From: Dr Ian C Baillie
Re: Your book has arrived

Great news Norman... I got home rather dejected as somebody broke into the lab on Saturday night and hacked into my computer to look up dodgy web sites for four hours and again on Sunday morning for twenty minutes...
But your book had arrived and I could hardly put it down for dinner! Great job, I've scanned all the 'Baillie' references and it reads like a walk on part in a Shakespeare play. Poor Baillie! I see what you mean Mom was a bit of an iron lady and Donny was her favorite. Still John paid for Baillie's education, which was nice and he ended up with a BA.
I'm still at a loss though as to why Baillie couldn't make a go of it in his own post war life, unless the 'family' like our Royals were too strong? I can see why he didn't want to hire a substitute as his Mother wished... it was his big chance to 'get away.'
No wonder I have Baillie's memories of the 5th! It would have been the most exciting time of his life and one that was so strong that even physical death couldn't block them from resurfacing in another time! Wow!
Ian

> **Thanks for making my Millennium. I shall read your marvelous tome avidly over the break and digest the detail. It is very well written from what I can see, well done you must be very proud? The condition is very good and I particularly like the blue dust cover and stylish cartoon of John McIntosh Kell on the front.**

Coincidence is exactly how the Universe functions, it functions on interconnections, as all things are one. This self-same coincidence was at work in our stories. The tail end of Norman's next e-mail gave a good example of this:

> Hope you like my book, Ian. I spent a good deal of time becoming acquainted with the Kells and am so glad that I had the privilege. My advisor-professor at Duke U. had planned to write the book himself but was close to retirement and passed along the project to me. How fortunate can one be!
> Bye for now,
> Norman

Exactly, he had instinctively given the right job to exactly the right person. Serendipity, Fate call it what you like, it had happened. I was beginning to realize as I became more aware of my own story and past that all human beings in the Matrix are doing the same thing; following their own stories, with the exception that most do not realize that they are indeed doing it. Occasionally we stop and say, 'Well what a coincidence?' But we soon forget and move on. We function as automatons in the Matrix, but by becoming aware and looking for the connections, coincidences and such like, we become more in tune with ourselves and others. I am not unique, perhaps my story is, but we are all accessing the past and maybe the future to some extent, as time has no meaning in higher dimensions. Time is merely an artifact of the 3D space that we live in. James Redfield in his excellent book, *The Celestine Prophecy,* was the first popular author to make this known to the public in general.
Together we reflected on the scene in the Christmas card of the lonesome Baillie standing in front of his home:

> Very nice picture, Ian! I think it's great that finally someone is thinking about the forgotten 'little brother' of the Kell family. And wouldn't Baillie be pleased! Good work!

> **Thanks, that's exactly how I feel. I realize now that it was the family**

that nearly broke 'poor Baillie' not the war. The war was the most exciting thing that happened to him, it gave him his freedom - and he never forgot it. The whole terrible experience of death and destruction was tempered by the excitement of riding with the 'Knights in Gray'

That's why he strangely refused to pay $100 for a draft substitute as his mother wished. It was his ticket out! A chance to escape from mother just as his brother had done. He loved his brother; Donny paid the college bill. I bet they had many adventures when they were young messing about in boats on Doboy Sound and the inlets. A bit Tom Sawyerish crossed with Swallows and Amazons.

The nice refined neat ladies would soon have put a stop to all that nonsense!

Your book is a treasure! I shall cherish it forever, as I said I shall read it Christmas. That is the fitting time to read such an important document.

I was thinking about Baillie's fiancée, did she have blonde hair? I suppose we will never know. Shame it was nice seeing a picture of Blanche and the kids. Not a great beauty, but wholesome and honest. Funny thing is that the women in my life are always telling me the correct and sensible thing to do - trouble is they're usually right! Sometimes I just want to run away and do the opposite - just like Baillie. That's the Rebel in me!

Yours Confederately, Ian

Ian Baillie: 2nd Amendment to the Constitution 'Every citizen shall have the right to keep and arm bears!'

I was beginning to ask the right questions, the first stirrings of what would be unleashed five months later were beginning to rise from the depths of my subconscious.

The coincidences continued on cue:

Ian,

I'm in the middle of correcting final exams, but want to ask one question: Do you know Stephen Hawkings? It dawned on me that the subject of your research touches on his specialty, too, the origin of the universe. Steve is a fan of Hawkings and another physicist, Feynman, I believe, who is now deceased. I'll bet that you can make science interesting, and even FUN.

For now, Norman

Exactly right Norman, I do not know him personally, but I have read his book. Our ideas go way beyond Hawkings. He does consider them, but in his position he is careful in what he says. That's why scientists never talk on the news groups - in case you quote them! Peer pressure is such that they are scared stiff of losing their credibility and more cynically their meal ticket. It is strange that we are all stifled in the pursuit of truth by the very mechanism that should be encouraging new research and ideas. The status quo have always been in favor of burning the new kid on the block at the stake! So we have always traditionally explored our ideas through the medium of science fiction.

I used to be very careful about what I said for fear of losing my job. My wife would always remind me so. But along came the X-Files and at first I could not believe that they could screen such stuff - so near to the truth (especially series one) After three, it went down hill. Since then I can mention things without batting an eyelid. In fact the kids at school already seem to know many of the things that I have discovered! As Jung put it we are all tuned in to the collective subconscious. In fact it is the Universal Internet if you like. If Steve likes Hawkings then I'm your man! Interesting especially as he is a creative writer. I wonder why he likes Science and from which perspective? Here for example is a geometric diagram which gives the true ratios of Earth, Moon and Mars correct to 99.9%

This is known as the New Jerusalem diagram and is the floor plan of Stonehenge and several gothic cathedrals. It's a subconscious thing we just know it! Oh and it also squares the circle an ancient geometric conundrum in that the circle circumference and the square's perimeter are the same! 44 units.

The moon is not an accident it is a design as is everything else.

E.g. Just down from Darien, Georgia, is Folkston, with the River St Mary's running through it, to St Mary's on the coast next door. I was born in Folkestone Kent in 1954 and I work now at St. Mary's Westbrook, which used to be a convent two years ago. Spooky!? Nah not really it's just how the Universe works.

Baillie and I share the same soul memories. I am 99.9% sure that we are the same consciousness, just in different physical bodies. Time is just and illusion, which we perceive from our 3D perspective. I think that from a God's eye view it would look more like a bubble or donut and that we could be several physical beings at once! It's just from a geometric topological view it looks like linear History!:) Physics is FUN!

The Universe is simply a multi-dimensional holographic illusion!

How does that grab you?

Yours Confederately,
Ian

'The Universe is simply a product of the interactive harmonic resonance of complex waveforms; created, ordered and sustained by consciousness'
ICB97

Interrupted by the millennial celebrations our dialogue continued from where we left off:

Date: Tuesday, January 4, 2000:
To: Dr Ian C Baillie
From: Dr Norman C Delaney
Re: Happy New Year

Hello Ian - here's wishing you a very happy year 2000 in every way. I was glad to receive your e-mail this morning when the college opened up again (although classes don't begin for another two weeks). And I'm especially glad that you and Stephen were able to get together during his break. He enjoyed it immensely, despite the short time to be with you in Canterbury and to see some of London's attractions. He arrived back in Tours at 9:00a.m. on Monday expecting to meet his classes, but instead learning that classes don't resume until tomorrow! That was good news!
By the way, regarding Canterbury Cathedral and Thomas Becket: I understand that Henry VIII removed the body and looted the place for his own ends, but were Becket's bones ever returned to his tomb? Come to think of it, what ever happened to Cromwell's body? I know that he was disinterred after the Restoration and his head exhibited as a 'criminal' for all to see. I hope that Becket did better than that!
Steve mentioned that you are another devotee of Dr. Who. And he must have mentioned the X-Files, too. I'm sure you two had a lot to talk about. I'll end this for now.
Best wishes, Norman

You beat me to it! Happy New Year.
Pauline banned the computer over the holiday so we have been indulging in family activities such a Monopoly, Cluedo and Trivial Pursuit plus seeing all our relatives.
Stephen and I had a quality experience in Canterbury and I found him to be excellent company! We hit it off from the word go... I met him outside McDonald's near the bus station at 11:45 on Dec 29,

Becket's Anniversary and we headed straight for a Pub with log fire and I made sure that he was fed and watered! With Steak and Ale pie and real ale to drink (the best of English for the weather and time of year). We spent an hour chatting during which I told him about the Kell connection and the Physics of it all. I then shouldered his bag and we set off for the YHA, which I had previously reconnoitered. Leaving the bags we then went to do a tour of the sights starting with the Cathedral in all its magnificence, which was the highlight and with a bonus service in full swing. We had an extensive architectural tour of the city and discussed the English historical perspective. Especially why the English are so darn English! Finally we went and sampled city shops by foot and returned to my car, which I re-parked in the city as it was now 18:00 hours and traffic OK. We made for Pizza Hut as it was a known quantity and enjoyed our meal together. We then retired to the same log fire chatting there until just after 22:00 hrs, we put the world to rights! Then we drove back to the YHA and I said Abientot! I presented him with a copy of some of my book notes as a souvenir (Intro plus first three chapters) as I feel they may in another guise turn up in one of his creative SCI FI novels in the future?!!! An excellent day had by all! :) Talking of books I must congratulate you on the 'John McIntosh Kell of the Raider Alabama'. A first class read... it flowed beautifully and would make an excellent film. I recognized several sources and quotes, which were accurately and seamlessly threaded into the story. Brilliant stuff, I now have a much better idea of 'poor Baillie's' situation and his movements. My Christmas picture was correct in its sentiment, in that he did indeed return home in late November 1864, but to Retreat near Walthourville, Liberty County to see his brother & mother, there after being impressed into the defense of Savannah. My favorite bit was 'Baillie, however, was either unable or unwilling to buy a substitute; any rate, he was soon back in the army as a private in the 5th Georgia Cavalry'. This said it all, his one chance for escape and adventure!

As for Becket, 'print the legend!' I shall ask the Rev Richard Wood at school. He will know for sure. Cromwell is indeed true and there are several skulls claiming to be the original.

Best wishes Ian

Regards from Doc Baillie 'Happy New Millennium... MM'

Gosh, I must be more careful with my addresses. Yesterday I sent one off to docbaillie.demon.demon.uk and it was returned with the comment that it contained 'fatal errors.' Trouble is my eyesight sometimes does tricks on me. What I had commented on was your

visit with Steve and how much I would have enjoyed being with you two! Yes, science and history, a marvelous combination, at least in the hands of the right person like yourself. In case I haven't already indicated, you and any member of your family have a standing invitation here in Corpus Christi, which would mean all the more since nobody ever visits us here so far removed from anywhere here in South Texas. So thanks again for your kindness to Steve. I was about to comment on 'English hospitality,' but I'm also reminded of Laurel Grove in the good old days of typically Southern hospitality.
Best wishes, Norman

You are too kind Norman!
The spirit of the South lives on, a warm hearth and a good welcome, are things Scots the World over appreciate. When will you make it across the pond? Surely you must come and see where the good ol' 290 was built!
Oh I asked the Rev Richard Wood today about Thomas a' Becket and he said what I suspected that we just do not know where his remains are buried. Shame.
The older I get the more I am aware of how little remains of our passing. We are but footprints on the beach of time, soon to be washed away by the sea! That was my impression of Darien last summer not just a town, but a whole civilization and culture vanished... amazing. The great thing about your book was that it breathed life into those characters. The other references are very third person, but I now feel that I have recaptured the characters and faces of the Kells. I really can't explain how marvelous it was to read of those events and the photos too. I have some of John with Admiral Semmes on deck from the William C Davis book. The Civil War photos have always held a magnetic fascination for me. It's as if the long sitting times required meant that a part of the person's soul was left behind in the image. I think they are some of the most powerful and stunning images that I have ever seen. Ken Burns obviously thought the same way!
Well back to the chalk face... we had an ICT inset course today... the one word missing was 'money'! The techno haves vs the techno have nots a new class divide. Interesting stuff, but you have to have access to the kit. Mine is now at home and the baby flies! We do not have masses of money, but we know a good thing when we see it!
Oh yes Harriet my 11year old daughter was elected Form Captain (President) today, which was a nice thing.
I do hope that Stephen will pay us another visit this year and stay with us, he is such a nice young man. You both must be very proud

of him, I know that I would be if he were my son. He told me about your severed head antic for the French Revolution at College... way to go Norman... that's got to get them interested, first you capture their interest and then you teach them something.
Time to tuck Harriet in.
I've lots of detail to discuss re Baillie's appearances in the book, but I will keep them for another day.
Until then Abientot,
Ian

Our conversation broadened, as Norman became aware of the web site that Ashley and Tommy had put together. The Internet had proved invaluable in enabling such complex research to occur so quickly, years of work compressed into a few accessible files. In the final part of my quest I would have needed several lifetimes to accomplish what I had achieved in five short years or quite simply this wondrous discovery would never have happened.

Ian, I was browsing through the Internet web site of the 5th Georgia Cavalry and am quite impressed with what's been put together. It's the spiritual home of a lost age. I noticed the name of James Pierpont, the chap who wrote 'Jingle Bells'.

Yep that's true not a lot of snow in Georgia though!

So all of the pertinent information seems to be there, and there is the possibility that more will be added. I especially appreciated your tribute to Baillie, along with his picture.

Thanks to you Norman, otherwise it never would have happened. Oh and I'm going to alter it with your suggestions soon. Plus new details from your excellent book!

But tell me more about your participation in re-enactments. How long have you been doing this?

Since I was 11 years old

Is this with other 5th Georgia descendants?

Only if they live in the UK? I related to the cavalry early on and joined the 43rd Virginia Cav. you can read it in my intro if you like?

Where do you go and how long do you spend when you come over to the States? Does it give you time for travel? I'm wondering if you could include South Texas in your itinerary.

I hope so I want to shake your hand for giving me back the past. I was a bit like an amnesia case, partial memory, but no more. I gave up when I started work 22 years ago; life was just too hectic. But I have re-kindled my interest, because of the picture and the re-discovery of my roots. So you are to blame so to speak! But it did conclude my search for a meaning to life, So I shall be eternally grateful for you putting pen to paper in that article 1988.

And, oh, what about your horse? Where do the horses come from?

They come and go. I cannot spare the time to look after one personally. At the moment I have secured the services of a beautiful blonde 17 hand filly named Claudia. She is 5 years old and stabled near Canterbury. I ride in Denge Woods at the top of Stone Street the old Roman road. The woods remind me of Georgia/Tennessee, but on a much smaller scale.

Sounds like great fun!

There is nothing to beat the thrill of a Cavalry charge. When I joined the Roundheads in 1975 I was at the Battle of Brill that summer, 3,000 re-enactors. We charged a Royalist Hedge of pikes. The commander just said, 'Stay on and hack at the pikes with your sword, the horses know what to do. They've been trained!'
The horses were just like performing dolphins, they spurred into the gallop and I thought 'Oh my God we are not going to stop!' They stopped all right, just before we hit the infantry. I nearly went over the neck. The horses were trying to intimidate the foot soldiers.
I started hacking and looked down at this guy's red cursing face by my boot. He was swearing and saying, 'Come on then I'll have you!' The horse took his hat in its teeth and tossed it in the air! The man's face lost total color and drained to white. The horse then lunged left and grabbed a fellow by the elbow of his jacket, lifted him into the air and shook him before throwing him to the floor!!!
Panic ensued. With that the hedge of pikes disintegrated like butter before a hot knife and they all ran away! Like frightened rabbits. Martin Savage the Colonel looked at me and said with a wink, 'I told you they've been trained!' :) Being on a horse is like being a god on the battlefield! That's why the cavalry have that crazy elitist attitude

that has got them into so much trouble throughout history. Always be on a horse - never be in the Infantry (Hence the acronym PBI. Poor Bloody Infantry!)

Hope that all goes well during this term. Ours has finally begun.
Bye for now. Norman

Ours is in full flight we have already had mocks last week and I've applied for a lecturing job in Canterbury. Regards Ian

It was at this time that I embarked on producing paintings from memory. I was using my feelings and emotions. The aim was to externalize for the benefit of others what I could see in my mind. The technique improved quickly and I kept Norman up to date with the latest pictures as they happened. I had also pulled out Baillie's records from Princeton and I found a tremendous piece of confirmation as to my character. On a photocopy of a scrappy piece of paper was this gem of information as to the nature of Baillie's character:

Date: Sunday, March 19, 2000:
To: Dr Norman C Delaney
From: Dr Ian C Baillie
Re: Classe de Neige

Hi Norman
Ian here... just back from the 12 day 'Classe de Neige' in the French Alps. Great time had by all. Snow was good, as was the sun...
I pulled Baillie's records from Princeton and I was pleasantly surprised to find a copy of their 1965 letter to you among the photocopied documents! How thorough! There was the letter from John about Baillie and the railroad, a letter from Blanche regarding his death, an obituary from the Princeton newspaper and a marvelous quote, 'Suspended for throwing fire balls in the entrance of the North College' Oct. 22, 1849!
This sound amazingly familiar, I have spent most of my life doing similar stunts, but I didn't get caught!
So history repeats... a nice little fragmentary insight into Baillie's and my psyche.

Hope you are all well, we have two weeks to Easter vacation. Harriet has to work until the April 12th (Sumter!), but I shall be free to pursue the next adventure!
Best wishes Ian

Hello Ian
It was good to hear from you after returning from Spring Break. You had a much more exciting time than I did one reason being that my wife and I were both recovering from colds and didn't feel in the mood for travelling. We'll try to make up for it in May after Steve is back. Right now he's trying to pin down a teaching position in the US, where (hopefully) he can finally make some money for a change. We hope that he can find a position not too far from Corpus Christi. Hey, Ian, that's great about Baillie and the fireball at Princeton that brought about his suspension! They never sent me that information when I enquired about him all those years ago. I never did understand why he left Princeton for the Kentucky Military Institute. What else did you find out about him from the letters and obituary? Darn those folks at Princeton who never sent me the information they had! Isn't it something, having a new view of Baillie Kell as prankster! But what exactly was the 'prank'? Apparently, quite serious if it resulted in his suspension. That's all for now.
Thanks again for your letter.
Norman

Dear Norman
Sorry to hear that the dreaded bug got you, we had it at school, but I seemed to have avoided it this year (fingers crossed!). Hope Steve finds a job back in the good ol' US of A. He is a great lad and sure to do well!
Baillie's records have probably been updated and the filing system is now computerized, I should imagine. Anyway I can scan the details in and send them if you are interested. John's letter is particularly well written in his own hand. Blanche's too, plus the form she filled in for Princeton records. The other documents are mainly type written circa 1914. They obviously loved him and cared... that's all I really wanted to know.
I knew intuitively immediately what the 'prank' was, knowing my pyro tendencies! Having access to kerosene (paraffin) or whale oil for lamps the boys would make balls of rag and soak them. These could then be set alight at will with matches and hurled (using) either a leather glove or as one of my students today exclaimed 'tied with string, whirled about the head and slingshot!' at the opposing team much like a snowball fight! This would have been done at night for a much better effect! Result, much dodging, singed hair and a lot of excitement... plus a suspension for may be a couple of weeks to cool off!
I once witnessed some of my Rugby friends 'Faggot racing!' at a stag

night (I was best man). They stripped off naked, clenched rolled up newspapers in their buttock cheeks, set them alight! And then proceeded to run around the garden in a circuit until only one was left! The scientific principle being 'the faster you move the less likely you are of being burned plus the flames are reduced; a bonus!' Needless to say all were completely worse for drink and as I had just driven from Germany and arrived near midnight stone cold sober I was not in the mood. However it was totally amazing to witness! And lasted several minutes... I hasten to add that in English faggot means a bundle of kindling wood or in this case newspaper! Not in the American slang sense!
Sort of thing used on Jean d'Arc by the dastardly English; she's one of my favorite ladies. I have a thing about strong intellectual French ladies with a bit of spirit! Being a Scientist and having a logical mind I learnt Dutch pretty easily 20 years ago at University and when I worked at the Gezondheidsdienst voor Dieren (Animal Health Laboratories) in Boxtel, Provincie Noord Brabant. 1976. I soon then got to grips with German when I worked for the Forces in Germany 1984 to 1987. I have also studied old English, Anglo-Saxon and Icelandic as a hobby, because I like history and the Vikings. But French I was 'scared' of! I studied 4 years at school reading & writing no trouble, but speaking!!! Tongue-tied, all those unpronounced letters. However after 5 years of exchanges with Ecole Charles Peguy school in Lille and 3 years of Classe de Neige with Ecole Jean d'Arc, Calais my phobia is ended! Hurrah, so another dragon slayed!

As for Baillie and non-graduation... I feel let down, either he didn't make the grade, Princeton is pretty high powered and he flunked (John would have been mad at that, having funded him) or he was ill and didn't sit the finals. Either way finding an alternative venue to complete the degree satisfied honor. The Kentucky Mil Institute nearer home? (Virginia would have been equally as good). I thought that Baillie studied History for his degree, but it looks like it was Civil Engineering? He may have switched courses I don't know what the final BA was for. But we have always had strong Scottish warrior tendencies in our family plus Religion, so a Military Institute sounds fine, especially as John was in the Navy.

Well time to go! I will e-mail some more!
Best wishes, Ian

Well the answer to the question, *I never did understand why he left Princeton for the Kentucky Military Institute* was to wait a whole 12 months before a solution could be found. In a pile of documents Norman gave me in January 2001, was a letter stating that Princeton simply did not offer a degree examination in Civil Engineering until 1878. Baillie therefore had to finish off his studies at the Kentucky Military Institute, graduating fifth in his class of eight and gaining a BA in 1852. I knew exactly why he graduated only fifth. It was to do with the mathematics as I have the same problem. I can do the math given enough time, which is not good in an examination situation. I had a similar problem with population dynamics this time around! The detail of the curriculum matched exactly my interests in this lifetime, including ancient and modern languages. Finally, I did complete the fireball experiment. It worked perfectly the flaming balls of rag made a great whooshing sound as they coursed through the air. I had also got up to my usual habits of having a good time, this was to be confirmed in the letters about Baillie that were sent.

Date: Monday, March 20, 2000:
To: Dr Norman C Delaney
From: Dr Ian C Baillie
Re: Confederate Drinking Habits

Hi Norman Confederate drinking habits! How's things?
Just got back from Classe de Neige 12 days in the French Alps with our school and Ecole Jean d'Arc, Calais. Great time introduced the French teachers to Confederate drinking practice when off duty! You have to wear the cavalry kepi, then give a rebel yell and down a shot of Jack Daniels in one, slamming the glass upside down on the table to signify finishing. Get it wrong and you have to do it again! The kepi is then passed to the person on your left and repeated ad infinitum. After three or so rounds the kepi gets thrown about a bit as people try to avoid having to have a drink...great fun had by all, the French were very impressed. I showed 'em Baillie's photo and we had Old Glory and the Stars and Bars out on the table too. Each night at the 5eme repas, each member had to introduce a new drinking experience!
We had G and T night, Tequila 'slammer' night, Drambuie night. The French had Kir royal night (Champagne and cassis, Super Champagne night (Champagne and Cointreau), Calvados Moonshine night.
Good time had by all!
When I came back I had a nice letter from Princeton with Baillie's records. Turns out he did three years 1848 to 1851 and was

suspended for 'throwing fireballs in entry of North college' Oct 22, 1849! Sounds horribly familiar as I was known for doing very similar things at University with my home grown firecrackers!
So History repeats. Baillie then went to the Kentucky Military institute where he gained his BA in 1852. I didn't get caught and I graduated straight... So an improvement I think!?
Baillie would have loved the bangs and smells of combat and despite the horror of it all... the excitement would have been quite intoxicating; Gunpowder and Horses!
Well better close now. I have some more pictures in the pipeline and will e-mail them when ready.
Best wishes
Ian (Doc Baillie)

The next e-mail was to identify the nub of the problem Baillie never got married? This was the very heart of the mystery and we were about to break through to the answer in dramatic style!

Date: Tuesday, March 21, 2000:
To: Dr Ian C Baillie
From: Dr Norman C Delaney
Re: Fireballs!

Ian, it's GREAT! I LOVE IT! (Baillie would, too!) As for the information about Baillie and the fireball throwing, it really helps in humanizing him. I'm glad it turned up. Unfortunately, the timing of the incident was bad. That was the year that John was court-martialed and expelled from the navy, so he and the rest of the family would not have been amused. John took credit for supporting his family at Laurel Grove during that period, so losing his salary for that year would have been quite a loss. I don't think that poor Baillie had many opportunities for skylarking after that incident, or could I be wrong?
Norman

Well, it's all part of that being away from the 'gals' routine. Really the 'old gone a' Viking' bit a chance for the boys to play away! Baillie certainly enjoyed Princeton as Blanche wrote after his death. The club life and the intellectualizing. He joined Clio Society 1848 so it says. Having visited the Princeton web site and got a feel for the place I would say that he was in his element! But may be the socializing got in the way of the studying?
I am really disappointed in him for not graduating, especially after John's sacrifice. It may be that he didn't really know that John was

funding him. Margery would have kept that close to her chest I feel. Perhaps Baillie would have tried harder if he had known.
(We now know that this was not the case, as mentioned above)

John's court martial was a fine example of highland/Southern spirit. Semmes recognised that and ultimately it was that quality that made John the man he was to become. The Southern cavalier image, gallant knight, jolly japes making the ladies giggle. That was Baillie, that is me! It is an absolute conundrum as to why Baillie in the end never married? Did the family cramp his style? The war was boys' own adventure; Robert Louis Stevenson/Walter Scott/Alexander Dumas stuff. The reality of losing being quite something else. Yet Baillie is getting oxen, talking with the Yankee troops at Laurel Grove just weeks after the end of the war. Soldiers can relate to soldiers... So he was not sitting idly by depressed by it all.
His fiancée is probably the key... she the one he adored, his paramour throws him up as useless. Rejected big time he loses the will to hunt down another female... and settle, make a life outside the family. Time running out John and Blanche come to the rescue and provide a home for him. Uncle Baillie; the kids would have liked him, stories of his adventures with the 'Knights in Gray/ Gray cavaliers.' Three musketeers all over again! One for all and all for one! A thrust with a saber here and a pistol shot there, hurrah for the Stars and Bars and southern rights... Gone with the wind eat your heart out!
This would make a really good film! 'The Captain and the Cavalier' a tale of two brothers... wow we might even win an Oscar! Dr Norman Delaney Historical advisor/consultant! :)
Ian

The very next picture entitled *Duty calls* was the tin opener that opened the can of worms. I had worked hard on this picture and I was now closing in on the cause of my trauma. I really felt confident that I had captured something special in the past life of Baillie, my remote viewing skills were going off the scale. Again all the detail was to be stunningly confirmed by actual letters in July later that year.

Date: Thursday, May 18, 2000:
To: Dr Norman C Delaney
From: Dr Ian C Baillie
Re: Duty Calls!

Hi Norman
What da'ya think? :)

This one's called 'Duty calls' and shows Alexander Baillie Kell taking leave of his Mother and two sisters at Laurel Grove Darien GA. He refused to pay $100 for a draft substitute as his mother wished, and leaving came back saying that he would pay $100 for an over-seer to look after the Negroes on the plantation. A typical IB/AB compromise I can never just leave an argument and walk out, but always have to return to resolve the situation! Typical me...
I think I have got very near to the look of Laurel Grove. The basket (empty) shows that Mom really cares and has packed him something in the saddlebags. The flag stands ready to be defended and his Captain (William Brailsford) waits adjusting his hat ready for the off.
It also shows what Baillie aspires to, but never reaches.
Fighting the Yankees becomes the priority and thoughts of glory and promotion a passing fancy.
I have also remembered the identity of his young lady, blonde Southern bombshell fiancée that dumped him after the war!
She was none other than Sarah (Sallie) Spalding! The teenage daughter of Randolph Spalding, his brother in law's brother.
The blonde lady in blue is maybe her or maybe a sister the choice is left to the audience!

I have a few pictures to paint on that one, which are already in the planning stage! They will be cracker's I can promise. Sallie broke his heart and did much more damage than the Yankees. She dumped him because he could never keep her to the manner that she was accustomed to! The little ***, she was beautiful, intelligent, artistic and the reason behind Baillie's hurry to buy Rushlands, become an Officer and win his princess. He fell hook line and sinker for her and then she dumped him... Very much like 'The History of Mister Polly' by H G Wells... I related to that with overwhelming empathy as a boy; to be continued... Call it past life therapy or what ever, but I need to settle the account before moving on!!!**
Regards Ian

Eureka, we had reached the Holy Grail of my existence; Sarah Elizabeth *Sallie* Spalding had broken my heart all those years ago. This was the real reason I remembered everything, ***the blonde lady,*** wouldn't you know it? At the base of this profound quest to unlocking the secrets of the Universe was an amazingly beautiful women, how original!

Ian, your picture of Baillie's farewell is TERRIFIC! I LOVE IT! And the STORY that it tells, and who could tell it better than YOU! Say, now, this is getting better and better. But tell me more about Sallie; how were you able to connect her to Baillie? It all seems to fit so well. Ian, maybe you should have been a detective; well, actually, you ARE a detective.
Well done! I'm looking forward to hearing more about Sallie Spalding. Who did she wind up marrying? Little snip. Baillie should have found somebody else. I wonder why he didn't. Thanks, Ian!
Norman

The floodgates were now open and out poured the terrible secret and whole story in a cataclysmic week of body shaking trauma wracked emotion. The answers to Norman's questions were about to be graphically and profoundly displayed in Technicolor detail. Hastily I went into the attic and dusted off my old art folders from the 70's. There in graphic detail was displayed the whole story of Sallie and Baillie in every detail. I was absolutely stunned at the comprehensive data logged all those years ago, without knowing the subconscious made manifest. Rosie was the witness as I took my art works from the 70's to school on the monday morning. At lunchtime I displayed and related the whole story to her in the Physics laboratory, her reaction to the event was so emotional that I had to share it with Norman. This was something special, very special and it was unfolding before my eyes.

Date: Monday, May 22, 2000:
To: Dr Norman C Delaney
From: Dr Ian C Baillie
Re: Email from Rosie!!!

Here is Rosie's impression of today:

'I'm just so overwhelmed by this - I'm in a state of overload- it's going to take a while for all of this to sink in. We have unlocked a door to the last 20 years of your life!! So far you have written two chapters about your war memories - years 11-23? But now the story of Sallie and Baillie is so much more powerful, tragic and emotional. This is your story from 21 to present day. This is colossal Ian. I'm absolutely blown away. Thank you so much for asking me to be with you today. I'm truly humbled - to witness all these images that have held you in their grip for your lifetime. I've witnessed your 'awakening' to your memes! What an honor! I keep thinking of the word KEY. Unlocking

the subconscious that is so powerfully revealed in your pictures. They have been there. I can see links. The roots of the 'pain tree' beg you to delve deeper, shout out of a pain that tore your/ Baillie's soul apart. The haunting haunted figure looking out to sea, to Sapelo, to the lonely tower. But the saddest picture is seeing the fierce warrior standing between you and your dream, a powerful black force, black knight standing between you and the girl of your dreams.
There is so much here I will let these thoughts have time-I'll write them as they come to me. Clannad's song keeps drifting in and out of my mind. The posters show you really know where my evolution is taking me. Thanks to your help.'
'In Lake 'ch'
Rosie

Norman was quick to join in with the revelation that Baillie worshipped Sarah Elizabeth Spalding; *Sallie*. All was now so clear and the connections throughout my life just kept on coming.

Well done, Ian, now all we need is a picture (or painting) of Sallie to make her even more real. Considering her family's wealth, there's bound to be a painting, and most certainly photographs. Whom did she marry?
What was her life like post-Baillie? Children? Correspondence? I wonder if she and her family are mentioned in CHILDREN OF PRIDE (Myers?) that huge collection of Jones family correspondence (Georgia Coast, contemporaries of Kells). I'll certainly want to check it out. Ian, you have certainly taken Baillie's life out of the shadows!
Norman

The picture expanded into glorious life, a bygone age of chivalry and decadence, antebellum America in its splendor, yet paid for by the nightmare of slavery. It was at the same time so ironic that the system was propped up by an institution, diametrically opposed to the sacred ideals of freedom that Scottish folk hold so dear. Yet we were accessing the truth not some comfortable fantasy of fabrication. We had to take the information at face value no matter how ugly and painful that may be.

Date: Tuesday, May 23, 2000:
To: Dr Norman C Delaney
From: Dr Ian C Baillie
Re: Wow... Revelation!

Sapelo Sallie 1861: Baillie's happiest memory of his ideal love.

I am going to scan some of the pictures in and photograph the big ones.
I have written a short article on the decoding of the imagery which will give any psychoanalyst (joke!) a field day... It's all there! The whole story!
This would never have come about with out your input... I have relived the whole thing several times in my own life. I would still be doing this now, but I/we have broken the cycle. I can move on...
Thank you Norman!

Together we had broken the spell of *Sapelo Sallie*, and I was now free at last from the haunting of this subconscious obsession that had survived physical mortality. The specter had vanished when exposed to the daylight of conscious reality.

Update from Buddy Sullivan: In a nutshell...

Date: Thursday, May 18, 2000:
To: Dr Ian C Baillie
From: Buddy Sullivan
Re: It's a Southern thing!

Hello Ian!
Thanks for the pictures and the updated information. Sallie sounds incredible! How I wish I could go back in time to 1866 before she has a chance to marry Archie McKinley. I would happily join the long line of those trying to woo her! It is easy to see why Baillie fell for her the way he did. I believe all of us men in this part of America have experienced at least once in life what Baillie went through. There is always that one special woman in our lives. Sometimes we get her, but often as not we don't. It's a SOUTHERN thing you know! I have a number of color photographs of the Sapelo Lighthouse taken after its restoration was completed in 1998 - the way (colors and banding) it would have looked at the time of your story. I will be happy to send you a few for your perusal if you would like. Let me know. Also send me your address again, as I am unable to keep up with things with so much going on.
I am working on a new History of Georgia under commission to the Georgia Historical Society - hardest book I have ever written, trying to consolidate 400 years of history into a reasonably concise narrative. I am accustomed to dealing in detail, rather than the broad overview approach! Interesting about the Sullivan woman. As far as I know I am not related - my roots are here in coastal Georgia, most of my family came from this section, via Charleston - Sullivan's Island at the entrance to Charleston Harbor, where many English, Scots and Irish came into America, is named for one of my direct ancestors. You mentioned a Patrick Sullivan. Would you believe my son who lives and works in Atlanta, is named Patrick!
All kinds of coincidences in this life...
Talk to you later.
Buddy

Chapter Three
Letters

As the story unfolded the synchronicity of events accelerated, Norman was able to provide a unique insight into the character and personality of Baillie, with an overlay of historical events and background. He had retrieved the stored letters and documents from his attic, placed there thirty years ago and miraculously saved despite not knowing that one day they might come in useful. That day had arrived and with it I unlocked the door to my past. As I read and re-read each new piece of detailed information one word kept echoing in my mind, same, same, it's all the same!

All of the information described me perfectly in vivid mind shattering detail. This was confirmation indeed that Baillie and I are one and the same person in mind and spirit if not physical body. It was as if the Matrix was willing us on. Precisely the right piece of information would arrive at precisely the right time to spur us on to a new discovery. Our minds were working in synchronous harmony on an entirely different plane. Explainable as all things are connected in the Matrix and thought is faster than light. Right on cue and without prompting in July 2000 Norman fired a burst of data from the records, which confirmed all of my paintings from memory and findings. Baillie was revealed from archival documentation and excitingly the five most important letters he had penned himself. *Oh my goodness, he had written himself and they still survived!* I was ecstatic at the thought of possibly seeing my own writing from 140 years ago. As I read and re-read the evidence I was determined to extract copies of the real letters from the *Kell papers collection*, Duke University, Durham, North Carolina.

In August I penned my own copies to compare the handwriting and signatures for when they would arrive. Yet another experiment was in the making. I knew that I probably even wrote as Baillie, for I had deliberately changed my style from cursive script to a more upright stance when approximately fifteen years of age in imitation of my mother; a deliberate conscious act. I guessed that my original style would be the closest to Baillie's own writing. I was not to be disappointed, in October I examined and compared the originals and I did in fact write the same, the only exception being the letter **'r'** which Baillie wrote the old fashioned way and I the modern. The most noticeable factor was that I wrote most like him when in a hurry and quickly. This was to be expected from my findings, as this is the state when the subconscious has the most control and can flow freely, exactly as with the paintings. Even my signature was a modern version using the same strokes, constructed in a similar fashion, again the elaborate **'B'** began its construction differently, but was completed the same as my own. I instantly could replicate the signature perfectly. I understood intuitively its construction from first principles. The hand movements were entirely natural for me and the **'aillie'** part of the signature was identical to mine, as were the underlining emphasis with strokes at either end. The action was the same.

I have replicated Norman's e-mail copies of the letters, as they contain the essential relevant information. A full text version of the important letters and documents can be read in the appendices. Many family letters include only a line or two in reference to Baillie and although I have them in my possession for handwriting analysis and interest, I have omitted them from the records at the end of the book.

Date: Tuesday, July 18, 2000:
To: Dr Ian C Baillie
From: Dr Norman C Delaney
Re: Letters in my attic...

Ian, those are really great pictures! Looks like you're having a lot of fun! I'll continue with more of the information I've turned up. First;

A letter written by Baillie to Blanche, dated June 21 (1864). He gives his address as Troop H, 5th Georgia Cavalry, Wheeler's Corps, Army of East Tennessee, Atlanta, Georgia:

'I write you a few lines more to inform you that our cavalry had a severe fight with the enemy two days ago, about two thousand strong on each side, but our squadron was not engaged in it. The loss in the two squadrons engaged was 4 killed and 25 wounded, in the other cavalry there was only two killed and I don't know how many

wounded. The Yanks were finally driven back with great slaughter. (He encloses a few dollars for Blanche to buy him a pencil.) I suppose Nath's regiment is on the left (Nath was Blanche's younger brother) as all the forces are being concentrated there and towards the centre, as Johnston is doing his best to bring on a general engagement.
Gen. Lee has telegraphed Gen. Johnson (sic) that he has given Grant the most complete whipping of any General that has been in command of that army and our army here has all confidence in Johnston and the opinion is that he will serve Sherman as he did McClellan before Richmond, having retreated over a hundred miles and had it not been for Magruder and Huger, the whole Yankee army would have been compelled to surrender.'

I'm not doing this in order. The next Baillie letter I'll send is dated August 14, 1862. Will follow later.

Brilliant... it's got the feel of correctness! :)
I never knew Baillie had written! He obviously thought a lot of Blanche!
Ian

The possibility of performing another experiment loomed:

Norman,
It occurred to me that you might have copies of Baillie's handwriting I would dearly love to analyze the script would it be possible to photocopy or scan copies of the documents to me. I will be more than glad to cover any cost involved. The originals are now worth loads of dollars. I saw one of John's letters on the Internet for $3,000 !!!!
How incredible! Yet I would pay it for Baillie's if I had the money and the originals were available. I am on holiday now and going over to Granpa's by the sea at Herne Bay, North Kent, time to get the boat out, weather's been very cloudy though.
Harriet presented the flowers at Canterbury Cathedral in front of her whole school at the Commemoration Service Friday... a proud moment for the Baillie's... timeless too amongst all that history.
I thought of Steven's visit at Christmas, please give him my regards. Becket and the Norman Kings looked down on humble Baillie, but in the end we are all equal in the sight of God.
Regards Ian

The next piece was a little puzzling to Norman, but not to me. Whilst working on the railway one day in 1974, I found that I could make some easy money by carrying peoples bags. So I set to with enthusiasm and rapidly accumulated over £3.00 for very little effort and a lot of politeness.

Oh, one other thing to add from a letter of **Margery to Blanche, February 24, 1863,** from the Retreat. This piece really surprised me:

'Baillie in camp and makes some money for himself waiting on other Gentlemen.'

That strikes me as VERY strange!
Ian, here's some more great Baillie stuff, this next a letter written by Baillie to Blanche from

'Camp Davant, dated August 12, 1863. I copied verbatim most of it.

'I received your answer to my note today and thank you kindly for giving me the desired information about the strings so promptly. Please get me three treble E and one B, which is the next largest and of the violin strings, you may get two of the first and one of the last, which is the A on the violin. (He has enclosed $10 for Blanche to buy the violin strings.) Gen. Evans of South Carolina has arrived with his brigade from Mississippi and they are now encamped on the island, but the General's headquarters are in Sav and as he outranks Gen. Mercer, he will be in command of the department and Gen. M will take the field. (He mentions having attended Christ Church and also having dined with the Bishop.) There has been a great deal of sickness from typhoid fever and a number of deaths, but I have never been in better health. Our tents are moved out now, entirely clear of the stables, which I think will cause an improvement in the health of the regiment. In going to Cos. Charles's you get off at Quitman about half past six in the evening, where you take supper, but Valdosta, ten miles this side is the regular supper house. At Quitman you get in a four-horse coach after supper and you arrive at Retreat about 11 o'clock, right upon the road, 11 miles, from Quitman. Tell Munroe that Roanoke is at Rushland and he is so old that I have given him his freedom. I shall have to go on picket to Sav in a very short time.'
(NOTE: Quitman is on the Savannah Albany & Gulf RR, 26 miles from Thomasville in Brooks Co., Ga.; fare from Macon to Savannah is $10; fare from Savannah to Quitman is also $10; leaves Sav. at 6a.m., arrives in Quitman at 6p.m., Retreat is 10 miles further.)

Baillie had played the **violin** and the **guitar!** I had taught myself to play the guitar from the age of eleven and I had carried it everywhere with me through out my travels. Interestingly Baillie is requesting three top strings, which keep breaking. With modern day metal wound on nylon strings it is the D that keeps breaking, I had bought endless D strings. I checked with a picture of an actual Civil War guitar and sure enough the picture showed the top string to be missing. It all checked out.

My sister had put me off of playing the violin, because of her incessant scraping and poor forming of notes. She learnt piano and later took up the guitar much to the relief of all concerned. The tune *Turkey in the Straw* had been going around in my head since I was a boy, I would often find myself whistling or humming it. I instantly recognized that this was the source of the tune, Baillie had played it on the fiddle in camp with the boys of the 5th, or as we were to find out later, on the *Sully farm* in 1870 when he had met Mary Sullivan.

Another thing that I noticed was the familiarity with giving direction in the latter part of the letter was also typical me. I have a good sense of direction and a grasp of travel. The directions were clear, concise and accurate. The generosity of spirit and compassion towards the faithful Roanoke, an aged servant, was also exactly in accordance with my nature and humanity.

Next letter from Baillie to Blanche: from Camp Davant is dated August 24, 1863:

(He has received the violin strings.) 'I suppose it must be an undoubted fact that brother is in command of her (CSS ALABAMA) now. I do not feel at all uneasy, or never will about him, especially since the Vanderbilt has been destroyed. (Hopes to get a 5-day furlough so he can visit Blanche.) I shall see the Col as he knows me now so well and he is so friendly to me; but there are some men in our company who have not got a furlough for twelve months, and no furloughs are given now at all. I will let you know after sounding Mars' Bob (the Col). He told the Capt. that he was trying to get me an appointment, from the Sec. of War, in his regiment. I shall carry in my diploma that I received at the Ky Mil. Institute, and tell him to make every use of it that is in his power for my promotion. How nobly has the garrison of Fort Sumpter behaved.

(Here I go again: Poor Baillie! That promotion would have meant so much to him! more follows)

Our Donnie: This is the image Baillie had of his brother as he wrote this letter. Both brothers were now determined to play their parts in the escalating struggle.

The *promotion,* this was the key; I realized in a flash that I had re-enacted this when I was fifteen years of age! I even had the photographs to prove it, how utterly amazing. The Matrix was providing exact confirmation to match events documented on film in my early life. This was certainly also the reason behind my seeking a Queen's Commission in the army this time around. In the end I settled on a Captain's rank and three years in Germany with British Forces as a Physics teacher. It was all there, the same, absolutely the same! I was reliving my past in this present physical lifetime, yet totally unaware of what I was doing. Then it hit me! This confirmed my assumption that the promotion would have meant he could have married Sallie. He would have obtained the correct social rank to marry his young lady. It all fitted, Sallie was the reason for everything, the prime motive in everything he/I did. I had at last found the fountain of motive from whence all events flowed. The emotional euphoria of discovery was so intense it had to be true.

Then Norman posted the all important promotion letter. I knew then for certain that Colonel Robert H Anderson had after all recommended Baillie to become an officer, here was the definitive proof. This was pure gold dust, beyond all possible value; absolute vindication and I had the photographs to prove it. Undeniable evidence that memory is transferred between physical beings. The Matrix had come up trumps again and this was the big one:

Head Qrs 5th Regt Ga Cavalry Savannah, Ga. August 30, 1863
General S. Cooper
Adjt & Inspector General C.S.A.Richmond, Virginia

General
I have the honor very respectfully to request and to recommend that Private Alexander Kell of H Troop of my Regiment be appointed a Second Lieutenant of Cavalry in the Provisional Army of the Confederate States, and assigned to duty with my Regiment as a Drill Master. Private Kell has been in the ranks performing his duty in a faithful and soldierly manner ever since the commencement of the war. He is a high toned honorable gentleman, and has received a military education, being a graduate of the Kentucky Military Institute, and one in every respect worthy of and deserving a commission.

Respectfully requesting the favorable and earliest convenient action of the War Department in this matter.
R. H. Anderson
Col 5th Regular Ga Cavalry

comment added:
Res. subj. to the Sec. of War
The services of a Drill Master should not be required at this advanced period of the war. The regiment has its full complement of officers.
By order
Ed. A. Palfrey
Lt. Col & Adj.
9 Sept. 63

It was all so very clear, Baillie had been a 3rd Lieutenant in the Militia and then had enlisted as a private hoping to gain promotion in the field. He had been an exemplary soldier as the recommendation for Drill Master shows. But who would want another additional officer at this late stage in the war? Gettysburg had just been lost and Vicksburg had fallen, the idea of a Drill Master was patently absurd. If the Colonel had put something more relevant Baillie would probably have got his commission and he might have married Sallie and I should not have had the deep emotional scars that caused me to remember. In fact I doubt whether I would have remembered it at all, for it seems to be that it is only with extreme emotional circumstance that people remember their past lives. Many cases show this to be true and usually once the person is aware of the past emotional or physical trauma they begin to rest easy and continue with their present life. I was sure that I could now rest easy for the rest of my life. We had discovered my dark secret and I knew that I had made every attempt subconsciously to make right the story this time around and I had succeeded with out knowing. The emotional relief was so profound and deep that I knew I was at last completely healed. Tears filled my eyes for weeks; they still do at the thought of all that has transpired. Poor Baillie, one twist of the cards and fate condemned him to a life of bitter loneliness and unfulfilled ambition. The Matrix can be a cruel mistress, but we learn from it, boy do we learn!

The Commission letter: This is the original hand written letter recommending Baillie for his commission. The promotion meant everything and Baillie would have been able to marry Sallie had he succeeded.

Ian, here's a little gem from a letter to **Blanche from Hetty, dated Rushlands, July 12, 1862.**

Most of it concerns war and family news, but this piece will interest you.

'Baillie brought over four of his companions in arms night before last, and gave us a treat in the way of music, they sang charmingly (underlined) together, and one plays finely on the piano, they staid (sic) until half past eleven singing and playing and then rode back eight miles to camp - it was amusing to see them how they demolished their supper. Baillie gave us notice the day before so we were prepared for them.'

Wow! This fitted like a glove; I had spent all my youth doing the same things; a good meal, good company and a good singsong. Yes, this was me all right, no doubt about it.

Ian, I'm going to try and finish these Baillie related letters this week. They are certainly giving both of us an even better understanding of the man.

Here are excerpts from a letter to **Blanche from Hetty, 'Rushlands,' June 12 (1862?)**

'I am going to ask you to send me the money you have in keeping for me. I begged Baillie to give me his $50 bounty money to keep for him and that with some of mine and what you will send me makes $100 which I will send Mr. Gue to put out for us in the shape of a Confederate bond. . . . I have persuaded Baillie to give me all he can spare to keep for him, for he is so regardless of money. . . . Please take from my money enough to get me two pieces of music. I saw the names last night when Baillie and I were singing - My Maryland, Beauregard's March or Quickstep at the Battle of Mannasses(sic). I forget which, and Baillie has carried the music to camp this morning so I cannot refer to it . . . . then I want Marsellaise, by Herz or Beyer whichever you think best.'

This hit a home run again, I have always been unconcerned about money, not wasteful, but I have always regarded money as a vulgar subject and one that we simply do not talk about in polite society. This fitted exactly, my character, my attitude. A core personality description, so precise, so perfect, again Baillie had to be me.

Letter from Baillie to Blanche, dated August 14, 1862 from 'Rushlands'

(Baillie acknowledges having received a package from Blanche.)
'Our camp is situated on a river, in a beautiful oak and hickory grove, an hour and a half's ride from home. I have fine fish for dinner everyday and all the other good things that are to be had out of salt water and of all things, that would not have suited me better, we have a quartet of singers, in which I take part and I flatter myself that our singing is hard to surpass. Our Savannah members of the company are

> nearly all of them, men of great musical talent. (Comments on family matters, on Brother John) May his cruize on this new Steamer be as successful as that of the Sumpter's of which I have no doubt it will be if she is as fast a Steamer as the Sumpter. The Nashville is still lying under our battery at the mouth of the Ogeechee, awaiting the opportunity to escape, and I hope that she may be soon favored. (Comments on weather, extreme heat) I expect shortly to go down to Sapelo with the Capt. and twenty men to bring back some of the Negroes on the island that have gone from us, and I do hope that I may come across some of ours. I never should allow any of mine, if we should be fortunate enough to get them back to remain three days on the place, but take them right away and sell them. We are to go down at night with muffled oars in three boats, then to reconnoitre the island to find out the strength and position of the enemy, if there are any there, before any attempt is made to rescue the Negroes.'
> (Kell Papers, Duke)
>
> (I don't get this. Are they being 'rescued'? Didn't they run away?) Norman.

Oh dear, I had been afraid that something like this would come up. The word rescued is a euphemism for recapturing the Negroes. Baillie had been involved in the hunting down and infamous shooting of the runaway escaped contrabands on Sapelo Island. Captain Brailsford had justified the action, 'as the Black men had been found in arms against the Whites.' Unfortunately several had been killed in the firefight that ensued and the Yankee gunboats had retaliated later by burning the Captain's plantation on Sutherland Bluff at a later date. This celebrated action, being well recorded and documented in Buddy Sullivan's book, *Early days on the Georgia tidewater*. The action was also used in some small measure, to try to justify the burning of Darien in June 11, 1863. The 2nd South Carolina and the 54th Massachusetts Infantry, both Negro regiments carried out this act. War can never be pleasant and these ugly episodes mar the gallantry displayed early on in the conflict. I felt sure that Baillie was not proud of this.

To Blanche from Hetty, 'Retreat,' May 25, 1863

> 'I suppose Mother wrote you Baillie was stationed at present on the 'Isle of Hope'. We feel so relieved to think the regiment has not been ordered to Tennessee as we heard at one time... you know this part of the country is a healthy pine forest - no rice fields to dread.'

A small snippet from a letter; I have always dreaded mosquitoes, they are the one insect that I will go out of my way to kill, as I do not wantonly destroy that which I can not create. But mosquitoes and other biting insects I have always given no quarter too. This phobia seems to be a result of living in close proximity to them last time around.

An earlier letter **(February 7, 1864) from Margery to Blanche has this morsel:**

'You mentioned getting Mr. Sims (Tadie's Husband; Tadie was Blanche's sister) to interest him in getting a situation for Baillie, but he seems so satisfied now that you need not trouble yourself. He has got so accustomed to the hardships of a private's life that he does not mind it and since his Negroes are hired out he has enough to live on which his Soldiers pay did not give him. Col Anderson expects to be promoted and if so, says he will take Baillie on his Staff, until then he will remain as he is. I would be very sorry to have him join Morgan. I should never hear from him and he would be constantly in so much danger. Now I hear regularly once in a week or ten days. I suffer so much from having one beloved away with but little probability of ever seeing him again that I must try and hold on to this one'
(Kell Papers, Duke University)

Here in this letter, Baillie is fondly thought of by his mother and certainly he might not have returned, if he had joined John Hunt Morgan's raiders. In the event the 5th stayed with Joe Wheeler's section of the cavalry, fighting around Atlanta and then raiding into Tennessee in the fall.

To Blanche from Evey, 'Retreat', Feb. 25, 1864

'Baillie took us quite by surprise day before yesterday, his regiment has been ordered to Florida, and they had reached Valdosta the night before, so poor fellow, he could only get one day's leave, and rode on horseback 18 miles to get here, he arrived about one o'clock in the day and started on his return between 8 and 9 at night. It was a great pleasure to see him even for a few hours. Mother busied herself at once seeing to what clothes he had brought being washed and mended and **I got up all the nice things I could and filled his haversack for the next day's march.** He looks thin and his horse looks badly too. He has had to do a great deal of riding he says, which has worn down both man and beast, but he looks healthy and in good spirits...' More coming, Ian.

This refers to the Olustee campaign in Florida, February 1864. The Confederates fought a pitched battle with the Union forces around Lake City in an effort to curtail their march on Tallahassee. The Yankees were soundly beaten and retreated back to Jacksonville and safety. The 5th Georgia entrained men and horses in South Carolina and was transported to the battlefield. The stop over enroute took place in Valdosta, so Baillie took advantage of the lull in proceedings to visit his mother and sister's staying at Cousin Charles Spalding's retreat plantation near Quitman on the boarder with Florida. The 5th arrived at the end of the battle, one company seeing action, but the remainder acting only as a grisly burial detail.

I then realized that I had correctly painted the haversacks being filled in the painting *Duty calls* again it was mentioned here in actual verifiable letters. I had also accurately painted Baillie looking thin as described in the same letter. The following letter described the tedious picket duty that had to be performed in case the Yankee's returned to the field.

To Blanche from Evey, 'Retreat', March 18 (no year) probably 1864.

'Baillie is near Jacksonville and we have been dreading to hear of another battle there, but by the last reports the Yankees have gone to Pilatka - he writes in low spirits poor fellow, do write him, he seems so dull and is going thro' many hardships, and he enquires so affectionately of you in all his letters and begs us to let him know whenever we hear from you, and says you have always been so kind and affectionate to him - when you write direct to Capt. Brailsford's care, company H, 5th Geo. Cavalry, Lake City, Fla. Among other duties his regiment has been going out on picket duty, the whole regiment at a time, alternating with one another and they stand bridle in hand by their horses 12 (underlined) hours at a time, and only three men allowed to be absent at a time - it must be most fatiguing there. He did not take **Jim** with him either, thinking it would be troublesome to get him there, as no transportation was allowed for him and he sent **Jim** to Rushlands - so I suppose he has to attend to his own horse, unless he has been able to hire some one to do it'.

(Kell Papers, Duke)
Believe it or not, Ian, MORE coming!

Incredibly I had painted *Jim* the groom in my picture *Duty Calls*. I instinctively felt that I should paint him holding the horse and now that had been confirmed as true and we now knew his name.

> Ian, take care of yourself! I'm sorry to learn about the latest setback. Hope that all is better. I'm way behind this week so will have to delay most of the remaining Baillie related material. I do have time to mention another letter from:
>
> **Baillie to Blanche, dated June 18, 1864,**
> 'To the front 6 miles from Marietta.'
> Most of what I have are my own notes rather than direct quotes. Here it is:
>
> '... Regiment extreme right of the army; only cavalry there; no one allowed to leave camp out of hearing of the bugle; expects at any moment to hear boots and saddles sounded; some skirmishing day before yesterday; equipped with Enfield rifles 'the best that is in use anywhere'; 'spoiling for a fight'; regiment had left Augusta week ago last Saturday, arrived in Atlanta the following morning; met Mr. Pinkerton, who took him to his house until next morning; promised to bring Johnny a Yankee pony; wonders when the great battle will come; can hear the booming of cannon and firing of small arms; Col. Anderson has been given command of a brigade; intends to use 5th Cavalry for charging only, with sabres and revolvers.'

Apparently Blanche has expressed her concern that Baillie could be wounded. After the deaths of her two children she served as a volunteer nurse in a Macon hospital. Baillie writes:

> 'I am very much obliged to you for your kindness and will certainly avail myself of your offer if I have the opportunity of being sent to the Macon hospital.'

This turned out to be another star letter, for when I obtained a copy of the original from Duke University it described in full detail one of my paintings, *Battle of the Saltworks*. But the picture actually shows the events mentioned in this important letter, the memory was of hauling cannon up a mountain and then firing down on the Yankees from a tremendous height behind rocks. The feeling was one of overwhelming security and safety knowing that the Yankees would never get near. This was the Battle of Kennesaw Mountain June 1864, all correctly shown in the painting. Baillie mentions also that he is armed with the Enfield musket, this was the reason why I had made a working rifled musket when I was fifteen years of age and had then made a full size cannon. It was all described in this one letter.

> Ian you're going to find this interesting, portions of a letter of **Margery Kell to Blanche, dated July 5, (1864).**
> Margery is depressed because of concern for Baillie and also the close proximity of the Yankees. She writes:
>
> 'This morning I got two letters from Baillie, and I am glad to see he writes so cheerfully. He says he has not had a dry stitch of clothes or a dry blanket in two weeks, but still his health is good... I wish Baillie could meet your brother, but a private has little time or opportunity... Poor Baillie writes me he is **barefoot** and no prospect of getting shoes. **He has been supplying himself altogether** and I must try and get him a pair made here, but I don't know how I can get them to him...'

The weather was extremely wet for June 1864, the roads muddy and this is mentioned in all reports of the Battle of Kennesaw Mountain. I was drawn to the comments about being bare foot for I have always had a love of good shoes and boots for riding. Several times I have made my own boots for my re-enactment uniforms, supplying myself exactly as described in the letter. So another home run is scored! It all fits so beautifully.

> That's all I have on that letter. Jumping ahead to a letter written after the war:
> **To Kell from Sister Mary Kell, from 'Rushlands,' Feb 21, (1866); it contains a really strong put down of their brother. (How many put downs can the poor guy take!)**
>
> 'Baillie's judgment(sic) is so poor - not that it is his fault at all (last two words underlined) - but he has not the capacity (underlined) for managing a plantation as well as it should be and if we lived near you he would be guided entirely by your advice and judgment(sic).'
>
> (So, they are all going to wind up living in Spalding County close to John, but will that change anything? I'll make every effort to finish this next week. Only a few letters left; none from Baillie)

From this important letter I later came to realize that Baillie had given up. He had lost all hope of marrying Sallie. Immediately after the war he was busy trying to salvage the plantation, gathering oxen and ploughing to get a crop in. But Mary Bass Spalding, Sallie's mother has dropped the bombshell that Sallie was to marry Archibald Carlisle McKinley. Baillie was devastated and heart broken. His sister Mary does not understand and pens this sad letter to brother John.

> Say, Ian, I have some interesting information about Baillie that you should know about. I turned up copies of letters of his and references to him by other family members in research material I had from my study of Kell. I hadn't seen this stuff for years and had forgotten about it. This will fill in some of the missing links in your own research on Baillie. I'll give you some of it now and continue over the next several days. Here's what I have regarding Baillie's broken engagement found in Kell Family Papers at Duke University:
>
> **letter to Blanche from Evy, Jan. 24, 1871:**
>
> 'I am glad to hear that you have a white cook as well as nurse. I should think you would get on easier with them than white and black together and the white farm laborers too, I cannot but hope will do well on the Sully farm. I am glad your eyes are opened to C.M.S.___character. I never really liked her altho' I tried to do so after Baillie's engagement. Brother's opinion has been the same of her for some time past. I suppose you will not be much thrown with her now, as her home at Mrs. Varner's is broken up. Who really owns that house now, Mrs. John Varner?'
>
> (So, Ian, who is C.M.S.????)
>
> **To Tadie (Blanche's younger sister) from Evelyn Spalding, Chestnut Ridge, Nov. 25 (1871?)**
>
> 'Baillie has been very busy getting in the corn and fodder at the Sully place, and expects to finish tomorrow - poor fellow 'hope deferred' makes him groan and sigh. I think, altho' I do not say so, that his engagement will come to nothing. I have never felt sure (underlined) that his 'ladye love' was in earnest, so I have had very little to say to him or any one else about his engagement.'
>
> These excerpts from two letters are all I have on Baillie's engagement

that never materialized, so now it's time to do some more detective work and try to identify C.M.S. I'm assuming that her last name is Sully. I can try looking her up in the 1870 Georgia census. Could this have been a second try for poor Baillie? A second rejection? Oh, no! How much rejection can a guy take! Sorry I didn't find this stuff sooner. Until next time, Norman.

This crucial and informative e-mail will be discussed at length in another chapter so I will refrain from reiterating the details here and move swiftly on.

Ian, a very interesting letter from **John Kell to Sister Evy; Sunnyside, August 6, 1876**

'My first and principal delay in writing was on account of Baillie's indecision, and I believe he is today as far from any fixed plan of action for the future as he was the day I received your letter; this morning only he handed me Het's note to him and after reading it I asked him if he thought of going down the country?
He replied that he was afraid he could not stand the warm weather down there and besides living at the Grove House and planting at the old garden would be too great a temptation for the surrounding black population, and taking it altogether he did not think there was much money to be made by him down there: yet I believe up to this time he has had a strong desire to return to McIntosh Co. Just before the receipt of your letter Henry Reese made us a visit for a couple of days and I think **Sallie Wylly** sent a message by him to Baillie to beg him not to think of returning to McIntosh, as she could speak feelingly of the difficulty her Brothers had to earn a living, and I think Henry also tried to dissuade him from going down, as I did myself, dear Evey, from the belief that he could not make a living there, and would be a tax upon Cousin Charles and yourself.
I offered him a room at Rocky Knoll and land to plant for himself, but he declined it, upon the fact that the land was too poor without heavy manuring and also it would take capital to lay out for plants, which he had not. I offered to help him with the manure and then he wanted about sixty dollars to lay out for strawberry plants, which I told him I had not to spare. He has now decided to go to Griffin tomorrow and see a Mr. Rhea (who is said to have some money and owns a nursery and vegetable garden in the suburbs of Griffin) and go into business with him if he can do so satisfactorily. I do not think he will succeed.

I have had many anxious thoughts dear Evy about Baillie's lonely

condition and his unsettled frame of mind, he is at times painfully low spirited and again with young people in the house he forgets it all, with music and games to divert his mind. I wish I could do something for him, but I have no money to give him: later in the season if he makes up his mind to go to McIntosh (for I think it will result in that, and it may be better that it should be so) I will pay his passage down and help him as much as I can, and after trying it there if he should not succeed, I will pay his passage up again to live with us, where I think he will be better contented.'

(In a postscript Kell mentions that Baillie had returned from Griffin but had been unable to see Mr. Rhea. 'I think he is quite full of getting in with Rhea and nothing more can be done until he hears from him.')

Of course we know how this sad story will finally end, with Baillie living with his brother's family. Still more to come.

This interesting letter describes Sallie Wylly, sister to Alexander and William Wylly, Baillie's friends from Company H, 5th Georgia Cavalry and also a cousin to Sarah Sallie Spalding! It may be that the letter contains more than what is being supposed. Baillie is still thinking of his blonde sweetheart Sallie now married to McKinley and Sallie Wylly could be attempting to put off his return so that he does not upset the status quo down on Sapelo? John is oblivious to this, yet worried about his condition. The description of playing games etc. again is an absolute fit to my character and nature. I have spent most of my childhood and adult life playing War games, role playing games, adventure games and of course video games, at home and with the children at school. Another home run without a doubt, Baillie and I are the same person!

As we later discovered Baillie had also lost his fiancée Mary Sullivan in 1871 through lack of money and Mary's own lower social class. He had also lost through infant mortality 'Lil' May,' Margery Baillie Kell, his six years old niece and name sake in 1873, so all in all things were looking pretty desperate for the poor guy! Lack of prospects, lack of money, lack of hope. The warm weather bringing out the mosquitoes and the thought of being just a stone's throw from Sallie at the old ruined Grove, it was all too much to even contemplate.

Ian here's part of one more letter before I call it a day. All of these certainly tell us a lot about the poor guy!
To John Kell from sister Evey, from Ashantilly, January 1, 1878

'Baillie has just returned from **Rushlands** where he had gone to collect rent from his tenants but got little.'
The truth is the Negroes do pretty much as they please with Baillie, and I believe he is conscious of it, for he never likes to speak of his management's with them. I tried to find out from him what they would pay altogether, but he said it was impossible to tell... that he would take part cotton from John, and that Sampson had offered to give it out when he has ginned his own, with the foot gin. I suppose he may realize something from it by March, which was the time, Sampson says, he paid the rent last years.'

Another home run! This letter describes exactly my temperament with the pupils at school. I find it very hard to be the tough *boss man* disciplinarian. I like the pupils too much and regard them as friends. We achieve results through co-operation and amicable agreement. Sometimes they take advantage, but I am always aware of this and operate a policy of give and take. In the end Baillie couldn't take money off of his childhood friends. The very people he had grown up with and played with, known all of his life. Everybody in the rural South was poor and had very little cash flow. So how could he be ruthless with those who like him were struggling just to survive? Baillie was not a money orientated Yankee businessman, he was first and foremost a true Southern gentleman. This was how he was brought up and this is how I am, it is all in the blood and you can't help it. It is just what you are!

Ian, there's no sequence to what I am doing, but you can sort them out after you get them all. This one is a real eye opener! What's going on!

From Blanche to daughter Tibbie, from Sunnyside, Ga., March 29, 1888:

'I suppose I ought to write to Uncle Baillie tho' he was so hateful before he left. I was glad to be rid of him. I trust he will keep his RR place headquarters at Americus.'

Trouble, trouble. Can you read between the lines? I'd say that Baillie has turned out to be a very lonely and even embittered fella, probably long before 1888. By that time there's probably no chance of finding love. Compare his life with that of his brother John and his brood.

This was the big bust up with John, over money and all the emotion of Baillie's condition. Baillie now sixty years of age probably wanted to leave his railroad job and move back into Rocky Knoll with his brother and their family, but there was no room and so the monumental argument ensued, but this time there was no reconciliation. My capacity for coming back to sort out a compromise had been lost. Baillie would only move in with Blanche after his brother's death in 1900.

Ian, I've got time enough for one more letter before I leave for the day. This one is absolutely devastating!

From Blanche to daughter Tibbie, from 'Home' November 6, (no year but I had put 1894 based on some reason or other)

'Papa is so much worried besides public affairs that he has no farm arrangements made for another yr.! And Mr M - frets him more and more everyday, being naturally suspicious he has now concluded that he has sold all the good corn as his half and left us all the nubbins. I begged him to let Baillie see to the division, but he said B' had not the character enough to make him divide squarely.'

What a concentration in a few words!!'

(Nisbet Papers, Duke University)

Obviously the animosity still persisted even at this late date. I was not surprised at Baillie's description by John, as I am always trying to give people a good deal and find it very hard to be a tough businessman. Another home run in describing my character.

Ian, do you have Baillie's pension papers (from the Georgia State Archives)? In looking them over, I notice that some of the forms are in his own handwriting, explaining his physical ills and need for financial support. Interestingly, he used his friends Alexander and William Wylly, who also served in the 5th Georgia, as witnesses to back up his claims. It's 1899, and poor Baillie is claiming 'No employment', 'No family', and 'Supported almost entirely by friends'. He is applying for help on the basis of 'infirmity and poverty.' Lordy! To have reached such a low! Why didn't he turn to John for help if he was that badly off!!

The answer has been given above, Baillie had argued and fallen out with his brother. He had then probably not spoken again to his brother and regretted this profoundly when his brother had died in 1900. He was determined to make amends as he did by the following action. It was the *squaring of the Matrix* that I put right when I met and shook hands with Norman on January 24, 2001. Baillie had been reunited with his brother and at last could put right the dreadful fallout from the argument that had occurred.

Ian, how's this for a final irony, a reminder to the end that he was the younger brother of a famous Confederate. I have a note here that on March 23, 1901 Baillie (residing in Sunnyside) had applied for a Confederate Cross of Honor. He was a member of JOHN McINTOSH KELL UNITED CONFEDERATE VETERANS CAMP #1032.

Baillie was a founder member of the camp named in his brother's honor. It is in the second photograph that we see him standing resolutely in the foreground, proud and erect. The sadness in his eyes showing the emotional turmoil that has taken its toll on him. Ironically immediately behind him to the left is Archibald Carlisle McKinley, Sallie's husband and to the right Alexander Campbell Wylly, commanding officer of H troop after Captain Brailsford's capture in 1864, both Lieutenants and both responsible for his condition. That of losing Sallie to marriage and the blocking his promotion respectively. Yet all united by the cause above everything else.

Here goes!
Blanche to daughter Tibbie, dated 'Home,' April 9, 1912
'Baillie continues very weak and infirm and helpless (underlined) - no mummy (underlined) was ever so skin dried and drawn - as since the grippe left him, and his cough like a consumptive - but he still says he is going to the reunion! And if he finds he cannot (underlined) go I think it will kill him. If he goes and recruits any, I may go to Tifton but as it is, to leave him here in the condition he is would be disloyalty to yr Father and his poor old Mother who was always so kind to me and expected (underlined) us to take care of him.'
(Nisbet Papers, Duke)

Here at the close of Baillie's life we see the devotion and fanaticism given to the cause and the cavalry that drove him even when frail and ill. This is all he has left. It is no wonder that such a strong urge and drive would survive physical mortality and resurface in a future generation. The entire experience of those four terrible years was indelibly written into memory. The memories formed were strong enough to survive even death.

The following are excerpts from Blanche's diary: Mon. Sept. 30, 1912
'Baillie died at 1 o'clock today! all (underlined) so kind and attentive and he so calm and resigned. God has received his ransomed spirit. he was a devoted Christian.'
Tues. Oct 1, 1912
'Baillie buried St. George's Church at 3 o'clock. Tibbie and Gazzie (?) came - and many friends gathered to do him reverence. How he loved religion and the Church.'

Back from holiday and I've been thinking...
The letter saying about the horrible things Uncle Baillie said is the big bust up with brother John. The worm finally turned and told John his fortune. Baillie then kept clear until John had passed away and then made up with Blanche. He was a founder member of the John McIntosh Kell veteran's lodge and this may have been some way of making it up with John although after his demise or just before he died.
I will check.
I'm now looking for a Publisher to publish the story entitled, 'Rebel Spirit'; Evidence for the continuity of consciousness.

I have also e-mailed Duke re: Baillie's letters
Best wishes Ian

With that, the close came to a remarkable once in a lifetime week, centered on July 20, 2000. A week of unforgettable revelation as e-mail after e-mail arrived on time and in synchronicity with the events that were unfolding in England around me. Norman had shown himself to be a star researcher of the first order. I had to meet him. I had to stand over my own grave to show that I was a true rebel, that I had beaten the system, I had broken the Matrix.

Thinking through it all, I sat at Herne Bay in the big white house on the sea front in August, recovering from kidney failure induced by the intensity of this roller coaster of remote viewing and inter-dimensional hopping that had lasted almost six months. I had spanned two worlds for too long. The toll had been too great for my system to endure and I now had to take time out to recover. Yet I had with Norman and Rosie's help, completed the impossible, cracked the physical Matrix of our reality and accessed the data of my past. All was now so clear. I understood everything about myself in transparent crystalline detail; exactly who I was, what I was and the titanic events that had shaped my being. I now had it all. Euphoria coursed through my veins and I wore a permanent smile on my face. I would heal myself. I was a time lord. I could do anything...

I resolved to make plans to meet this remarkable gentleman that had found the photograph and had rendered so much assistance to solving the puzzle. I would give up my job and make plans to see Norman! I had to *square the Matrix.* It was the cosmic mission of a lifetime, so profound, so beautiful. I would give it my all.

Part Two:

The Witness

Chapter Four
Rosie-Mary

In January 2000, I knew that I was about to undertake the greatest experiment of my life. Frustrated at being so near to the answers posed by the photograph, yet so far I had reached a point of total stasis. The sheer desperation had resulted in my contemplating hypnotic regression the previous summer. Three times I had almost crossed the threshold of this road to find the answers to my past, but each time I had turned back or the Matrix had intervened externally to prevent it happening. I was also aware that using such a heavily criticized technique might jeopardize the scientific validity of my conclusions should I reach them using such methods. The answers had to be discovered by my own conscious effort.

It was then that I had a chance encounter with a fellow colleague Rosie Lagrue, Head of Religious studies one friday at the end of the day. I poured out my story and intrigued, she began to help me. The process evolved rapidly from that point, I wanted to explore and externalize the reoccurring images in my head that I had seen ever since my present life had begun. This effort was to be further prompted by my wishing to repay Ashley Pollette with images for his excellent 5th Georgia Cavalry web site, a small token gesture of appreciation for the tremendous amount of data he had provided for my research into Baillie. I quickly began to appreciate that I would need a principal witness of unimpeachable integrity to guarantee that I had not hoaxed or faked the evidence of these images. The images would be painted first from my mind before any evidence to substantiate them was sought. That way they could be viewed as genuine hard physical copies of my memories. Thankfully Rosie agreed to moderate the experiment and to ensure a fair test. The following is her testament, in her own words as principal witness to what unfolded over the first six amazing months of a brand new millennium and the final quantum leap in the search for Alexander Baillie Kell.

Rosie-Mary: This picture of Rosie Lagrue, nee O'Sullivan shows what Mary Sullivan probably looked like in 1870, on her 18th birthday. The big house in the background would be the Varner's place of which, she was housekeeper. I predict that if ever we are fortunate to discover a photograph of young Mary she will look similar.

When I first met Dr Ian C Baillie in 1997 I realized I had met an exceptional man. For here was someone who understood the workings of the Universe and could put our microscopic human daily life into the perspective of the bigger scheme of things. Not only was his understanding of time and space different to the average person living in the Matrix of life but, also he could lift a person out of the ordinary and help them view things from the viewpoint of his twenty years research. At this time Ian was working on his book, *The Intelligent Universe,* which he was willing to share freely with his fellow teaching colleagues. I consider myself lucky to have benefited from three years of staff room lectures. Morning and lunchtime breaks became a hot house of intellectual debate on such topics as Ancient Knowledge, Sacred Geometry and the Intelligent Universe. Einstein's view that Science is lame without Religion, Religion blind without Science, became vividly clear as my own twenty years of teaching Religion took on a whole new outlook.

At the start of the new millennium, January 2000, Ian shared with me his find of the photo of Alexander Baillie Kell. As a teacher of Religion this has been an opportunity of a lifetime. We affectionately dubbed our work together over this year, as 'Mission 2000'. It has been an experience of a lifetime, a cosmic unfolding, not only of the life of the Confederate Alexander Baillie Kell 1828 to 1912, but of how Dr Ian C Baillie's own life story mirrors in incredible accuracy this life story. For Ian and myself this has been a roller coaster ride of emotion and energy. As soon as we unlocked the details of Ballie's life, Ian found he had been driven to relive this same experience, but to a happy conclusion. Each time we felt we had reached a landmark in the story, a new clue would turn up leading to another unlocking of Baillie's life and in turn its parallel link with Ian's life. To discover that your choices in life have not been your own, but governed by the emotional life of a Confederate soldier whose life was devastated by the American Civil War, and who had loved and lost, is a discovery that does not come without a cost. Ian, normally a cool calm and collected scientist, has lived through a whole range of emotions, with each new discovery, eventually suffering near kidney failure from stress. As the following e-mail records my role has been as witness and record keeper of the events as they happened.

Date: Monday, May 22, 2000:
To: Dr Ian C Baillie
From: Rosie Lagrue
Re: Today!

Thank you so much for asking me to be with you today - I'm truly humbled - to witness all these images that have held you in their grip for your lifetime. I've witnessed your 'awakening' to your memes!!!
What an honor! I keep thinking of the word KEY, unlocking the subconscious that is so powerfully revealed in your pictures - They have been there - I can see links the roots of the 'pain tree' begging you to delve deeper - They shout out of a pain that tore your/Baillie's, soul apart. The haunting haunted figure looking out to sea, to Avalon? To the tower of hope - But the saddest picture is seeing the fierce warrior standing between you and your dream. A powerful black force, black knight standing between you and the girl of your dreams. There is so much here I will let these thoughts have time - I'll write them as they come to me.

Date: Friday, August 4, 2000:
To: Dr Ian C Baillie
From: Rosie Lagrue
Re: The Book - Mission 2000

Good morning Ian,
The book describes your mission - your life story is one for all to hear. It is a beautiful mission. It is cosmic. The last 7 months has been a tidal wave. Tres magnifique. Such a privilege for me to have been a part of. And for you I can only begin to imagine the exhaustion of this experience and sadly some of the bumps along the way - Emotionally exhausting.
But I pray that once recovered you will feel all the benefits.
Grow strong again Ian
Roisin Daub

At the end of this period of experiment we came to the conclusion that Ian's complete lifetime is just one giant experiment, which provides evidence for the continuation of consciousness and emotion after death. The following is my own eyewitness account of the unlocking of Ian's subconscious.

Gazing into the looking glass of time I spied a familiar reflection

In 1997 Ian's school and mine merged, to become St.Mary's Westbrook, Folkestone. (Coincidentally, there is a river St. Mary's in Georgia. On that river is the town Folkston.) Inevitably it was a traumatic time for all concerned. Despite the close proximity of the two schools, historically we did not mix, tending instead to seeing each other as rivals. With the merger every one's jobs was on the line. It was a very tense time. I stood by helpless as much respected colleagues, friends, were maneuvered like pawns in a game of chess. The tension eventually became unbearable as I began to spot the tactics being used! It was at this point that I picked up the phone to talk to the Union Rep. for the *other* school. So came about my first conversation with Ian Baillie. The conversation flowed for the best part of an hour. In that one hour Ian gave me a completely new understanding of the way the Universe worked! He described the merger of our two schools, as a microcosm of what was happening in the world around us. All the upheaval mirrored the increasing tumultuous change being experienced everywhere. The forces of global power were asserting control and dominance as never before and we too would experience such control on a smaller fractal scale. Putting things into the greater perspective Ian explained how many centuries ago the Mayan's had predicted an end to this cycle of civilization in 2012. But we could learn lessons and prepare for it at this time, by adapting to change, bending, and letting all flow passed us as we surfed and rode the wave. Those of us who learnt to survive change would be ready for our next stage of evolution. As the conversation came to a close, I felt everything falling into perspective; there was nothing to fear. I began to look forward to getting to know the person behind this great and wise mind. From this one *lecture* I was equipped to rise above the troubled times that lay ahead.

Adapting to change was the key phrase for the next three years. Despite the turmoil, I spent short breaks in Ireland, in search of my roots, aware of the strength of their call. During this time conversations with Ian were rare, but none the less equally pertinent. Until one unforgettable January afternoon at the beginning of a brand new millennium.

The weekend looming, the staff room emptied leaving two people. As I prepared for monday, Ian approached to tell me the story of how he'd found the photo of Alexander Baillie Kell. I listened entranced, immediately understanding the great significance this had for him. As he spoke, his eyes filled with emotion, the language of the soul. I listened fascinated as Ian proceeded to tell me of how he had even put the book back not daring to believe! Yet this was a photo he had never expected to see. Here was a man who not only shared the same name, with its own Scottish spelling, but also looked like him. To add to the intrigue, Alexander Baillie Kell had fought in the American Civil War. The connections were immediate, but daring not to believe Ian played safe, putting it down to mere coincidence, he returned the book to the shelf he had found it.

In the following days the pull to return to buy the book, to have it in his possession, to look again at that remarkable face, an unexpectedly familiar reflection, and to read the life story of Alexander Baillie Kell, became too great. Ian found himself drawn to return. This was a book that seemed to hold answers to the many questions that had haunted him. In time the significance of the find would sink home. This was like winning the lottery!

Finding Alexander Baillie Kell started to make sense of Ian's life. My patience could hold out no longer, this seemed such a remarkable story.

The questions came fast and furious. In response Ian described his childhood. A childhood spent re-enacting the American Civil War, playing War games, and making weapons. He had even made a cannon! Remarkably Ian's father seemed to be in on this for he provided his son the freedom to explore this connection. As he sat resting in the sitting room a flash of light lit up the newspaper he was reading, and he lifted his head to see a flame shooting across the garden. Ian had fired a shot from his cannon!

A picture emerged of a wise man who had given his son freedom to explore this drive that seemed to fill his every waking moment and probably flooded his dreams too. I had never known anything quite like this. More questions followed. Amazingly Ian's father too had experienced a connection with the sea, and ships which had awakened a dormant sense of a past life. He therefore understood the drive within his son, the connection with the American Civil War. I was filled with respect.

For twenty years teaching Religious Studies I had kept an open mind to the belief in reincarnation. But as a Roman Catholic I taught it as a belief I didn't share. This story was already pushing me to question this stand. I knew from the start that this was an experience that was the answer to every Religious Studies teacher's dream. I didn't have any answers right there and then, but I was sure going to find out. I wanted to know more. I wanted to know answers to this amazing story. What was going on here? What was the reason for this great similarity between Alexander Baillie Kell, and my colleague and science teacher, Ian Baillie? I resolved to respond by sharing in an equally honest way. The next monday morning I left a note in Ian's pigeonhole in the staff room.

And so started a voyage of discovery into the nature of consciousness, transmigration of the soul, and an unraveling of this story that neither of us could have possible imagined back in those early days. My mind was ready to find out about how the Universe worked and Ian had the answers! For twenty years he had researched the workings of the Universe and was in the process of writing his book *The Intelligent Universe.* Three years before we had talked of how Science was on the verge of proving mathematically the existence of life after death. This was my field of study, and I knew nothing of these things. And what a wealth of knowledge! The lesson had begun. I was a signed up member of the class. For the next six months I became an avid student devouring everything Ian could teach me, Sacred Geometry, Ancient Knowledge, the workings of the Universe.

But the holding fascination was in knowing more about Ian's life story, and the connection with Alexander Baillie Kell.

That very same monday Ian penned what I call his first lecture- *Emotion is the Language of the Soul.* I was on the first stage of my journey to understanding how the Universe worked! We spent every spare minute over the next six months on this most amazing journey of discovery. At the end of it we know we have uncovered a story of cosmic importance. And I know it is a story for the world to hear. A story with the potential of awakening all that read it, to the implications it holds for us all.

The first major question I put to Ian was 'What was it that formed us into the people we were?'

So many of us seem to be carrying things from the past. Do we carry genetic memory from our ancestors? Attending Ian's *Intelligent Universe* lectures provided answers.

The first lesson to learn is **matter is an illusion!** Hard to believe, but true, Science reveals there is nothing inside an atom! Everything exists in waveform. Like looking at the grid of dots on the TV screen that make up the images we see.

'I am a fractal of intelligence a fragment yet complete
Charged with the energy of vibration
I explore the Universe of Creation
Sonoluminescence...
Let there be light'

ICB95

What we believe as real is in fact illusion. Buddhism teaches that all matter is transient, passing. Both Science and Religion tend to suggest that the realms of the soul and emotion are eternal, unlike the physical objects people spend a lifetime gathering around them.

The emotional trauma deep rooted in my family tree was a weight I found hard to bear. Here too Ian was able to give me an insight that enabled me to lighten the load. In his first lecture Ian wrote:

Cause and Effect - We all live in the aftershocks of Emotional Crisis e.g. Northern Ireland, Bosnia, etc. All are one. We share the experiences we produce. Everything exists in waveform. Emotional trauma ripples through time. We are all caught up in the aftershocks. This related again to the Buddhist teaching about Karma. And began to explain how the past affected the present.

Crucially Ian's explanation of time began to make sense of my questions.

Time is not a line it is more like a bubble even a doughnut - Time just looks like a line, it is simply a product of the architecture of 3 dimensional space. In higher dimensions there is no time!

Time too is an illusion! Our minds are too restricted in this 3D-matter illusion. Barriers of time, space, matter started to go down for me. I was beginning to piece together my own early experiences of reality in the spiritual, an existence outside of time and space, with Ian's scientific explanations of matter, time illusion, and the reality of inter locking dimensions, it all fell into place and made sense. As we walked through the historic sacred site of Canterbury Cathedral we discussed this concept. Old perceptions discarded the new paradigm shift opened us up to an awareness of parallel existences, dimensions of time happening at one time, not in the linear sense, but as a multidimensional holistic event. All life experiences happening in parallel. I looked around the ruins, trying to picture them whole, monks walking their rounds of office, fourteenth century and twenty-first century pilgrims visiting the holy site, oblivious to each other.

Leaping out of all of this was the significance of emotion in this experience we call Life. I started to read Ian's thesis *Intelligent Universe* and discovered his explanation of the role of emotion.

The 3D physical matter Universe is a holographic illusion, designed with the express purpose of allowing fractals of the one consciousness to interact and experience a variety of novel situations in order to learn. The earth is therefore a school for emotional experience.
Dr Ian C Baillie

Matter is an illusion, but this *earthly* existence is an opportunity to experience emotions in all their complexities. This is far more in keeping with the Buddhist teaching of lives being soul journeys. We were a meeting of Science and Religion, Ian's twenty years of scientific study of how the Universe worked complimented my twenty years of study about Life, Death the Universe and everything.

Date: Wednesday, May 24, 2000:
To: Dr Ian C Baillie
From: Rosie Lagrue
Re: My eyes have been opened!

Hi Ian,
I'm really enjoying reading your book I can't put it down. I have always thought these ideas beyond my understanding - only for brains like Stephen Hawking! You definitely have the gift. I hope others get the chance to appreciate it.
Our first phone call was the start of this journey - who could have known it would have led to such a discovery. We have traveled a long way, opening doors that I never knew existed. You always knew this place was significant. This has been a mission. I am honored to have been a part of it. The map shows it was all meant to be. Truly 'Soul Quest 2000'!
My eyes have been opened. I was asleep, but no more. The horizon is eternal. No more tunneled vision.
All boundaries are cages; they've been leveled. A new dawn breaks more beautiful than before. Reaching for the stars
'In Lake ch' I am another yourself - Mayan Wisdom
Rosie

Above all was the help Ian provided in assisting me to release myself from the chains of the past Sullivan/McCarthy experience that had engulfed me. I saw evidence of the aftershocks in my family line. However knowing about them somehow released me. I was learning from this experience how to survive.

I had long been fascinated by the hold the past held over us. Ian introduced me to a recent discovery. *Memes* provided an answer to why people had particular behavioral characteristics, interests and hobbies. There are a number of different opinions on how memes are accessed. One viewpoint is that this is genetic memory, the memories of our forefathers being carried down through the genes, propounded by Richard Dawkins and Susan Blackmore. Another popular theory is that memes are accessed through the individual and collective consciousness, an idea expressed by Carl Jung. However Ian's preference is the explanation I feel most happy with.

In the lecture *Emotion is the language of the soul* - Ian explained how memories might pass from one life to another, from one personality to another. The Spirit is a multidimensional being which inhabits 3 dimensional space/time through DNA. Deoxyribo-Nucleic-Acid being a double helix based molecule formed on a ratcheted dodecahedron with pentagonal side structures provides through sacred geometry a mathematical mechanism for the imbedding of the Spirit into matter. Memory survives through this same mechanism using the familiar *Golden Mean,* phi spiral to allow data to be transferred between physical bodies without loss of integrity. In this way the individual soul memory can survive death. All of this allows memories to be stored and accessed from different dimensions and times. The phi spiral breaks through the barriers between dimensions allowing information and memories from fourth dimensional space to be experienced in three dimensions. In other words, allowing memories of past-lives to be experienced in our present lives. Bodies come and go, but it is the mind and soul memory that remains constant, ever developing, ever evolving.

Emotion seemed to shout out from the pages of Alexander Baillie Kell's life. This was a story of gunpowder, guns and war. In historical terms the American Civil War was a watershed, *the last romantic war,* the first modern. The Southern States at a stroke lost everything as a result of this horrendous conflict. A complete way of life was destroyed as well as any hope of ever recovering lost status and wealth. The golden days were over. Times of honor, of the life of a Southern gentleman and lady were wiped away, never to return. A civilization had vanished. Baillie as he called himself, was never to recover. Every effort to make good of his life failed. *Poor Baillie,* as his sisters wrote ended his days working on the railroads, alone, unmarried. The emotion of such a tragic life rings out for all to see. Here was a tragic hero, who somehow managed to hold on to his gentlemanly qualities. Those same qualities that I recognized in my dear colleague Ian, standing physically before me in the staff room that friday afternoon.

Surely such emotion and tragedy was the stuff of how memes would be formed. Memes strong enough to survive death, and transmigrate with the soul.

As Ian uncovered Baillie's life it became clear that there was an unbreakable link between Alexander Baillie Kell and Ian Charles Baillie. It was like looking into a parallel life. Throughout Ian's life he had felt driven, drawn, to fulfil very specific goals, all connected with the American Civil War, and to marry a blonde lady. Thorough painstaking research into the life story of Alexander Baillie Kell was revealing amazing parallels with Ian's life. Now all those unanswered questions were beginning to make sense. Ian was discovering each and every drive could be linked back to an original experience in Alexander Baillie Kell's life one hundred years before. The phrase *just the same* became familiar. As we read Baillie's life and letters another striking parallel hit. Baillie's characteristics were remarkably similar to that of Ian's. Not only did they look alike, but also they had the same personal traits. Ian carries the air of the Southern gentleman about him at all times. Honor and duty is paramount in all his dealings with everyone he meets. It is a trait, which distinguishes him from most men who are focused to *getting on* in this fast track, materialistic, business world in which we live today. Such focus on bettering ourselves materially often leads us to neglect the relationships around us, and to be unaware of the true concerns of those around us. Not so with Ian, his ability to be ever conscious of others' feelings is always paramount. It is this, which comes across to students and staff alike, and the real reason for his great popularity. As both teacher and parent in the school, it felt that not a day would go by that I did not hear a parent, pupil, or member of staff talking of Ian with affection and warmth; about another amazing experiment and fun that was being had in the science lessons. Dr Baillie was the name most often said. And always with such high regard. This sense of duty was most noticeable in respect to his family.

Looking at Baillie's life pre-war, during the war, and following the war, the signs of this sense of duty, and same attitude to people were very strong. Baillie's mother, Margery Kell, pressed on this sense of duty when it came to Baillie signing up to the army. Her wish was for Baillie to stay to protect his women folk, Mary and Hettie, on the plantation. But on this occasion it was Baillie's sense of duty to defending the cause of the South, which prevailed.

Date: Friday, June 23, 2000:
To: Rosie Lagrue
From: Dr Ian C Baillie
Re: The Protectors...

Here's a new one - Guess who the blonde girl is... This is how Baillie felt towards Sallie. The child also represents the helpless citizens of Georgia and the role of the Cavalry in trying to protect them from the scourge of Kilpatrick's troopers and Sherman's marauders
'We fought to the end and surrendered in good order as Southern Gentlemen should... Hillsboro, NC April 26, 1865'

Ian,
Thanks for the picture... The theme is quite appropriate, especially in light of the attachment to this message... The 5th was all that stood between the people of Georgia and Sherman/Kilpatrick's thugs.
Rosie

As Ian passed on Baillie's letters to me via the e-mail, I found myself focusing on what could be gleaned about Baillie's character, from the family letters, and description of the family. Sure enough the similarities came to be obvious. Ian had quickly realized that events in his life mirrored Baillie's life. For example Baillie spent some years working for the railroad. Ian worked on the trains before his teacher training. Baillie worked on the family plantation and post war, with Negroes working the land. Ian studied agriculture and farming at University. The tales of Baillie's time on the plantation seemed to mirror Ian's time here at school, especially as we had a number of Nigerian boys as boarders, some of them Muslims. The children flocked around Ian his popularity springing form his obvious concern and consideration for them. They knew Ian as a teacher willing to give up a great deal of his spare time, simply because he enjoyed their company and was interested in their welfare. War games were the most popular activity in the school alongside video games, both run by Ian, in his lunch hours and after school. Ian often talked about how the pupils felt so comfortable in his presence, but that they sometimes ran rings around him

Date: Sunday, July 23, 2000:
To: Rosie Lagrue
From: Dr Ian C Baillie
Re: Baillie's Letters

Baillie has just returned from Rushlands where he had gone to collect rent from his tenants 'but got little.'
The truth is, the Negroes do pretty much as they please with Baillie, and I believe he is conscious of it, for he never likes to speak of his management's with them.

Other letters written by members of the family say of Baillie that he treated his Negroes well. Here was another link; Ian's popularity was based on a sincere interest in the rights of the children. He feels passionately about the rights of children, ever conscious when children are being subjected to unjust treatment.

Date: Friday, March 2, 2001:
To: Rosie Lagrue
From: Dr Ian C Baillie
Re: The kidz

Tell them I miss them but to go forward into the Matrix and be excellent! Also... This is my version of pop stars!!! Also 'They gave me the confidence to be more than I was' Teachers are all talk... kids do... I learnt from them... Especially Sadiq and Tito. Sadiq is better than Craig David and Eminem -loads better he should be on Top of the Pops making millions! Oh and John'o can be the director of the film and be in it! Remember Kidz 'get educated and then get even!' Doc B says!
Trivia- you know I keep going on about Doc Holliday-and I used to say 'It's like Doc Baillie and the gunfight at the OK Convent! Well guess where Doc Holliday the gunfighter, TB ridden, dentist, died at 36, came from? Answer a little town called Griffin, Georgia! A coincidence not!

Dr Ian C Baillie; 'Coincidence is the Norm in the Matrix!'
ICB01

All of the evidence showed that part of the reason Baillie could not follow the success of his elder brother was because he did not have the business like approach with the Negroes on his land. Even the lure of making money did not change his heart from feeling for the needs of the freedmen. Having seen the strength of Ian's sense of protectiveness for the children in his care at school, it was possible to see how this would have worked against Baillie when trying to eke out a living from the land after the war. He clearly did not have it in him to be forceful with his workforce.

Then there was the sense of loneliness and loss, which Ian carried around with him, despite being happily married to his lovely blonde wife Pauline. Reading this letter from one of Baillie's sisters-in–law to another, it was becoming clear that the reason was not related to Ian in this lifetime.

Date: Sunday, June 23, 2000:
To: Rosie Lagrue
From: Dr Ian C Baillie
Re: Norman Delaney writes:

To Blanche Kell from Sister Evey, Nov 25, 1871

> Baillie has been very busy getting in the corn and fodder at the Sully place, and expects to finish tomorrow... poor fellow
>
> 'hope deferred' makes him groan and sigh. I think, altho' I do not say so, that his engagement will come to nothing.

When talking of Baillie's life Ian's eyes often filled with emotion. The phrase *Emotion is the language of the soul* is a phrase Ian uses to round off his e-mails to Norman and myself.

Dr Ian C Baillie: ' Emotion is the language of the soul': ICB 1997.

In the family letters when Tabbie asked whether John McIntosh Kell, Baillie's brother, was handsome, Blanche replies that *a pleasant face showed that he had a soul.* When in April 24, 1855 Kell spent two weeks with Baillie, John called Blanche the, *little lady of my heart.* Again when describing Baillie's mother, Blanche wrote, Margery Kell is a *very hearty whole-souled person.* These references to the Kell's as *soul full* people, resonated with me. My first, and continuing impression of Ian, is just the same. Ian's phrase *Emotion is the language of the soul* for me epitomizes Ian. He is a man who speaks from his heart and soul, who lives from his heart and soul. A man, who, in this life time, would not hurt a single soul. A man who speaks with such passion about the cause of the American Civil War and of these people and events, that his eyes fill with tears. Here is a very real connection. Blanche herself is made of the same stuff, an honorable lady, who suffered much in those hard times. Eventually loosing three of her children. Blanche remained ever thoughtful and mindful of the plight of her brother-in-law, *poor Baillie.* The many letters that went between Baillie and Blanche are very touching and sincere. The first two children to die, died during the war, at the time when John was missing, presumed dead. It was Baillie, Blanche wrote to, and received letters from, at this desperate time.

It felt like looking at a mirror reflection, but this was a looking glass in time, one hundred years apart. What was true of Baillie was also true of Ian. Instinctively I knew from being with Ian that Baillie was a warm, sensitive man who was very appealing to women. I began to wonder if Baillie had broken a few hearts along the way, not knowing of his impact on them! It became clear from Blanche's letters, that they had had a close friendship as brother and sister-in-law, but also that he spent a lot of time with his nephews and nieces. I knew instinctively that he would have been a very popular uncle, making toys, games, just as Ian Baillie was doing here in the school. Despite this apparent image of domestic happiness, I felt Baillie had been robbed of his own wife and family. There was something still waiting to be uncovered. Then there was the photo of Alexander Baillie Kell. Something about Baillie's eyes told me that this was a man capable of great love. It could not have been that he was not the marrying sort. Baillie was a man who had had social standing before the war. I also felt it was not a good thing for Ian to have to live with. The question began to become a burning issue. What had happened to prevent Baillie marrying his fiancée? Had she *dumped* him? My instinct was aroused. There was an emotional story here lying buried deep in Ian's subconscious.

Every Picture Tells A Story

Ian's paintings seemed to express the sense of being at war - *Mount up, Draw sabers and Charge!* He was drawn to externalizing his emotions through painting. And all the scenes were of a conflict 140 years earlier. It was as if his past life experience as Baillie and that experience of the American Civil War was being relived. Even more striking was that most of the paintings were of battle scenes in which cavalrymen were attacking infantrymen. The infantrymen were definitely the enemy. The Confederates were invariably cavalrymen the Union, Yanks or *Feds* depicted as infantrymen. I quickly learned how these paintings were filled with all the sense of emotion that Ian was feeling with this present frustrating situation. We became very used to the sounds of loud bangs that came from the play ground, as yet another group of children were treated to a pyrotechnic display - what a great way to let off steam! It was as if 140 years had faded away, and Baillie, the Southern gentleman, the cavalrymen was very much present in all Ian did.

Date: Thursday, January 13, 2000:
To: Rosie Lagrue
From: Dr Ian C Baillie
Re: Spirit of the 5th

Anyway we can always blow off some gunpowder Southern style, those Yanks are too d** serious about everything. We have been through this three times already!**
Here's a picture 'Spirit of the 5th' that sums up how we deal with the invaders...
Now does that sound familiar?

Spirit of the 5th: Later we were to discover that this picture reveals my subconscious aggression towards Archibald C McKinley. I realized that the picture was really a cavalryman attacking an infantryman, not just a Confederate attacking a Yank. McKinley was the infantryman. This is based on one of three very similar pictures that are my *favorites* in the 88 strong Civil War card collection from 1964.

The painting *Spirit of the 5th*, depicted charging Confederate cavalry, sabers drawn at the attack The Yankee infantrymen met the avalanche of cold steel and fell crushed to the ground. The ferocity and feral energy of the attack was apparent. The Confederates though vastly outnumbered, were fearless and more than ready for action.

Ian's paintings were improving and becoming more atmospheric. As they came up on my computer screen I felt a sense of seeing the world Baillie lived in, Ian's parallel existence! In the staff room we explored Baillie's life. Ian was so aware of Baillie's feelings of loneliness, of loss, of having failed. Our interest lay in finding out why he had never married. Ian was aware that Baillie would have been healed in his own lifetime if he had found a loving partner to share his post war years with. I knew this sensitive man would have made a loving husband and father. This indeed was a tragic tale. And Ian carried it subconsciously around with him. I began to be aware of how this puzzle was simmering below the surface. Up to this point in Ian's life it seemed the only memories of Baillie to surface were of the war, gunpowder, horses and war games. Yet something vital was missing. Where were the women in Baillie's life? Ian felt that meetings with eligible partners in backwoods rural Georgia of the 1850's and 60's were few and far between, but we knew there was still something waiting to be uncovered. The previous summer Ian had made an appointment to see a local hypnotherapist in Herne Bay. When he called, the gentleman was not at home, much to Ian's disappointment. It seemed the puzzle was going to have to remain unanswered.

The next painting to come through was filled with a deep significance for me.

Date: Sunday, June 23, 2000:
To: Rosie Lagrue
From: Dr Ian C Baillie
Re: Defenders...

New picture 'Defenders of the faith!' The women folk attend even song whilst the boys are off to protect the homes and sweethearts from the Yankee invaders. You could say that this picture was inspired by you!!! Faith keeps cropping up lately.

Every picture tells a story, 'Defenders of the faith' completes the picture - it's just great! My favorite, if I can have one - I like them all. Atmosphere is right… You are letting us in to Baillie's world - and I like it! This completes the circle. It feels complete - really nice.
Rosie

The women folk had appeared on the scene! The fuller image in Ian's subconscious was beginning to unlock. This painting, full of color, was filled with the sense of why the South was prepared to give their all, in defense of land, family, and sweethearts. The cavalrymen turned to watch their women folk attend Evensong, praying for the cause of the

South. All was at stake. The emotion of the moment was tangible. I was experiencing it as I looked on.

Defenders of the Faith: This is the first picture that showed a real event of which I had no possible conscious knowledge. Tommy commented on this and I drew a second version with the correct Midway church called, *A Time to Pray.*

As I wrote in the e-mail, *Every picture tells a story.* I was beginning to experience my intuition coming into play as the pictures appeared on the screen. Ian was letting me into Baillie's world. I was beginning to experience the emotion of these people, a people who had lived in the 1860's. This was the world Baillie inhabited, a world of romance and gallantry. The last romantic war, in which men gave their lives for their sweethearts. Baillie had to have had a sweetheart. He probably even carried her picture around in his pocket! But having come this far would we be able to find out any more?

The end of term staff dance at Ward's was the setting for my intuition to fully come in to its own. Through Ian's paintings I was beginning to experience Baillie's world of grandeur and elegance. But it was at this dance, that the parallel world Ian so obviously relived began to be tangible to me as well. Standing beside Ian I sensed the presence of Baillie, the Southern gentleman, as a separate identity. But like the pictures, this let me into his life story; it led me to sense, to feel details about his lost sweetheart.

Then on Sunday May 7, came the *Eureka* moment. The information had come through to me - Baillie had formed a relationship in the golden days before the war. Losing everything in the conflict had left him unable to offer his hand in marriage when the time came.

Date: Sunday, May 7, 2000:
To: Dr Ian C Baillie
From: Rosie Lagrue
Re: Baillie

Good morning Ian,
I have just had a 'Eureka' moment!! I think Baillie's problem with his fiancée was financial?
They would have both been used to finer days. He could no longer offer her the life of her pre-war expectations. He would have wanted to marry a 'lady,' but he could no longer offer the big estate, servants, etc. So marriage became out of the question. She probably turned to someone who could! Oh dear that is a sad ending. What do you think? It feels right to me.

YES! I think so... He was one to be ever loyal and that would fit... no more good times so bye bye... Touch of 'Gone with the Wind.'
I have memories of Southern balls! In the grand fashion... but on a more modest smaller scale. She was definitely blonde and broke his heart! The tune 'Turkey in the Straw' keeps haunting me. I thought it may have been the Regimental tune, but it could have been from the dances.
However after the war Baillie would have then dedicated his life to engineering, enjoying the practical 'hands on' approach - and being good at any thing he did. Family came to the rescue... He never married so it was her or nothing! I think he then played with trains a lot to forget her, a return to childhood independence!!!
Yes, thank you spot on I feel.
Ian

Shortly after Ian e-mailed his friend and author Dr Norman C Delaney he had made the major breakthrough! The whole story poured forth from his subconscious.

Date: Sunday, May 7, 2000:
To: Dr Norman C Delaney
From: Dr Ian C Baillie
Re: I know who she is!!!

Last Thursday night I reasoned in the bath late at night and the Spalding name popped into my head. I checked the Buddy Sullivan book for a possible cousin or a friend of Hettie's, that liked painting and drawing... there on page 137 was Sarah 'Sallie' Spalding's name.

As his subconscious memories surfaced Ian recalled Hettie (sic), Baillie's younger sister enjoyed art. They probably all spent time together drawing and painting. It all felt right. As Ian turned the pages of the Buddy Sullivan book he found her! There was the artwork of Sarah *Sallie* Spalding. From that moment everything fell into place. And I do mean *everything!* Not only details about the unknown areas of Baillie's life, but also the whole pattern of Dr Ian C Baillie's life fell into place, like watching a jigsaw put itself together.

I know the answers to this because my life has followed the same pattern and game plan in frightening detail!
It's all to do with money and security. The Kell's although respected did not possess the wealth of their peers. When Thomas Spalding died in 1851 so did the miserable puritan ideals that he held. A renaissance blossomed of fun and frolics led by the two Spalding Brothers. Charles Spalding was already family and married to Evelyn West Kell, Baillie's eldest sister, so the links were already forged. Baillie who revelled in the high society life having tasted it at Princeton and the Kentucky Military Academy, attended many of the sumptuous entertainment's of music and dance at South End on Sapelo.
The Young Sallie maturing into this society as she grew made a devastating impact on Baillie's attention. He was a Philosopher, a Romantic artistic type, well versed in History, drawing and cultural chitchat. She was young beautiful vibrant and full of energy! Plus blonde... oh yes!!!
As she reached her teenage years 15 to 16 the relationship blossomed into something a little more passionate than drawing the odd picture on the beach by the lighthouse! Baillie would have been the perfect gentleman and never have taken full advantage of her innocence, although she may have been perfectly willing? Flirting is one thing, but sex in that rigid aristocratic society... no sir that would have to wait until marriage and everything kept well above board.

And so the story flowed out of Ian's subconscious. The Spaldings were the most influential family of that area of Georgia, most significantly of Darien and Sapelo Island. Reading the lives of the Kells and Spaldings, Ian experienced the memes that had previously been hidden deep in his subconscious. This was Baillie's life story; a story Ian quickly realized had been a major driving force throughout his life.

But alas money talks and despite all efforts the promotion never came, the top jobs went to the wealthy and powerful in the Scottish tradition. And our poor Romantic soldier poet/philosopher couldn't match the poker stakes... Always with the picture of Sallie in his head... A noble cause worthy of fighting for. But the whole thing went belly up, Georgia got stomped on, and we lost. Not giving up though Baillie returns not afraid of the Yanks whom he regards as fellow soldiers doing a job and gets on well with at the Grove and immediately gets oxen and starts ploughing and replanting... he can still win Sallie even if the war's lost. She gives him a couple of years, but tiring of his lack of wealth dumps him (she's now around 25 he's 40!) The gap seems to have grown and being one to look out for herself finds another more wealthy and younger catch! :(

This was written before we discovered that Archibald C McKinley had married Sarah Elizabeth *Sallie* Spalding in 1866, just one year after the end of the war.

Baillie is devastated she has inflicted much more damage on him than any number of Yankee horsemen and bullets. The heart broken he becomes more lonely and unsettled... the result of rejection, the dream is shattered.

Ian immediately realized how much the drive to marry a blond lady had been as much a driving force in his life as had cannons, and gunpowder. His entire life had so far had been a re-enactment of Alexander Baillie Kell's. Up to now the connection with the re-enacting of the Civil War was clear, but now Ian could also see that there had been another, much deeper subliminal drive. From a very tender age he had been drawn inexorably to blonde women. Through childhood days of watching Lady Penelope of Thunderbirds, to the final clinch of marriage to Pauline Elizabeth Danter, his blonde teenage sweetheart.

Sapelo Angel 1860: Sarah Elizabeth Spalding aged 16. This painting was based on my daughter Harriet and the photograph of her I kept on my study desk. I somehow knew that this is what Sallie looked like, later I was proven to be correct when two photographs of Sallie were found in Buddy Sullivan's book.

Date: Tuesday, May 16, 2000:
To: Dr Norman C Delaney
From: Dr Ian C Baillie
Re: Marrying Sallie

My life has been the same... But this time the game plan worked! I married my beauty and avoided the Army, only working for them briefly for three years. I avoided the hot headed beauties and found a much more level head young lady that although extremely beautiful with rich parents was also kind generous warm-hearted sensible and intelligent, my wife and best friend helping through all these years to heal unknowingly the scars of the past. So I can't blow things up too much or ride horses as often as I would like... But who cares they are only passing distractions. In the end it is love that counts and I finally married my Sallie. I am indeed a very lucky man... This time!
Ian :)

The revelations didn't stop there! The link with Sapelo Island started to become highly significant. For this was where Sallie lived. A realization hit home that the lighthouse was a place of rendezvous during the courtship. From that moment everything started to take on a momentum of its own. For as soon as his subconscious threw up its long held secrets of Baillie's courtship with Sallie, Ian began to realize the image of the lighthouse was central to many of the paintings he had produced as a student.

Date: Monday, May 22, 2000:
To: Dr Norman C Delaney
From: Dr Ian C Baillie
Re: Slaying Dragons!

And then I saw the picture of South End drawn by her and it all came together! Baillie, Sallie, Hettie all liked art... I then realized that my paintings from the 70's have a lonely tower theme, which is in fact Sapelo lighthouse! I then retrieved my folder of art from the 70's and was totally amazed that it tells the whole saga in subconscious imagery. It is all there in minute painful detail... the longing, the pain, the warrior images, the Yankee hordes, the gallant defenders the lot!!! Today I presented the whole lot to my colleague Rosie Lagrue at school who has been working this through with me and she was blown away...Sarah Sallie Spalding is the nub of every hang up and trauma that has been in Baillie's and my life. TODAY

we slew the dragon of Sapelo and laid to rest Baillie's hang ups and mine... It has taken 140 years to clear the air but we have done it! I am finally free of her...
This would never have come about with out your input... I have relived the whole thing several times in my own life. I would still be doing this now but I/we have broken the cycle. I can move on...
Thank you Norman!
Ian

The deep significance of the Sapelo tower image was beginning to hit home. This very same image shouted out of the paintings Ian had produced in the 70's and 80's. He had been driven to paint the image over and over again. It had become the central theme of all of his artwork. He had even painted it all over the walls of his student digs while the other student friends fixed motor bikes on the sitting room floor.

In the early years after Sallie's marriage to Archibald McKinley, Sapelo lighthouse had held sway over the mind of Alexander Baillie Kell, torturing him, always present, always visible. Taunting him with the unfulfilled promise of his beloved *Sapelo Sallie,* yet overwhelming in its refusal to let this passion have free reign. And again exactly one hundred years later the image had come back to haunt Ian Baillie. Again it held this tantalizing power over Baillie's subconscious. This new unraveling of the story was revealing monumental parallels within his life. The revelations were evoking emotions. Perhaps the source of these emotions was Alexander Baillie Kell himself. For certainly with each new subconscious meme surfacing, Ian was experiencing massive emotional shock waves.

Date: Sunday, May 21, 2000:
To: Rosie Lagrue
From: Dr Ian C Baillie
Re: Emotional tsunami - big time!!!

I'm still reeling from the shock of it all... the emotional intensity is so incredible to experience... normally I am so in control. The cool scientist! Blood guts etc. no worries but this! Blonde ladies have a lot to answer for! I think the little white house held a lot more memories than the one he lived in with his brother. I think I might take a trip to the lighthouse at Dungeness with Harry in the week on the steam train... just for old time sake!

> **I feel like a giant infected wound has been lanced and the healing is beginning. Images just keep hitting me, which I want to paint so the story will heal.**
> **I found last night that you could see clearly in a 5-mile line across the marsh and Doboy sound to the lighthouse. So Baillie was forever reminded that he could see his love from his doorstep at Laurel Grove, probably from his bedroom window and definitely from the roof which John's wife used to look for John returning from sea. He would have yearned to be with Sallie, whist eating with his Mum and Sisters, all the time the flashing light would remind him of her at night. 'There, there is your happiness so near yet so far.'**

The following day Ian arrived with his artwork from the 70's. He strode into his science lab. A man filled with a mission to *slay the dragon* that had enslaved him, taken hold of every decision related to the affairs of his heart in this life time experience. It was time to rid himself of the hold Sapelo lighthouse had held over him, for two life times. Sapelo lighthouse, the place of the secret rendezvous with Sarah *Sallie* Spalding,

Opening his portfolio I stood back, amazed, transfixed, speechless! For there, in every picture, was the recognizable reoccurring theme. Standing out in the majority of this clearly artistic work was a large tower and side lower building that I instantly recognized as Sapelo Lighthouse, with the white house that stood beside it there on Sapelo Island, Georgia. How could this be explained? We had only uncovered Sallie and Sapelo lighthouse this May 2000. Ian had only discovered his connection with Alexander Baillie Kell as recently as 1999. Yet the imagery, down to correct perspectives, clearly leapt out as central to all of this artwork. More than that the deep level emotion shouted out with the pain of a broken heart.

Observing the paintings I was filled with a feeling I had last felt when watching the film *The French Lieutenant's Woman.* It was a sense of the tragic. In the film a sad deserted figure of the French Lieutenant's women stands on the cob at Lyme Regis, waves crashing over her head waiting for her lover to return. Her wait unsuccessful, she becomes an image of the broken hearted. The pain, the tragedy that leapt out from every painting was equal only to this sad deserted figure. Here was an equally haunting image repeated over and over again in Ian's 70's artwork. The deep sense of a broken hearted figure watching and waiting for his lovely sweetheart to return, always frustrated, barred from even a fleeting secret meeting, but living in hope.

Rainbow Bridge: One of literally hundreds of images of the *Lonely Tower* as I called it, this one shows a badly painted rainbow bridge of happiness leading to the lighthouse beyond which Sallie lives. These were rejects that survived, as the tower is too wide at the base. Many people liked this image and kept the paintings. The other is much darker and disturbing, a Black Knight on horse back prevents a small cat with wings from getting to the island. Sallie and the island are no longer accessible.

Some of the artwork depicted images I quickly named as *pain trees.* As I looked at picture after picture with the same haunting theme, the same feel of the pain of a deeply broken heart, I was filled with a sense that I was witnessing an outpouring of emotion, but was this emotion Ian's or Baillie's. The artwork told a clear story. This was a story of the maiden being held prisoner in the castle. While the lover looked on, separated by a stretch of water and a bridge. On the bridge stands a figure in black, mounted on a horse. Ian had painted this same figure at the top of the stairs of his student digs to scare off unwanted intruders - a powerful black wraith – an insurmountable defense, preventing the lovers meeting. And so the hero stands always facing out to the tower. A lonely, sad, love torn figure, utterly dejected broken hearted, helplessly standing by, looking on knowing his love is there, *so close and yet so far!*

The story told Ian's desire was to slay the dragon that had held him prisoner for the main part of his life. Lighting the fuse, sealing the ritual, the little model cannons exploded leaving our ears ringing and my mind racing. The sheer emotion of all of this was overwhelming. Hours later I was still left speechless, aware of how much all of this signified.

Ian Baillie had experienced this exact same yearning, heartbreak for Sapelo Sallie. He had been compelled to comply to his subliminal drives to retrieve her memory from the depth of his psyche, but it was Alexander Baillie Kell, who had lost his love Sarah *Sallie* Spalding to Archibald McKinley following the American Civil War in 1866 not Ian Baillie in 1977. How could this be?

As Ian sounded the cannons, he celebrated the release from the hold that all of this had had on his life. Now he knew what had driven him with such a passion. His emotion was obvious; all the frustration of realizing he had been helpless, to this overriding, overruling memory evaporated in a cloud of gunpowder. This was what was needed to finally set this tragic story to rest.

Ian left me, as he did so, he gave me the music tape he had played continuously in his TR7 in 1982 after his treatment in hospital, 'Greensleeves' (*lyrics: It's only been an hour - since he locked her in the tower!*)- by Ritchie Blackmore.

That night I wrote:

Date: Monday, May 22, 2000:
To: Dr Ian C Baillie
From: Rosie Lagrue
Re: Today! Slaying the Dragon... Wow!!!

It's all so amazing - it's mind blowing! One door opened has unlocked so much - and the connections are out of this world. Re - living the same story, going through the same tragedies - but working it through in this life- to be aware of the memories - you can see why people say memories haunt them - more that they are so real yet not in this life but in the previous. It wasn't that long ago that you were talking of hypnotism - it hasn't been necessary - the doors are opening - there'll be more - and the connections then with your life this time around will be complete - incredible!!!
Rosie

Searching for meaning in all of this we began to see that here was a story that had a life of its own, and that would work its way through. Ian had been powerless, totally in its control. The gift we all hold as the right of all humans created by God, the gift of Free Will, had apparently not been an option in Ian's life this time around. He was compelled to re-enact the past, the past of another person with the same face and the same name, **Baillie!**

The next question that begged to be asked was if he hadn't been able to make free choices in his lifetime, what about the rest of us? Were we all in fact, like Ian, reliving a *Story* from a previous life, trying to bring it to a happy conclusion? Just as in Ian's early years re-enacting had been an overriding *hobby*, a *hobby* that was about creating everything, making guns, rifles, a life size accurate flag, even a cannon. Now we had discovered that Ian's student years had been filled with a sense of a love that was not his own, but that of Baillie for his sweetheart Sallie.

Windows of Time

The find of the photo of Alexander Baillie Kell provoked a drive to paint, to externalize the images Ian saw in his head. The painting unlocked recollections, but not just memories came flooding back, more importantly emotions came flooding back too. Without any preparation Ian was thrust into a roller coaster of emotion, as the story was unlocking. At the same time I found my own gift of intuition bursting forth. As Ian transferred his artwork to computer and forwarded them on to me, I began to experience a sense of time travel, of entering into the picture and through into Baillie's world, of 1860's and 70's. The heat hit me, my senses were awakened, the rush of the romance, the sounds, the emotion, the feelings.

Looking back it became clear that there were certain times in Ian's life when the memories of his past life as Alexander Baillie Kell, had been bubbling under the surface. It was at these times that he was driven to paint. Student days were a time of love and emotion, and so the memories were aroused. College mates must have wondered what on earth was going on as Ian covered the wall of their shared flat with paintings. But Baillie's story remained hidden. Unbeknown to the artist the subject of each and every painting told the story of Baillie's tragic love affair. At key points in his life Ian was driven to re-enact these events. In the year 2000, Ian was again driven to paint, at a rate of two or three pieces a week. But this time there was the knowledge that the drive came from Baillie, and this was definitely related to Baillie's life story. This time working together through the Internet we were unlocking the memories. The combination of the painting process our gift of intuition was leading us to interpretation. Now at last Baillie's story lay revealed before us! We had cracked the code!

Date: Sunday, May 28, 2000:
To: Dr Ian C Baillie
From: Rosie Lagrue
Re: Good times at the Big House

Every time I see one of your pictures I think, 'this is the best yet.' And again I say this is the best one - but they are all so good, because they are windows to your memes.

Try to imagine the Officers and Ladies arriving by boat for the ball at the mansion!

I see a night time scene - a hot night full of expectancy of the occasion - lights of lanterns on the boat - light from the tall windows of the house - laughter echoes, good times are made of moments like this - the thrill of the dance!

As Ian scanned through a photograph of Sapelo Landing he set a scene. That was all it took - the scene came alive before my very eyes. More than that I felt taken into the very picture. I could feel the occasion I described. I could feel that romance, was there, looking on as Alexander Baillie Kell strode from his boat to take his place beside his blonde Sallie for an evening of dance, entertainment, romance at the Big House, South End.

Date: Saturday, May 27, 2000:
To: Rosie Lagrue
From: Dr Ian C Baillie
Re: New Pictures

I have drawn two train pictures to photocopy and paint. This ones called 'Last train to Olustee' Hope you like it? Ideas keep flowing... I'm researching Alexander Baillie Kell's Links with the railroad! Baillie worked for the Rome and Carrolton Railroad after the war and he always liked steam trains! Plus he got to ride 'em with the 5th in the War.

Images just keep hitting me, which I want to paint so the story will heal. All of this shed's light on Baillie's life, I must find out what happened?

Meanwhile we had understood Ian's drive to paint. The urge was a channel for Ian's subconscious to break through, for the story itself to be revealed. Hypnotherapy was no longer necessary. Ian felt this to be part of the healing process.

Date: Sunday, May 28, 2000:
To: Dr Ian C Baillie
From: Rosie Lagrue
Re: Sigh!

I love the dresses in the ballroom picture! So colorful and glamorous... YES how absolutely beautiful!! What a dream - if only... to get a chance to step inside the frame in costume, in style!! I would give anything to be there just one evening to watch it all and dance to the music - wouldn't that be grand, just breathtaking. Sallie would be the one in blue/lavender with her back to the view! Sigh! Tres, tres belle, la belle mademoiselle. Thanks for this glimpse into Baillie's world - very romantic.

Date: Tuesday, May 30, 2000:
To: Dr Ian C Baillie
From: Rosie Lagrue
Re: Subliminal Sandcastles

Checkout this image from the 1983 Ibiza hol... Shades of close encounters I think?! Amazing what a relaxed state can bring forth from the depths of the mind! I will scan in another from the same time zone you'll see why the memory surfaced. This is mind blowing - the tower and the little white house so obvious - a hot sunny day - and the little white house - fireworks - for sure!! Ibiza would have been the right temperature to bring back the memories of the sentiment, romance, and love.

There's the beach, the blondes Baillie, so all that was missing was the tower and white house - it has to be. 'Legacy from the Stars' and the X-Files episode 'The Field' confirm that regressions are centered around powerful emotional memories.

Subliminal Sandcastles, Ibiza 1983: I had subconsciously recreated the shape of Sapelo lighthouse with its attendant white wooden keeper's hut in sand. Blonde-haired girls, including my wife and a family with three small children surrounded me. It was for them that I had built the castle. The sun, the heat, the sea, combined together with the blonde hair had released the memory.

Here's why the memory was so strong
Just count the number of blondes in shot! Yet I didn't have a clue at the time!!!! No - it is all such powerful evidence of the subconscious at work.

Like a detective, once he knew the identity of the blond bombshell that lay behind the magnetic attraction to blondes in this lifetime, Ian was then able to discover her life story. The husband was soon discovered to be Archibald Carlisle McKinley, 1st Lieutenant of the 57th Georgia Infantry Regiment, Baldwin County. Here was an eligible marriage, for a family wishing to continue its power and dynasty.

A thunderbolt of recognition hit home instantly! For low and behold amongst Ian's 1970's paintings, recently retrieved from the loft, was a hand drawn image. The heavy dark lines and expression clearly revealed anger, rage. It warranted no explanation. Ian knew this was in essence Baillie. And this was how he really felt about Archibald McKinley, the man who had stolen the one true love of his life, the one and only Sarah Sallie Spalding!

The rage was clearly visible in this 1970's drawing and it was still just as real for Ian Baillie, now, May 2000! As Ian stormed into the staff room picture in hand, he blurted out everything he had since uncovered about McKinley. This was the man who had come between Baillie and his sweetheart. This was the man who had broken Baillie's heart, and left him unable to truly love any other women. He was the reason Baillie died, unmarried, unhappy, a man whose heart still burned for his Sapelo Sallie.

More than this - This very same angst had passed on to Ian Baillie. With the uncovering of the story came a reawakening of the painful memory of Baillie watching his last dreams of happiness fade before his own eyes.

Date: Thursday, June 1, 2000:
To: Dr Ian C Baillie
From: Rosie Lagrue
Re: The Lonely Tower

Your art in the 70s, music of the 80s, all bring out the pain of the broken relationship of Baillie and Sallie; Baillie's despair of loosing everything after the war, and so not being able to secure the one love of his life. She was his one and only true love, and perhaps it was also the fascination of the power and wealth - there could be no other - so in this life time it had to be Pauline. You couldn't risk loosing this blonde young beauty with parents offering the 'Spaldings' power and wealth. You married Pauline, to correct Baillie's pain.
Au revoir gallant Time Lord

Finally it was the questions from Norman as to the fate of the marriage of Sallie and McKinley that led Ian to put the last pieces of the jigsaw together. Further forays into the archives revealed a slightly less optimistic conclusion. Poor Sallie lost her one and only baby at birth in 1867. Very little else could be discovered other than her position on the island as postmistress. As for McKinley, he had written a diary that was now on record. Reading this, Ian was to discover that this man was after all a decent enough guy, but certainly no romantic! A man that seemed to spend the best part of his time away on hunting trips, receiving letters from Sallie, but very frustratingly not talking of their contents! As the real story fell into place the rage seemed to abate, they too had had a very hard life. Ian picked up the paintbrush, as an opportunity for healing the pain of the past; it all now became so clear to him.

Date: Saturday, June 3, 2000:
To: Rosie Lagrue
From: Dr Ian C Baillie
Re: Hardtack!

A Hard Tack to Swallow: I found this picture incredibly hard to paint. I still find it difficult to forgive McKinley. In fact I even found it a struggle to include this picture in the book. I would really rather just forget it or destroy it, so bitter are the emotional memories.

This is possibly the hardest picture that I have ever had to paint spiritually! It shows Alexander Baillie Kell Co H 5th Georgia Cavalry giving his only last hardtack biscuit to Archibald Carlisle McKinley 1st Lieutenant, 57th Georgia Regiment. The smoke rising is from Bentonville, NC, last battle of the War for them both. The symbolism is that the biscuit represents Sarah Sallie Spalding, Baillie's one true love being willingly given to his rival; the person that she marries in 1866 through family power pressure. He's younger richer and more acceptable to the Spaldings. Baillie is distraught at the fact and it ruins the rest of his life, but the acceptance in this lifetime will heal the hurt of his soul.
With this picture I accept that he was a worthy rival and a brave man wounded at Vicksburg in both shoulders, paroled but returned to fight at Atlanta through to the bitter end at Bentonville. He married the family and lived on Sapelo with Sallie until they both died, Sallie 1916, McKinley 1917, a hard tack to swallow!
Ian

Hi Ian. New picture 'Hardtack!'
'There is no greater thing that you can do, than to lay down your life for a friend.' A gallant act, from a truly gallant and honorable man the supreme act of love, is to set your loved one free to follow the path destined and chosen for her. Baillie was asked to make this greatest sacrifice, and he paid the price. You are who you are. These memories have survived, because of the intensity of the heartache, a broken heart, that could never heal. This painting shows Baillie as made of the same stuff, as worthy in this life as in the last.
Arise Sir Knight you have fought your battle of honor and come away the victor.
Rosie

Emotion is the Language of the Soul

Date: Saturday, May 27, 2000:
To: Dr Ian C Baillie
From: Rosie Lagrue
Re: X-Files

Hi Ian,
I've just watched X-Files, 'The Field' - it sent shivers down my spine, goosebumps - and it is the emotion that floods back with the regeneration - between Sarah Cavanagh, now Elizabeth and Sullivan Biddle, now Mulder.

So your reaction of intensity of emotion that has survived 130 years!! Baillie's and Ian Baillie all rolled into one - very powerful!! No wonder:

I'm still reeling from the shock of it all. The emotional intensity is incredible to experience... Normally I am so in control. The cool scientist! Images just keep hitting me, which I want to paint so the story will heal... I am sure that this is the imagery of the tower pictures...

The whole story is filled with emotion, I can feel the tragedy and the sadness, the mighty fallen, the broken heart, the harshness of life after the war, the dashed dreams, hopes, passions, desires.
Love is such a powerful emotion - this is indeed the Universal story of the eternal triangle!! - Very appropriate, geometry there too! No wonder there is so much to heal, the pictures of 74-78 show it all, and the music, the tower... but the healing can start now. Good luck with the paintings, the healing touch of the brush. I have a great interest in Blanche - I would like to know more about her. 'The Field' has set me wondering - the same people brought together in different life times.
Enjoy the experience of the steam train to the lighthouse - never too far away in both life times! I would like to know how you feel during that re-visiting.
Take care, and bon nuit.
Rosie

Finding Sallie, putting a name to the lady, who had *dumped* Baillie, realising who she was, felt incredible. Ian had made a find as equally significant as finding the photo of Baillie in Waterstones bookshop. But it swiftly brought with it a rush of emotions. I watched helplessly as Ian was filled with one emotion after another. The question had been answered, only to be replaced by others, 'Why had Sallie dumped Baillie?' Ian appeared to be filled with outrage.

Date: Saturday, May 13, 2000:
To: Rosie Lagrue
From: Dr Ian C Baillie
Re: Sapelo Angel

Hi Rosie
This is the little vixen that drove old Baillie nuts! Sarah 'Sallie' Spalding aged 17 in 1861 'How could you?'

Filled with this emotion Ian's mind was racing as another realization hit him. Baillie had experienced a romantic entanglement with this young beauty, but had lost her love. This sense of fear of loosing the love of Baillie's life, Ian now realized, explained the irrational fear that had driven the early years of his relationship with his lovely wife Pauline. This discovery explained everything about Ian's romance with Pauline. The drive to find a blonde sweetheart had dogged him from the tender age of ten years old.

Lying behind all of this was the deep emotion of love. Alexander Baillie Kell had worshipped Sarah Sallie Spalding with a passion so intense that it could not be forgotten. Even after the last fifty-two years of his physical life and the intervening forty-two years between his death and Ian being born! It was still overwhelming. Sallie had given him a photo. A photo Baillie carried around in his pocket during the three years of the American Civil War. (Just as Ian has carried a photo of the love of his life, his beautiful wife Pauline in his pocket, since the 1970's). On his return after the war he made his way back to Sallie, but he no longer held the pre-war status. His financial future looked bleak. The following year Baillie desperately tried to improve the financial prospects of his land- to no avail. The year following the end of the war, Sallie married Archibald McKinley. Sallie's mother introduced this man into the family as someone with a future, an officer with status, with prospects, with standing in society. McKinley, also a younger man, had all the prospects that a young, beautiful girl, such as Sallie could hope to look forward to. They were married the following year, 1866. Baillie's heart lay broken. The Spaldings had prevented him from fulfilling his dream. The dream of marrying his young sweetheart, the love of his life lay shattered around him. Baillie's one and only sweetheart, the girl who had carried him through the last four terrible war torn years was now the beautiful bride of another.

Date: Monday, May 29, 2000:
To: Dr Ian C Baillie
From: Rosie Lagrue
Re: X-Files: The Field

I am still amazed 'Legacy from the Stars' and the X-Files episode confirms that regressions are centered on powerful emotional memories. Elizabeth and Sullivan Biddle had been separated on 'The Field' by his untimely death as a Confederates fighting the Unionists - The regression was the emotion of his dying in her arms-heartbreaking. Then the pattern was repeated - this time her turn to die an untimely death he could not stop. Same story relived to the same sad ending! - Sound familiar?

Of course... they sure knew their stuff those writers. There was so much too fight for here on the fields of battle, in the American Civil War. With our hindsight we can now see the real people.

Your new picture spoke to me of people who knew each other perhaps since childhood holding on to everything they had - all at stake, fighting for their loved ones, for their future with them, all their worldly possessions, source of livelihood, all at stake, to lose now would be to lose everything!!!!!!
Emotions must have been running so high.

On the result of the battle field all was lost. We lost big time!

It is mind blowing - I find myself 'seeing' Baillie and Sallie's story - the glory days before the war - the dances, the white house - haunting in their contrast, just as they must have haunted Baillie - hence as you say the nightly calls to Pauline from University

The emotion of the loss of Sallie hit hard. It was as if Baillie was pouring out all the anger, turmoil, and heartache from the past. More incredibly Ian was now experiencing this. It was Dr. Ian Baillie experiencing these powerful emotions when in May 2000 we broke open the story. He experienced the same pain Baillie had experienced with the loss of his beautiful blond sweetheart. Along with this came all the other emotions. Perhaps unsurprisingly, there very soon followed awareness that one of the emotions passed on was one of intense jealousy for Sallie's husband McKinley. There was a great sense of anger too, that had come across in the paintings of Ian' s student days as far back as the 1970's. Ian was also experiencing Baillie's frustration and pain, as the hand of his young Sallie was given to another, and Baillie's sense of powerlessness as the powerful Spaldings prevented him from seeing the love of his life!

Date: Tuesday, May 30, 2000:
To: Dr Ian C Baillie
From: Rosie Lagrue
Re: X-Files: Haunted Images

> Your pictures of the haunted figure looking out across the waters to the tower, are so compelling, they hold such a fascination to me - they speak the emotion of 'The French Lieutenants Woman' the lonely figure of Baillie! Heartbreaking
>
> **This image is spot on I can almost taste it and feel it! Baillie was a romantic twit!**
> **Head in the clouds... the crash of reality was a mortally hard blow for him... 40+ years to think about it... then... Emotion is the key to memory!**
> **Now we know why he had to move away to Spalding County near Atlanta with his brother and family. He would have probably gone to the Wedding being family and watched her getting married in 1866. After that then Laurel Grove burnt down in 1867? Coincidence??? And in 1871 after Margery his Mum died, the only mention of him is being with his brother.**
> **Darien would have truly haunted him!**
>
> This part of the story, the haunting sadness is clear in your 1974-1978 pictures and the music you were listening to in the 80's.
>
> **They say 'it never rains but it pours' - but it must have broken Baillie - thank goodness for Blanche' s kindness - and for the children, they will have kept his mind off his misfortune when he was with them, they would have been bought closer by the hardship.**
>
> It seems her children laid the foundation for your role as teacher, children are great healers - by their sheer innocence of anything outside their own world.

A love such as this, a broken heart such as this, must be the stuff of memories that are able to survive death. Here was all the evidence, if any more was needed, that Alexander Baillie Kell had died a broken hearted man. These memes had survived death. Here was the stuff of Ian's memories, in this lifetime. Up to this point Ian had been compelled, driven, but was totally unaware as to why. The events of the American Civil War had been the driving force from Ian's childhood days to present day, driving him to re-enactment. In his teenage years and later in early years of marriage, the emotion of the loss of the love of Baillie's life, the memes, images, had surfaced. The Sapelo lighthouse image had come to represent all of Baillie's love for his sweetheart, Sarah Elizabeth *Sallie* Spalding. Well before he knew anything about

Alexander Baillie Kell, this image had come out in Ian's 1970's paintings.

The Story has a Life of its Own

No one could have prepared us for this experience. Usually if a person has an idea of having experienced a past life they go to a hypnotherapist. The hypnotherapist will then attempt regression under careful, controlled conditions. But we were doing this without having first tested our wings! I had not been trained to help Ian if he found himself having difficulty separating his past life memories from the present, and even more extreme if he found himself caught in the persona of Alexander Baillie Kell. In the months of June and July, the beginning of August I found myself looking on with a mounting fear as I realized in horror that this experience of unlocking memes was taking its toll. The summer half term had been an emotional one for Ian. It was as if all of Baillie's broken heart, sense of loss, of having nothing to show for his life, had hit Ian. It was he now who was experiencing all of these emotions. I stood by helpless not being able to do anything.

I was aware too of extraordinary things happening. The synchronicity factor and coincidences started to accelerate! In May our conversation over the e-mail regarding Stone Age Man's use of stone circles had led to Ian telling me that John, his friend in Holland, had a copy of *Pi in the Sky.* Incredibly as soon as he told me Ian received a phone call from John who was ringing to say he would be coming over the next week, offering to bring the book! When planning my weekly thursday assemblies each time I turned to my text books the page would fall open onto a page that was about the subject we had just finished speaking about! I never failed to be amazed. In time the frequency of this became more and more incredible.

Date: Friday, June 23, 2000:
To: Rosie Lagrue
From: Dr Ian C Baillie
Re: Fractual Patterns of Coincidence

All that has transpired was meant to be... Remember Folkston St

> **Mary's on the Georgia map! You are right it is a healing place... Amidst the turmoil and chaos! Eye of the mote of the storm...**

I felt we were being given indicators that we were on the right path. Ian kept his birthday a secret, but one June morning he came into chapel with a card in his hand, in a state of amazement. His aunt had sent him a birthday card of a lighthouse that looked so like the Sapelo lighthouse and the beach scenes depicted in Ian's, 1970's paintings. Yet she knew nothing of the story or the process of discovery we were making. Some of the most amazing experiences occurred around train stations, and train journeys. It was not until months later that we began to realize that train journeys unlocked very powerful memes, and emotions. That indeed it was Baillie's own experience of the painful parting with his real fiancée Mary Sullivan at a train station December 1871, that was being re-experienced first by Ian on two occasions in July, and later by myself on August 2.

Our Deputy-Head, Carola Timney arranged a school trip to the Eiffel Tower in Paris. Early that morning I arrived at Ashford International Train Station with my son Joseph who was going on the trip. We all stood there restlessly checking passports waiting as one parent phoned to say she would be late as she had left her daughters passport in the school safe. The farewell delayed, the atmosphere started taking on an eerie nature. We joked about waving white handkerchiefs, and I caught Ian checking his timepiece. I had already mentally dubbed this as a Baillie timepiece. Ian did not wear a watch, but had a waistcoat with a chain and an old-fashioned pocket watch kept in a little side pocket at waist level. The delay made him restless, and uneasy, I could sense that he was starting to feel uneasy. The hustle and bustle of organizing the children soon took over, and eventually they all set off. As I left I found the image of Ian looking at his timepiece in my mind. It felt as if I was looking back in time. That side ways serious glance as he ushered the children forward looked unexplainably familiar. When he returned he was strangely quiet.

The next train journey was even more significant. The week before Ian received his much-prized Confederate uniform. Excitedly he brought it to school mentioning that Pauline had been shocked when she had seen him wearing it. She wasn't sure what to make of it. Ian brought the entire uniform and the full equipment to school saying, 'Do you want to see a ghost?' And that he would like to try out an experiment after school, please would I act as witness and at some stage write down the results. He explained, 'All experiments need a witness.'

As he got ready to put the uniform on I started to feel nervous. I had not told Ian, but the first time I looked at the photo of Baillie in the book, I found myself feeling strangely emotional! Baillie's eyes filled with emotion, as he obviously gazed at his darling sweetheart Sallie. These were the eyes of a man in love. I felt drawn to those eyes in the photograph in a way that begged understanding. I found myself asking why the picture stirred emotions in me, emotions I did not dare tell Ian about. They could not be explained by any rational explanation at that point. But as I waited for Ian to appear dressed in Confederate uniform I found myself looking forward to this meeting with Baillie, Alexander Baillie Kell! The Baillie whose life we were uncovering. The Baillie, who was a Southern gentleman, used to the life of the grand balls at the rich and powerful Spalding's mansion. Where he would meet his beautiful Sallie in her electric blue ball gown, in the heat of the evening, to the sound of the music, romance filling the air. It was this Baillie I felt I was now going to meet. I was filled with excitement and nervousness. I was aware that this was not just Ian appearing in soldier's uniform. There was much more to it than that. This was something Ian was driven to do. It was as if Baillie was so very eager to have an opportunity to appear as himself!

I was nervous, Ian was excited. A moment such as this heralded a cannon blast. These small cardboard cannons were amazingly noisy - just the ticket! That smell of gunpowder, the sound of the blast in our ears, all very evocative to the memes. With the smoke of the cannon still filling the air, Ian walked back into the chemistry lab in full Confederate uniform. And to me here was Baillie before my very eyes. This was Baillie in full uniform with water bottle, gun holsters, full leather black boots and kepi. What an amazing sight! I sat back spellbound taking everything in. Here was Baillie in his element, so much more at ease with himself than the Ian Baillie I knew. Now at last Baillie was getting a chance to be the real *Baillie*. I tried to get a feel for what I was seeing here, ever conscious of being the witness. Without a doubt I was looking at a man so much at ease, confident and at home at last! The man I knew as Ian Baillie was now transformed. Yes I was now seeing Baillie, the Southern gentleman, and soldier with a familiarity and enjoyment of a man whom has long wanted to be able to do these things again. The real Baillie was at last present and free to be himself, thinking of getting back on the horse, firing his guns, fighting for survival and ready for action.

The AB/IB experiment was so stunning that my only possible conclusion was simply that time had to be an illusion!

Baillie 2000: Recreating Baillie, the AB/IB experiment after the end of the Summer term.

Ian was planning to join the school party in France, that weekend travelling by Eurostar. Walking on air, Ian was finding a healing that had been long over due. I can only describe it as a religious experience. This is my field of study. I was aware that Ian was experiencing a spiritual awakening. Kindness was irradiating from him. But life intercepts and things at school were stormy. Ian came down to earth with a colossal bump, more like a crash, just as he was heading off to France by train. The train journey was like a nightmare!

The next week as the staff gathered for a barbecue Sandra Cook, our French teacher described how she met Ian off the train white as a sheet, in much need of a stiff drink! Later Ian told me how this was an emotionally charged train journey. This was an experience that appeared to be linked with the putting on of the uniform on the thursday previous. At the time it was an euphoric experience, but the very next day Ian was feeling the negative effect and all the upheaval of the Celtic emotions. Waiting at the train station was absolute turmoil, as Ian experienced a depth of emotions that had no explainable reason to anything that was happening in this life. This begged explanation. I was learning very quickly that an appearance of the real Baillie was liable to result in emotional turbulence and high drama. This was a very painful experience. I realized Baillie's facet was more emotional. Baillie was a true Celt, vulnerable to the highs and lows of emotional turbulence. As we near the end of our great experiment, bursts of revelation were still coming through. The emotion in this e-mail was so tangible.

Date: Saturday, June 17, 2000:
To: Rosie Lagrue
From: Dr Ian C Baillie
Re: The Protectors...

She ain't heavy she's my sister! To misquote a famous song...!! :)
I am only glad that in some small way I can repay your generosity and help in solving the Baillie puzzle. We make a good team and spark off of each others energy. I have never had an intellectual relationship of such electric chemistry!
I have always been alone in my quest of 20 years like the warrior in the snow, but no more you have brightened my world and cured the heart that was broken 140 years ago!
Nobody can understand the loneliness of this quest... Pauline barely guesses at its enormity... many times she has been totally at a loss as to why I have driven myself on so...
But now I feel different, spiritually rested and uplifted thanks to a certain little Irish lass that has completed the circle!
Remember Baillie was a Kell (It would be perfect if the Kell's originated from the same place as the O'Sullivan's!! How rich, now that would be closing the circle! I've got a funny feeling that this might be so, but I shall have to research it!... sister dear!!!)
Just now I found where John's wife was at church in Griffin. Guess what? Yep. St George's! Couldn't be anything else a real 'well what do you expect you silly fool... Everything is connected!' So John's buried in Oak Hill Cemetery Griffin and I bet Baillie's led alongside him... Blanche would have done that...
So I'm going to e-mail St George's to find out if they can help?

Meanwhile rock on sister... If I can make you smile occasionally then all is not lost and you can cope with the slings and arrows etc. Tomorrow will be glorious... Barbour wellies sun tan cream... lunch! perfect... Oh yes guns!!!! lots of bangs
YES!!
Hoist the Confederate flag and we're almost there!!
Ian =;^D

Ian was right, Baillie had been buried alongside his brother. It was to be another seven months before this was to be proven by actually visiting the cemetery in Griffin. But the prediction was spot on. We were beating down the doors of the Matrix big time.

Date: Sunday, June 18, 2000:
To: Dr Ian C Baillie
From: Rosie Lagrue
Re: AB/IB

Bon soir Ian, IB/AB
I am struck by a realization - which makes Thursday and Friday all fall into place. Baillie's facet is one of great emotion - the Celtic spirit at its most romantic and yet tragic - On Friday you said many times that you felt like Baillie - and were even at the train station feeling like Baillie. All of this follows my meeting of AB/IB on Thursday. I am convinced the story has a life of its own and we are servants to it.

I tried to make sense of this incredible experience by putting together all Ian has told me, and all the events I have been witness to. Trains, train journeys were definitely painful experiences, for some reason. Baillie must have had a painful experience connected with a train station and train journey. I could think of no other explanation than that his meme was being relived on this occasion, and in full. The previous experience I had witnessed had just been a taster; this fresh experience had been traumatic. Days later and Ian was still shaken.

The conclusion I reach is that this is real evidence that Ian experiences the memories, experiences of Alexander Baillie Kell. He experienced the painful turbulent emotion that left him shaking like a leaf and white as a sheet, as a completely independent witness, Sandra Cook testified. Yet she knew nothing of this and still does not.

A second conclusion I reached was that *the story had a life of its own* Ian was reliving the story. It was unfolding as it always had done throughout Ian's life, so that Alexander Baillie Kell's life was being replayed in this life time. Ian has no control over it. Experiences had to be relived, probably to find a happy conclusion.

At this stage this was clearly an experience we knew nothing about, but was clearly emotionally traumatic. I was not interested in discovering the historical event behind the meme, just how it was affecting Ian. And that this was clearly memes at work. Memes bubbling to the surface and emerging as he set out on a train journey across and under the water, in the Eurostar! This felt very X-Files to me. I was determined to make sense of it all. It was definitely linked with the thursday uniform display. I was already wary of what might happen at future appearances of Baillie. Was this what spooked Pauline? Perhaps she was aware that there was more to this than met the eye.

Date: Saturday, June 17, 2000:
To: Dr Ian C Baillie
From: Rosie Lagrue
Re: Slaying the Dragons

And now I have met AB/IB wow what a wonderful experience - Time lord brother I thank you for giving me this magical experience. But for my biggest concern is for AB/IB not to be re-linked with the experience of the time of trains and pain - I wish I could erase this!!!!!! 'The 'story' has a life of its own and will be relived - we are servants to it.' We know it is real because it is being relived and you can 'feel' it – BUT this time 'all will be well, and all will be very well' I pray you found good company in France. The train must become a transport to good times.
Roshean Daub

We had reached a stage where it seemed that we would never fully understand this last mystery, when out of the blue Norman e-mailed Ian, with an amazing new piece of the puzzle. A discovery which was not only to give us a whole new incite into Baillie, but an amazing new incite into the relevance of our teamwork. A partnership we had affectionately dubbed *Mulder and Scully on the case!* This new vital piece of historical detail was to lead to solving the mystery of the turbulent emotions associated with train journeys.

Date: Wednesday, July 19, 2000:
To: Rosie Lagrue
From: Dr Ian C Baillie
Re: Baillie (of course!)

Check this out Rosie. Norman has turned up a second engagement with a CMS
Interesting! Baillie didn't stop trying!
But he picked the wrong wench again! Not liked by the family!
The name Catherine Mary Sully popped into my head as I read the initials and pondered?

'These excerpts from two letters are all I have on Baillie's engagement that never materialized, so now it's time to do some more detective work and try to identify C.M.S. I'm assuming that her last name is Sully. I can try looking her up in the 1870 Georgia census. Could this have been a second try for poor Baillie? A second rejection? Oh, no! How much rejection can a guy take! Sorry I didn't find this stuff sooner. Until next time, Norman'

Well I never Ian, just so amazing and of course 'Sully' was another of my nicknames!! From O'Sullivan, Rosemary O'Sullivan, with a sister, Catherine Mary, And wait for this, now Catherine Mary Alexander!!!
Time for the X-Files music!! What do you make of that?!
It is truly amazing that this name came to mind! There might be something in it - a meme.
I will share this with my Catherine Mary how incredible!! And the letters have such an insight on our dear Baillie - I will enjoy reading them - very evocative - learning more about Blanche and Evy's characters. They don't like anyone who is going to hurt Baillie good for them. But love doesn't seem to enter marriages then - it seems to be based on money and power- Baillie couldn't offer either.

The next weeks were so eventful, that at their culmination I wrote everything down in a letter to my sister Clare:

Date: Thursday, July 27, 2000:
To: Clare Sheenan
From: Rosie Lagrue
Re: Mary Sullivan

Hi Clare,
Just when I thought that Ian and I had found out as much as we could

about Alexander Baillie Kell and Mary Sullivan, I have found myself discovering the final stage of their relationship.
It's the kind of information that I thought I would never know! But it has all come about by a string of realizations, events that have unlocked my own subconscious memory, that I now think of as genetic memory. A series of events have triggered off deep-rooted memories, memes, though that are not mine! I've discovered the story of Mary and Baillie unfolding! It's an amazing experience especially as soon as something has been unlocked I have discovered that it mirrors my own life! Definitely X-Files!
During the summer I set off on a train journey to London. From the out set of the journey I started experiencing very unpleasant emotions. It felt as if all my instincts were on overdrive! I felt as if my sixth sense was warning me of something I could know nothing about. The whole overwhelming experience stayed with me throughout the next day. It was very unpleasant, quite oppressive. Yet I'm not even now absolutely clear what I was being warned about, and why I felt so strongly. Last week my memory was triggered off again. I started to remember these turbulent emotions. This time I started experiencing images of the front of a large black steam train! The emotions and train seemed to be linked. It came to me this was connected with the story of Baillie and Mary, and was to do with the ending of their relationship. I felt it had been pretty dramatic, and to do with a train.
For a number of weeks before this I'd felt compelled to understand more about Mary Sullivan. Looking at the Census returns for 1860 and 1870 I noticed again that Mary's mother Easter was replaced by another lady called Mary. It suddenly became clear to me that Easter had died in childbirth. Mary was a new wife, with two sons being born to that marriage. In 1871 Mary was engaged to Baillie. We had discovered from letters between Baillie's sisters–in-law that Mary was living at the Varner's house, these being Blanche's aunt and uncle. Unfortunately the house split up because those who were living there could not pay their way. Evie wondered what Blanche would think of Mary now. It seems she was not a very popular choice of fiancée as it was! John was not at all keen. Which probably explains why he did not help his brother out financially.
Mary moved back to her family's farm, where Baillie helped get in the various harvests. Evie talks about Baillie groaning and sighing at hope deferred - probably by November of 1871, it was clear the marriage was not going to happen. Baillie had not improved his lot. He was still unable to set up a home for himself and Mary. It must have become a point of tension with the father Patrick. It could not have been easy for Patrick's second wife having Mary, now 20, living under the same roof.

I guess and feel they made a decision that it was about time Mary left home. I guess Patrick made arrangements with Mary's aunt, probably living in Atlanta, for Mary to move out there to find a living as a teacher. The train station was the scene of an emotional parting as Mary headed off after breaking off the engagement. The emotion must have been running so high. Mary and Baillie still loved each other but could not marry, as he could not offer a home to support her and a future family. Times were tough back then!
The sheer turbulence of the emotion I experienced along with the ominous image of the front of the distinctive steam train had led us to breaking open the story. This was Mary's emotion and memories I was experiencing!
Confirmation for all of this came as Ian painted the picture. At every stage of the story Ian had found himself driven to paint the image as it would have been in Baillie's time in the 1860s/1870s. Just as with all the other occasions as I watched the picture unfolding I felt I was being let in through a porthole of time, a gateway, window. I was being let into the scene.

Seeing the scene of Baillie and Mary saying goodbye at the train station, I could feel this event as if it was my own memory. I could feel the heat, smell the smoke; feel that awful emotion. But then I was hit with another incredible realization. The dress Mary was wearing was the exact same style I had designed for my wedding dress back in 1982! When designing my dress I knew exactly what it was to look like, without looking at a costume book. I had no doubt in my mind I wanted a particular style of sleeve, a very distinctive 'leg of mutton' sleeve, and a bustle, with full flowing dress. My little white hat was quite unique.

Now as I looked at this picture, I was amazed to see Mary dressed in the exact same outfit, but with hoops to fill out the full skirt! Even the hat is the same! The phrase 'too many coincidences' started going around in my head. As I selected photos of my wedding dress to show Ian at school another incredible parallel hit me. On the day of my wedding, Peter did not have a job, or any money, we did not even have a house to go to after the honeymoon. Three weeks before my wedding day August 14, 1982 my foster father Edwin had pleaded with me to reconsider- it must have seemed like madness for us to go ahead. Edwin had a partnership in three building firms. Had worked hard to get where he was. And now I was marrying with these incredible odds stacked against me!

Rosie's Wedding Dress: A perfect subconscious emotional memory made manifest. Doubly so as this is probably the most special day of a young girl's life. It was this evidence that convinced me that Rosie had the subconscious memory of Mary Sullivan.

Now I'm left with an amazing conclusion.
In my last life as Mary Sullivan I was prevented from marrying the love of my life, Alexander Baillie Kell because he had no money, no home to offer his wife, and no work to speak of. In this lifetime I, then Rosemary O'Sullivan, went ahead and married Peter, despite him having no money, having no job, or house! And despite knowing Edwin's views on the matter. All the details about Mary's choice of teaching came from my own realization that there was never any other choice for me. I always wanted to be a teacher, leaving my little farming village at the age of 18, to go to teacher training college in London. I never contemplated anything else. Just as I had to play the piano. I taught myself to play, until I was given piano lessons. Its all so

amazing!!!! To add to my sense that I have uncovered the story as it happened, Ian has also often experienced emotions that were not his own at train stations, and to do with train journeys. Life re-runs the same story over again to find a happy ending! I'm sure I was subconsciously trying to find and marry Baillie, the love of my life in my past life.

I wonder how many other people are doing just the same and yet are, unaware of these hidden agendas, driving forces they have no control over! It is truly incredible!

Love Rosie xxx

Date: Friday, June 28, 2000:
To: Dr Ian C Baillie
From: Rosie Lagrue
Re: Soul Quest 2000

Hi Ian,
Our first phone call was the start of this journey - who could have known it would have led to such a discovery. We have traveled a long way, opening doors that I never knew existed. You always knew this place was significant. This has been a mission. I am honored to have been a part of it.
The map shows it was all meant to be. Truly 'Soul Quest 2000'!
My eyes have been opened. I was asleep, but no more. The horizon is eternal. No more tunneled vision. All boundaries are cages; they've been leveled. A new dawn breaks more beautiful than before. Reaching for the stars.
'In Lake ch' I am another yourself - Mayan Wisdom

Rosie

Update from Rosie: July 15, 2001

Looking back on the painting of Mary and Baillie's farewell scene at the train station, Griffin, Georgia, it all becomes more and more remarkable. During Ian's research trip to Georgia, February 2001, he found an old photo of Griffin train station, and struck lucky. He himself was amazed to discover the architecture of the platform buildings matched those in the painting he had drawn using his subconscious emotional painting technique. I had recently experienced an unlocking of my own memes. Sensations of a highly emotional and distraught parting connected to a train station had been dogging me like a recurring nightmare. When finally, I was able to make sense of this experience and realize that the train that loomed large in this memory was the front of a large black steam train, I realized that this was not a memory from this lifetime. I now knew how Baillie and Mary parted back in 1871. It was a highly emotional parting of an engaged couple still desperately in love, but unable to marry due to family intervention, and lack of money. On sharing this all with Ian it clearly was hitting the mark with him too. He was midway into drawing the farewell scene between Baillie and Mary. He asked me to tell him the story again, as I did so, he became lost in thought as he let the picture of the scene pour forth from his subconscious. Incredibly, at the time we were sitting at table in the school dining hall, with the noise of the children all around us. Ian was able to block all of that out as he, with a blank paper and pencil started drawing the scene from memory. But, again this was a memory of 1871; it was Baillie's memory. I also realized that Ian too had experienced this turbulent emotion at train stations in the past and that we can now associate this with the parting.

I sat spellbound as Ian filled the paper in a matter of moments. He focused first on Mary. As he did so I took a deep breath in, for there in front of me Ian was drawing my wedding dress! A dress I myself had designed from an image in my head back in 1982, but at the time I didn't even question as to where this idea had come from. From there Ian moved to the front of the towering black steam train that loomed so large in the nightmarish images that were haunting me. Yes, his image and mine were the same. I was beginning to realize we both had the same image in our minds. Ian's drawings and the images in my mind were cross checking as the same.

From the train Ian moved to drawing Baillie looking at his timepiece, as I had seen Ian do at Ashford train station, and thought at the time this looked familiar. Ian's pen was flowing effortlessly as the memory was releasing. Next came the train station buildings. As he drew them Ian himself was puzzled, he didn't feel that they could be accurate as the perspective was all wrong. This was a building with the upper story overhanging. Also they seemed to fall into the picture, falling in on the couple standing by the train, with storm clouds gathering in the distance. Unknowingly Ian was getting across that same nightmarish quality my own images brought with them. Ian was not satisfied that the buildings could be accurate, but he took the picture away to paint.

Baillie and Mary: December 1871: This was to be the last painting completed, it told the tale of a terribly emotional farewell at Griffin Station. Baillie never saw Mary again and any chance of female companionship vanished as the train left. His hat and watch are accurately depicted as can be seen in the 1901 photograph that was found February 2001.

Eight months later Ian's research trip provided the most striking piece of evidence for the accuracy of this technique. Ian uncovered a photo of Griffin train station, as it would have been in 1900. The architecture was accurate just as Ian had drawn it from memory; a large disproportionate structure sat on the roof of the main building. He had been so puzzled by the lay out and the over hang, for it wasn't at all like any train station he knew from this lifetime, but there it was Griffin train station. And there we had the scene of Baillie's parting with his fiancée.

After the discovery of the photo of Alexander Baillie Kell the main questions that remained unanswered and that was troubling Ian was, 'Why hadn't Baillie married? Why had his fiancée dumped him?' It was at this time when these questions were surfacing that Ian shared with me the find of the photo, and *Mission 2000* took off; a mission that was to help Ian unlock the subconscious memories of Alexander Baillie Kell. Six months into our work, we were to make a most incredible discovery thanks to Norman, the name of Baillie's fiancée. In 1870, Baillie was engaged to marry a young second-generation Irish girl, hailing from county Cork. Her name was Mary Sullivan. My maiden name coincidentally is Rosemary O'Sullivan; I too am a second-generation Irish girl hailing from Cork. Around this time I discovered, that I too had my own subconscious memories. In meeting me, Ian and I had set about discovering the details of Baillie's emotional life. It is perhaps the biggest coincidence of all that, just as Ian wanted to know the identity of the fiancée in Baillie's life, that he indeed met the fiancée. I was therefore the one person able to provide the answer as to why they hadn't married. Simply, because on review my own life has followed the same pattern as hers. I coincidentally have worked through the life of Mary Sullivan, just as Ian has worked through the life of Baillie to find a happy ending. Incredibly all of this is foretold on the map of southeast Georgia, with Folkston and St Mary's being clearly shown? As Ian met me at St Mary's in Folkestone, when our two schools merged in 1997.

Part Three:

Baillie Returns

Chapter Five
Shadows

'Well, Mr Baillie, I'm afraid you have cancer. The biopsy has shown that you have had a malignant tumor, but the good news is that it's treatable and we can give you remedial therapy.'

The news hits you like a sledgehammer in the abdomen and your whole existence recedes into a shadowy nightmare. I had just turned twenty-five years of age and it was a Wednesday towards the end of July 1979. I was sitting up in a hospital bed in Margate, Thanet. Three doctors stood at the end of my bed. With dead pan expressions they delivered the dreadful news. Well, what do you do? I sat there, took a deep breath and calmly accepted my fate. I was sun tanned, healthy and totally without a clue as to what life was all about. I now had an eight-inch scar on my lower right abdomen from the operation on the previous monday and I simply had to accept the doctors' verdict as to my fate. In an instant my whole life had been irrevocably turned upside down.

My world changed just like that. One minute everything was normal, the next minute, suddenly, there was no normality. You just have to get on with it, accept what you are given.

I thought back to the previous week. I had just finished my first year of teaching, a newly wed, and I was busy working on my bungalow building a garage, doing all the things that young people do. I was fit, played rugby, but I had a lump.

It had appeared almost a year before. But, being young and stupid I did nothing about it. I thought it was just a simple problem, a rupture, or something similar and I decided that as I was going back to Boxtel, Holland in the Summer holidays to earn money working for the Encebe Varkens Slachterij (Encebe Pig Slaughterhouse), I would go and get it checked out. The job involved loading pigs into lorries, extremely heavy work at thirty-five kilos per side of pig multiplied by eight hours! One four hour shift on a saturday morning I had lifted the equivalent of fourteen metric tons. I had developed muscles on my muscles, but the pay was very good; the equivalent of three times what one could earn in England at the time. It was a veritable gold mine and I was young just getting started, building a home, I needed the money.

It was a wednesday when I went to see my GP who on examining me said, 'I don't like the look of that, you need to see a Consultant.'

I replied in an irritated voice, frustrated at the collapse of my plans, 'Well, can't it wait until I come back from Holland? I've got a job lined up to earn loads of money.'

'No,' he replied, 'I really think you should have this looked at.'

That was when I realized that this was important, because I had an appointment with the Consultant within two days and that never happens unless it is something very important. By the friday I was sitting in a waiting room in Ramsgate Hospital, Thanet.

The Consultant examined me and said, 'I don't like the look of that, you'll have to report to hospital.'

'Can't it wait until after the summer? I'm going to Holland. It's very important'

'No, this is even more important!' He emphasized.

On the sunday afternoon I reported to Margate Hospital, Thanet, I was resigned to my fate. I sat in bed wondering why I was there.

Three different doctors came around each with a different verdict as to what was to be done. The first pronounced in a professional tone of voice, 'Well, we're going to try this.'

But the other as if to contradict came back with, 'Well, we're going to explore this and have a look at that.'

The third doctor added in a quivering voice, 'Well we're not quite sure what we're going to do, but we're going to do something,' as if trying to reassure me, but failing miserably.

So like a condemned man I awaited my fate.

On the monday morning I had my pre-med, went in to the operation quite cheerfully, not knowing what to expect. I woke up later that day with a stiff sharp pain feeling as if I had had my leg sawn off! I nervously looked under the sheet to discover an eight-inch scar on my abdomen just above my right leg. It was this that was feeling very tender. Well, they hadn't warned me about that! But at that moment, still drowsy from the anaesthetic, I was simply happy to go back to sleep.

I was woken at six o'clock the next morning, far too early for my liking, to the loud voice of a nurse saying, 'Mr. Baillie, out of bed, I want to make the bed!'

I replied incredulously, 'But it's only six o'clock! I don't even think I can walk, my leg is so stiff.'

'Never mind, off you go to the TV room.' She retorted in an efficient tone.

I tried to get out of bed, but nobody offered to help me. Nonetheless I had been given an order. I had to get out of bed! It felt like my leg was going to drop off at any minute and the tissues had stiffened wonderfully! I had to walk a good sixty yards down to the TV room. It seemed more like sixty miles. Finally sitting alone, gingerly on the edge of an upright day seat and looking at a picture on a wall, I tried to get my head around the events of the last twenty-four hours. Wondering what the hell life was all about? The painting was a scene of a ship upon a storm tossed sea. For some reason, though not surprisingly, this started me thinking about the uncertainty of life. What does one do at a time like this when your world has crashed around your ears? It's not supposed to be like this. It just isn't fair! Suddenly my emotions took hold and that empty knotted feeling hit my stomach. After an hour or so of lonely contemplation it subsided. I made my way carefully back to bed and like a drowning man grasped for the security of the bed, my National Health lifeboat, collapsing gratefully into its secure embrace. Later that day two nurses tried to comfort me, 'Well don't worry about it you'll be all right.' It was reassuring to hear such a matter of fact opinion from two attractive young women. Perhaps my disfigurement would not be so unattractive to the opposite sex after all? Only time would tell. I would have to wait and see what my young wife would say.

The biopsy results were due in on the wednesday. Being a trained scientist, I was able to detach myself from the situation and look at it in the third person. Scientists always have a way of looking at things in the third person. It's how they cope with the horrors of physical reality. A technique developed over the centuries, to cope with the more unpleasant side of life. I therefore threw myself into other diversions. I had taken two books in with me to distract me from my thoughts. One was about the English Civil War and the other the American Civil War

- a War gaming book by Terence Wise. I busied myself reading and re-reading the tiniest of details in these and thinking abstractedly, deliberately trying not to think about the obvious pronouncement that would come all too soon.

Wednesday came round horribly quickly. I was healing up, but still felt very sore. The three wise doctors in white coats stood at the end of my bed and delivered their message. I will never forget that darkest of moments.

By the end of that week they had literally thrown me out of the hospital. I was healing up very fast, as you do when young and vibrant. They said, 'We can't do any more for you, off you go home, stay in bed and don't do too much.'

Great! I went back to my father-in-law's place the fish and chip shop in Minster. I felt sorrier for my dear wife Pauline than I did for myself. There we were, married for just a year, and now this terrible thing. The words of the marriage ceremony a year and a half before echoed in my mind. 'In sickness and in health,' 'In sickness and in health,' 'In sickness and in health.' Around and around it went in my mind, and it slowly started to dawn on me just what that phrase, uttered in a matter of fact way somewhere in the ceremony, really meant.

Two weeks passed and as I lay back in bed, the district nurse came in to pull out the last few remaining stitches. In no time at all the wound had healed, I was genuinely amazed at the capacity of the body for self repair after such trauma. One day shortly after this Pauline and her parents locked themselves out of the house leaving them unable to return through the external gate. Ever the adventurer I hit upon the only solution, I would climb out of the window! Undoing the window I stepped out into free space. Oh no, I had misjudged the height to the ground. Not a clever thing to do with an eight-inch scar in your side, especially as I had to stand on a chair and stretch to get out the window. But I made it. Oh well, it was the only solution. I made my way back to bed thinking it will heal up again.

What was I to do now? There was nothing much I could do but await my fate. We had planned to go to Holland, so as not to be cheated we followed our plans and headed off for our holiday, all the time amazed that this was happening just four weeks after my operation. The plans were to stay with Mevrouw Endstra my Dutch *Mother*. I had met them on a train in 1975. They seemed to appreciate my humble efforts to practice my Dutch, for out of the blue they had invited me to visit them in Holland. From that time on Mijnheer and Mevrouw Endstra treated me like a son. This bond became stronger when I started teaching English to their youngest daughter, José (Johanna Josepha Francesca Maria Endstra). José was blonde and five years younger than I was.

It was the opening of a great doorway of adventure. I had spent the wonderful long hot summer of 1976 working at the Gezondheidsdienst voor Dieren, the Animal Health Laboratories in Boxtel, Noord Brabant. The hot weekends were spent on the Noord Zee coast at Vlissingen in Zeeland. I could speak fluent Dutch now and the monetary remuneration had helped tremendously with my life. I had earned a lot of money the previous year 1978, working in a slaughterhouse loading pigs in to lorries, but all that seemed a hazy dream now. I had to get on with day to day reality.

At last we were back in Holland again. As soon as we were there we met up with my friends at an exhibition in s'Hertogenbosch on the Eighty-Years War, celebrating the 350th anniversary of the Siege of Den Bosch. We traveled up the Rhine, and stopped at a café at Königswinter looking down the river from on high. But despite it all, reality wasn't reality any more; it felt surreal. I was used to reality being normal, but this no longer felt normal. I looked around at all the other people and wondered just how many other people had problems like I had. Perhaps I was the only one.

We came back to England with a jolt and in the first week of September when I should have been back in school, I started the radiation course. I received a little letter saying that I would have to report to Canterbury and they explained to me that this was an insurance policy, that's all. They were going to use radiation to knock out any cells, which may have escaped. I came to learn very rapidly that it was a specific sort of cancer caused by cells having been knocked into a place where oxygen is abundant and they then can grow freely, causing the lump. The danger was that the lump might have broken up causing secondary cancers in the lymphatic system.

I had walked around with this for a year without knowing! Oh my God how stupid I was. The people in hospital said incredulously, 'You're lucky to be alive! With some people the cancer goes all around their body, up into their lymphatic system to the stomach and neck, in four to six weeks. How come you're still alive?'

I quite naively replied, 'Well, I have been so busy with my life that I really didn't have time to die!'

I duly reported to the Radiotherapy Unit, Canterbury Outpatients, every day each week for four weeks, monday to friday. A nice Australian girl fitted me up with a shield made of lead blocks and jokingly tattooed my stomach. I had to lie on a trolley two inches from the ground and on wheels like a giant piece of toast. They turned me over after two minutes of gamma radiation and then gave me two minutes on the other side. Then, just like a piece of toast, I was done. It was then back home to wait for the effect. Every time four hours later, sure enough, right on cue I was throwing up down the toilet. Radiation is not a fun thing and if anybody tells you that a limited nuclear war might be OK, ignore them.

At the hospital they asked me to fill out a form with a long list of questions asking what could I do following the radiation treatment? Could I think? Could I follow instructions? Having had an interest in all things military and being a history buff I knew exactly what they were asking, why they were asking it and who was doing the asking! I exclaimed, 'There is no way you can follow any coherent instructions when you have had a high dose of gamma radiation like that. You just want to curl up and die.'

They said, 'Oh, right OK. We can give you some tablets for that.' It wasn't really the answer they were looking for, but it was honest. At least they then gave me some anti-sickness tablets, which alleviated the symptoms.

It's amazing is it not? They never actually tell you these things. You have to find them out from experience. They only give you things if you ask. The universal phrase among the suffering outpatients for whatever complaint they developed was, 'It's the treatment you know!' We felt just like experimental guinea pigs in some insane Nazi concentration camp where they were busy doing obscene experiments testing the limits of our endurance. I was amazed at the stoic resignation of my fellow humans as they suffered quietly under the most horrendous physical abuses. In years to come one can imagine the incredulity of students as they listen to the catalogue of medical practice for the latter part of the twentieth century!

One day I met a strange little man while I was there. Most of the patients were elderly and I always felt awkward, but he was kind. His name was General Wolfe! At first I couldn't believe that he was called

General Wolfe, but he was. He showed me his birth certificate, which he carried around with him. His father had had a very good sense of humor and named him General, because his surname was Wolfe. This had caused endless amusement throughout his lifelong travels and had earned him many a free drink.

Once he had visited the Quebec Arms, somewhere in London. The landlord had asked him to drink from a special glass tankard. 'If you drink out of this glass you can have free drinks all day.' He had told the amazed General. The very next week he went back in and the glass was in a special oak cabinet and on the cabinet in large letters it said, *This Glass Was Used by General Wolfe.* 'Well, that is no lie.' He said with a chuckle. It was little anecdotes and camaraderie between the inmates that made the experience bearable. The human spirit is an amazing thing. It reminded me of how it must have been waiting in the trenches during the First World War, waiting for the whistle and certain death. General had been there, but survived. He told me many stories of his life experiences and we passed many an hour in the corridor waiting to be fried by the infernal machine. I realized that he like all of us was a walking talking time traveler. He gave me glimpses into a long forgotten world that I had only seen in history books, yet he had lived it, been there, experienced it. I did not realize at the time, that all these experiences were altering my perception of reality. I was waking up, starting to perceive the true nature of time and space.

So, we persevered. I had many an adventure in the back of the ambulance going to the hospital. I produced and painted some Dutch toy soldiers and I translated the Dutch diaries of the Siege of s'Hertogenbosch, 1629 as a little exercise to keep my brain going. I later produced the translation and artwork as a small book.

I also built a chicken house in the back garden. On her daily return from work my wife would say, 'That looks like a chicken house. That's not a chicken house is it?'

And I would reply abstractly, 'No, no, no, it's just a place to put the tools.'

Not satisfied with my evasive answer Pauline would reiterate, 'I'm sure it's a chicken house.'

Each day she came home from work I had added a little more and each day she would say, 'Looks very much like a chicken run to me.'

I replied again, 'No, no, no, it's just a place to put things in to keep them safe.'

Finally she came home to find some chickens in the run. Exasperated she exclaimed, 'It is a chicken run!'

There were four little chickens sat contentedly in the little run. I, using my coaxing voice whispered, ' Ah go on, let me keep them. I've always wanted some chickens and I'm not very well.' Reluctantly, finally she agreed.

I learnt a lot from the four little chickens. I had time to study them in detail. I had never had that luxury before. Being like most people always busy with the mechanics of living, too busy by far to see the wonders of life. I learnt that the little animals were individuals, very different in personality and temperament. I had been taught the party line in agricultural practice, that all biological organisms were just organic carbon based machines. I had rescued these chickens from a battery farmer who was intending to sell them to a restaurant. Once they had stopped laying two eggs a day at around the time they were eighteen months old they were ready for sale. In business profit had to come first. When I first bought them they just sat there in the rain, not even knowing that they could move inside. They had been conditioned by their treatment to not move. I had to physically lift them and carefully place them one by one inside the dry brick chicken house I had built. I had prepared it for them with great pride and so was amazed that they did not take the opportunity to use their new home, even after several hours and when night fell. They were so used to their confined quarters that they didn't even know they had a choice. It dawned on me that my fellow human beings were just like the chickens so conditioned to the system that they never questioned it nor thought outside of the corporate paradigm.

But, within a week they had adjusted to their new environment and they became normal chickens - scratching, developing a pecking order and characteristics. All four were very different. They became part of my new reality. I now appreciated how beautifully intricate all living things truly are. I had made a quantum leap from the sterile mechanical view I had learnt in Biology.

Faced with radiation and an unusual situation you start to think about how things work. You realize that things like green grass, sunshine, the blue sky and the honest laughter of children are really the important things in life. And that all the things I used to think were important, such as money and business and stuff like that, were really not that important; necessary to our every day life yes, but not that important in the overall scheme of things. Earning a living is something you have to do to get along in our society. So your values start to change and you become a different person.

I had suffered twice the lethal dose of radiation to the abdomen, but somehow I had survived. I was now not so fit but well enough to go back to the *chalk face.* In early October of 1979 I went back to school. I had made a fateful prediction at the beginning of July and said to the children, 'Isn't it nice, I won't have to change jobs any more. I'll see you all in September.' Having enjoyed my first year at the school I wasn't planning to change jobs.

How wrong I was, but the Kent Area Education Officer reassured me saying, 'Don't worry. We have a local Headmaster who has a brain tumor and is in a very similar state to you. We understand. You haven't to worry about money; we will pay your salary and get somebody to do your job while you are ill.' They were so good. I had no financial worries. Kent Education Authority paid my salary, not only for six months but also for the complete year. I shall always be grateful to them for that. I'm not certain that this would be the case now.

I went back to work for two weeks in late October. Everybody was glad to see me. But very soon a letter arrived from the Royal Marsden Hospital in Surrey saying they would like to see me. Dr. McElwain a big jolly fellow greeted me, he was second in charge of the Unit. 'We recommend that as you are young and fit, you should undergo chemotherapy as an insurance policy.' He continued, 'You are an unusual case, because normally patients have the chemotherapy first and then have the radiation as a back-up, but Canterbury have seen fit to do it the other way round.'

I had various other tests done such as a lymphangiogram. This is where they insert needles into your feet by cutting a small nick in the surface of each foot. The nurse then uses a machine to pump radio opaque fluid under pressure into the lymph system and lymph nodes. Afterwards the X-ray machine takes a picture to see if any escaped cancer cells have produced tumors in the lymphnodes. I also had a Gamma camera test for liver function. A radioisotope tagged chemical is introduced into the blood stream to be metabolized by the liver. In the test they allowed me to watch my liver light up on the screen! You can actually see the scintillating specks of green light caused by the radioactive decay outline your liver. As they injected me with the radioactive fluid. I became aware of the tremendous pressure that the heart exerts and the sheer speed of circulation. The nurse said that I would feel a tingle just like pins and needles as they injected it into me. With one mighty whoosh the sensation shot down my right side and with the next up my left side. I then could comprehend the enormous pressure that the heart has to exert. Being a scientist I found this all incredibly fascinating.

I also had a CAT scan while I was there. This is where they put the patient in a cylindrical multiple X-ray device. The computer then rearranges these X-rays by density to give a composite view of the body in two-centimeter slices. At the time the scan cost £3,000 per hour - it gave me an excellent view of the inside of my body. I persuaded them that, being a scientist, I would find it interesting. They showed me slices of my body right the way through, like little road maps, something that most humans do not get to see.

The treatment continued. Dr McElwain said, 'There is a risk you may go bald.' I had seen all the bald people walking round the hospital and I thought, 'Yes, for sure that's breaking it gently!'

He added after a pause, 'It may not happen to you though.'

But I knew the odds were high, after all why should I be any different? The treatment causes that problem. It is a side effect. He continued in a matter of fact tone, 'The treatment is very aggressive, but you are deemed young enough and sufficiently strong enough to take it. It will attack all the body cells at their most vulnerable, at the point when they divide.'

My scientific mind started sifting through this new data. So that means all the cells that divide rapidly, like sex cells, hair cells, skin cells, epithelial cells including the cells in the lining of the stomach, will be attacked, and my hair may fall out! Apart from that I will be fine, nothing to worry about. A chill descended on me and I shivered at the prospect.

'Will I be able to carry on at work?' I asked trying to be practical.

'What do you do?' Dr McElwain inquired.

'I'm a teacher.' Came my reply.

'Forget it!' he said with no hesitation in his voice.

At this I was a little apprehensive wondering how long I would be off school. So I tentatively asked, 'For how long? Two or three weeks?'

'Six months.' was his reply.

My heart sunk it was like receiving a death sentence. At that we exchanged formal parting pleasantries and I left to walk back to the car. It seemed a very long way and the silent two-hour drive home endless.

I arrived home and cried. I had to tell the school that even though I had been back but two weeks, I was now going to have to disappear again. I reported for my first course of chemotherapy at the Marsden in early December. I turned up, the new kid on the block. Right to the top of the building I went, up to the seventh floor. The Staff Nurse after making me comfortable left me saying, 'You've got Bob Champion next to you. He likes horses.'

I replied in an annoyingly cheerful voice trying to be positive, 'Oh, I like horses too.'

The little ward had six beds, three per side of the room, a pleasant view not at all like the normal hospital ward I associated with childhood. This was much more comfortable, up at the top of the building, and Bob Champion was in the next corner bed by the window.

I turned and uttered nervously words now forever etched in my memory, 'Hi Bob, how are you? I hear you like horses, have you got one yourself?'

Bob groaned. He had been throwing up after chemotherapy. He turned to me and mumbled trying to smile. Later I found out that he was a famous Steeplechase jockey and that he was on his fifth dose of chemotherapy. And if that wasn't enough to be coping with he had just heard that his favorite horse Aldaniti, might have to be put down because of a fractured fetlock.

Another patient quietly put me right and I shrugged my shoulders. Turning a neat shade of claret I thought, 'Oh my goodness! He must think me really strange.' Imagine asking such an obtuse question like that to a jockey! But then, I didn't know he was a famous jockey. To give him his due, Bob was a nice guy and often pulled my leg about the faux pas on subsequent occasions. He was never a very happy person in hospital and hated the treatment profoundly. He was also extremely miserable leading up to the treatment. The poor man was hypersensitive to the terrible lethal drug cocktail and if that wasn't bad enough he had to face six doses, but had prepared himself for four!

My turn soon came around. After the blood tests I had my first day of a five-day course. The only way to describe it was a living nightmare. It is very similar to being in one of those old-time horror movies, except it is real and you're the star performer. First of all they fit you up with a cannula. They find a convenient vein in the back of your hand, forearm or even foot if they run out of options. They insert the inch long stainless steel needle and bandage it up so it won't move, and then they hydrate you with at least two liters of saline solution. Several times we were allowed to visit the local pub for a last drink or four. Having a few pints helps to hydrate you. Well that was our excuse and we were sticking to it! Eventually the landlord would not allow us in as the sight of so many bald people with bandaged arms was putting off the locals. When the pub closed we would arrive back at the hospital and the nurse would fit us up with a drip. This was the start of the one hundred hours of hell. Next day, midday usually, they administered the first dose of drugs, a lethal cocktail of platinum and bleomycin. They also gave you several anti-sickness tablets, which in my case did not the slightest bit of good whatsoever. You would then spend the next ten hours throwing up continuously, retching, even when there was nothing in your stomach to retch. Until finally you collapsed into a fitful sleep from fatigue awaking periodically to be sick yet again. You exist in a sort of semi-conscious under world. A drug-induced stupor designed to get you through the horrendous ordeal.

I always had a terrible metallic taste in my mouth. It was a bit like chewing stainless steel, that is the only way I can describe it. I used to suck glacier mints to try and get rid of the taste, but to no avail. I ended up hating the flavor of glacier mints. In fact, glacier mints still make me feel sick if I have one now, twenty years later. This is termed aversion therapy in scientific circles.

So, I would throw up for ten hours on average, always on the first day. On the first occasion I came to at about ten o'clock in the evening to the ward in semi-darkness. I mumbled to the nurse, who spoke in a kind angelic voice, 'You may have anything you want.'

I knew milk was a good healer to adjust and buffer the acidity in the stomach, so I asked in a parched rasping voice, 'Can I have some milk please?'

Immediately the ministering angel replied, 'I'll get you some milk, but I will put some *build-up* in it.'

Wow, that was like offering a dying man water on a battlefield, so thoughtful, so trivial in the scheme of things, yet at that moment everything and never to be forgotten. *Build-up* is like a chocolate milk shake, which gives you proteins and necessary essential nutrients to put back into your body. So I started to learn that the ritual was to be sick for ten hours, then rebuild yourself by drinking two pints of build-up and then back to sleep. The next day they would give you the next dose, but then it wasn't so bad, you weren't so sick. I used to lie there, wondering what the hell was going on, as the world passed me by. The third day was the same and the fourth and the fifth. But on the sixth day we saw the finish line, end of game, one hundred hours from to start to finish. You observe what is going on around you, but you are not really part of that reality. Still bloated from the hydrating process drip, not really with it, I would stumble into my normal clothes. They felt inordinately alien compared to the sweat stained salty pyjamas that I would discard. An imprint of my body was left like the Turin shroud to be expunged ritually at home. My body had suffered another crucifixion, yet I had lived to fight another day.

At the end of it all they would say in a jolly voice, 'Right, off you go. Come back again in seven days for your next lot of tests.' I was told these tests involved a blood count to see how low my red and white blood cells would go. If this was OK I would be given a booster to make the treatment more effective. Then after eleven days I would be checked again. My heart sank! 'Oh God, I've got to come back in between all of this!' The thought caused my stomach to sink. The journey between my house and the hospital was two hours both ways with all of this waiting at the end of the line. My morale reached rock bottom.

By now it was getting closer and closer to Christmas. All I could think of was spending a normal Christmas at home with my wife Pauline. But after seven days I dutifully returned. By now my blood count had reached such a low point they could not give me the booster. I had been hit so hard that my count had gone to one quarter of the normal number of red and white cells. When I returned on the eleventh day I was suffering a high temperature. I had difficulty climbing stairs due to lack of available oxygen in the blood transport system. I pleaded with the hospital, 'All I want to do is to go home for Christmas. Just let me go. I have had the blood test, just let me go.'

But the reply was worse than I was expecting, 'Oh no, not so fast. Let's have a look at your temperature. You are burning up.' The thermometer read 104 Fahrenheit, one below fatal. I was dizzy, sweating profusely and burning up with fever.

Dashing my hopes they told me, 'I am sorry Mr. Baillie you are not going anywhere. You are going straight to bed with a drip.' So they stuck yet another large cannula needle in me and put me into an isolation ward with a broad-spectrum antibiotic drip. I was diagnosed as having viral pneumonia verging on full pneumonia.

My wife had to go home distraught and alone. I was alone in bed feeling awful. I was however relived that someone was doing something. Once I had accepted my fate it was OK. My gums became swollen and I could hardly talk. My body defenses had gone right down to almost zero and the enemy bacteria had started to overrun.

Amazingly I made a speedy recovery. The doctors had quickly identified what strains of bacteria were causing the mischief and hit me with a specific antibiotic. It was Christmas Eve 1979 and I was in bed alone. But in amongst all this chaos something happened to cheer me up. The BBC was putting on a theatre production of Henry V as part of their definitive series on Shakespeare. Again, I was able to divorce myself from reality and to look at something more abstract, to throw myself in to it and to watch it, to feel the passion, to rally the soul. I identified with the bedraggled English army defiantly trudging through the fields of France. It was soon to become one of my favorite plays as it rekindled my love of history linking that with the Bard. Being a linear minded scientist I had concentrated my efforts for the most part on my discipline. Now I was broadening my outlook.

I woke up on Christmas Day feeling awful. I staggered to the mirror in the corner of the room looking up into its mercuric sheen. A ghost looked back at me, haggard and worn, shivering still from the aftershocks of fever. I looked awful. I was white, pale beyond recognition, an apparition. I put my hand up to my head and touched my hair. A big clump of it fell out into the sink. I tugged limply at the rest of my hair and it too started to come out in handfuls. 'Oh my God what a Christmas present!' I thought.

The nurse came in, she saw the hair and said, 'Oh dear, shall I get a razor and shave the rest off?'

In a hollow emotionless voice I said, 'I think that is probably a good idea, its all obviously going to come out.'

I sat up in bed with no hair, completely bald. A very novel experience. I was used to having long copper colored Celtic locks. Gathering my thoughts I suddenly announced to the nurse with the razor, 'It's Christmas Day and my wife is coming to visit me. This is going to be the worst Christmas present we have ever had.'

She kindly replied, 'I will try and get you a wig.'

A lady came up quite cheerily and showed me a selection of uninspiring National Health wigs. She kindly put one on me. Looking in the mirror I decided I looked like some demented peasant from the Middle Ages with a rat on his head. But this had to be better than the alternative. For Pauline to walk in the door and see me with no hair would be an enormous shock, too much to cope with.

Later that day, Pauline arrived. She walked into the room, took one look at me and burst into tears. I said, 'Oh never mind, you might just as well see what I look like,' and I pulled the wig off and threw it into the corner of the room. And I never, ever, put a wig on after that.

I can honestly say that, that was the worst Christmas Day I have ever spent so far in my life. To cap it all, there was a snowstorm on the way back in the afternoon and my wife had trouble on the motorway. She had to get a kind truck driver to lead her up onto the M2 from the Detling hill interchange, she nervously following in his tire tracks as the blizzard raged.

It is at times like this that you realize who your friends are. People I thought were my friends disappeared and yet some that previously were just acquaintances turned out to be really good friends. One such person was Clive Dorrell, an old school buddy. We had completed a Rocket Project together for our public examinations. He now working as an engineer for the British Airports Authority regularly turned up to visits even though we had just been acquaintances at school. He lived nearby and came to see me - I shall never forget him. All my real friends had disappeared. Later on they would say things like, 'Oh, we didn't want to upset you.' 'We thought you would be busy.' The plain fact was that they just couldn't handle it. Being ill with a cancer is like death, a taboo subject difficult to talk about. Best to sweep it under the carpet, pretend it doesn't exist.

Finally after a week I was discharged and went home. I spent New Year's Eve with my family at the fish and chip shop in Minster; 1980 had arrived. I can remember looking through the cold rain soaked panel of the upstairs window above the shop at the people making merry with a piano, in the street across the road at the Saddlers Arms. Seven short years ago I had been a nervous prospective boyfriend in the same room, trying to impress my future in laws. I was still at school studying A level's with my whole future before me. Now I was a shattered wreck facing nothing, just the next dose of chemotherapy. I held Pauline's hand tightly she was my rock, the only thing I cared about in the whole crazy messed up World. 'Life is not supposed to be like this!' I thought somewhat irrationally.

I was just starting to make a recovery when it was time to return for the second dose. I was dreading the second dose after the experience of the first. This time I was in a ward on my own with a Royal Marine called Simon. He was a real marine and was much more positive about the situation he found himself in. He knew the soldier's mentality - you had to eat to survive. If you were getting hammered, if your body was taking a bashing, you needed to eat to replace the nutrients. The staff at the Marsden had this philosophy - you may eat and drink as much as you like whatever you want. So, we had Guinness and Marmite sandwiches, Marmite toast - anything to take the taste away from your mouth.

I was sick the first day, as usual, but I was learning to cope. My body was starting to get used to the treatment, just like an alcoholic I was getting used to the punishment. My body was becoming a little more immune to the physical effects of the chemical beating.

I didn't know much about the second dose of treatment apart from that it went fairly swiftly. One hundred hours flew by and I was quickly back home. But as before my blood count went down. My arm was getting more used to the needles going in. We had to carry a card in case the police stopped us and thought we were drug users. We had too many needlepoints in our veins, a dead give away, or so you would think not knowing our predicament. We used to play a game called *Hunt the Vein.* As you become more physically abused and low in your body fitness, so they find it harder to find a vein in your arm, foot leg or what ever to stick the needle in.

The third was the same, but my memory of the fourth course is of a nurse who tried repeatedly to stick a needle in my arm all the while I was wincing and getting very annoyed. She said, 'Oh, don't make a fuss you baby.' But when it didn't go in she pulled the needle out to find it had a burr on - it was actually blunt! She had been trying to stab it into my vein and it was blunt! I said in a very controlled voice my teeth gritted, 'Go away and get me somebody more competent before I get very annoyed.'

The best nurse was a Philippine nurse. She was very good, one little ping and the needle was in - excellent.

And so the course of treatment continued. I went back for the fourth dose. This time I met a cockney guy called Bob - 'Bob the

Cockney.' I had seen Bob Champion in passing, but he was no longer having his treatment. He had finished his sixth go and had been off to Miami recovering and I envied him. It must be nice to be able to do that.

Bob the Cockney was totally the opposite. Bob sat up in bed. His doctors and the Consultants would call him Robert and they would say, 'Good morning Robert. How are you?' and Bob who could not stand being called Robert lying there, feeling very sick, would pull back his pyjama top to reveal a T-shirt which said *'Eff off'* in big letters. The nurses would go red and hurriedly try to hide it. The rest of us thought it most amusing. The patronizing Consultants, who looked quickly at their notes, then called him by the wrong name were a favorite target for Bob. Because everybody knew he was Bob not Robert except 'them' of course, so Bob could have his wicked little joke.

Bob was a brilliant character. He called a spade a shovel, in fact an *'effing shovel'* to be more precise! We had one chap in the room who spent three days moaning: moaning, moaning, moaning, and moaning at the nurses, moaning at the treatment, moaning at everything. All of us were suffering from his negativity, we all felt awful. On drugs your sense of reality blurs and if you have a nuisance or an itch you scratch it. So Bob quite simply said to the guy in the corner, 'If you don't *'effing* well shut up moaning we're going to throw you out the window.' Well, I thought that was a somewhat excessive statement from Bob, surely he did not mean it literally? But he did! Then I too thought, well who the hell cares? We've all had cancer and we are all on this infernal treatment and they can't do anything more to us even if they kill us. It won't make any difference. Some of us might not make it anyway.

The guy said, 'What's it got to do with you?'

That was when Bob said, 'Right lads that's enough, let's go and get him.' Luckily I was in the end bed near the door and merely witnessed the bizarre proceedings that followed. I was thinking, 'Well perhaps this isn't such a good idea.' But the other three boys, dragging their drips, got out of their beds. They rushed over, grabbed hold of this person who had moaned non-stop for three solid days and hung him out of the seventh story window, dangling him by the ankles! By now the guy was screaming. Two nurses ran in and said, 'What the hell is going on?' Bob turned round and said, 'We are throwing him out of the window, because this bastard keeps moaning. We've had enough.'

It seemed like a good idea at the time. The nurses however begged to disagree with the drug-induced logic and said firmly, 'You can't do that.'

Bob said, 'Why not? We don't care. We have already got cancer. You can't do anything to us.' I can remember thinking at the time that may be Bob did have a point.

So, they grabbed the moaning man, still moaning, by the ankles and pulled him back into the room. Somewhat disheveled they then whisked him off to his own little room for his own safety and put the boys all back into bed. Nothing else was said about the incident, the nurses obviously understood how we all felt.

That was the first time I started to question my values on the subject of reality. I had been trained and disciplined by the system not to question, but now I started to think. Yes we are all held in our places by fear; fear of retribution from society. Society is however an artificial structure glued together by a consensus of opinion. If there is no fear we are free. It may be a totally irrational act, but what the hell, lets just do it. Bob had demonstrated just how easy it was to slip into anarchy. Yet the concept appealed to the hidden rebel in me. It was another lesson in this bizarre University of horrors that I found myself in. I felt like Alice adrift in Wonderland, a cosmically surreal playground of experimentation. I was a willing student. The Matrix was teaching me. So I learnt a lot from Bob.

I learnt a lot more lessons. One day I was asked, 'Could you go and talk to the children who have got leukemia?'

In the Children's ward I started to make friends with a little girl. She was five years of age a lovely little girl. We talked about things, what she liked, where she lived. She was on a drip, the same as I was and I thought, what is this all about? What has this beautiful child done to deserve this? Me, I'm an adult, I can rationalize my situation. When they do painful terrible things to me I can say to myself they are doing it to try and help me. But all the children do is look and say, 'Make it stop, make it stop.' And you can't make it stop. The nurses can explain all they want, but the children see only pain and fear. We were very good friends her and I. We didn't bother asking each other our names. We were just people sharing a common experience in the Matrix.

A month later I was back in for the fifth time. After the treatment and when I was feeling better I went down to the ward. 'Where's the little girl?' I asked 'Where is she?' They just looked at me and said, 'I'm afraid she didn't make it.'

I was extremely emotional and had a long discussion with the nurses as to why such innocence had to suffer. They told me that even babies get cancer a fact that I was shocked to hear. I then realized that I had no right to expect anything, I was the lucky one. I was still here. There had to be a rational explanation for this appalling state of affairs. How can such innocence be slaughtered? My cancer was operable and treatable. They tried to save her but they had no chance. She was too far-gone her condition too advanced. After that I didn't bother going back, it was too upsetting. I talked to other patients who were far worse than I was and I realized even though I was ill I wasn't so bad as the others. It was the most humbling experience and I resolved to study this so that if I ever made it through I would make a difference. I would seek the answer and prove the point. There has to be more going on in a sane Universe than this? This is all wrong. We are not meant to suffer the agony of not knowing what happens when we face death. I wanted to understand!

The pauses between treatment got longer and longer as my body couldn't take it anymore. Being short of breath I could hardly get up the stairs. In fact I could hardly breathe, the slightest exertion made me faint. I fought it and made myself eat. I ate boiled fish and milk and when I came out after five days of hell I couldn't sleep. I was like a battery, fully wound up, fully charged. I used to sweat out pints of salt water onto the sheets and towels that I had on the bed at home. I used to get up and put loud music on in the middle of the night. The Tourists, *It's Great to be back Home*. I would play it really loud at 3 o'clock in the morning and jump around frenetically, despite my short breath in time with the music - I was just so happy to be back home. That was all I wanted to do, be home. I was alive! I was surviving!

I became very aware that our so-called reality is not as real as we imagine. We are all in fact half-asleep. We don't realize what the true reality is and what is really important. Relationships, emotions and being loving to each other, that's what's important. Everything else is garbage. Our society has got all its values wrong. Now I understood I was right, society was wrong. I had to change this; I had to wake people up. This was my mission in life; I had been spared an agonizing death to carry out this mission. The Matrix had a job for me and I resolved to carry out the will of the Matrix with all my power and resources. I could make a difference. I am the Matrix and the Matrix is me! I am one with the Matrix, now I understood.

I struggled on to the end of my treatment. One final blow was that I, like Bob Champion, had to go through to six doses. I thought I might get away with four. Nowadays they do give you four, unless it's exceptional and then its six. Back then when I went through the mill we were all guinea pigs - they gave us six to be sure, unless you were exceptional. That final one, getting that final mile six months later, was terrible. I came out a wreck. I went in fighting fit, healthy. And six months later I was a wreck. It was my twenty-sixth birthday, fourth of June1980. I thought back reflecting again, what has this experience been all about?

Fortunately during the early part of the treatment it had been the one hundredth anniversary of Albert Einstein's birth. I had been greatly impressed by a book called *Violent Universe* by Nigel Calder and a programme of the same name that had been on BBC television. *Violent Universe* was about Albert's theory of relativity and Albert's famous formula, $E=MC_2$. And I threw myself into the series, mind and soul. I didn't want to know about my everyday reality. I wanted to know how the Universe worked. I wanted to try to understand, if I was going to die, I wanted to know where I had been? What had I experienced? What was this life all about?

Through these marvelous television programs and the associated book I found the answers to these questions. And then I suddenly thought, 'Why wasn't I taught this at school?' This is so important. I had studied Physics, yet I didn't even know why it was called Physics. Teachers hadn't even bothered to explain the title! It is about the **physical laws** of the Universe. I had repeatedly written it on my schoolbooks without knowing this. I was a slave of the Matrix unquestioning the obvious, wishing not to look foolish before my peers. I had learnt all the formulae. I had learnt all the experiments. I had taken all my Ordinary levels at sixteen and my Advanced levels at nineteen. But I did not know what Physics meant and now at last I knew what it meant - revelation! I now realized this was important and that if I ever made it back into teaching I would make it my mission to teach this knowledge. I wanted to pass this wonderful view of the Universe on to children, because they are the ones who need to know. And, just like that little child who died in the bed aged five, they might not have the chance to learn.

I wasn't the only person developing a new sense of purpose form this terrible experience. When I was in the same hospital ward with

Bob Champion I asked him two questions. It is difficult to make continuous polite conversation when you are both together for five days and both feeling sick most of the time. It was he who started the proceedings completely out of the blue by saying to me, 'Do you find this puts you off sex?'

Somewhat taken aback and bemused by the abrupt highly personal question I replied, 'Not really Bob.'

'It does with me.' He confided.

I wanted to keep this extraordinary conversation going so I asked, 'What are you going to do if you ever get out of this Bob?'

He replied unequivocally, 'I'm going to ride again.'

I can remember thinking, 'Yes! That's good. But I bet there are lots more young jockey's in the stables who are just waiting their chance to take your place.'

But Bob was determined he was going to ride again. His horse had been saved too - Aldaniti had survived despite the odds. Sure enough, two years later I saw them win the toughest steeplechase in the World, the famous English Grand National. The year was 1982. I deliberately withheld betting on the race, so as not to jinx the result. I never did have much luck in those days and I didn't want him to lose. But he triumphed against all odds in a fairy tale finish both he and Aldaniti won! Both rider and horse had beaten the system. The system had nearly beaten us but the human spirit prevailed. They even made a movie called 'Champions' about Bob's story, with the actor John Hurt playing the lead role. You come out of that kind of experience, forever changed nothing is ever going to be the same, but you know how to beat the system. There is no other training like it. The determination on his face, he was going to do it. The horse was going to do it. And he did it. There is no other experience that can set you up like that. This is the ultimate training. I had had the same training. I too was determined to make a difference.

I decided what my mission would be. The one television program that I used to look forward to in my one hundred hours of hell was on a saturday morning exactly halfway though the treatment. I had turned the psychological corner and I was just starting to feel better. thursday and friday, day one and two just disappeared in a stupor of sickness. By saturday morning I was on the mend. That program was called *Tiswas.* It was three hours of total anarchy, three hours of custard pies and mayhem with Chris Tarrant and the gang. I thought, 'Yes, kids should have fun. That's what's its all about. When I go back to school I'll make sure the children have fun and I'll teach them how the Universe works. They'll never have time to be bored, Physics will from now on be amazing fun. This is the way to get the message across - a winning combination!'

By now I was walking round again, and they threw me out of the hospital. The final day came very quickly. It was mid June1980. I was twenty-six years old. I was called into the Consultants office all the time dreading the thought that I would have to under go another operation. I had had enough of knives - I had had enough of needles - enough of drugs - enough of hospitals - enough of nurses - enough of doctors - enough of the whole damn shooting match. I sat in the office and I gripped the chair, Dr McElwain looked at me and said, 'The good news is, we can't find anything.'

I said quite stunned, 'Pardon?'

He continued in a matter of fact manner, 'We've looked at the CAT scans and we can't find any scar tissue or any other dead material to remove. So you don't have to have any further operations and I burst into tears with joy I really couldn't take any more.

I said, 'What do I do now?'

He replied in a soft voice, 'You are free to go, go home.' He continued, 'We'll keep an eye on you now, but that's it.'

So I went home and cried. I was free from the months of hell. Eleven months of pushing myself through an endless nightmare trying to cling on to hope. Watching my wife watching me go through the sort of physical torture and abuse that is only normally seen in the worst prisoner-of-war camps in history. For one-year life had stopped completely, time had ceased to have relevance. We hadn't bought any clothes, records, or furniture. Nothing had happened we'd just survived. Very much like a war.

I went home and I started my recovery. My body had become used to fighting the enormous damage caused by the continual punishment of the treatment. But as soon as the treatment stopped I put forty-eighty pounds on. In six weeks my body ballooned. My metabolism was in hyper-drive. I had been so used to fighting the drugs and the damage the drugs were inflicting on me as soon as the drugs stopped my body just ballooned out of control.

Around this time I received a call from the school. They wanted me to come in to meet my new form for September. The parents wanted to meet me. I had to put a suit on and I was bald. But on a warm July evening after an absence of a year to the day I walked into the School Hall at St George's Church of England School, Westwood, Broadstairs and was greeted by a sea of faces. Over a thousand people had gathered for the event. I felt and looked like an alien being that had just droped in from a space. The gaze of the assembled multitude suddenly confronted me and in an embarrassed timid voice I just said, 'Hi!' and they all gasped.

I looked to all intents and purposes like some freak dressed in a three-piece suit and I was going to be responsible for the well being of their children come September! The parents immediately started a clamor and voices were raised objecting. The Headmaster Norman Morland rapidly ceased the moment and explained all, which had the desired effect and quelled the dissent.

After that I didn't wear a three-piece suit again. The suit just didn't suit! I wore jeans and my leather bomber jacket. I looked like a skinhead then, that was trendy and all right. I looked *well hard* as they say and got very little grief from people in the street. Within six weeks I looked like an escaped foreign legionnaire from a special-forces unit.

I had recovered, but one thing was for certain, my mind had been changed forever. My attitude to reality had changed. I had stood on the edge of the abyss and looked beyond into the dark void of the Universe. I had stared death in the face for a whole year and walked away. I had seen what was really important and I was now mentally prepared for anything. My only question, the one all important question I asked was, 'Is this one physical life all we get, or do we get another chance?'

Mankind has struggled to answer this same question from day one. Yet I had set myself the ultimate challenge, I would set out on a voyage of discovery to find the answer. I would seek the grail, I might not get there, but it was a journey that I would undertake at all costs.

I had made it through alive, but I had seen lots of people who hadn't made it. You get born, you die, is that all there is? There had to be more to life than that. I was now very anti-religious, because for me religion was full of contradiction and riddled with falsehood. I had been forced to conform as a young person. I had attended church schools at St George's. St Lawrence drummed religion in to me as a junior, but I had rejected it. I had very firmly chosen science, logic and reason as my tools. Now I would wield them with a new sense of urgency and purpose. I would push my intellect to the limit in order to answer this one all consuming question.

I had chosen the scientific method at eleven years of age, to try and solve things by experiment. To actually *prove* fine theories not adhere to them regardless of evidence. To formulate mathematical equations that sum up Nature's Laws. Religion was for me this time around a non-starter. I had seen so many religious *do-gooders* try to wheel cancer patients into church and the chapel at the Marsden to try and help them in their final hours. Yet without a shred of comprehension as to what exactly they were doing. To me they were mumbling words they didn't understand; it was a blind meaningless ritual. They thought they were doing some good. Just like the art lady who was trying to get patients to produce simplistic meaningless paintings by squashing paints together, who was terribly insistent. I am afraid that I flipped at one point and I was most abusive to her. I said that I had better things to do with my time than to squash paint together at that moment. Squashing paint can be great fun, but not in that place and at that time. I was busy using my time on more pressing problems, to try and work out how the Universe works and Albert Einstein had given me the clues I needed. My urgency was paramount, as I did not have a clue as to how much time I had left in this physical realm. He was now my hero. Filled with zeal I had become an *Einsteinian missionary* ready to spread the word of relativity, to darkest corners of the Earth. To spread the gospel according to Albert!

I had perfected my plan; first you give a young person the picture on the box lid of the jigsaw puzzle. Then they can find out how the bits fit into it. The trouble with my education was that I had learnt all the bits, but I didn't know what the picture was. I couldn't fit them together. My teachers scratched their chins thoughtfully and would incoherently mumble, and say things like, 'I understand it all now, it is all clear to me now. I can see how it all fits together.' But they would never tell you how it all fits together. I had to sit there in frustration saying, 'Please Sir, tell me, what does it look like?'

I therefore resolved to take the opposite approach. I would show the children the picture of the Universe, the picture on the box lid first. Then they would be able to see clearly how the bits all fit together. That way they would understand from day one of the course where we were going. I learnt very rapidly never to under-estimate the capacity of a child to absorb information. I was sure that this would bring success.

I remember my Art teacher giving me a lesson when I was seventeen, about the Golden Section and about the proportions of classic paintings. Afterwards I kept thinking to myself, 'Why didn't you tell us this when we were eleven? We struggled for six years to try to compose and draw pictures, and if we had known this one lesson before, we would have known what we were trying to achieve.'

Mr. Joy simply answered, 'I thought you wouldn't be able to understand.' Never under-estimate what people can understand. Even a small child can understand how the Universe works if the concepts are explained correctly. Very often they have a far better idea than adults do. Adults get clouded by the everyday reality and minute details that prove to be completely irrelevant. They forget the important things. Children go straight for the jugular with simplistic honestly. We all forget this as we grow older and become more complex in our behavior, perhaps we should remember to be more child-like in this respect.

So twenty years ago I began my quest, and the quest is now over. I have successfully answered my own question and the contents of this book are the direct product of that answer. For the distilled results of all those experiments, all that understanding, all that investigation has been poured into these pages. I present to you the ultimate demonstration that we indeed all survive physical mortality. I give you the story of my present life in the physical Matrix, which exactly parallels the life of another physical being present in the Matrix over eighty-nine years ago.

Update: March 2, 2001

Yesterday I reviewed my research trip video to Baillie's grave and subliminally absorbed the knowledge that, Margery Baillie Kell, 1867 to 1873 'Lil' May' as she was known died at six years of age. Blanche, Baillie's sister-in-law lost other children. But the death of his favorite niece who had shared his name would have had a profound emotional impact on Baillie.

Later that evening I was editing this chapter and again I was touched deeply by the little girl dying in the Royal Marsden Hospital. At 5:00a.m. this morning I awoke, I couldn't sleep thinking about events. Then I realized that this was the reason I had chosen to come back. The reason was to help answer the question, 'Why do innocent children die?' It will be of comfort to know that this physical plane of temporary existence is not all that there is in the Universe. I was then inspired to write the following lines in pencil least I forget by the morning. This feels right, very right, my mission, and my higher purpose in this lifetime.

At 5:22a.m. this morning I wrote...

I came back to prove that we survive. I saw so many children die for no apparent reason through illness, that I needed to prove the point. Just like the little girl in the Marsden triggered my resolve. That's why Baillie loved Religion and the Church. I chose this mission no doubt about it! I came back into the Matrix to prove the point.

Baillie

I intend now to go back in time in order to demonstrate how upon review of everything that has transpired, my life has been influenced overwhelmingly by the personality, character and life of Baillie. The myriad coincidences and events that have enabled me to put right the tragic events of the past. I have played my part, but more incredibly the Matrix has set the stage, provided the actors and supplied the props. Even the place names and images surrounding me are the same, Folkestone, St Mary's, Dover, Dungeness can all be found on the map in Georgia. The very latest find discovered yesterday is a house called *Rocky Knoll,* just at the bottom of our drive! *Rocky Knoll* is also the name given to John and Blanche's house. A complete coincidence you say? Well yes exactly, but that is how the Matrix works, all things are interconnected and coincidental. Coincidence is the norm in the Matrix. You will discover as I did that I have apparently had very little free will in my life. *Now let us together explore my past, but with the knowledge of knowing the whole story of Baillie, Sallie and Sapelo Lighthouse.*

Chapter Six
Gunpowder

I shall now go back into my own distant past, in order to demonstrate the remarkable parallels in my physical life with that of Baillie. I shall examine the subconscious motivations that have driven me forward into this present point of time and space. So let us now go together back to where I was born in Folkestone, Kent on June 4, 1954 at 12:09p.m. Imagine if you will Folkestone, a little seaside coastal town on the Southern coast of the United Kingdom, just across the sea from France. My earliest recollections are of playing Davy Crockett in the garden. The garden backed on to the railway line and I would run to greet the *Golden Arrow* as it steamed hurriedly past every morning at 8:10a.m. precisely. The damp hiss of the white steam and the smell of the coal burning intoxicated my young senses. I had a passion for live steam trains even at that age.

Baillie spent the last twelve years of his life 1900 to 1912 at Rocky Knoll alongside the Central Railroad of Georgia track, five miles north of Griffin, Georgia. So as I ended, so I began. We lived in Dunnett Road - 'Done it' Road, literally!

My favorite toy was a popgun. It had a black cold metal barrel and a warm tan colored wooden butt. I loved my gun. I used to load it with gravel so it became a childhood scatter gun which was much more interesting than firing corks and much more effective! After all corks have a rather low mass, which means that they didn't have a lot of hitting power! They tend to lose momentum due to their light density; of course at the time I was unaware of the precise science behind my love affair with the popgun. It was simply a very cool toy!

In the garden we had a number of railway sleepers, Americans called them railroad ties. I used to arrange these ties, when I was three, into various patterns. I would construct log forts to keep the imaginary invader at bay. My father would come home and find the sleepers all over the garden, having left them all neat and tidy the previous evening. The neighbor, a kindly lady once went into the toyshop in Cheriton, Folkestone and asked, 'Have you got any toys for a little boy that throws railway sleepers around?' These were my halcyon days of blissful innocence.

Davy Crockett rides again: A young Ian Charles Baillie, aged 2, prepares to ride again. Folkestone, 1956.

As an older boy I was very much taken with the power of chemicals, especially gunpowder. Gunpowder is a magical substance that has held an almost hypnotic fascination in the affections of many a small boy for generations. I know that this love affair was for me triggered off by the traditional celebrations of November 5, Guy Fawkes Night, with the making of a Guy effigy and going out on to the streets to collect a *Penny for the Guy.* We used to make our decorated Guys, go out, collect charitable donations from passers by and come back with usually a small amount of loose change. Sometimes we would do this three or four weeks in advance and then eagerly buy up stocks of fireworks, such as *penny bangers* and *threp'nny cannons,* the bright red ones! I always had a penchant for the exploding fireworks as they represent better value, *more bang for your buck, so too speak!* Rockets were another favorite of mine. But we didn't just put rockets up into the sky, being more inventive we made *bazooka* rocket launchers, which we would aim and fire horizontally. Often we would engage in childhood *gang* fights, small but intensely emotional affairs with some of the local neighborhood ruffians. We improvised an impressive arsenal of weaponry and being less in number would try to outwit them with our superior technology. It always worked, prepared only as they were for hand to hand combat, our firepower was a surprise and certainly scared them away from pursuing their bullying tactics and intimidation.

'Door chime' carbine: Several made for the 1970 Civil War movie shot in Blean Woods near Canterbury, Kent.

So we experimented and technological advances were made. When not using gunpowder from Bonfire Night, I made muskets from tubular door chimes. Rather gratifyingly we found that if we dropped the *penny bangers* down the barrel after lighting them, they could be fired horizontally. Then in a quantum leap we discovered the joys of weed killer sold in the local garden centers of the time. In those days you could buy a large one pound tin of weed killer for very little money. Modern day weed killers do not have the same pyrotechnic properties as forty years ago.

The experiments gathered pace. They moved into loading door chimes full of the mixture and making a rather effective flame thrower instead of a musket, which ejected a rather large two or three foot flame, bright yellow, for at least a minute or two. Advancing this new exciting technology we discovered that we could use this for our own rockets, so gratifyingly we experimented with a rocket shell. The grainy, powdered mixture was a bit too dense, so after experimentation we put the dissolved weed killer directly onto newspaper, soaking it in and letting it dry in the sun. Then rolling up the newspaper we packed it carefully into our homemade rockets. With an air of excitement we would then try them out by firing them in the local field. Some worked, some didn't, but on the whole they were always most spectacular.

The trouble with rockets is that they usually do one of three things. They either don't work, in which case they are extremely boring, and everybody groans, or they explode, or even take off successfully and behave as rockets really should, which is usually a novel bonus. Then they are quite exciting and spectacular, zooming off in various directions, ending up in neighbors' gardens. At the bottom of our house was an old disused railway embankment, the old Ramsgate/Margate line. We would at any opportunity escape up and onto this cherished playground of mystery and adventure. There we would build our elaborate camps and traps and imagine ourselves as Wild West pioneers fighting against incredible odds.

I was always influenced by American ideas yet they came somehow from within and not from the media. I never really felt English. I always felt at home with American ideas. Some people may suggest that this probably came from films, such as the famous 1950's John Wayne, films, but there always seemed to be more to it than that. For I was never one to watch television apart from, the Gerry Anderson puppet series, *Supercar, Fireball XL5* and *Thunderbirds.* In our games there seemed to be a certain amount of detail which we couldn't quite have gleaned from the films of the time.

By the time I was fifteen I was moving on to bigger and better things. I made a three-band working musket with bayonet. I constructed the barrel at metalwork and the stock at woodwork with

Mr. Bones, finally putting the two newly fabricated pieces together and thereby making my own musket. I used a toy pistol mechanism for its action and got it to work using red match heads as the percussion caps. This was somewhat slow on ignition, but effective none the less. Gunpowder provided the pyrotechnic propellant. Not satisfied with just recreating this long-arm of a forgotten war, I progressed to making a side arm percussion pistol. I had the feeling that one always has to be fully equipped!

My father assisted in the fabrication of the barrel by helping to solder a back plate on with a *touch hole*, to a large bore copper pipe. He did this on the gas cooker, much to my Mother's dismay! The barrel was then attached to a cut down toy diecast .45 Colt *Peacemaker* with a jubilee clip, which also secured the wooden shaped ramrod to give the pistol that authentic Civil War look. The whole assembly was then painted black with wooden hand carved grips. The finished product whilst not a true revolver did look and feel like the real thing. Needless to say I was most proud of this achievement and set about making a holster for it. When fired it functioned perfectly although with a slight time delay on the combustion of the red match head, to produce an authentic puff of smoke. We made it specifically to be used for special effects in the film and for our battle re-enactments. It was not enough to just make uniforms, one had to have the correct equipment. **Little did I know that, I had subconsciously recreated the weapons that Baillie used, as described in the letter dated June 18, 1864.**

So by the summer of 1969 I had recreated a bayonet, a musket and a pistol for some deep strange reason that would only finally become clear thirty years later. Thinking back the handgun experiments had begun very early on. One of the earliest attempts was at the age of ten. This comprised of merely a cut-out piece of plywood, shaped as a Colt .44 caliber Civil War pistol with a piece of half amp fuse wire and some gunpowder. The half amp fuse wire was attached to a piece of lighting flex, which was then plugged into the mains. I held my new toy out the window and turned the mains on with my other hand, it duly exploded rather gratifyingly with splendid effect. I hasten to add that **I do not recommend that any reader attempt to recreate my experiments!** I count my self-fortunate to have survived intact from these childhood adventures with all appendages still attached and functioning. I did use a lot of common sense, knowledge of safety procedures and safe loads. But accidents do happen and the purpose upper most was to produce special film effects not to engage in any criminal activities with full charges and real bullets.

I thoroughly recommend that those wishing to shoot safely join a recognised shooting club and gain the correct certificates from the authorities. Shooting as I do now proper reproduction Civil War percussion revolvers as a hobby is both educational and more importantly safe.

I also had an air rifle with which I could hit anything in the garden. It was a .22 caliber *Tornado* under-lever German airgun, a breechloader, which was immensely satisfying to use and quite powerful. I was always very good with it. I could place a single old penny coin at a distance of 75 yards and hit it without trouble. The gun can still be seen in my photographs of the time. Still restless with this subconscious drive, I set about making an American Civil War film with my friends.

My next self-appointed task was to build a full-sized cannon for the film I had planned. The cannon was quite a major construction. I had desperately wanted to make an American Civil War film since joining the hiking association at school. The weekend forays into the woods around Canterbury had sparked a deep passion to relive the excitement of this particular conflict. My friends all twelve of them would often play the equivalent of modern paintball, so I was quickly able to encourage them into taking this one-step further by making uniforms and equipment. My friends with my prompting became enthusiastically interested in the American Civil War. We managed to persuade a builder to part with his cherished old handcart. In those days builders still used wooden handcarts with wooden wheels. At first the builder wanted quite a bit of money, I think it was something in the order of £2.10 shillings, but being only children we had no money.

On going back several times and quite frankly being a bit of a nuisance, he gave in and donated it to us free of charge. We were most grateful and duly pulled it all the way home from Ramsgate town center back to my house.

With the help of one of my friends we then set about converting the handcart into a passable gun carriage by sawing the center sections out and clamping the two outside pieces to the middle central trail piece of wood, driving in 6 inch nails to hold it firm. I then trimmed the wood and, using a cast iron drainpipe for the barrel, carefully managed to drill through and pivoted it on the carriage. My father had said, 'There is no way you could drill through that without cracking it.' But somehow I managed. I then fitted all the accoutrements, an old bit of chain we found in the road, old bits of garden stuff that we got from our shed, a galvanized bucket, we made the ramrods out of old broom handles, and finally the cannon was complete. Sealing the breech was quite a hard job. We achieved this by pouring molten lead onto stuffed newspaper, which worked jolly well and made a good gas tight seal.

Finally the big day came when we decided to try it out. It was a saturday morning and the sun was shining. We went out in the garden, loaded the barrel with the weed killer mixture and then lit the touch paper made from loo roll. Standing back admiringly, the monster blazed away and came to life. Issuing forth from its mouth a 30-foot jet of yellow flame and smoke belching across to the neighbor's garden. At that moment my father was sat in the lounge reading the newspaper. Years later my father shared his memory of that day. I will never forget his words. 'I remember that day vividly. I had come home from working the saturday morning shift, sat down in the lounge to read the newspaper, and the room suddenly lit up with a bright yellow glow! I thought, what the hell is that? I looked out into the garden and there was the cannon with a 30-foot yellow flame and you standing there looking admiringly at it. That is one of my most cherished memories of you.'

I think my dad quite admired it actually despite the several bald patches left in the lawn from the spewing concoction! He had been in the regular army from 1926 to 1938 although he had joined as a band boy at fourteen years of age. A total of thirteen years service was spent in the Royal Ulster Rifles. As a rifleman he had marched all over the world - Shanghai, Egypt and even Belfast! All this before the great conflict of World War Two. Luckily he was discharged in 1938 as Neville Chamberlain the then Prime minister descended the steps of the plane waving his famous piece of white paper from the Munich agreement with Herr Hitler and saying, 'Peace in our time'. My father then signed up for the Palestine Police. Being an orphan he had nothing to lose and the Government were looking for adventurous characters to sign up, for what one can only term as a *suicidal job*. So he went out to Palestine and became a Palestine policeman for seven years. I was indeed proud of his comment, for even having seen such service, I think he genuinely admired my acumen in producing this rather splendid beast. Unfortunately the cannon proved to be too large to wheel out into Sturry Woods near Canterbury, where we had planned to make our American Civil War film.

With my twelve fellow classmates in what was called Randall's Hiking Association at school. Chris Randall and his brother had set up a club the previous year and I now persuaded them that it would be a good idea to make a film. As they had already built several log cabins and played the equivalent of paintball using dried pea shooting pistols, it was but a small step away from donning uniforms and re-enacting my script. Luckily they all agreed to help me.

I was always mysteriously attracted to Blean Woods to the north side of Canterbury, between the city and the sea. It was a marvelous place; it had inspired and invoked many memories. Rushing around in the undergrowth triggered off things in my mind. We used to play the games with BB guns that fired ball bearings or spring-loaded plastic pistols that fired dried peas. We used to play War games! Two sides engaging in skilful combat, usually with a flag or objective to capture. The aim was to try to win despite all the traps, pitfalls and enemy soldiers. We had to actively avoid the Forestry Commission people, if they had ever discovered us they would have sent us out of the woods, an added bonus to the excitement of the game!

We would spend our saturdays there, having planned it all week at school. This involved endless drawing of maps of Blean Woods and talking about what we would do on the saturday. Come the weekend we would don our kit, get on the train and then hike out to the woods we knew so well. The base was a sturdy log cabin that Chris and his brother had started to build in the early days before I had arrived on the scene to join in. They had spent a long time on its camouflage. Unfortunately it wasn't very camouflaged in the winter, because all the greenery had dropped from the trees and it tended to stick out a bit like a sore thumb, but it was certainly camouflaged well in the summer. Many times walkers would pass several feet away but not notice the cunning construction. We would then eat our rations, continue to build the cabin, or make the camp bigger and more interesting.

We had a long history of building camps in those days and it continued from our activities as children *up* the railway bank and *up* the allotment. We had a whole series of tunnels built by digging out earth and by putting corrugated iron over the top and then putting the earth back over. We were much like an adept pack of ferrets, skipping around these tunnels at a great rate of knots. Armed with candles to light the little chambers full of dried grass. The girls used to enjoy the excitement of the chase and we had many a happy time underground!

So, having assembled my troops, I then set about arming them because they needed some weapons. The only thing I had was four or five sets of old door chimes, which were quite useful for the purpose. In order to make the number of weapons needed, I had to saw the tubes in half. This was a nuisance, because they would have looked better with longer barrels. But we needed at least eight weapons. They therefore came out looking more like carbines than muskets, but that would have to do. It was only a film and carbines were after all quite useful at close range, especially in a wooded situation.

Two sides were then formed. One group agreed to make Yankee uniforms and the others Confederate. I would film it, having only a cameo role. So we went out in the summer term of 1969 in order to film an 8-millimeter epic of four minutes duration. I even persuaded St George's Boys' school to pay for the film. The film may still be viewed as I now have it stored on videotape in addition to having the original celluloid version in the attic. It is a vital historic document that mutely testifies to the extremes that my subconscious memory went too in order to recreate Baillie's past in those early years of my present life.

But that is not all, for my re-enactment days had started somewhat before that. At the age of eleven, I had become so enthralled in the American Civil War that Dave Pilcher a friend of mine at school had persuaded me to join the Confederate High Command; a new re-enactment society of which he was a member. He happened by coincidence to be in the cavalry, more specifically the 43rd Battalion Virginia Cavalry. The cavalry appealed to me because for some unknown reason, I really had a passion for horses and I was especially fond of the colors gray and yellow. I had always been in the yellow team at school. To me, gray and yellow went naturally together, it just felt right.

In 1966 I joined the 43rd Virginia Cavalry, Mosby's Rangers. I was one of their youngest members. At the age of thirteen, I went to camp in Chatham, North Kent. It was at this camp during Easter 1968 that the crucial Polaroid photograph was taken. The pose was that of me advancing under fire with the Confederate cavalry standard. I had donned Sgt. Major John Cullis' uniform to complete the image. It was an image that I was intensely proud of. The 43rd Virginia Cavalry was a very useful outfit and I reveled in their accurate portrayal of the legendary *Gray Ghost's of the Confederacy.* Their tactics of hit and run were my tactics; exactly fitting the subconscious memories that I had, yet at the time were not aware of. They had a variety of weapons and access to shotguns and various other firearms that I could experience and my ears were always attuned to picking up more information.

Captain Baillie CSA: This picture taken in 1970 shows the completed uniform that I had painstakingly made from scratch. I wore it with pride on many an occasion.

My most treasured book on the subject at the time, bought with my own pocket money, was *Arms and Equipment of the American Civil War* by Jack Coggins. I had saved up all my money for a number of months. I was only aged thirteen so it took a long time at 7 shillings and 6 pence a week. Finally, I walked down to the Albion Bookshop in Ramsgate and asked if they could order it for me. It was a staggering £2.12 shillings and 6 pence. Unsure of my seriousness as a potential customer the kind man behind the counter enquired with an air of incredulity, 'Are you sure you can afford it, because I have to send to America to get it?'

'Yes, I've got the money, I've saved it up. This is the book to have.' I replied.

He was duly convinced after some earnest discussion and the fact that I had already purchased several paperbacks on the Civil War from him. So he agreed to my request. Two months later I received the book all the way from America. The volume still sits on my bookshelf today a poignant reminder of a small boy's hopes and dreams, more than just another book in its nostalgic value of distant days.

I had learnt about the book through a series of articles, in the Airfix Plastic Modelers magazine, of autumn 1967. They had detailed the American Civil War over five issues and I still have those precious five magazines tucked away with the bubble gum cards in my collection. One of my lasting treasures. They were basically a series of articles written by Michael Blake explaining how to convert War game figure for the American Civil War.

The Civil War really was more than just a hobby. I ate it, slept it, and lived it every waking hour. But I didn't know why? I never even questioned this obsessive urge to relive the past, one hundred years on. I can remember being quite disappointed at the thought that had I been born in 1854 I might not have been old enough to participate in the struggle. It was a strange thought for a boy being brought up as I was in the swinging 60's, surrounded by the Beatles, pop music and the trappings of modern progress. Firing muskets, blowing up things with gunpowder, was all an inseparable part of my daily life. Studying the drawings enabled me to build the muskets. Using the red match heads as percussion caps, worked effectively although somewhat slowly and enabled me to fire my weapons authentically.

It was autumn 1968 and my pyrotechnics adventures continued. I was now a member, with my father, of the *Little Group Cine Club*, in Ramsgate run by Wally Smith with his friends and his son Colin. Derek was the stills cameraman and Pete the creative prop making genius and there were others in the gang. My father had joined, because he was interested in cinema and making home movies on standard 8-millimeter film. I was usually busy constructing props and uniforms. We never really had any money, so most of our things were home made. A marvelous guy called Pete carved a German Mauser rifle out of a scaffold board, with a moving bolt. He then made a hand grenade out of a piece of chalk and some boot polish. He was the sort of guy that you would find in a Prisoner of War camp, making things that looked extremely real out of almost any piece of household rubbish or junk. With a penknife and some skill he was an extremely accomplished craftsman. He made a whole set of German helmets in fiberglass, making a mould in a cardboard box with newspaper and plaster and an old German steel helmet as a template. I learnt many useful manufacturing techniques from him.

The Southern Cross: This is the flag that I made in 1968 aged 13. My father was astounded, as I couldn't even sew when I first started the project. Yet a few weeks later there it was, my subconscious had driven me to manifest a powerful memory. The yellow fringe edging is the same as the original 5th Georgia Cavalry flag in the Atlanta History Center.

I was always interested in special effects and pyrotechnics; anything that went bang or made a flash would draw my attention. I produced a first class rocket project for my CSE Science in which I gained top honors. NASA was busy putting man on the moon, it was 1969 and we were all inspired into rocketry, because of that epic achievement. I wrote to NASA and got a rather handsome set of books and memorabilia sent back. Exciting little paperback pamphlets, photographs of the moon and one lovely little book on home made rockets. It had a favorite cartoon image called *Don't be a Basement Bomber* showing a pipe bomb rocket zooming out of a basement window. I never actually managed to destroy my shed, but I did have several near misses. It was also in this historic shed, my first laboratory, that I manufactured the first toy soldiers of many I have since made.

It was now Easter 1971 I was older and more independent. My school friends and I decided to have our own Confederate camp for two weeks up on Dover Cliffs, flying the Confederate flag, a popular symbol of youthful rebellion at the time. I had flown the second battle flag that I had made at all of my camps since 1970. The camp was a great success and we decided to go to Chilham Woods the other side of Canterbury the very next year and repeat the experience, Easter 1972, this time I recorded the events on film for posterity. The guns and uniforms went everywhere. It was part of our essential camping equipment. We would take our Confederate uniforms and our flag and with other like-minded friends we would go out camping rough. We would skirmish and re-enact battles and generally having a *good old time* reliving simpler days.

I progressed from the *Little Group Cine Club,* to teenage rebel, to academic student. Advanced Levels cut in and I didn't have as much time to spend re-enacting as I used to. But the *hobby* just evolved into a new dimension as I went to University and the pyrotechnics continued unabated. I think I became quite famous for my pyrotechnic epsiodes at University.

Imagine my delight when I discovered some twenty-five years later that my otherself Alexander Baillie Kell had been suspended for 'throwing fireballs in the entry of North College' Princeton October 22, 1849.

All of this I feel is evidence indeed that I am the same personality reliving the same events as my illustrious predecessor. He had used balls of rag soaked in lamp oil, matches and leather gloves to have a flaming fireball contest with his fellow students. I have recreated this experiment to demonstrate the efficacy of the technique and the fun that may be had by a group of similar minded undergraduates wishing to escape the academic pressures of university life.

Many years later I would continue with my adventures. I had

formed an association with what I can only describe as the most famous duo in this part of East Kent, a legend in their own minds! The Hemming's brothers, Larry the older brother, and Colin the younger, were a bit like Wild West heroes. Of the two brothers, I was mainly friends with Larry, because of his arty connections. We had formed a friendship when I was studying my A' levels. After which I went up to university. Larry came around Europe with me immediately after I had worked on the railway in 1974. He had also been to Spain camping with me the year previous. But really, Colin the younger brother was the real pyrotechnic wizard and was famous certainly for rather large special effects, the largest of which was to blow approximately 50 feet of chalk cliff into the sea at Pegwell Bay in Thanet! Colin regarded explosions as an art form, but on this occasion the special effect device was a wee bit too big and he actually succeeded in finding a fault in the chalk and then most impressively the cliff disappeared! I think that that was one of his more famous exhibitions.

One day I went back to Larry's house where I discovered that Colin had joined a gun club and Colin now had a black powder revolver to go with his shot gun. It was a .44 calibre Dragoon model. I know I was absolutely in awe of it for I had only made models of these firearms when young. I did not even know that such replica Civil War revolvers existed. I had already been clay pigeon shooting, but my heart really was in the gunpowder and especially the black powder weapons from the Civil War period. And there it was, Colin actually had one! In a hushed tone I asked Colin, 'How did you get that Colin?' He replied that he had just joined the local gun club. After the initial probationary period and on becoming a full member he was able to purchase the revolver and shoot authentic black powder. I immediately signed up for three months, dutifully attended and after approval by the committee I became a fully-fledged member and still remain so to this day. I applied for my FAC (Firearms Certificate) and then went out to buy my first black powder pistol a Colt Navy .36 replica made by Uberti of Italy.

The Colt Navy .36 had a special pride of place in my mind for some strange unknown reason. I had made a model of it as a child and it is displayed in the photograph with my flag that I made aged thirteen. The Confederate battle flag, as you can see in the illustrations, turned out to be a subconscious copy of the 5th Georgia Volunteer Cavalry flag as I was to find out later on. And now, in my hand, I had the real .36

Navy revolver. I was enthralled actually to own one. I could also actually shoot it and smell again the evocative scent of fresh burnt powder and caps.

The Colt Navy .36 was something else. It held an elusive fascination that haunted me holding echoes of a distant memory that I was not yet consciously aware of. It was so familiar in its crisp action; the stripping, cleaning and assembling all seem second nature, so easy. Yet how could I know all of this, for I had only made models and toys up to that point?

In 1984 to 1987, while I was in West Germany I joined one of the eight local German Gun Clubs (Schutzen Verein) so that I could shoot in the evenings and at weekends. Unfortunately and much to my disappointment I was always working when my Army and RAF colleagues were shooting. But shooting with my German friends was great fun and always interesting. They taught me to reload correctly and I was able to increase my pistol collection from home. But always pride of place was my .36 Navy. Another of my most prized purchases was a Colt Walker, the largest handgun ever made - 4.410lbs of steel, .44 caliber. Firing 60 grains of black powder it makes a sizeable bang. It was the specially created and chosen sidearm favored by the early Texas rangers, I refer to it as the Confederate artillery on the range. The .36 Colt Navy of course, at 17 grains of black powder, seems a bit *whimpish* compared to the Colt Walker, but it was a nice handy gun, shooting from horseback. Years later, when I came back from Germany in 1987, I went out and bought a second hand Colt Army .44, Uberti. It was a very elegant state of the art gun for 1860, the 8 inch barrel points and shoots jolly well, exactly the sort of thing the cavalry would use in a close hand to hand scrap.

In time I ended up teaching Chemistry along with Physics. Chemistry gave me access to the whole world of pyrotechnics. Wow what better thing is there to do! And I continue to do, to this very day. Two years ago I developed my own successful fireworks course, poacher turned gamekeeper at last, what delicious irony? The annual pyrotechnic fiesta in the United Kingdom is known as Bonfire night, November 5. This has always been my favorite night of the year. Firing the school display for the last ten years has been a great privilege. One does not often get the chance to let loose so many expensive fireworks and not have to pay the bill.

So it continues, carrying on into the future with my War games an unbroken chain of events from an early age until present. Two years ago I developed a very small paper cannon, I term it, *a penny pyrotechnic*. I developed the idea just after Christmas. It was a 1:32nd miniature cardboard cut out Model 1857 Napoleon 12-pounder. To which detachable paper barrels can be inserted and lit, these thereupon blow the toy soldiers over in our miniature battles. Everybody's schoolboy dream come true. I was inspired by the *Addam's Family* television program many years ago. Watching my very first episode in black and white I was thrilled by the sight of Gomez blowing up his model train set, bridges and railways lines. My interest in trains and explosives coming together in one program! It was one of those things that I really felt that every child should be able to do.

I now have over 600 *Britains* 1:32nd Civil War figures and I have been playing War games for thirty-six years with friends, colleagues and pupils. I have perfected the game as popularized by H G Wells in his classic book *Little Wars*. Wells developed the game whilst living locally at Sandgate near Folkestone between 1900 and 1909 and like the master I have large armies re-contesting old battles such as Gettysburg. The cannons all lined up on a freshly mown summer lawn blazing away, the smell of gunpowder and the whiff of grape shot as Napoleon would say, dispersing the troops as they make their long desperate charge across open ground. All the while the music and the video from Gettysburg playing loudly in the background. There is always that hushed air of disbelief when the children come to view the battle and say, 'Do they really fire?'

And I reply with a smile, 'Yes of course!' Then I light the fuse and we all stand back, the cannons burst into life with a startling loud **bang!** Then the paper cannon balls knock the Yankee horsemen off their horses much to the delight of the audience. You then get that timeless whiff of gunpowder, the sulfur and the charcoal burning together, mixing with the burning cotton string. Totally intoxicating in its excitement and of course, totally authentic as any good Civil War soldier knows, yet we must break this destructive passion in real life.

We have to develop a healthy disregard for jingoism, because in the end, war is not an exciting adventure as portrayed in the movies. One has to experience the reality somehow in order to understand that it should not happen. We try to capture the color, the smell and the raw emotion of the combat scenarios in our miniature battles. But again the fire of the cannon endlessly kills the *poor bloody infantry,* as they charge bravely with futile hope across the field, only to lose once more. We all should re-fight lost battles with miniature figures in order to understand why war is such a terrible thing. Just as H G Wells, the great pacifist wrote in his 1913 book *Little Wars.*

'You have only to play Little Wars three or four times to realize just what a blundering thing Great War must be. Great War is at present, I am convinced, not only the most expensive game in the universe, but it is a game out of all proportion. Not only are the masses of men and material and suffering and inconvenience too monstrously big for reason, but-the available heads we have for it, are too small. That, I think, is the most pacific realisation conceivable, and Little War brings you to it as nothing else but Great War can do.'

I endorse this sentiment wholeheartedly. For we must break the vicious cycle of war, violence and conflict on this planet. Otherwise as my story shows, we may be doomed to endlessly relive the experience over and over again.

Chapter Seven
Horses

Horses have always figured large in my life. I always wanted to own one, but never quite got round to it. Money is the root of all problems on this planet. Horses are very expensive they take a lot of upkeep. Motorbikes, on the other hand, don't. Motorbikes are mechanical horses, motorbikes go in the garage, don't eat food, don't need mucking out. You can leave them for six months and they don't mind. A horse is a seven-day a week job. You really have to be born to it, you have to live it and you can't take a holiday. You have to find somebody to look after them. All their needs, feeding, exercising, mucking out, it is all so very time consuming. But, one essential difference between horses and motorbikes is that horses have a soul, horses are real beings with character. Riding a horse you form a bond, you and the horse are one. When you are riding the horse understands what you want to do and you understand what the horse wants to do and what it is capable of and you don't ask any more of the horse than is really necessary. You always have to look after your horse. If you are a cavalryman in the Confederate army and you lose your horse you have to walk, which means you join the damned infantry. No one will catch me in the damned infantry! So you look after your horse, make sure it stays all right.

Looking back on my early life, horses and motorbikes have both had a big influence. I joined a re-enactment society and the 43rd Virginia Cavalry, when I was twelve and went to camp with them when I was thirteen. My interest in girls started when I was fifteen. From then on I like most other younger men was interested in meeting girls and if you are going to impress the girls you have to have money. So I started working in Boots the Chemist in Ramsgate. The problem was the discos always used to turn into fights and I always used to get picked on by the skinheads, who were the local nasty guys and seemed to take delight in trying to beat people up. As for me, I was only interested naturally in girls.

Barn dances were in vogue during the early 70's way before the modern trend for line dancing. Everyone was dressed up in fancy dress and it was very pleasant. I went dressed as a Confederate Cavalry Officer. We danced the Virginia Reel and some other square dances. It was a memorable experience, yet I seemed to be out of place, in a world of my own. The other people at the dance were a little spooked at the accuracy of my uniform. But as for meeting girls, well Barn dances are not conducive, especially at that age. It was nonetheless an interesting experience, evocative and strangely familiar. It was never going to be the place to meet girls so I was going to need a successful game plan.

Quite by chance my sister used to go horse riding. One Sunday she said, 'Why don't you come up to the riding stables with me?' I thought, that sounds a jolly good idea, somewhere to spend my money, for I was only fifteen and not interested in public houses or discotheques yet. So I walked up to the stables with her and they said to me, 'Have you ever ridden a horse before?'

'Yes, sure, no problem,' I replied nonchalantly being somewhat circumspect. I was determined to look as though I knew what I was doing for there was no way that I was going to go around in circles in a paddock for weeks on end! I mounted the horse. To my utter astonishment, I found with in a minute or two that I could ride the horse! I knew exactly what to do. I was so comfortable on the horse. I found this amazing. I did actually feel quite a strange shiver of familiarity at the time. How on earth did I know how to do all this? How could I just get on the horse and ride it? Around this time I even wrote a small scientific paper on genetic memory in an effort to explain this amazing discovery. We went off riding from Brompton Stables, Broadstairs, along to Margate. I enjoyed it immensely. It was fantastic, exhilarating; I loved being on the horse. And the real bonus was that there were lots of nice, young rather well to do ladies, mucking out the stables. Well, I really thought that I had it made.

Sundays at the stables and riding became a regular event. I had a great time. But times changed and I progressed to my mother's moped to get around as I was now sixteen and I could have a driver's license. I still went up to ride horses on Sundays and met the nice young ladies, but they were not very interested in me. At other times in the week I would ride my mother's moped, but the street credibility rating on this machine was minimal if not negative! Due to its low power I used to drive it at full speed, a bit like a speedway rider, putting my boot out to go round corners. One fateful day at the bottom of our road I managed to go round the corner a bit too fast, hit a dust trap in a hole and came off it. This was my first accident, one of many. No helmet, no protective clothing, I scratched up my jeans, but mercifully was unhurt. I picked myself up, but I had put a dent in my mother's moped. Rushing home, I hammered the dent out of the mudguard, rushed down on my pushbike to the bike shop, and bought a can of *mushroom* paint. The moped was a rather horrid beige color. I quickly re-sprayed it. By the time my mother came home from work she never knew the difference.

I soon realized that mopeds were a bit of a liability, because they had no power. One day while I had pulled half way across the road a car came hurtling towards me travelling at 100 miles an hour down by the viaduct in Ramsgate, at the top of Whitehall Road. I just about made it into the gutter before falling off again. I then realized that my Dad's adage that you need a bike that is powerful enough to get you out of trouble, was a good piece of advice. So, having talked to my Dad, we went out and purchased a Triumph Tiger Cub. We rebuilt the engine with a friend of my Dad's. £30 it cost altogether, £15 for the bike and £15 to rebuild it. New big-ends, new small-ends, re-conditioned engine, and a re-sprayed tank. The bike was now completely rebuilt and a nice maroon two-tone color, maroon on top and metallic light blue on the bottom half, with the proud Triumph logo shone up, it looked terrific.

I had arrived. I had finally made street credibility. I had joined the cavalry, no more foot slogging for me! At school I was no longer a whimp, walking around in flared trousers and zip-up boots, getting beaten up by the skinheads, most of whom resided in the year below me. I was a prefect and I had my motorbike. I also had my leather-flying jacket. I paid £1.00 for it second-hand, a real bargain. The bonus came when we watched *Easy Rider*, the *in* film of 1970, with Dennis Hopper and Peter Fonda riding across America on their Harley Davidsons. The immortalized chopper bike with the American flag on the tank. Absolutely brilliant, it struck an instant chord with me, somewhere in the depths of my soul! Dennis Hopper was the sidekick going all the way across America from California to New Orleans having many adventures. They were rebels with iron horses. I decided right away that I would repaint my tank with a Confederate flag motif in imitation. My friends and I decided that this was our life. We were young, just sixteen at the time. So, investing in a cool pair of tinted spectacles I mounted my machine, wearing my leather jacket with the sheepskin collar, my tight jeans and leather cavalry boots. Off we went and rode into history, legends in our own minds, my friends and I.

Knight of the Road 1970: Baillie joins the mechanized cavalry. Street cred rating 100%.

Motorbikes were brilliant fun. Spontaneous adventures - we would zoom off down to Folkstone, Dover, to the all-night cafe and up to Tontine Street, by that little narrow road. I was always able to find and remember my way around. Like a lone horseman or in small patrols of three or four we would travel the highways and byway, back roads and lanes of East Kent. Even then I felt that I had done this before, not on a motorbike, but on a horse. It was a reoccurring feeling that I couldn't quite nail down at the time. It all felt so familiar, the emotion and the camaraderie. Our enemies were *skinheads* and usually they outnumbered us. They rode motor scooters, but had more infantry support in the towns. We were the dashing cavaliers, knights on iron horses, rescuing maidens and doing good deeds, despite our formidable appearance.

We had many adventures. We used to sleep out under the stars with a small fire for warmth, usually by the sea at Pegwell Bay. One night Tim Cramp and myself were camping there between our motorbikes, at around 3:00a.m., when the mother of one of our friends at school, Lindsey Marshall, came along. She wound down the car window and said, 'Have you seen Lindsey?' We were just going to sleep by the bikes exactly as in the *Easy Rider* film. I'd just passed all my exams at school, gained four Grade 1 CSE's and four O' Levels, the first person to ever score that number. I was always the gentleman and very polite when talking to parents. I enjoyed the fact that looks can be deceptive, so I walked quietly over and recognizing her said, 'A very good evening to you Mrs. Marshall.'

Quite taken a back at my politeness she exclaimed, 'Aren't you Ian Baillie, the one who has just gained all those exam passes?'

'Yes, I am actually,' I said in a casual voice and smiled back again politely.

I told her not to worry and that I had just seen her son not fifteen minutes earlier returning home. He was on the back of John Lycett's Tiger 350 zooming past at about, well I didn't tell her the speed, because I did not want to worry the dear lady.

We had quite a large gang going at that time. We used to ride over to Minster to meet at the Youth Club. But mostly we would all gather down by St Mary's Church. Minster became the *in place* to go to. Minster is a little village - villages are nice and quiet, there are not too many police around and it happened that a lot of the kids from our school lived in Minster, so it was natural to meet there. I often rode on my bike and went over there frequently on my own. I seemed drawn to the place. The biggest gathering ever was about thirty bikes, again down by the church. A lot of the guys had Japanese bikes, which were being imported into the country and were very good, but with very high-pitched whining engines. We all laughed at that, because we liked the solid throb, the real rumble of the British bike, the throaty roar of the four-stroke engine! We didn't like the tinny sounding two-stroke stuff the Japanese were producing, even though ironically they were far superior and far faster than our bikes.

We would meet with all the other bikers and attempt to steer clear of trouble. We would all go off on a ride, a spontaneous adventure. We imagined ourselves as the *Rebel* cavalry. Then one saturday evening in early September 1970, I tempted fate by saying, 'Why don't we all meet back here next week, same time, same place and do this again?' Of course having waited all week, I went back again expectantly the next saturday. And, guess what? Absolutely nobody turned up. I was stuck there on my own. I waited for an hour and I was totally miserable. I thought, what a waste of time! It just goes to show you that spontaneity is the key to life. If you plan something too much it goes wrong. People are ill, they don't turn up. The best party is the one where everybody just says let's have a party and they all rush off somewhere and all have an impromptu party usually for three days, everybody gets into it and everyone says, what a fantastic party. You just cannot plan something like that.

On this fateful day I had ridden all the way to St Mary's Church, waited an uneventful hour on my own. Feeling a little fed up, I drove up the High Street and parked my machine outside the local fish and chip shop. I was fascinated at the time by the illuminated ***lighthouse*** signs at either end of the shop. These were glass signs that I later found out had been put there, because the Fish Fryers Federation used the lighthouse as their symbol. Many car rally enthusiasts on treasure hunts would try and find the Lighthouse in Minster!

Walking into the shop I laid eyes on my future wife Pauline for the first time. Pauline was a vision; she had stunning waist-length blonde hair and a brown smock on. She was serving, head down, busy, but she was breathtaking. She was so beautiful, her long blonde hair stuck in my mind. I asked politely, 'May I have cod and chips please?' She served me with a smile and took my money. Where upon I walked out, ate my fish and chips and went back home. I felt a lot better. Needless to say I soon forgot about my first encounter with the enigmatic blonde lady from the Lighthouse.

Unknowingly I had just re-enacted the first meeting of Baillie and Sarah Sallie Spalding, 110 years previous. History was repeating itself, I on my iron horse and the lady from the lighthouse, heiress to the estate.

As progress would have it, the motorbike had replaced the horse, but it had served its purpose. I had found my soul mate. I didn't think any more of it at the time. I just carried on horse riding, going up to the stables on my motorbike. I graduated from wearing leathers to being a little more sophisticated. I was still working in Boots the

Chemist and I wanted to be a pharmacist. I had always wanted to be a scientist. I loved chemicals, but at that moment I wanted to be a pharmacist. A chap called Don, who was at university, working at Boots during the summer vacation now became my hero. He had a 650 Triumph Thunderbird with twin exhausts. He used to roar up the High Street making a hell of a racket at 5:30p.m. He was the man - he was my idol. I used to follow him with my bike, making not quite as much noise as his Thunderbird, but certainly it was quite impressive with the two bikes. He wore an old RAF jacket, surplus Officer's issue, and I took to modeling myself on him. I was naturally drawn to the *Officer* image. So I went to Newbury's secondhand *rag and bone* merchant in Ramsgate and found myself a conscript RAF Officer's jacket with the four pockets, in RAF blue. I was very familiar with this establishment as I bought most of my clothes for Civil War uniform conversion there. I wore the jacket all the time and when I went riding I put the jodhpurs on. I wore my jodhpurs and boots to the stables. I used to also carry a riding crop with my helmet as I still rode at Brompton Stables in Broadstairs. I felt very much like General Patton with thes jodhpurs on and my motorbike! When I arrived, the girls there would all look at me, because now I had a motorbike, I felt really cool. And I went riding on horses, which was even cooler. It all seemed to fit. Little did I know that, with the exception of the motorbike, I was instinctively following a previous pattern that I had no conscious knowledge of, to me it just felt right.

Not thinking about my chance encounter with the *blonde lady from the Lighthouse*, I became much more academic focusing my attention on my studies. My adventures on the motorbike and horses suddenly came to an end. I loved my Triumph bike, but sadly I had to sell it, my life had changed. My parents were somewhat relieved at this decision. Motorbikes are naturally every parent's nightmare, yet I had emerged unscathed despite several minor mishaps. The whole adventure had lasted just under a year, yet to me it had been a lifetime.

I progressed. I had gone from horses to motorbikes and suddenly I was into cars and being a student. But the horses and motorbikes would not die away. They would come back another day and in the next chapter you will see why the chance encounter with the *Blonde lady from the Lighthouse* was to change my whole life.

Chapter Eight
Women

Baillie was desperate. I was always a very shy boy and very awkward around girls. I had a sister and I knew lots of girls. Girls were fascinating, they thought differently to boys. They were civilized, clean and jolly good company. One could talk about art, music and literature with girls. Boys weren't all that interested. I had had many adventures, but nothing serious, all very innocent, and gradually I progressed to learn that the best thing was to go out with girls who were slightly younger than you were, not older. Going out with older girls was a bad idea; they always used to run rings round me. But I always had an attraction for blonde women. Ever since I was young I had been programmed to marry a blonde woman.

It all started with the early episodes of Fireball XL5 by Gerry Anderson in 1964. I was nine years of age and in love with rockets and space, but the series had a character called Dr Venus, she was the medical officer. The other characters for those who are nostalgic were Steve Zodiac the pilot, Professor Mathew Matic the navigator and Robbie the robot. I only had eyes for Venus though and later on I learnt that Gerry had based the character on his wife Sylvia Anderson. Luckily all these images are available on the web for those that wish to check out my ideal woman. There was some thing about her blonde hair, articulate manner and intelligence that attracted me. As we now know from the first part of the book, she was a Sarah Sallie Spalding look-a-like. Fireball XL5 graduated into Thunderbirds and again the archetypal Sallie was Lady Penelope Creighton Ward, again based on Sylvia Anderson. Knowing she was a puppet was devastating I just had to find a girl like that! Then one day I chanced on a real life Sallie look a like.

I used to walk home from school with a girl called Ruth Offerman, who was slightly older than me, and her young sister Rachel Offerman, who I ended up teaching later on in my first teaching post. Their father was a doctor and I used to go up to the surgery and see him, so walking home with his two daughters was quite a normal thing to do from Junior School. I was only a little lad, about ten years old. They lived off St James's Avenue in Ramsgate, a more select area than where I lived in Lorina Road just off Whitehall Road, Ramsgate.

Incidentally I can not help noticing how Lorina Road rhymes with Laurel Grove, Baillie's home in Darien, Georgia. Constant reiteration makes the point - coincidence? Whitehall could easily be a description of Sallie's Big House at South End Sapelo Island!

My good friend David Ellingworth lived in Whitehall farmhouse just across the road, a big lovely house, with a big dog called Prince. I had many adventures with Dave. He also had three cousins, Gary, Pete-ie and Stevie, who were all Americans with their short crew cuts and I loved them, because of the American connection I guess. I always had a thing about America. We used to play board games and they had this marvelous game called Railroader.

The American's had much more imaginative and innovative board games than us British at the time. We used to play such fantastic board games. They were so lucky because they had a PX, the US equivalent to our NAAFI and they could get access to all sorts of cool American stuff.

St James' Avenue was just around the corner at the top of the hill by Dave's house. Now just off St. James' Avenue was Beverley Way, which was where Ruth and Rachel Offerman lived, I quickly noticed that there lived opposite a rather stunningly attractive girl called Diana Price. She quickly became the object of my every fantasy, so struck was I with her. She had absolutely natural white, blonde hair, which she swept back in a bun when going to school. She had porcelain features, absolutely flawless complexion and impeccable manners. She dressed perfectly and I just couldn't help noticing her. She also went to Ruth's school, St George's Girls,' and was in Ruth's class. She fascinated me from the first instant.

I was a little ten year-old lad, but so entranced by this incredible beauty who lived opposite Ruth that I actually went up to Diana's house one Easter holiday. I walked all the way up there without telling my parents, which broke all the rules. With my heart in my mouth I rang the doorbell. There was no reply so I rang it again. Pausing, I suddenly thought to myself, 'What the hell am I doing? What am I going to say? I'm only ten!' With a total loss of confidence and out of sheer embarrassment I just stood there. Luckily for me there was nobody in. After ringing it twice I suddenly thought that it was probably a good idea if I just ran away. As it was summoning up my dignity, I walked all the way home quite disappointed.

Girls came and went, yet every relationship was half hearted or with the girls very much in charge. I always went for the blonde Sallie *look-a-like*, mostly to be let down as they dumped me after a few dates if that. But my confidence increased. Finally I became mobile with my motor bike. The next blonde lady I saw who was anywhere near Diana Price's perfection was Pauline. I met Pauline, as you are now aware in her father's fish and chip shop. Nothing came of that meeting, but the Matrix had other ideas, I was just absolutely stunned by her blonde hair.

One year past, and one evening my mother decided I had to go to my sister's open evening at St George's Girls' School. Oh whoopee, I thought, how exciting can that be. Yet I dutifully went, with my mother and father and we walked around looking at the displayed work and the departments, I remember clearly the microscopes in the Science Labs. I liked the Science Labs. But it was all getting very tedious. Then we went into the hall for the concert. My sister was scratching away on the violin, making an absolutely hideous noise. Then amidst the assembled mass I spied a blonde beauty radiating like an angel. It was exactly like the scene in the sport hall of the film *American Beauty*; everything faded except for the focus of my unwavering attention. There was Pauline with her long waist-length blonde hair, playing the bass recorder. I sat entranced for the rest of the performance just looking at Pauline. She also played timpani drums and I couldn't take my eyes off her. She just shone like an angel. The performance ended and we all went home, but the image was impressed on my brain. I kept thinking about her blonde hair.

I was busy working on my A' levels and studying. We went to discos and parties with all my new chums at Chatham House Grammar School, but nothing ever resulted. saturday night was usually disco night. I was in the rugby team now and was more interested in singing songs, drinking beer and doing what rugby players do best - that's causing mayhem usually! We all went on to become vets, doctors, dentists and teachers. We were all destined for university it was just a question of time. You were expected to go to university, but we made sure that we had a good time along the way. I was getting a little bit fed up with studying. It was now 1973 and coming up for A' levels, the university entrance exams. I suddenly thought, why not punctuate the tedium of study by challenging some of the local girls to an inter-school basketball game? There were lots of very pleasant young ladies that worked at my saturday job in Boots the Chemist. They always had a nice class of girls in Boots! Other shop assistant girls' were somewhat rough diamonds for want of a less polite phrase, but Boots girls were the best. And I was the only guy working there, which was quite embarrassing actually. They were usually older than I was and they used to take pity on me, I think? The regular shop girls would give me hints and tips on presentation and dress, they were very kind. Unlike my contemporary peer group that regarded me with disdain, extremely cutting in their refusal to countenance a date. I quickly found that *the school of life* is far harder than any academic institution and many a rejection followed.

Yet, my confidence improved, I became older and wiser, so now I threw down the challenge. I challenged the girls from Clarendon House Grammar School, Ramsgate to a basketball match, because they were a spirited bunch of intelligent young ladies. But, I was still subconsciously interested in blonde hair and another young lady Mary Brogden by name did have blonde hair, but strangely she just wasn't my type, although she was very pleasant. Mary managed to round up a team of sporty friends from St George's Girls' school and bring them down to Chatham House Boys' grammar school in Ramsgate. It was coming up for Easter 1973. They turned up and in amongst the team was Pauline, with her long blonde hair. She had blue, flared jeans on and a rather cute blue T-shirt with an apple appliquéd motif. Her long blonde hair reached down to her waist. I felt sorry for her really, because she was obviously out of place. She didn't like sport at all. The Matrix works in mysterious way its wonders to perform. Pauline only came as an after thought to make up the numbers with the more sporty girls such as Mary.

I liked Pauline straight away and wanted to attract her attention. So I kept giving her the ball to help her out. After the match we dutifully said, 'Let's do this again next week.'

I asked nervously, 'Where do you live?'

And she replied coyly, 'I live in Minster.' I had quite forgotten about the fish and chip shop where I had seen her and I had also forgotten about the concert where I had seen her a year later, this all seemed new to me. It was only upon reflection that I was to remember these things when writing this very book.

The Matrix has a funny way of working with coincidences, you don't quite know what is going on at the time, but you put it together in retrospect and it suddenly all makes sense.

I walked her back to the railway station. On the way there, I spontaneously rushed in to my house in Station Approach Road. In a flash with out pause for breath I blurted out my request, 'Dad, Dad get out the chair quickly. Can you sit with me whilst I drive this rather fantastic girl home to Minster?'

He said, 'What? I've just got in from work!'

'Dad, come on let's go, get out of the chair.' And grabbing him, I rushed to the door talking him into it as I went. Pauline sat in the back of our old Austin A40 and I drove manfully over to Minster and dropped her off very politely, saying a quick hello to her mother and father.

The next week came and the same thing happened again. After school the girls all turned up and we played basketball again. We had a good time. My best friend, Malcolm Hasler also escorted his young lady, Sue Penny home, coincidentally one of Pauline's friends. Pauline came back with me again. I walked her back to the station and this time I rushed in and said, 'Dad, dad can you take me in the car and drive Pauline home over to Minster?'

He replied categorically, 'No, I've only just got home from work, I'm tired and I'm not getting out of the chair.' I was frantic; I really wanted to get this girl home to impress her. Malcolm had already passed his driving test. He had a little red soft-top Triumph Herald, which was impressive then.

Crest fallen I had to go out and tell Pauline that the car had broken down. I walked her to the station and waved her off. But while we were waiting for the train, we made our first date. The following saturday night Pauline arrived at 6:00p.m., she was wearing a suede leather mini-skirt with suede boots and matching tasseled suede handbag. She had beautiful long legs, hair that came down to her waist and she had a tight tan brown Erica Budd sweater on. She looked absolutely stunning. She was an angel, a vision.

The rugby players all went to the Hotel De Ville in Grange Road, near the Western Undercliff beach area in Ramsgate. It was a Mecca for the rugby players in Thanet obtaining legendary status in our impressionable young minds. Ted the landlord had welcomed us with open arms despite our high sprits and loud signing! I was drinking Newcastle Brown at the time, which coincidentally would influence my university choice, ultimately. Pauline came over; she looked dazzling. She stood in the doorway lighting it up she didn't need sunshine she was just radiant. Dave Cookson our school rugby coach and the entire rugby crowd were there and I will never, ever forget the look on their faces when I walked in with Pauline. Dave said with his typical Cumbrian bluntness and distinctive accent, 'Bloody hell Rocky what have you got there?'

I proudly declared, 'Actually it's my new girlfriend Sir,' trying to be polite.

Needless to say the boys were well impressed with my good fortune. Pauline was quite bemused by all this as she had not mixed with rugby folk before and didn't know quite what to make of it all. She knew they were all reasonably intellectual, especially when they weren't drinking and playing silly games or crawling under the tables. Pauline and I sat there making polite conversation and got to know each other. My first big surprise was when I said, 'What would you like to drink?'

She replied quite confidently, 'I'll have a Dubonnet and lemonade please.' I knew instantly that this was no ordinary young lady.

We had a couple of drinks and then walked all the way to my house and I saw her off home on the train again. I had absolutely cracked it! This was like my best dreams of Diana Price, but this was real! Our relationship blossomed and developed and, of course, I had to meet mum. I had to go and be polite. Immediately I scored lots of points with mum and dad, because I was always very polite and well spoken, especially with parents.

One always had to get on with the mother. I had somehow had this drummed in to my mind and I now know why, because in the past life experience of Baillie it was Mary Bass Spalding who ultimately decided to whom Sallie her daughter would marry. It all went horrendously wrong then. One has to get on with the future mother-in-law. Fathers, yes, you can get on with them, no trouble, if you say the right things, but mothers are the key - you must get on with them. They are the ones who say yes or no to their daughters getting married. I was desperate for this relationship not to fail, so I went over there determined to repeatedly score lots of points.

Pauline simply liked me because I looked like Jonathan King, who was in the Top Ten on *Top of the Pops* then, plus I had the right length trousers, they almost touched the ground! That was her only criteria. If I hadn't had the right length trousers that would have been the end of the relationship! But, I did, thank goodness and so I was in. With her mum and dad it was another thing. They were conservative self-made business people. Luckily I voted Conservative, straightaway I scored some points! I was at the Grammar School - excellent, I scored some more points! I wanted to be a medical student or a pharmacist – I scored even more points. I was doing really well, talking politely. To top it all Pauline's mum made the most excellent roast dinners I had ever had. She had real roast beef, with real Yorkshire puddings - fantastic. In one stroke I had acquired a girlfriend and a mother-in-law who could cook! Life doesn't get any better than that!

We had many adventures. We went out with Malcolm and Sue in the back of Malc's Herald, laid down in the back because there are hardly any back seats in one of those. A little car, mostly string and wire, but it was great fun.

Everything in the Matrix was going so well, in fact too well! I had known Pauline just two months and then I had a panic attack. I was going to go camping in Spain with my school friend Larry Hemmings for a month and my father and sister would join us for two weeks out there. Then suddenly out of the blue, I had this totally irrational emotional gut feeling, a real *stomach churner*. I was certain I would lose Pauline! It was horrendous, all consuming, so overpowering. I had never experienced anything like this before ever. I was convinced that she would forget me and go off with somebody else. Desperate for a strategy to manage this unbearable thought, I decided on a pro-active approach, so on a hot June evening in 1973 at the South Eastern Tavern just off Station Approach Road, Ramsgate, I proposed to her. Somewhat taken aback she said, 'Yes,' much to my relief. We agreed that we would wait formally until her 18th birthday in the October and I would of course ask permission from her parents at the first available opportunity. But, we effectively became engaged to be married, I was elated at this decision of commitment on her behalf. I resolved to write constantly from Spain in order to maintain contact.

This is a very important episode in my life as it clearly demonstrates the impact that my subconscious was having on my behavior and physical body. Baillie had made a similar agreement with Sallie, but of course he did lose her to McKinley whilst away on service in the cavalry. The memories continued to dictate my physical actions in a most tangible way, reinforcing and proving the point. Interestingly, Baillie came from southeastern Georgia and again the railroad connection, trains played a large part in his life; South Eastern Tavern, Station Approach Road, was it just coincidence?

My next action was to unknowingly re-enact Baillie behaviour in 1861 with the fateful photograph. I had an enlargement made of our engagement photograph and gave a copy to Pauline. I was particularly proud of how I looked in this photograph and I wanted Pauline to remember me while I was away at university. I knew that I would be going away for maybe three years or more and I needed to give her this image, as a memory of me.

The Engagement: October 1973, I made sure that Pauline had a copy of this photograph so that she would remember me whilst I was away at University. I had repeated history without knowing it. **This photograph is therefore the exact counter part to the Baillie 1861 photograph!**

I knew then that my fate and destiny were sealed. I was going to go to university the very next year. I had been given the place. I left school in January 1974. I played my final fourth season for the 1st XV. Things were looking good. But, I needed money and I needed to work. I had to get a job. My father had a word with the station manager in Margate and the Matrix took over again, the Matrix said, 'Yes, time to work on the railway!' I had loved steam trains from the time I was a very small boy. As with most small children, I had model trains as a kid. My father even worked on the railway. I didn't know why I liked steam trains, I just did. We all carry on doing the same things in the Matrix.

Chapter Nine
Railroads

A guy has got to have some money and if he is going to impress his girl he needs to have some money and a set of wheels! I was aspiring to a rather aristocratic beauty that I had got to know and I was busy trying to impress her well-to-do parents. So I needed to have money and a car. My dad provided the car. It wasn't a very good car, but it was all right. Things were going really well.

Does all this sound familiar? Just another time and another place! Baillie had felt and thought the same way about Sarah Elizabeth *Sallie* Spalding, now it was my turn to feel the same way about Pauline Elizabeth Danter, my Sallie. This time I would not make the same mistake. Money was important I had learnt my lesson. I was determined to succeed.

It was 1974 and it was time to knuckle down and do some work. Off I went to Margate Station dressed in a suit for an interview with Mr. Nuttall. Mr. Nuttall was a short gentleman with ginger hair. He shouted a lot, like the Fat Controller in Thomas the Tank Engine, a very accurate character portrayal! He was very abrupt and brusque, but he liked me, I think! I think he liked my dad too. He said to me, 'You are exactly what I need. I can offer you a six-month job on Broadstairs Station, which will allow me the time to look around for somebody more permanent. In that way I won't have to be rushed into appointing somebody. So I am very pleased to offer you a position as *Upside Railman* at Broadstairs Railway Station.' Gosh, I was chuffed! I didn't ask about the wages or anything.

Looking back now it all looks so much like the hand of the Matrix at work. Baillie had gone to work on the railroad in 1876 after his catalogue of personal disasters. Losing the promotion, losing the war, losing Sallie to McKinley, losing Mary his fiancée due to lack of money and worst of all losing his little niece Margery Baillie Kell aged six to infant mortality. Yet this time the railroad would pave the way to securing the practical financial aspects of winning his/my bride.

I didn't really know anything about money. All I knew was that I needed money and later that it was £25 a week, but being tax free I could earn £600 in a tax year without paying tax so it was worth doing. Luckily enough the job started in January, which would allow me to earn £300 before the tax year in April 5, 1974. And then to earn £600 afterwards, but I decided that as soon as I started paying tax I would pack it in. I did not want to give the Government any more money than I had to.

Hettie (sic) his favorite sister had been worried about him all those years ago. She wrote:

> 'I begged Baillie to give me his $50 bounty money to keep for him and that with some of mine and what you will send me makes $100 which I will send Mr. Gue to put out for us in the shape of a Confederate bond... I have persuaded Baillie to give me all he can spare to keep for him, **for he is so regardless of money.**'

I was determined subconsciously not to make the same mistake this time around. With money I could win Sallie!

And so I went to work on the railway. I didn't know what to expect. This was my first real job in the real world. Boots had been very civilized. I had parted company with Boots on amicable terms, they were a bit disappointed that I wasn't going to be a pharmacist, because I had decided to read Agricultural Zoology, but I was doing something I liked doing and wanted to do. Everything seemed to be going along smoothly in the Matrix.

Baillie worked on the railroad. I was going to do the same. Baillie never seemed to have much success with plants in agriculture. I too did not want to go into the plant science side of agriculture, I instead opted for the zoological aspect, studying animals and livestock. Again I had learnt my lesson.

The railway job began in the January of 1974. It was seven days a week, with double time on Sundays, 6:00a.m. to 2:00p.m. and 2:00p.m. to 10:00p.m. The job was quite simply to make sure that nobody fell on the tracks and to ensure that all the doors were shut on the train before it left the station. The other duties included sweeping the platform, polishing the brass, of which there were three items, one doorknob, one hand plate on the sliding gate and one brass tap. Polishing the brass was even on the duty roster. The morning duty man was responsible for seeing the commuters off on the train. The little robot-like people that boarded the train every morning would soon look around to complain to someone if the train was more than three seconds late! As I was dressed in a British Rail uniform - a porter's jacket with a hat on - they would make a beeline for me and start making abusive comments. Meanwhile, I would try to ignore them and carry on putting the boards up. The London trains would come in very fast in the mornings and that was where the commuters were heading. Once past 9:00a.m. things slowed down.

Mornings were always very busy. You then had a lot of time on your hands. During this time there were two trains an hour up to 2:00p.m., and the odd parcel to process, which the guards were always reluctant to take. I felt at the time that people working on the railway seemed to make an art of doing nothing. They spent their long hours trying to fill their time. I couldn't believe it to start with. My father used to tell me stories, but they had it off to an art form. It really was quite amazing. They were trapped in the Matrix. In the end I found that one had to learn how to pass the time. My father said that he had seen people roll cigarettes and spend half an hour making one and smoking it, which again is an art form in wasting time. You weren't allowed to read books. I tried reading books, but they frowned on it. Far too intellectual, you're supposed to be a porter on the railways, so what are you doing reading books?

One had to find ways of passing the time. I suppose it was here that I developed my cartooning techniques, because I started drawing in my little British Rail notebook, cartoons about life on the railway. I still have the cartoon book. It looked as though I was actually working, so I drew cartoons of railway life, and things like that. I invented my famous cartoon character.

My first cartoon character was *Newcalithic Man*, who was an extremely dim caveman. He came about because I was going to Newcastle. He was based on the drink Newcastle Brown and to me at the time every invention mankind had ever made was to do with Newcastle Brown! He then evolved into *Railman Ron and the Broadstairs Gang*, which was a satire on my colleagues. There were six of us working on the station, two on my side of the platform, the upside, and two on the downside, of which Gordon was the archetypal railman. He used to shuffle around and had a little Hitler-style moustache and glasses and his hat. It was impossible to understand what the hell he was saying! He would come to the rest room and do something totally bizarre like taking a frying pan and frying cod's roe, smoking the place out. The rest room really stank afterwards and it looked more like we had just had a major fire than lunch, but it tasted beautiful!

I liked trains, but these weren't steam trains, these were electric trains with a live rail - having no steam took all the fun out of it. Steam engines were powerful roaring lumbering beasts with individual character. I always had a thing about the old prototype Wild West trains, with the big black smokestacks. My favorite is the old *General* 440 locomotive. Years later I had a big G scale model of the General over my black board in the Physics laboratory. I had even altered the shape of the smokestack to make its profile more accurate to the original, complete with nameplate and the paintwork of the W&A RR.

After visiting the real General locomotive in the museum at Big Shanty, Kennesaw near Atlanta, February 2001 I discovered that the General had been used for track laying duties during the period of Baillie's employment as a civil engineer on the railroad. It is entirely probable that my attachment to the locomotive stems to this period, as Baillie would have seen the locomotive daily in his work routine.

At that time I did absolutely nothing really, except count my money, because the money rolled in and I was busy saving. I had to save to acquire funds for university and for Pauline. I literally went to work, went home and slept. The only bonus of the job was the 6:00a.m. to 2:00p.m. shift. This provided the luxury of spending the afternoon chatting with my dad and having memorable long conversations about the war and his life. This proved to be invaluable father/son time for sadly he was to die the following year while I was away at university. It happened completely out of the blue. He suffered a massive heart attack and then a stroke. He was only aged sixty-four. My father like many of his generation was a heavy smoker - he smoked as a soldier during his early life and had tried to stop, but couldn't. In the end the smoking killed him - I was glad that I had had all those afternoons with him. It was a really precious time.

The job continued. In the mornings and evenings you could see the foxes at the end of the platform. I responded to their presence and they taught me about nature and survival. They became my friends. Then there was a guy called Bob. Now, Bob turned out to be one hell of a character! He was a man out of place. He was far too intelligent for his job. We became good friends. He had been stuck in the job for fourteen years and he realized that he was stuck, that was the tragedy. He was too bright. He lived at home with his mum. He was a very handsome looking guy, always immaculately turned out in his uniform and the women liked him, but he was stuck in this dead end job. He had a totally manic sense of humor, which was absolutely brilliant for whiling away the long hours on duty.

The many, many practical jokes we played relieved the boredom and broke the day up. They were fantastic fun! Bob became my hero on the railway. The tannoy announcement was the scene of most of these pranks. Bob would announce the football results on saturday, followed by the weather forecast. The passengers on the platform would all applaud. I would then follow on announcing the trains in French and in English and deliberately mumbling announcements! Sometimes the train would slow down to go through the station, but not actually stop, then it would speed away. The passengers would be sat on the railway platform with their bags waiting expectantly for their train. Each time the train would almost stop, but then the lights would go green and it would speed up again. So, as the train came in I would say over the tannoy, 'The train arriving on Platform 2 (and they would all stand up, grab their bags and shuffle forward) ... *pause...* - is not stopping at this station. Please do not attempt to board the train.' They would look totally amazed and all sit down again. At the time I found this most amusing!

I learnt a lot from that experience. All you had to do was to sound as though you actually knew what you were doing and have a certain air of authority and you could get away with absolutely anything. Especially when wearing a uniform. People always expected things to be properly done by people in uniform.

Another thing about the illusion of the Matrix is that everything is supposed to be proper and people are supposed to act in proper ways. When somebody does something totally unexpected the normal reaction from the average person in the Matrix is to ignore it, or to pretend it doesn't exist. So long as one does it with an air of authority you get away with it.

Back to my friend Mr. Nuttall, the *Fat Controller,* he would always try and catch you out to see if you were not working. He would only inspect the station, once a week, but one never knew quite when he was coming. He would try and catch people on the hop, not doing anything. Most of the average railway employees there had very little imagination. They would suddenly grab a dirty rag and start polishing a window to look as though they were actually working. But, I had worked out a scam. I would hide in the Gentlemen's rest room and flood the floor with water and bleach. Then scrub it up to a nice big lather with a stiff bristle broom. I would then stand there amongst all this foam, waiting for him. I could hear him rummaging about, trying to find me. Suddenly he would burst in to the rest room and I would be scrubbing away up to my armpits in foam, looking so impressive. He would say, 'There you are Baillie, well done an absolutely fantastic job, really spick and span.'

I would reply courteously, 'Yes Mr. Nuttall, I try and do my best sir!' He was suitably impressed with my endeavors, because he hadn't seen anybody like me. He would then say, 'Well done, carry on,' and disappear rapidly. As soon as he had gone I would get the hose pipe out, spray all the foam down the trough and then walk out feeling rather pleased with myself! Simple as that! That was one of my perfected techniques for impressing the management. It worked every time.

Life continued on the railway very satisfactorily. I spent a lot of time planning escapes as I worked seven days a week. Inevitably I would take time off, catching the late train to Dover, boarding the ferry to Holland to see my friends. In those days going abroad was considered something you only ever did in your wildest dreams, so even if I had explained what I was doing to people, they wouldn't have understood. Now of course, thirty years later people travel all over and going to Holland or Belgium is not a big deal.

I was very proud of this escape route I once worked fifty-two days on the trot all the while planning my escape. I think that was the longest I ever did in one stretch and by the end of it I was starting to go a bit crazy with the same old routine. I would sit there working out exactly what I was going to do, how I was going to do it and then the big day would come and I would make my escape. I was always very interested in learning other languages, because I could see a future with Europe, working in Europe, and also Holland is where all the blonde girls are! It was the natural calling of my subconscious. All told I made a total of three such excursions to the continent during my six months on the railway.

I was indeed fulfilling a subconscious urge. Sallie lived across the water on Sapelo Island. Baillie would have had the same urge to get across the water to see her. He would have traveled across when he could and on any pretext. In time the parties at the big house would be the ultimate goal. The association of happy times, a blonde young lady and travelling over the water would provide strong emotional links, which could not be ignored. Even my interest in the Vikings can be traced to this imagery, sailing the boat over to Sapelo and blond Sallie. Baillie also studied ancient and modern languages at the Kentucky Military Institute as part of his Bachelor of Arts. This same interest manifested in my *hobby* of studying Old English, Old Norse and Dutch at University. Whilst on the railway I started to teach myself Dutch in order to communicate better with my friends in Holland. I found it fairly easy to pick up and I conjectured that again this was perhaps due to inherited genes. The Scots had close links with the Lowlands and the wool trade in the middle ages. Also a family member by the name of William Baillie had been a General in the English Civil War for the Scottish Covenanter Army. Yet he had seen prior service as a professional soldier in the Netherlands.

One summer day we had some trains arrive carrying holiday makers. I remember all the passengers getting off with loads of bags. They were travelling to Broadstairs for their summer holidays. I found very quickly that you could earn quite a bit of money by carrying people's bags to the taxis. I think I made about £3 in one day, which was an eighth of my salary. I very quickly learnt how to take advantage of this situation. Finally, the railway job ended in June, so I decided to take a busman's or rather railman's holiday.

Coincidentally in one of the letters there is a puzzling reference about the way Baillie is making money during the war. In her letters Baillie's mother talks of Baillie's well being and how Baillie is managing to survive. In this letter it explains one of the ways he made money during the war.

> 'Baillie makes money for himself by waiting on the other gentlemen in camp.'

Just as I did in the summer of 1974!

I had successfully earned £900, which was quite a lot of money in those days. At the time we bought a bungalow for £8,000. Pauline and I decided to buy a bungalow, largely with the help of her father. My savings from the railway job meant I was able put down the £600 deposit. This was to become our first home. So Baillie did care about money in the end, although I was always taught that money was vulgar and one should never talk about it. Unfortunately we live in a monetary system on this planet and we have to cut cards with the devil, so to speak. So I did my duty and played my part in the Matrix.

I put some of the remaining savings aside to have an around Europe inter-rail trip with my friend Larry Hemmings. We had many adventures during the next month of July.

Baillie loved trains and travelling on them. This is highlighted in several letters. In one he gives very confident precise directions to his sister-in-law Blanche. Yet with regard to travel, Baillie never left his native Georgia except when on war service.

Chapter Ten
University

Robert Habbick and I boarded the train for our big adventure. We were off *up North* to Newcastle upon Tyne. Neither of us had been much further north than London, hence for us Southern boys going *up North* was a huge adventure. I had previously got a taste for it when I went up for my interview the previous autumn. But now it was late August early September 1974. I got myself ready and packed up all my gear, we were off on our big adventure.

Baillie attended the College of New Jersey later to be called Princeton University, so I went to Newcastle and Baillie went to New Jersey. Both north, both on the coast and a both a big adventure.

We arrived in Newcastle, which was a Mecca for us. We already knew what to expect, we knew about the brewery and the blue star, Scottish & Newcastle Breweries, St James's Park, the Hay market. We knew we were in for an interesting time. I remember the trepidation I felt as I walked into the Halls of Residence. I always feel a bit shaky when I do something new, because everything is different, but I usually very quickly settle into the pattern. Yet in the back of my mind I was still wondering, what I was doing here?

I had become engaged to Pauline the girl of my dreams, but I remained very worried subconsciously that Pauline would find somebody else and leave me. I always had that feeling of insecurity at the back of my mind. At the time I didn't know why, all I knew was that Pauline was the love of my life and this was the person I really, really wanted to marry. The drive to marry was always paramount.

Still the feeling of insecurity persisted. Yet I had done my best, I had given Pauline £600, we had bought a bungalow and I'd worked on the bungalow with my dad's help. We had mown the lawns, tidied it up and we had started putting household goods in our *bottom drawer* for when we got married. But you never quite know with relationships. All the best laid plans of mice and men can come to naught, if somebody else comes along and upsets the apple cart.

Now we know Baillie had experienced the exact same emotions. He had expected to marry Sallie on his return from the war, only to find that she was betrothed to another. For Mary Bass Spalding had been introduced to Archibald Carlisle McKinley an Infantry officer with some means. She decided that McKinley was a better match for her Sallie. In 1866 Sallie and McKinley married. To secure the alliance, his sister married Sallie's younger brother Thomas Spalding the second.

I walked into the Halls of Residence and found my little room. The first thing I did was to phone up Pauline, to tell her that I had arrived. This was to become a pattern and I used to ring Pauline up almost every night just to see how she was. Some of my friends thought this was quite bizarre, because when at university you weren't supposed to worry about practical things like relationships and money this was supposed to be the best years of your life, a time to be free from all of life's responsibilities. Most of my friends were free and easy and had no fixed relationships. For some reason I remained extremely worried about Pauline leaving me and especially about being left on my own again.

We settled in and straightaway went down to find the bar. We lived in Castle Leases, on the town moor, which we called *Leasditz Castle* because we imagined it to be a bit like *Colditz.* The accomodation consisted of three huge tower block complexes, three Halls of Residence all in a circle, surrounded by a wall just up from Richardson Road where the student flats were for the Second and Third year students. Then towards the city center there was the Royal Victoria Infirmary and the university campus. All within walking distance.

We were in Freeman's Hall, which appeared to be the last Hall of the three built. Eustace Percy was the posh Halls of Residence most of the girls stayed there. Havelock was fairly civilized having furniture and fittings and Freeman's Hall seemed to be where they stuck all the agricultural students as the accommodation was somewhat basic, especially the bar. But, it's not the surroundings that count it's the people you are with. Straightaway I took my guitar down to the bar and started playing some songs with Robert. Very quickly we made friends with lots of other like-minded individuals. We found that we all got on. We had about a week to settle in. We went to the *Fresher's do's* and signed up for various activities, getting to know each other, mainly through drinking in the evenings.

The pattern is all too familiar. We later discovered Baillie used his guitar in camp and enjoyed a drink with the boys. The social pattern at Princeton would have been identical. The letters show that he held his student days in high regard and now it was the same again.

This set the pattern and very quickly we formed relationships. There was Ian Henderson and his school friend Stuart B Easdon from Warkworth in Northumberland, Frank Carr from Malham in Yorkshire and Philip Moore from Norwich in East Anglia. Ian's dad was a dentist in Bedlington. Ian lived about thirty miles away near Lindisfarne. He was totally eccentric, with a wickedly chaotic sense of humor. Ian and Stuart had been together since their days at Whitley Bay Grammar School, so they were the local lads. We all got on instantly. Another guy called Gerry Price, who became one of my best friends, was on the same course as me. He was also very interested in folk music and played the guitar. Roy and Kevin were friends of Robert. We were all in the same communal Halls of Residence. We quickly became a unit and our adventures began!

I think I can honestly say that university is the best three years of anybody's life. I didn't have a lot of money in my pocket, but I didn't have any worries, apart from the feeling of insecurity with Pauline. And you can buy a heck of a lot of drinks, even on a student grant! At the time inflation was starting to rocket through the economy, because of the oil crisis of the previous year, so we were paying quite a lot of money at the start in our Halls of Residence. Other people were laughing; saying we could get a cheaper deal outside in a flat, but by the end of the year it was actually cheaper in the halls. Inflation had risen four times during the year, due to the oil crisis and the other students were finding it extremely difficult outside. We had fixed rates for the year so we actually did very well.

In Fresher's week, we all signed up en masse for the *Cavaliers.* This proved very popular, probably because it was a way to celebrate being English and was a return to past values. I joined because there was no American Civil War, Society and I have always loved history and re-enacting. I couldn't continue with the American Civil War so I joined the next best thing - the English Civil War society, the King's Army. The Polytechnics had provided the Roundheads, Montague's Regiment, and we at the university were Sir Thomas Tilsley's Regiment of Foote, Newcastle's white coats. Now, as I disliked the Infantry, I decided very quickly that I would be in the cavalry and as there was no cavalry I made my own. So I was a cavalryman attached to the regiment and I had my own uniform. I had always been very independent and very strong-minded like that and there was no way they were going to get me into the Infantry despite much peer pressure. I used to tag along and join in wearing my cavalry outfit. I even made my own helmet, armor and boots. In 1974, I had visited Elizabeth Castle in Jersey with my father and saw an English Civil War Cavalier's uniform. I modeled my outfit on that uniform. It was an orange russet wool jacket with slash sleeves and wooden buttons, maroon trousers and a light blue sash with a black lobster pot helmet, thigh-length boots and a cross band sword belt. Wearing this uniform all I needed to complete the picture was a pewter tankard, essential equipment for drinking, and we were set! I always took my guitar with me and we used to sing when we went away for battles.

The course was something that happened alongside all of the other things. As well as doing Agricultural Zoology I was studying five subjects in the first year. But university was opening up a world of possibilities. I also had other interests I wanted to pursue such as history and languages. With the facilities available at university history became more like a hobby. I was free to delve into the university library and research my great interest in the Anglo-Saxons and Vikings. In the same way I turned to the facilities and teachers in the Language Department as I had a real interest in learning Old English and Dutch. One Dutch lad in Spain 1973 said, 'Nobody ever speaks Dutch, because it is too difficult, it's such a small country and anyway we all speak English.'

I thought, 'It can't be all that difficult?' So I decided to teach myself. One day early in the first term I was in the University Language Lab using the Dutch tapes. Fortunately one of the technicians saw me using the tapes and asked, 'Why are you over here? You're an agricultural student aren't you?'

This was where I had my lucky break, because when I told him, 'I want to learn Dutch, because I'm thinking of working in Holland.'

He kindly introduced me to a lady called Els Streitman and said, 'She would be very pleased to teach anybody who actually wanted to learn Dutch'. As Dutch was a subsidiary subject for the students learning German, they tended to show little or no interest in the subject. This was a great pity. For her part Els really wanted to teach students who were genuinely interested in learning to speak Dutch.

I went along and introduced myself to Els. She was a lovely lady and was very pleased to have me as a student as I was genuinely interested. Lessons lasted for two hours on a wednesday afternoon, which was when the other students were playing sports. I had quickly given up playing rugby on wednesdays. You never knew who your teammates were so you very often ended up badly injured. But I pursued horse-riding and fencing. I joined the fencing club for a few months, which was quite entertaining. Being a member of the horse-riding club was really great because we used to go riding on Blythe beach.

After Christmas 1975, I can remember my first sight of the Northumberland coastline, the white beaches at Blythe. People always think of the Northeast as being cold and miserable, but we often had days of bright blue-sky. My horse was called Tom. With three or four members of the club we would take the horses along the beach at Kitty Brewster, near the power station. It was sheer magic. Tom was a twenty year-old show jumper that had been retired and he used to jog along with minimal enthusiasm. One week the stables said, 'Tom hasn't got a saddle, his saddle girth strap has broken, do you mind taking him out bare back?' I replied that it was not a problem. For some reason I always had amazing confidence even though I had never ridden bare back. I thought, 'How hard can that be? I can ride, no problem.' So I rode bare back. Unfortunately Tom had a very bony spine so riding him bare back was like bouncing up and down on a broom handle. We arrived at the beach. But instead of jogging along in an orderly fashion Tom went absolutely berserk and broke into a gallop. He seemed to be a different horse with no saddle on and shot straight along the beach and then straight out into the sea up to his chest. I kept thinking, 'If I fall off now I'm going to get wringing wet. Don't fall off!' He ran up to his chest and then stopped. I managed to control him and brought him round back on to the beach. We carried on galloping along the beach bare back. It was the most exhilarating thing I had done while I was there. This is what university is all about. University shouldn't just be work, work, work, you have to play hard as well and this was certainly playing hard. After two hours riding bare back I had actually scraped all the skin of my coccyx and I had blood running down the back of my jodhpurs. When I got back to the halls of residence I had to put some antiseptic cream on, because it was all rather sore. Also the horse sweat had gone through my jodhpurs and I stank of horses. But it was great fun and an extremely memorable experience.

I had always wanted to play a musical instrument. Unfortunately my sister had put me off the violin as an instrument. Her attempts to learn the violin were painful to say the least. Early in my life I had shown an interest in playing the guitar. But my dad wasn't so sure. I suffered from partial deafness caused by sinus problems, so he thought I was likely to be tone deaf. He was probably right at the time! But, as my sinus trouble cleared by 1970, I improved musically. Ironically much later on I realized that my continual sinus trouble, was actually caused by my father's smoking. That year I went to Jersey as a young boy of sixteen and I experienced one magical day that restored my musical confidence. We were camped by the main airport and often walked down to St Quen's Bay, which is the big surfing bay on the western Atlantic coast of Jersey. I was into surfing and beaches in a big way. I met a guy there with a guitar. The guitar was led against the wall and I asked him, 'Do you mind if I have a little go?' he replied, 'No worries mate!' and went off surfing. I picked up his book and found that I knew some of the chords and could strum along to the words of *Streets of London* by Ralph McTell. He came back after a while and told me the secret of playing, 'If you don't know the chords or you find a difficult one just sing louder!' Very good advice, my confidence returned immediately. The next day, I copied down my first seven songs from his book. Since then my personal repertoire has increased to about 100 songs. Over the next few years the guitar became a magical passport to making new friends and having fun on my many travels. For if you can sing a few songs and share a drink with people, no matter what sex, color or creed, you can create a party atmosphere and there by make your own entertainment. This was the key to success with my peer group, I was no longer a loner. Drinking and singing were very useful skills at university and I had rediscovered my own inherent abilities, in fact I had cured my own problem of lack of confidence; it was a definite case of, *Physician heal thy self!*

Baillie had perfected the self-same skills as described in the letter from Hettie:

> 'Baillie brought over four of his companions in arms the night before last, and gave us a treat in the way of music, they sang charmingly

> (underlined) together, and one plays finely on the piano, they staid (sic) until half past eleven singing and playing and then rode back eight miles to camp - it was amusing to see them how they demolished their supper. Baillie gave us notice the day before so we were prepared for them'.

University continued and I passed all my exams, because I had learnt how to pass exams. I had also learnt how to enjoy books, visualizing the images. Reading books was something that previously I didn't do. My father always said that he liked books, because you could imagine the story in your head. Films often were just a pale reflection of the imagination and he was often disappointed with films preferring to read books. Now previously I could not visualize the images from words, so my book reading had been limited. Limited very much to one Civil War story, which I had read twice, and one story about going to the Moon, which I had also read twice when I was in Junior school aged about ten. That's all I had really read, the rest I had learnt from television and reading the odd bit of reference material. I even managed to pass English Literature Grade I, because I liked the *History of Mr. Polly*. I identified with the Mr. Polly character, especially the scene with the young girl and the wall, which triggered off some of my memories. Mr. Polly, the older man, falls in love with the young girl, but the young girl is just playing around, teasing him. He discovers her friends are giggling at his folly and totally embarrassed he rides off flustered and emotionally crest fallen on his bicycle. I liked John Mills and I liked the *History of Mr. Polly*. I gained a Grade I, because I knew the story backwards. Analyzing the situation now, the story has eerie parallels to Baillie falling for Sarah Sallie Spalding. He the older gentleman of thirty-two, she the young beauty of sixteen 16. Again I had related to the familiar. My conscious mind identifying images and translating my subconscious memories into present day experiences.

It was at university that I was to discover the mystery my father had unlocked for himself, the true joys of reading. It all came about in a rather odd way. All the students at Castle Leases went down with an awful bout of food poisoning. It was the autumn of the first year and it was half-term. I was looking forward to going back home to Pauline. But of 1,000 students staying at Castle Leases, a full one third were suffering from the effects of food poisoning. It was one of the worst cases of food poisoning I have ever had in my life. Fortunately I just happened to have a copy of the *in book* that somebody had loaned me due to my illness

Baillie to the Rescue 1975: My summer job as a Safety Boatman was perfect. This is my favorite picture of myself and one could easily see in the image, young Baillie stealing away across Doboy sound to rescue his princess from Sapelo Island.

Somewhat disgruntled at not being able to go home I took to bed with the book *Lord of the Rings* by JRR Tolkein. I managed to read the book from cover to cover in four days flat, it was so imaginative and deftly written, that I just couldn't put the book down. My half term transformed from abject misery into revelation, I had under gone literary metamorphosis in the twinkling of an eye. Before that point in time I had difficulty visualizing and reading, but having unlocked the secret of speed-reading and visualizing, I could now read anything. My brain had made the quantum leap. Tolkein's story had struck another resonant chord in me. I was also a keen artist and became emotionally inspired by the epic characters and events. Later in my second year, I started to paint pictures prolifically. *Lord of the Rings* was unleashing subconscious memories of the Civil War and Sallie on a massive scale! Using art to express myself I launched into huge murals on the walls of our flat, *Watcher of the Stairs,* a 12-foot horsed *Ringwraith* was really the subconscious archetypal Yankee cavalryman on horseback. It was a hooded mysterious figure reminiscent of the terrifying Klu Klux Klan, but in black with a nightmare steed snorting hot vaporous steam. The hideous overwhelming armies of Mordor were in truth the legions of Sherman terrorizing and destroying all before them. The gallant band of heroes, outnumbered and out gunned were the Confederate cavalry. Of course the *Riders of Rohan* completed the image, chief among them Eowyn their Princess, with her blonde hair! No wonder that my subconscious was on overdrive during this period of time, it was a gift.

At school my best subjects had been Chemistry, History and Art, but I decided to be a scientist in order to establish a career, or so I thought at the time. But really I loved being the artist, so I freed my mind at night after my scientific studies, liberated my subconscious to explore and manifest my free expression. It was a glorious outpouring of emotion on a titanic scale. *Lord of the Rings* had opened my mind to reading and visualization.

Upon reflection, I related especially to that one character in particular, *Eowyn,* because there is always, as we now know a blonde woman at the bottom of all my angst. The character was so evocative - the horses and the blonde woman combined. That's really what took my imagination and the struggle of the heroes against the overwhelming odds of the evil armies of Sauron. This struck a chord in my mind and when my artwork of the seventies is examined, one can see why, because deeply buried in my subconscious was the story of Baillie, Sallie and the Civil War. Everything in the end goes back to that, absolutely everything. I still feel totally in awe at the depth and sheer force of this emotional memory. The fact that I had absolutely no control over my actions, no conscious awareness of why I choose to do what I did, indeed I had no free will.

As the first term drew to a close, we celebrated with a *Ceilidh* for our Christmas Ball. The theme was *Country and Western* so I dressed up in my Confederate officer's uniform for the event. I had written down Captain Ian C Baillie CSA on my invitation, but the man announcing the Ball, being ex-army refused to announce me. Even though I informed him not to forget to say Confederate States Army after the rank and name. I thought that he might not mind if it was clearly not a Queen's commission. Like my predecessors I had my pistol with me in case any Yankee sympathizers might rumble me. You never know when the opposition may have a go at you! There were also several Yankee uniforms in evidence and despite a truce being held in honor of this fine ball, what with all these here glamorous young ladies and the like, I was not about to take chances. The Yankee boys came over and surrounded me saying, 'Oh you've got your pistol with you Johnny Reb?'

'Yep, and it works,' I calmly replied with a smile, so to make the point I pointed it to the floor and fired! It went bang and made a nice cloud of smoke, which impressed the assembled crowd. The evocative smell of black powder always adds that certain sort of atmosphere to the scene. My friends although dressed, as civilians were well impressed. The only *Johnny Reb* there, I had maintained the dignity and honor of the South. Needless to say I was a hero with the ladies and the Yankee boys kept their distance from me for the rest of the night!

As you can see the essence of role-playing is to maintain the character at all times no matter how difficult or threatening the circumstances appear. The audience is then witness to a genuine piece of real life drama. The whole situation was totally unplanned and unrehearsed, I had merely anticipated what might happen and had pre-planned what I would do should the situation arise. I think that the lads might have tried to *de-bag* me or play some such other prank? But I was not going to let that happen, so I acted my part as it arose and stayed in character. Colonel John Singleton Mosby had acted much the same way during the real Civil War. Ever the individual and a similar character I had merely followed his footsteps!

I passed all my exams that year. The highlight of the summer of '75 was when the Cavalier Army descended on Brill in Oxfordshire, between Aylesbury and Oxford. We had a most glorious massed English Civil War battle there with about 3,000 people. The whole village had dressed up in English Civil War costume. There were Cavaliers, Roundheads, medieval instrument players, Mummers plays and Morris Men dancing all over the place. It really was what I can only term, one of those magic moments, because when you re-enact every so often you get a magic moment, a time shift. Everything comes together and everything is so perfect that you suddenly take a leap back in time. I can remember in the evening on the saturday there were people roasting oxen and music playing and the Morris Dancers were so drunk that they were dancing everywhere and anywhere. Children were climbing under the tables and dogs were eating the bones off the floor. Larry Hemmings had joined me for the event. We sat at one of these trestle tables taking it all in I said, 'This is just amazing. This is just like being on a film set or, even better, the real thing.'

I grew dissatisfied with the Cavalier Cavalry and defected in the end. They were just a bit too *cavalier*, for my liking. They were not very well organized and had no horses of their own. They used to try and hire horses, which was a complete disaster, because you need horses that are thoroughly trained. It was at this time that I met Martin Savage the gentleman that was in charge of the Roundhead Cavalry. They were far more organized and had the ethos that if you worked hard and helped, then they would let you have a ride. Martin Savage invited me to join in with the Roundheads saying, 'You can ride with us and see what you think?' The Roundheads were always looking for new recruits, especially people who could ride horses.

He had two rather large beautiful chestnut horses. On the Sunday morning of the actual final battle they were going out to practice when Martin said, 'Why don't you come along?' They had about five horses. We mounted up while he explained, 'We're going to charge the Royalist Infantry on yonder hill.' The Cavaliers had marched out flags flying and drums beating and formed a hedge of pikes with the musketeers on the wings in the distance. He said, 'We're going to charge them and have a little bit of a practice let us see what happens gentlemen?'

I replied somewhat hesitantly, 'What do I do Martin?' As I was aware that you've obviously got to look after the horse and make sure that the horse doesn't get injured. That's the primary concern, especially with firearms and pikes. With a wink he said, 'Don't worry, the horses have been trained, just sit on tight, don't fall off and use your sword to hack around at the tops of the pikes!'

We immediately lined up abreast, I could see the target ahead, and Martin shouted, 'Forward Company at the trot. Company Charge!' We spurred our horses on. The horses behaved immediately like performing dolphins. Their ears pricked up and they shot towards the target, straight as an arrow from a bow. The feeling was so exhilarating and as the target homed into view (this all happened in a very short space of time, maybe two minutes at the most) I thought, 'Oh my God they're not going to stop? We're going to hurl ourselves onto the pikes.' But, the horses, from a flat out gallop came straight up to the pikes and stopped, nearly throwing us over their heads. They then walked forward and engaged the infantry by nuzzling their heads in amongst the pikes. I dutifully began hacking away with my sword at the tops of the pikes, trying not to injure anybody, and I can vividly remember a red-faced chap shouting obscenities and getting really annoyed, like a football hooligan, at my boot.

This was when I was reminded of the power of horses. Horses are extremely large and extremely intimidating. Sure enough, what happened was the horse wove in with its head, grabbed hold of the man's hat to the left with its teeth and threw it up into the air. The man's face went white. The horse then went round to the right towards the guy that had been shouting at me, the horse bit into his jacket, lifted him up by the elbow, shook him and threw him onto the ground. The man's face just absolutely drained! The look of fear on his face was incredible. I was totally amazed at the transformation. I never knew my horse had been trained so well. Anyway, at the sight of this guy being picked up by the horse and thrown on the ground along with the other horses doing similar tricks, the whole unit just ran away and we were left there, masters of the field. The feeling of triumph was amazing. Martin looked around at me and winked saying nonchalantly, 'I told you they'd been trained!' and laughed.

We trotted back to our initial positions, the whole thing lasting no more than two minutes; that was my first cavalry charge - in this life. There is nothing quite like it in any other experience I have had since. That was one of my most defining moments, the excitement, the energy and the result. The sheer power of being a mounted soldier on a horse. It gives you such a sense of superiority over the infantry, no wonder people like being in the cavalry. I had always been a cavalryman, always felt like I was in the cavalry, and that's why. One doesn't ever want to be on the ground! The horse gives you such an advantage. You can never forget an experience like that.

The afternoon came. We had had some lunch around the campfire and a few sundry sword fights and skirmishes back at the camp and then we were back out onto the field for the battle. We had some secret weapons up our sleeves, because one never wants to get clobbered by the enemy. I joined the Cavaliers back again for the afternoon and Larry and I were doing our own thing. Larry had come up with a marvelous idea of putting a bag of pyrotechnic mixture inside a potato! A veritable vegetable hand grenade! He had his secret weapon and it was to prove very useful in the cause of events. We were suddenly cornered by some of the Roundheads, who were going to give us a going over, or so they thought. But Larry seized the moment and casually said, 'I say, wait a moment chaps, not so fast,' and with that lit the potato and once it was fizzing, tossed it to them like a game of catch. Needless to say they all ran clean away. Whereupon it suddenly went ***phut!*** Not too big a bang, but there were bits of potato everywhere, the whole effect was rather comical. The reputation of the Hemming's brothers was intact and laughing aloud we walked back to the ranks of our Cavalier comrades.

That really was the celebratory end of the first year at University. We spent the whole weekend there, friday to sunday and we came home through the Underground in London, back home, dressed in our Cavalier gear. Of course nobody bats an eyelid in London. We stood there in seventeenth century clothes and nobody bothered a jot. We turned up back home, the spell broken.

You can always get yourself out of trouble with psychology and a few pyrotechnic props. It's rather like the image of Clint Eastwood with a stick of dynamite. People are very wary of gunpowder. It's very useful stuff. I had learnt the power of explosives back at the Civil War camp in 1968, when we were sat round the campfire and a can of beans exploded in our midst! It was very sudden, extremely noisy and we were all totally covered in beans! I used to cook the beans in the tin on the fire, but I used to open the can first to let the expanding gases out. I guessed that the *rookie* Richard Sherwood didn't know that. Richard looked at me drenched in beans and I asked him politely, 'Did you put a hole in the tin of beans?' He replied, 'No, I didn't know you had to do that?' So his tin of beans had exploded and we all sat there amongst the carnage covered in beans. Needless to say his nickname became *Beans* Sherwood from that day on. It was a memorable introduction to the power of explosive devices and the unexpected.

Gunpowder and horses, beer and singing, figured a lot in my university days. They certainly were the best days of my life. Not a lot of women though, because I had already become engaged to Pauline and there weren't that many girls at Newcastle University, so I left that for the other guys. I was quite content to come home and see Pauline.

The second year at University was much more pleasant. It was not so intense, things had settled down and we weren't studying quite such a wide field of science. We had narrowed our subjects down to what we were actually supposed to be studying, rather than the more generalized subjects. These had included in the first year, Statistics, Agricultural Biochemistry, Chemistry, *Physical, Organic, and Inorganic.* The massive proportion of chemistry had been brought about by chance, because the Chemists basically had nobody to teach so they decided to teach the *Agrics* all the chemistry they knew. This was all right by me as I liked Chemistry, but many others found it taxing. Now, in the second year, we were into what I really wanted to study, Zoology. We also studied Pure Agriculture, which was fun as we got to go out on farm visits. There was a lot of interesting practical work involved, animal pathology and dissecting insects. The next summer, when I went to Holland it was quite amusing, because I was given diseased cows and sheep to dissect, whereas at university it was tiny insects! The Zoology Practical for the end of the second year was to dissect all the living systems from the ground beetle and label them. The beetle was only about half an inch long. I think they gave that as a joke really, but we had to do it. We spent ages dissecting it all out. That was our main practical examination - six hours with a ground beetle!

It was in the January of that year 1976, my father died unexpectedly. There one minute and gone the next. I was suddenly a man. I had to grow up. I couldn't just be me. My sister and my mother now depended on me. I was the only man left in the family. Quite a responsibility, really. You are trying to have a nice time and get on with your academic learning, but suddenly real life events overtake your ivory tower world.

I went to see my tutor on saturday morning and explained the situation. I traveled back on the sunday and it was a very sad journey back home. I looked out of the window of the train and my whole world had changed. I loved my dad very much. I had just got to know him as a friend. He had always been *my* dad, but over the last few years he had really become my best friend as well, especially when I worked on the railway and we had spent all those happy afternoons talking, telling me all about his war stories. And suddenly he wasn't there. On the monday morning I had to go down to the hospital and claim his things. I didn't really want to see the body, but I had to sign all the papers and bureaucracy took over. I had to take his entire things home, his razor, and his watch.

It is at times like this in your life, when you suddenly have to grow up and university was never quite the cavalier-spirited place again.

I passed my exams again, I had no re-sits, which was a relief and so I went off to Holland for three months. It was 1976 and extremely hot. Pauline came over to Holland to enjoy the weather and for a short holiday. Not one week earlier I had passed my driving test for a car and I had bought myself a Volkswagen beetle, which proved to be a nightmare. It was ten years old, dripped oil all over the place, had no working starter motor and I had to keep bump starting it; in short a complete disaster - but strangely I liked it. I took my mother up to Greenwich to the *American Revolution 1776-1976 Bicentennial Exhibition*, which was really interesting. It was a really hot day and I couldn't turn the heater off in the car, we had to have all the windows wide open, but still my mother ended up gasping with heat exhaustion by the time we arrived back home.

A week later I went to Holland. I progressed and built on my relationship with Mevrouw (Mama) and Mijnheer (Papa) Endstra in Holland and as fortune would have it, Mama managed to secure a summer holiday job for me at the local *Gezondheidsdienst voor Dieren*, animal health laboratories in Boxtel, Noord Brabant. I learnt later on that she had asked the under-director for the job, because I had lost my father and she was worried that I wouldn't be able to carry on my studies at university. I needed to earn some money, so the under-director had, as a special favor to her, given me the place. At the time I just thought, jolly good I've got it on my own merit. But, we all need help in life and a bit of luck and that was a big piece of luck. I shall always be grateful to her, for her kindness and generosity. I also helped José her youngest daughter, with English in the evenings. I used to paint pictures a lot, study Dutch and play the guitar. Coincidentally

José was very arty too and learning to play the guitar! I therefore became her guiding mentor and confidant.

This is interesting to note - that intense emotion and the need to let that emotion out triggered the outpouring of artwork. José aged sixteen, in effect with her blonde hair, looks and interest in art, became Sallie! She played the role perfectly and without knowing. I was, well I was Baillie. The hot weather, the trips to the seashore at Vlissingen on the coast, everything was right. The urge to paint came upon me. It was here that I began drawing the lonely tower. Separated by water from Pauline in England I drew endless images of the beach and the lonely warrior on the seashore. Even the music that I responded to contained the same lyrics and images. I was especially taken with *Uriah Heep* as I had seen them live at Newcastle City Hall that spring. I was deaf for *three* days afterwards, but it was an awesome experience! *Sunrise, July morning* and *Traveler in Time* were my favorites. All of them closely linked to the Sapelo story that my subconscious was trying to make known.

I was reliving in vivid detail Baillie's emotions and experiences.

This would accelerate into full creative expression upon my return to Newcastle in the October of that year. Whilst my other flat mates were listening to music, pulling bikes to bits, or reading, I used to paint. I would intensely paint all the images I saw in my mind. The one image I kept painting over and over again was a tower in the distance with a bridge to it. Sometimes the bridge was a rainbow as with *Bifrost* in Nordic legend and at other times it was just black, sad and horrid. The tower was always just out of reach, unobtainable. I therefore nicknamed it, *the Lonely tower.* I think I missed Pauline so much. It played on my mind so much, that something in my subconscious was triggered. I kept painting this image over and over again. Always the same image. Yet people liked it, it had a *Roger Dean* feel about it. At the time Roger Dean's art works could be found on the record covers for *Yes, Emerson Lake and Palmer and Uriah Heep*, to mention but a few rock groups. My friends liked my art, they thought it was quite good as it mimicked these popular styles. Unfortunately the two surviving examples I have left are rejects, because the towers are too big at the base - important point. The tower was very specific in shape, always much thinner. I wasn't happy with them when I drew them, but they survived for that very reason as vital evidence for this book. They do graphically tell the subconscious story, of *Sallie* and the *Sapelo lighthouse,* of which I had no conscious knowledge at the time. All these deep buried subconscious memories were coming through in my paintings, triggered by major emotional events, my dad dying, Pauline being out of reach and loneliness.

Vlissingen, Zeeland 1976: I have carried this photograph of Pauline at the base of Admiraal de Ruiter's statue in my wallet for twenty-three years. The subliminal imagery speaks for itself, Pauline is Sallie, the blonde princess of Sapelo. She is chained to the railings of the family, the imposing statue represents the power and might of the Spaldings and the cannons the Civil War. Baillie would have carried a picture of Sallie in his pocket just as I have.

When I came back to England that year it was still very hot. There had been an anthrax outbreak in Holland, which was an unusual situation caused by the weather. I had had many, many adventures; I now spoke excellent Dutch and even dreamed in Dutch! And so I came back to university for my final year. I used to amaze everybody by going up to Close House, where I took samples for my thesis project on spiders wearing my clogs, because I was used to farming in Holland.

Of course in Holland they wear that as normal kit. I was always an individual. The last year came and went, almost in a blur really. Three lectures a week, only three subjects and six months to construct a thesis. I wrote my thesis on spiders, because I liked spiders. I always liked to study things that I'm frightened of, because in that way you lose your fear. You face your fear and you learn about it. Humans are only frightened of things that they don't understand. Once they understand them, there is no problem.

I continued with my studies and I took my final exams and passed. I should have gained 2.1 Honors, but ended up with 2.2, because I had to sit a paper on *Population Dynamics*, which was basically mathematical statistics, an extremely difficult subject and I had no idea about Population Dynamics at all. I admit that I waffled my way through the final paper. The Entomology and Parasitology were no problem. I did very well on that. The Professors in the Department said I had submitted a very good thesis and I was offered a Ph.D. place to study spiders, but in the end with no money to continue studying, I had to leave.

Baillie suffered the same fate at the Kentucky Military Institute, graduating fifth out of eight in his class. Again due to the heavy burden of mathematics involved in the course.

The same again, all the time the same!

It was quite a sad day leaving. I remember a lot of the other students getting their results. They were all sat around in the Union bar thinking that university was going to look after them forever. They had been sucked in by the system and they hadn't realized that they were suddenly going to receive a piece of paper, which meant it was time to leave and get a job. I had been prepared for this, because I already knew what I wanted to do. I wanted to go back to Holland and work. I had had a good time at university and I was not worried about the future. I had taken part in all the extra-activities and I had had a really good time. I was naturally sad yet ready for the challenge and a change.

That summer was the final summer of being a single man. I had not gone to Holland in the summer. I would have to wait for the next summer to fulfil that ambition. The day of my wedding was September 10th. On that day we tied the knot. I was elated I had achieved my ultimate goal. I had realized my ambition, my dream. I had finally managed after 107 years to get married! That must be a world record, even if spread over two life times? All my friends came from far and wide. They had been away working in the summer. They all turned up around about 8:30p.m. on the friday night, September 9. There was no way they were going to get me drunk then, so we went along to the local pub, playing on the piano and singing, which sounds familiar! Then we sang *Blaydon Races* and all the old agricultural songs from the agricultural nights on thursday evenings.

They did however manage to get me drunk. I had five pints of Newcastle Brown, but unfortunately Phillip Moore, my Best Man, had been putting double vodkas in them. So I was a bit worse for wear. As soon as I hit the air outside, that was it, I was gone. The next day I was very shaky. They had all had a party and left me to it, asleep. I turned up at the church at 2:00p.m. I didn't know you had to get there early and I was feeling somewhat the worse for wear, but I managed to get through the ceremony. Pauline looked fantastic. The church was St Mary's Minster - September 10, 1977. All my friends were there. Even José and Mevrouw (Mama) Endstra had come from Holland.

This is an interesting piece of story detail too - I hadn't realized that José was very keen on me until I had told her that I had a fiancée in England. It was only then that I realized how upset she was. So José a year later watched me get married just as Baillie had watched Sallie get married. She even had to come across the water in order to take part. Exactly as Baillie would have traveled to Sapelo to watch Sallie marry McKinley. But five years later she too was married to her new husband. He too was a teacher and he even looked like me! But he was from a wealthy construction company. José had found her happy ending and did not suffer the same fate as Baillie. *The story has a life of its own* as Rosie says. Indeed it was the same summer of 1976 that Rosie met Peter, her husband on the beach at Hythe. And her Stepfather, Edwin was also a wealthy construction company boss! Parallels of coincidence.

The wedding reception was held at the Viking Motel, opposite the full size replica Viking ship, on the cliff top at Pegwell Bay in Thanet. My blonde lady and the Viking ship, all the imagery of my paintings, all assembled in one place, at one single point in time. We then drove off to the *Inn on the Lake* by the M2 motorway, near London. Next day we drove all the way to Cornwall and got there late at night. The caravan site was like something out of a Gothic horror film and Pauline really didn't want to be there. She took her wedding ring off and threw it down, saying she wanted to go home, right now! I some what taken aback said, 'Can we just wait until the next morning?' Because we had driven all this way and to drive back would be a non-starter. She had realized that getting married was a big step and we were starting out on a new life. The next morning the sun came out and the world brightened up. We got through the night and it wasn't so bad. We ended up having a beautiful week in Cornwall.

This new life included me needing to get a job and earning a living. I was offered two jobs; I accepted the post as the manager of a *Building Society*. I knew from the start that it was the wrong way to go. That job lasted only one day! After agonizing for two hours on the sea front at Deal, I decided that I would take my third option and study for a Post-Graduate Certificate in Education. It was relevant to my science training and offered me the chance of going to Holland in the summer vacations to earn more money and may be even secure full time employment. It was a great choice and a great year. I was a student again and able to enjoy all the benefits of being at Christchurch College Canterbury.

Teaching practices came and went, and that's how you really learn whether you can teach or not, because you are at the sharp end with the children. You can either do it or you can't, I found that I had a natural gift for teaching and especially communicating with children. My two teaching practices were at the Chaucer Technology School in Canterbury and Dover Grammar School for Boys. These I completed successfully with no problem.

We had to attend lectures on a monday morning and learn all about Piaget and various other educational philosophers, most of which have now long since been disregarded. The Education Theory Exam came around. Nobody was looking forward to this because if you failed that, you failed the whole course. In a complete reversal of expectations I actually managed to get a Distinction! Out of 7,000 entrants I managed to be in the top 15% to get the Distinction. So it showed that I could pass exams and I had become very good at that skill. I was quite pleased with that and left College to get a job.

Again the parallels continue - Baillie spent three years at Princeton, then the College of New Jersey and a year at the Kentucky Military Institute. I had subconsciously followed a similar pattern.

Luckily, I managed to secure a first teaching post at St George's Church of England Secondary School, of all places. By now the Boys had moved on up to the Girls' School at Broadstairs and amalgamated and so I started my first teaching post in 1978. The Sixth Form girls were actually only about five years younger than I was and I was teaching them Human Biology, which was quite entertaining to say the least. I used to try and get all the giggly bits out of the way first! Most of them went on to be nurses. That's when I met Rachel Offerman again, the Rachel, who was Ruth's little sister from all those years ago. I worked there steadily through my probationary year. The Inspectors came to look at me and I passed all my probation reports; and I was now a fully qualified teacher. It was then that I made the fateful comment in the July just before we broke up saying, 'It'll be so nice to be back here in September now that I have a permanent job and I don't have to keep changing any more.' But the Matrix had other ideas as you have discovered in Chapter 5 Shadows.

Chapter Eleven
Commission

Now I had finally re-joined the school. I was well again and it was 1980. I had gone through hell and come back. I was out to party, big time! We had purchased a TR7 sports car and were living life to full, but there still seemed to be something lacking? The military kept calling. I suppose if I hadn't been ill I would have taken up a natural military career. I had always had a thing about wanting to be an Officer and to gain a commission. It always seemed the right thing to do and it was still bugging me. It was still playing subconsciously on my brain. I had to address the situation.

The days out at RAF Mildenhall in East Anglia with the jet fighters of the USAF, the Mach 3+ SR71 Blackbird, the U2 spy plane, the F18 Blue Angels and F16 Thunderbird display teams, all reinforced my American calling and military instincts. I even took to wearing second hand German army shirts! The popular cheap conscript army shirts with German flags on, and wearing a dark blue naval officer's pullover with epaulettes. I always liked epaulettes, even when I was a Boy Scout. I was dressing more and more conservatively. To add to the army theme I had a shotgun and I would go clay pigeon shooting sporting my *Barbour and wellies*. My green moleskin trousers and short hair completed the country gentleman look. After having long hair with a moustache as a student and then losing it all with the chemotherapy I now had very short hair and a moustache. I looked every inch the army officer. It seemed to be my natural calling.

I always felt more comfortable with a moustache ever since I was a student. It again came as no surprise to see that Baillie had a moustache in his second picture aged seventy-two. It always seems to be the women folk who preferred their men to be clean-shaven and I guessed this was true of Baillie in his first portrait. With no lady to keep him under control and in true cavalier fashion, he had sported a moustache in the latter days of his life.

When I was fourteen one of my best friends was a boy called Gordon Whyte. We were at school together and he was also a Civil War enthusiast. Gordon's father had been Deputy Commander of the Canadian Air Force Detachment at Manston Airport, Ramsgate. We often used to stalk each other with our air rifles, rather like playing paint ball. The only rules were that you didn't aim at the face, because it was dangerous, so you aimed at the foot, especially the leather boot. If you got hit on the ankle, or the leather boot then you were deemed dead. I remember one day stalking in an orchard near Gordon's house, where I made a particularly fine shot, hitting Gordon with a lead pellet at a distance of a good 100 yards. Unfortunately it missed his boot and hit him immediately above the ankle, causing him to jump several feet into the air. He had a lovely little pink pellet mark on his ankle, which we judged a fine trophy of war! I was particularly proud of that shot, because he hadn't seen it coming and it was extremely accurate. It was just unfortunate that it hit him a few inches above the boot. For a distance of 100 yards that was a pretty good shot.

I then re-enacted the commissioning of my friend Gordon Whyte. Gordon of all my friends had been one of my best *Confederateers.* So I planned his commission in order to honor him as he was leaving for a place at boarding school in Hastings, East Sussex. I had already promoted myself to the rank of Captain in my own mind on the basis that I was now a veteran re-enactor of some four years and I had raised a *Company of troops - Baillie's Ranger's* from among my school chums. For the film project I held the rank of Sergeant, as can be seen in the actual movie and on the still photographs taken at the time. This was a deliberate act, as I had not wished to distance myself too much from my men. It just happened that way. I can not honestly recollect making a conscious decision to do this - it just fell into place. All I knew was that this was all just *a hobby!* saturday evenings after work were spent sewing whilst watching a Cowboy Western series on TV called *The Cimmaron Strip*. I had made the Cavalry Officers uniform over several weeks as a project, it was entirely hand sewn, with the three gold bars on the collar, the rank of Captain in the Confederate Army and with gold braid *chicken guts* on the sleeve. I had converted an old gray cotton overall from my first saturday job at Boots the Chemist and the most difficult alteration was the sewing of the braid on the sleeve, a very tricky procedure indeed. I think you will agree that this was extremely strange behavior for a fifteen year-old adolescent boy! Well nobody else wanted to promote me, so like every thing else in my life this time around; I did it myself! Now I needed a trusty Lieutenant, I felt deeply that he had earned the privilege and that I would honor him before his departure. Fortunately the whole ceremony was captured on film for posterity, thank goodness. Finally in the Easter holidays, 1970, I acting as Brevet Regimental Colonel commissioned my compatriot in the field, 2nd Lieutenant Gordon Whyte, an Officer in the Provisional Army of the Confederate States. I wrote out his commission, signed it, sealed it and then presented it to him in front of the all-important witness, my bemused sister.

This whole event is worth reiterating in detail, because I not only re-enacted what should have happened to Baillie in the field with the 5th Georgia Cavalry; but I even used the exact same language, as phrased in the historical letter of the proposed commission signed by the Colonel Robert H Anderson, *ol' Marse Bob* himself. **This one piece of evidence is in itself conclusive proof, beyond question and reasonable doubt that subconscious memory survives mortality!**

The Commission 1970: My good friend and best soldier Gordon Whyte is commissioned in the field to the rank of Lieutenant in the Provisional Army of the Confederate States.

The Commission 1970: The ceremony is now complete, Gordon has unknowingly played the part of Baillie and I have enacted the role of Colonel Robert H Anderson, *ol' Marse Bob.*

Baillie had always wanted to be an officer. He wanted desperately to get that commission. In doing so he would surely have won his bride, Sarah Elizabeth *Sallie* Spalding. I had re-enacted this completely when I was fifteen, without knowing it. Now I had won my bride, my blonde-haired lady, but there was still the niggling possibility that I hadn't quite fulfilled all my subconscious ambitions on the officer front. I therefore began a relentless quest to fulfil this emotional drive, this burning need to put right the wrongs of the past.

My interest in the army did not wane over the years. As I neared the age of thirty I started to feel time was running out. I had changed schools to Hartsdown Secondary School in Margate, and was having a wild time. The teachers' strike in 1984 was the final straw that helped me make up my mind, I decided to enquire as to the possibility of joining the army. My real goal was to gain a commission. I had investigated joining the Territorial's and gaining a commission through part-time soldiering, but as luck would have it our local Territorial's are historically the 3rd Foot Regiment- the *Buffs* - those damned infantry again! My subliminal phobia kicked in! Yet I was determined not to give up.

I was firing on all cylinders when I went up to Sandhurst the famous Army headquarters in Surrey for an interview. I was twenty-nine years of age, full of confidence and drove there in my TR7. The previous week I had been for an interview for the Service Children's Education Authority at Eltham Palace on the outskirts of SouthEast London. The Interview Board comprised of an Admiral, a General and an Air Commodore. Their first question to me was, 'Have you got a hobby?'

'Do you really want to know my hobby? It will take time to explain!' I replied with a smile.

'We have all the time we want, so fire away.' Came the decisive invitation.

I then went on to tell them all about the adventure games that I had organized together with my Customs Officer friend Jeremy *Jez* Lee. Pauline and I were very close to Jez and Claire Lee at the time, for we were all without children and so enjoying our social life to the full. Often we would have games weekends with another avid *gamer,* Customs Officer Dave Wright. The appointments board, were especially interested in the live action adventure game parties that we had played and developed. This evolved from just a few close friends discussing the proverbial; 'What if we tried to do this for real?' To involving the members of my after-school games club in *live* Dungeons and Dragons role-playing, with the Customs Officers, Teachers and Nurses who were my friends as participants. This was before these kinds of games became popular on television. We constructed traps, combat systems with custard pies and treasure/reward systems, together with many physical/mental problem initiative tests. The *games* generally involved hiking around the local marsh, or woodlands, building catapults, combating the *enemy* and collecting gold bricks as treasure. I had specialized in the pyrotechnics and I knew that they would be very impressed with this, because it was exactly what the Army wanted. The Army sought people who engage in this sort of thing, especially if they can organize and inspire other people to join in.

Having broken the ice they asked me a few other questions. I cracked the interview with one particularly memorable comment in reply to a question on the importance of reading, I said, 'Technologically speaking the future is in pictures! The F14 *Tomcat*, carrier based air superiority fighter, has a technological manual for its maintenance, which comprises of 2,000 pages of cartoons showing the ground crews how it works.' At that the Admiral lit up and said, 'Oh yes, he's absolutely right. I remember when I was on the USS George Washington that's exactly what they did.' They all laughed at that, because us *Brits* tend to think that we are intellectually more superior than our cousins. But actually it is the American Forces, with their massive air power and advanced weaponry that are more than a match for anybody; with the whole outfit run entirely by a bunch of *technicians*, using just cartoons and the power of pictures to make things work!

I had cracked the interview and they offered me a place straightaway to teach Physics in Germany. I still had an interview at Sandhurst, so I went there a week later to see about a commission in the Regular Army. I sat there in the office, quietly confident. The Officer interviewing me had a very pleasant informal manner and as I sat there in a big leather armchair, he turned around and said, 'Mr. Baillie, we will be glad to have you, if that is what you want to do. But, is it really what you want to do now? You are thirty, have been married several years, would your wife like to keep moving every eighteen months into new quarters?'

Well, this was a turn up for the books. They had offered me a commission, but it was really up to me whether I wanted it or not? Stunned momentarily I answered, 'Thank you very much, Sir.' The Officer said he would write confirming that they would offer me a place at Sandhurst and that if I wished to pursue this career option, then they would be really pleased to have me. Somewhat nonplussed with my brain racing to calculate the ramifications of the decision that I was about to make, I left the office.

It was certainly a strange feeling. I drove to the nearest Little Chef restaurant, by my grand mother's village of Ripley in Surrey, to think. I needed to think long and hard, 'What shall I do?' I had taken Christine, my mother-in-law, with me and we sat talking. The prize that I wished for above everything else, apart from my lovely blonde wife, a commission in Her Majesty's Armed Forces, was within my grasp. I sat there, debating everything in my head. I went to see my grandma and my auntie and then we drove back with the TR7, back to home in Thanet, Kent.

This would require some thinking about. Everything I had wanted was there, but dare I grasp it? I sat and talked with Pauline. She already had a career with Customs and Excise. She had put up with me being ill. We had got our life back together again. We had everything. Yet I had this urge. All I had to do was sit tight, but I couldn't. Our mortgage had dwindled to a very small amount. We had a bungalow, which we had expanded and put a garage and an extension on, doubling its value. And we were thinking about purchasing a detached house, which was everything we wanted. A detached house, with a detached double garage right next to the chip shop in Minster, where Pauline's mum could walk around for a cup of tea with Pauline. This was everything they wanted, to be close to one another as a family, yet I was still restless. The commission was dangling like a carrot in front of me.

A typical Baillie compromise was needed. After much thought I decided that the commission, well, that would have to wait, I couldn't be so selfish. And I would go instead for the three years to Germany working for the Service Children's Education Authority, Service Children's Schools, SCS, and take the place offered at *King's School,* Gütersloh, Nord Rhein Westphalen. As we sat on the carpet one afternoon in May, debating the issue, I made the decision - I would go to Germany. The miners' strike had been on for a year in England and the teachers were now working to rule, there was no way they were going to win against a Conservative Government, so I decided that I would go for it. I accepted the post in Germany, which then set into motion another chain of events.

We celebrated by going back to Ibiza. We had been to Ibiza the year previous, in the summer of 1983. That was when I had made that rather interesting sandcastle, which just happened to be a subconscious representation, much like *Close Encounters of the Third Kind*, of Sapelo Island Lighthouse. This was the lonely tower that I often used to paint still calling across time and space. Yet I had no conscious knowledge of this, but Ibiza was where we were happy, the sand the sea and the heat. *Marina del Torrents*, near *San Antonio* was idyllic. This was in the days when Ibiza was just starting to become popular. Ironically we liked it, because it was quiet.

I have just realized whilst reviewing this, that there is an interesting parallel here with Norman. Norman lives in Corpus Christi, Texas by the sea and often goes to San Antonio. With the heat, the sun, the sand and sea, we have another interesting Matrix coincidence! Baillie and Kell both enjoying similar emotional locations, all we needed was a lighthouse. I provided that by building one on the beach.

We went back to Ibiza and we sat on the beach and we had a very happy fortnight surrounded by our memories. We had some nice meals and I prepared myself mentally to go to Germany. We had already moved into our new house. In the event we actually only lived in the house for three weeks. Then came the fateful day when Jez kindly drove me with Pauline to Luton Airport, just north of London, to catch my flight. Pauline and I shared an emotional farewell as she waved me off at the departure gate. I experienced a peculiar feeling on the aeroplane for the entire flight. The parting had seemed some how so final, yet in reality it wasn't, as Pauline was going to join me in a month's time. It was only a one-hour flight, but again I felt the same as I did when I went to university. It was all very strange. Was I doing the right thing? It felt like the right thing, but it felt strange. We touched down at Hanover Airport and Colin Daines met us, he was the friendly faced, ever cheerful Director of Studies. And so along with a couple of other teachers who had arrived, I set off down the motorway to King's School, Gütersloh, and the life in the Officers' Mess.

I sat in my room in the Officers' Mess and for the first time I realized I was really on my own again. It would be a month before Pauline could join me. I had left my wife, my house and my car behind in England! What had I done? Driven by this insane desire to achieve a commission of sorts and to experience the military life. I was astounded at the lengths I had gone to make this happen. Nothing mattered; my subconscious was prepared to sacrifice all that I had achieved to fulfil that hidden ambition.

Looking back with the knowledge that I now have, I can see that this drive was so amazingly overwhelming in its intensity, that it leaves me speechless, in awe as to the power of the subconscious mind.

I decided then and there that I would leave my room and go to the bar, something was bound to happen. I had to be pro-active about my situation; after all I had made it happen! It was then that I chanced upon a dashing young officer of Royal Engineers, strolling by the lake, Alan Pateman-Jones and I struck up a warm relationship straightaway. Alan was a Lieutenant in 10 Field Squadron, Royal Engineers and like me he was waiting for his wife, Hilary. So we struck up a mutual friendship. We talked about all sorts of things, life, death, the Universe and everything. We had delightful evening meals in the Mess, silver service with a waitress and a wonderful English breakfast the next morning. I found him to be remarkably good company; he had tremendous general knowledge combined with excellent intelligence. As we were also sharing the mess with the 47 Field Regiment, Royal Artillery, *the Gunners* we had an excellent time. Alan was not a gunner and immediately joined ranks with the teachers in the friendly internal mess rivalry. Alan enjoyed the fact that the Engineers had saved some *guns* once from the enemy whilst in action and so he wore a blue lanyard in honor of that deed. Unfortunately the 47 had lost some *guns* once and conversely wore a white lanyard to their dismay and everlasting shame! On such amazing trivia is the tribal elitism of the British Army founded. I understood such things and together we made an excellent team, when out numbered by the gunners. Although even as a die-hard cavalryman myself I had always enjoyed cannons and the gunners were excellent company.

Again, we see the influence of the Baillie story in the re-creating of a synchronous parallel chain of events. These myriad coincidences created by the Matrix to bring about a complete similarity of experience, so perfect in their fulfillment, are breathtakingly stunning in retrospect. I relived the war in those 3 years in Germany, thirty to thirty-three years of age. Baillie was of a similar age thirty-three to thirty-seven. Saying good bye to Pauline at the airport was the counterpart of Baillie and Sallie parting in 1862. Hence the intensity of emotional reaction experienced on the airplane. I have no doubt that I was actually reliving that event.

I had really got it cracked. The car was ordered. This was the life. I was enjoying all the benefits of being an Officer, without having to go through all the pain of six months at Sandhurst. I really thought I had cracked it and time went by very quickly.

I often used to visit my Dutch friends Jan *(John)* and Agnes Sanders in Boxtel. I had met John's daughter whilst working in the Laboratory in 1976 and was amazed when she declared that her father was a student! John although thirty-seven at the time had decided to cease being a school administrator and to take up teaching. He was now a full time English language teacher and we had always got on well, with a lot in common. What's more, everybody mistook us for brothers! He had a moustache and glasses, as did I, for me this was a very high compliment, because I admired John immensely. To me he really did fill the role of a *big brother* and this friendship has stood the test of time until the present day. John is also a tremendously spiritual person and we soon found our paths of interest coinciding, we still do.

I realized when I discovered Baillie's story why I felt so close to John. He fulfilled the place of Baillie's own brother John McIntosh Kell in every way. In my subconscious driven search to gather the familiar, I had naturally bonded with him from the first instant. **He even had the same first name!**

It was very reassuring having him and all my old Dutch friends just a couple of hours down the road. Life settled down into socializing, working at school, partying and things like that. One worked hard abroad but, as in any community, especially with the army officers, there is never a dull moment. There is always a mess dinner evening with candlesticks, mess silver and full service of course. Mess evenings with just the officers were fun. We would line up the guns and have an impromptu firefight after the meal; much to the Staff Sergeant's bemused annoyance. I thought I was adept at handling explosives, but the army boys were really quite serious. They had an affinity with me, because I liked explosives, but they were the ultimate masters at causing absolute mayhem and I was in my element.

Several occurrences happened during my three years, some especially memorable. One mess meal the officers had clubbed together and bought a radio-controlled model King Tiger Tank, a large one, which they sprayed silver and put on a plinth. Halfway through the meal the Tiger Tank got off the plinth and started to drive down the table, knocking all the glasses over. Some of the visiting officers had already commented, as to why we had a Tiger Tank on the table when really it should be artillery, most of the mess silver consisted of various guns that the regiment had used. The boys' spun them a yarn about how the regiment had knocked out a King Tiger in World War II, which they swallowed. The Tiger Tank then rumbled along the table and turned it's turret with the barrel and pointed it up the Colonel's nose! The Colonel just looked at the officers and in a deadpan voice said, 'If that thing goes off you will all be on a charge monday morning!' So the barrel descended and the turret turned to normal position, the tank drove back up the table and onto its plinth and everybody thought it was a jolly good wheeze!

I was very privileged to share these meals with the Gunners and Engineers and I really joined in with the spirit of things.

There was another officer called Bob who had a BMW M3 and had a rather well connected girlfriend who lived down on the Brenner Pass. He used to go and see her some weekends. Bob used to blow things up quite regularly! In fact it became quite an art form with him. I think his most memorable moment occurred, when a local opera singer was singing in front of the General and the officers in the mess after dinner with a silver vase full of daffodils on the piano. Just as she reached a high note the vase exploded. It was a remote-control booby trap device that Bob had rigged up. The daffodils flew through the air, one of them ended up in the General's drink, and the woman went into shock. She wasn't used to army high jinx! I think that really nearly got Bob thrown out, but he managed to get away with it, as usual. He was always good at talking his way out of things. Everyone agreed afterwards that it was again a rather fine jape.

The officers were just like students, except that they had money and we had many excellent adventures. One Bonfire Night, Alan's Engineers had built a complete scale model of the Houses of Parliament out of cardboard boxes; it was absolutely huge. In their way it was another jolly jape, because it was slightly anti-government. This is because the British soldier is loyal to the Queen and not to any one Government. It is a fine institution, as it means the country can never be taken over by any one political party, as happened in Nazi Germany, in 1933. Parliament therefore is seen, as a legitimate target in the eyes of the army, for they really do not like political masters. All the best officers have a touch of dash and the old rebel spirit in them somewhere! But the important thing is to have style and this was perfect style, as in silhouette, the buildings looked so real; so up went the Houses of Parliament on November 5. The Germans could never understand why we kept having fireworks all the time, as they only have their fireworks on New Year's Eve. We tried to explain that it was a cultural thing, but at the time we seemed to have fireworks every other week, especially after mess dinners.

Two years into mess life the Colonel left. Colonel Douglas Withers, an officer and gentleman had been promoted to the rank of Brigadier General and was off to the Ministry of Defense, Whitehall in London. I was privileged enough to be asked to his leaving dinner when he formally was dined out. After the meal, officers and ladies only, he stood on the table, put his old parka on, and delivered his leaving speech, which was highly emotional. He was well loved for his generosity of spirit and excellence of conduct. It reminded me historically, at the time of Napoleon saying farewell to his old guard. Everybody had a tear in their eye. He was a fine gentleman and a damned good Colonel.

They took him outside and placed him in an armchair with his wife in another and then rowed him ceremonially across the lake in a rubber dinghy, whilst they played Richard Wagner's *Flight of the Valkyries.* With trip flares going off in the background all the while, to complete the atmosphere. To which were added a whole multitude of signal flares, maroons and all manner of other pyrotechnics. The whole thing was inspiringly emotional. Having got to the other side of the lake, the officers then picked him up with a mini, which they had chopped the back off, and with fellow officers on bicycles with swords drawn escorted the Colonel out of the camp. They then drove him around Gütersloh at 3a.m. for one last time. And so our beloved Colonel left. It was really quite a night.

The parallels kept happening, Colonel Robert H Anderson of the 5th Georgia Volunteer Cavalry was promoted to the rank of Brigadier General in 1864. Baillie would have experienced the exact same emotions then, as I was now.

It was all happening again, the same emotions the same scenarios! A complete synchronicity of time and events, Baillie had known the Colonel for two years before he was similarly promoted.

We were now coming to the end of my three years in Germany. Pauline was getting a little fed up with not having had a baby and I had taken her to the worst possible place, for the soldier's wives were having babies all the time. Looking back I had taken her away from her family and we thought we couldn't have any children, because of my chemotherapy. She had become more and more depressed. In the end I had to bring her mother and father over. I had not contemplated this turn of events. I just said in my naivety, treat it as a three year holiday, just one big holiday. But I hadn't realized that she wouldn't be able to do that. It was like watching a tiny caged bird wither and die. I became really quite worried at one point, but again I decided to be pro-active and to try to rectify the situation.

Once her mother and father came out it was all right. We now had our own house; officers quarters in Avenwede Bahnhof just north west of Gütersloh, with our own garden and things started looking up again. In fact her mum and dad spent six months out of the three years with us, on and off, because they had just retired from the fish and chip shop. We liked our house. We had a great time, with lots of friends, especially Nick and Claire Bishop from Gloucester, as they shared a common link with Pauline's Mum and Dad. Nick's Mum went to school with Pauline's Mum in Gloucester, another strange and wonderful coincidence in the Matrix. Once Pauline secured a job everything was all right materially, but still she wanted a baby. We had to do something about that. The story was incomplete. Seeing Nick and Claire with their beautiful baby daughter Charlotte, made Pauline's plight even more acute. Time was running out, I had to act. I had got my wish with the army, but Pauline hadn't become pregnant in ten years of marriage, so I had to think again what to do?

Again this is *the story* coming into play. Sarah Sallie Spalding had lost her only baby on the night that it was born. She had then remained childless for the rest of her days. The only thing she ever wanted was a baby! It had to happen I had to make it happen for her.

Whilst I was thinking we carried on having parties and elaborate dinners. We went on holiday. I even started buying Civil War soldiers again. I had already sold my collection in 1982 and now here I was in 1986 with a nice big garden, just right to play Little Wars, H G Wells War games, in the garden. What could I do? Well, I went to the toyshop and I started buying Britain's American Civil War figures. Over the next few months I bought up all the stock they had in the shop. I assembled my armies on the lawn. I even made little houses. So the old American Civil War raised its head again. I had played several games with my friend Simon Bamford, he was a rather eccentric mathematician and intellectual; an archetypal English professor as depicted similarly in the *Tin Tin* comic books!

I had been rather irrationally envious of Simon. Simon actually had a Queen's commission. He showed it to me. He was commissioned as a Lieutenant in the Territorial Army, so despite being a mathematics teacher at school he was also a territorial soldier. I remember looking at his commission and still wishing I had a commission. At the time the irrational emotional wave that came over me was totally inexplicable. We played our War games. Inevitably he was very good at it. Being a mathematician, he was very good at probability and we had a few close run games. He beat me a few times and I beat him a few times. He was an excellent opponent; good at abstract games and it was rather good fun. At one point our neighbors had some Germans visiting and they leaned over halfway through sitting out in the garden in the summer and said, 'Do you mind if we ask what are you doing?'

'We are War gaming, *Das kreigspiel, ja!*' They were quite intrigued at this, to see two Englishmen groveling around on their knees with little toy soldiers on the lawn, with all manner of scenery. It really did remind me of H G Wells. The 54mm chunky figures, approximately 2 inch Imperial size, 1:32nd scale, were really quite a nice size and to play with on the floor á la H G Wells, which is what we were doing. And that is exactly what eccentric English people should do, either that or croquette, which we played at the officers' Mess.

I ran a karate club at school, which was interesting and I played War games with the children. But I decided, that in the end I would have to come home. Pauline had to have a baby and I had to do my best to make sure we had a baby. So we decided that at the end of the three-year tour she would come back to Customs and Excise and we would move back to England. My dream of being an officer would be over, but it was a sacrifice I was willing to make for the sake of my wife.

When it came around to it, I was really quite glad to be doing something different and the three years, which had gone very, very quickly, seemed to have passed by in a blur. The next thing we knew, we were back on the boat going from Vlissingen to Sheerness, having a lovely moonlit dinner in the huge restaurant. Having booked into a pleasant cabin and with our new SAAB 900 car - we were on our way back. We arrived at Sheerness and it was cold. Germany had been nice and hot, 29 Celsius, but now we came back to England and we were back to the cold. It was actually 14 Celsius as we arrived in the early morning mist. We were in our summer clothes and had to quickly put jumpers on. We drove back to Herne Bay, to where my in-laws, Chris and John, had moved into their big house, *Hey Tor* on the seafront. The next episode of our life was about to begin. It was back to reality with a bump.

Coincidentally from the house on the seafront we could gaze across the Thames estuary to a place called South End. Sallie too lived at South End on Sapelo Island just across Doboy sound! Even the flashing light at the end of the pier reminded me subconsciously of Sapelo lighthouse. Not surprisingly I soon had the urge to paint again, this time I painted the end of the pier in oils. It was that lighthouse image again, pricking my awareness from the depths of my subconscious.

For five years in torment I sat and watched it blink at me, before one summer I cracked and bought a boat. But first we had to pray for a miracle...

Chapter Twelve
Miracle

We had come back to reality with a bump. We had left our quarters in Germany, a luxurious life in the Officers' Mess, all the socializing, and come back to good *Old Blighty,* freezing cold. Pauline's dad's house was an absolute shambles - no hot water, everything was being done, he had the builders in, and we had to go and wash in the sea. But it was a rather splendid property, with a little turret, right opposite the sea on the front at Herne Bay. John and Chris had admired the panoramic views of our quarters in Germany and in comparison their little bungalow didn't seem very pleasant. So, one January day, having looked at a property in Faversham, they came back, dropped off at Herne Bay to get some fish and chips and looked in the estate agents. There was a house for sale on the sea front. This house plays an integral part in the story, because of its positioning, its proximity to the sea, to Sheppey and to Southend. And now we come to the next major phase of our lives.

We had already bought a little house near Dover as Pauline was returning to Customs and Excise. I didn't have a job, but I didn't care - I was doing the right thing. I signed on for supply teaching and managed to get all my jobs done in the new house. Everything was brand new, Pauline was happy, the only thing missing was the patter of tiny feet. Somehow, some way, we had to have a baby. We had been told that the chemotherapy was going to leave me with a reduced chance to have children, but something had to happen. Something had to happen and I was going to do my best to make it happen.

It was in those early September days that I suggested to Pauline that we actually tried to get some help: with the modern technological advances it must be perfectly possible for us to have a baby. All we needed to do was to find out how to go about it. Our doctor recommended the National Health, but said it will probably mean waiting two or three years. We couldn't wait that long so he suggested

Harley Street as the place to go to get things done immediately. I managed to book an appointment.

October came around. We got on the train and went up to Harley Street in London. It all seemed so unreal at the time. It seemed very *techno* most people managed to have babies without really knowing it. But we had the opposite problem. I was certain we could do something, even if I had to keep going for a year, we would do it, we would make it happen. It had to happen.

It was late November when we went up again to Harley Street. After the appointment we went to John Lewis and had something to eat in the restaurant. We so wanted to have a little baby, just a little baby of our own. Now thanks to science we had the chance, would it work though? It was like playing the lottery they had given us only a 20% chance at the outside, but this was better than no chance at all. Anyway, we celebrated by having pancakes in John Lewis' Oxford Street, where we bought a small tree decoration, as Christmas decorations were on sale. It was a little angel with blonde hair entering through a white open window with a golden present and we called her *Angel Pancake.* When we came home we held hands, made a wish and put her on our festive tree.

Just before Christmas we were desperate to see whether we had had any luck. Nervously I went out and purchased a pregnancy testing kit. Pauline had missed her *time of the month* and our fingers were crossed. I arrived home and, being the scientist performed the pregnancy test, it was blue for positive, we were so excited. Being cautious and daring not believe the chemical results, I repeated the test. It was definitely positive, beyond doubt! Pauline was really excited. I cried. I couldn't believe it. It had actually worked first time. It was absolutely amazing. This was the best Christmas present that we could wish for. But, like most things, it was only the start of a rather long and complicated process.

Pauline continued working. But during the second month she suddenly started bleeding. We panicked and thought we were going to lose the baby. She was told to go straight to bed. We were distraught. She stayed in bed for a week. By then the baby's hormones had over ridden Pauline's own and the high-risk phase had passed. This baby was too precious to lose. We just called it the baby, we had no name yet, but the baby was everything. It was everything we wanted. We had a new house, we had come back to England, we had endured the hurricane of 1987, and now we were on our way to having what we wanted most, our little baby. The pregnancy went well, but nearing the end of the pregnancy Pauline had to take time off work, because she is not the strongest of people. At that stage in the pregnancy Pauline was the size of a balloon having to endure the heat of a hot summer. We went to pre-natal classes at Dover. I seemed to be the only man there because I was on summer holiday.

Just before Christmas I had had an amazing piece of luck. I had been offered a job at St Edmund's, Canterbury teaching Mathematics and Physics and at Dover College Junior School in Folkestone, teaching Chemistry and Physics. I had taken the Chemistry and Physics job because I liked bangs and smells! An added bonus to this post was being in a department of one. I was in charge of myself, so I had nobody to tell me what to do, which was a lovely feeling.

That Christmas I had a lot to celebrate. I went along to the school for the last three days of term and got to know everybody. This was like being back in Germany. It was a lovely school. It was full of very educated people, who spoke very politely, very nice children and the sort of place that I wanted to work. With the Headmaster, Nick Brodrick at the helm it was idyllic and so I took up my post in January 1988. I was able to tell him the good news that we were going to have a baby and that everything seemed to be working out. It was all a miracle. The whole thing was like a fairy-tale come true. The uncertainty had disappeared. I had a clear path. We had a baby on the way. We had a nice house. Pauline's mum and dad were enjoying knocking their home into shape and living in their ideal house by the sea. Everything was suddenly alive.

We were ready for it. We had had enough of socializing. We had so many gin and tonics in Germany, so many meals in the mess, that we really didn't want to go out and do things. We were quite happy to be at home, just us and *the baby*. The summer came, and we waited. D. Day, delivery day, came round, August 21, 1988. Pauline's mum and dad had come to stay with us at our house called *Cwichelm* in Eythorne, Dover. On the night the baby was due I cooked the dinner. I prepared steak in port and paté sauce. I was a bit liberal with the port and we were all absolutely away with the fairies! We had all retired to bed rather tired when Pauline started complaining of kicks and sat up, counting. I said, 'That's all right, there's at least ten minutes between each contraction, for the moment don't worry.' But by 4:00a.m. in the morning the contractions had become much stronger. We went downstairs half asleep, counting contractions. When Pauline's mum got up at around 8:00a.m. she said, 'Oh my goodness, how long have you been sat there?' We said, 'Since 4:00a.m. in the morning.' She said, 'You'd better get down to the hospital, this is going to happen quicker than we think.' I had taken the advice of the course too literally, because they said *stay at home as long as possible* and I was counting the contractions, but I was making mistakes, because I was only counting the large contractions and not the small ones in between! We were actually down to four minutes between contractions, in which case it was action stations!

Bundling into the old Saab, which belonged to Pauline's dad and was a bit worse for wear, we drove to Buckland Hospital. We got there at just gone 8:30a.m. Pauline was examined as soon as we arrived the nurse said, 'I think you'll have this baby pretty quickly Mrs. Baillie.' The nurse then asked me to take Pauline to the loo?' But Pauline really was close to having the baby and she started having the baby in the loo! My God, it was do-it-yourself time. Being an agriculturist I was used to this, but it is quite different when you are dealing with your wife, plus I didn't have my wellington boots on! We got her on the trolley down to the delivery room at 10:30a.m. By 12:30p.m. it was all over. It was all going along at an amazing rate of knots. I still hadn't realized the enormity of the occasion. Breathing, pushing, breathing, Pauline did it all without gas and suddenly another little human being popped into existence into the room. Suddenly we were not alone, no longer two, but three, our daughter had arrived. It was the most wonderful, wonderful experience actually to be there.

The doctor gave me the baby to hold. We knew straight away that she would be called Harriet. We had decided what the girl's name would be if she was a girl. The nurse said 'It's a girl!' Without hesitation we said together, 'Her name is Harriet Lucinda Elizabeth Baillie.' We had already decided. So the nurse gave me Harriet, who was quite stress-free, crying a little bit, and I cut Pauline's nightie with the scissors from my Swiss Army knife, a touch of the old backwoods there, *I never go anywhere without my Swiss Army knife*, and put Harriet on her breast. That was one of the happiest moments of my life.

The story has a life of its own. Ten years after the event, I was to learn exactly why Harriet had to be born. I knew Harriet was special, I knew we had to have a baby. Everything seemed to make it happen. Later on I was to learn why.

So, we were in possession of a little miracle. After three days we then went home to get used to having a new little person in our lives. What do you do? There were no instruction books for this; you have to make it up as you go along. Everything you read is only a preparation. You have to learn the hard way. We just got used to our roles. Everything was concentrated on the baby.

Two weeks after the birth my mother asked is she could visit. At the time we thought it was a bit of a nuisance, but it was a good job she did, because a couple of days after that she passed away. Life is full of ups and downs. We were on an enormous high. We were up as high as you could get one minute and this brought us crashing down the next. My mother had been to visit my grandmother and my auntie and then came to visit us for a week. While she was with us she got to know Harriet she even bathed her. She slept on a camp bed in my study. We found it all a bit stressful, because we were trying to get used to having the new baby. But it was as well that we did, because the week afterwards I received a phone call halfway through teaching in the morning and they said I had to go to Margate Hospital as my mother had collapsed. I thought, 'Oh dear, I wonder what it is? They didn't seem to be stressing it very much so I said I would go over at lunchtime, because I had to teach my lessons.

Unfortunately another phone call came urgently telling me I had to get to the hospital straightaway. That was when I realized it was really serious. The drive over to Margate was very tearful. When I arrived I went into the Pulmonary Unit to find my mother, who had had a mild heart attack five years previous, on a monitoring machine. She didn't look like my mother, but I sat by the bed. She was breathing heavily through her mouth with a breathing tube and oxygen. Her features were hardly recognizable. An hour later I was given the message that my wife had arrived with my sister and my brother-in-law. Pauline and Harriet were out in the waiting room. Ann my sister had Jonathan, my nephew with her. We were all shaking, trying to discuss life, what life is all about. I left them to go back to mum. As I walked into the room the doctor took me to one side and told me, 'I'm afraid your mother has just passed away.' There was nothing we could have done for her. She had had a massive heart attack; the muscle was too badly damaged.

Even if she had survived she would have been in a wheelchair, and that is not much of a life.

I walked over to the bed, sat down, prayed, held her hand, which was now cold and stiff. I looked up to the ceiling and spoke to her. I wished her well on her journey. I was always a spiritual person and I knew how to handle death. The rapidity of it all had been quite a shock, but unlike my father I had managed to get there. I then had to go and tell the folks outside - my wife, sister and brother-in-law. It was a very difficult thing to do.

Life somehow has to continue on as normal. I had to return to school. But the next weekend we needed to visit my nan. My sister and I went together. It was one of the hardest things I've ever had to do to tell my grandmother that my mother was dead. She knew it was something serious, because we both walked into the property through the back door at the same time and we never go in two's. We always visited on our own, or with our respective partners. But this particular day we were together.

Shortly after that Pauline and I took the baby to see grandma, to show that life continues. The cycle continues, as one person arrives, another person goes, that's the way it seems to be.

Anyway life moves on. Harriet grew up and joined our school at the tender age of two coming through the Nursery to the Pre-Prep. I had the joy of watching her play and grow whilst I did my job. The job wasn't easy, we had lots of changes in leadership, changes in name, changes in management, changes, changes, changes, but I was privileged to be able to watch Harriet grow up. See my own darling little blonde-haired girl grow up, running around in the playground, at the back of the hall, playing with the rabbits. She loved animals. She was baptized in the same School hall. One sunday evening service we had her baptized with the boarders present. We really were part of the community. The school meant everything to us. Harriet and I were immersed in it. Pauline used to make cakes for the Fêtes and join in the social events, helping with the mothers, and life was really quite idyllic.

Financially we were stable. My new teaching position was working out well. For the first time in my life we had financial security, which was a great feeling. I never felt financially secure, ever. Again, years later, I was to realize subconsciously why I never felt financially secure, Baillie had died in poverty.

I had always wanted to go to America. America was in my blood. Now I had the financial ability to do it. So as soon as we were able, in fact Harriet was coming up for eighteen months old, I said to Pauline, 'Let's go on holiday.'

'Where to? Shall we go back to Ibiza, or Spain'

'No, Harriet can get free air travel up to the age of two, so let's go to America. Let's go to Florida, to Disney and Mickey Mouse'. I had remembered *Mickey Mouse* from when I was a child and the Mickey Mouse model at Margate in the 50's, the old magical clock, so I had Mickey Mouse in my head. And I had Florida on my mind, I was drawn to America and Florida was the in place. It was becoming cheaper to go to Florida in 1990, so we looked at teletext and booked our first flight that Easter. We were off to Florida. We had a magical two weeks.

For me it felt like going home. It was like going home in more ways than one. Later on I was to realize that it really was going home because 100 miles up the road, in Georgia, there had been just eighty years previous another Baillie, who had the same face and the same name as me. At this point in time, 1990, I had not a clue that the other Baillie existed, but my other self was there. All I knew was that it felt right. I had made it to America. I had always wanted to go there. I had always felt that was where I belonged. I didn't feel English yet I was born in Folkestone. I had started to feel Scottish and to try to look at my name as being Scottish, but even that didn't feel 100% right. At the end of the day I always felt American. I couldn't explain it, it just was! Mildenhall had raised the specter to more prominence. It had been like going to America for the day and now, here I was, actually in America. We stayed in Kissimmee, at a little motel. It was a dream come true. We went to the Magic Kingdom. It was really magic for us despite all the clichés. There we all were on a hot sunny March day going across the lake in a steamboat Harriet in a pushchair, Pauline my blonde-haired wife, and myself. Everything was there. The steam trains at Central Station. Walking up Main Street. The same old Wild West trains. I realized it was like a dream come true. Everything, the whole jigsaw puzzle, had come together. I didn't know what the jigsaw puzzle was, but it just felt like I had arrived. The feeling was right, it was fantastic.

We only went to the Magic Kingdom for one day just to try it out, because we had decided that we would definitely come back. No sense in doing too much, it was very hot and we had a baby to look after. For me it was just enough to be in a diner, with an American waitress, using American dollars, eating American food. It was all so familiar. We drove down to the Gulf coast for the second week and stayed at Treasure Island, which was magic. It had the big clear beach on the Tampa Bay side, the Gulf of Mexico. The pelicans were wheeling their way in the sky like prehistoric monsters. Flights of pelicans, it was just wonderful. We bought kites and played on the beach and had pictures taken. We had arrived home!

After that all I wanted to do was to get back to Florida. But we live in the Matrix and the realities of life kick in. I returned to school and worked very hard. We had four months holiday a year, which was great. I knew if I worked hard and saved my money I could go to Florida. All I wanted to do was to take Harriet to Florida, to go to America. I had got the bug!

The very next summer, 1991, we went to Pennsylvania and Virginia. I had always wanted to see the battlefields of North Virginia. The battlefields of the Eastern Theatre of the American Civil War made famous by General Robert E Lee and the Army of Northern Virgina. Gettysburg had drawn me like a magnet. I was still playing War games. I had a War games club with the pupils at school. My good friend, Roger Lewis, was Deputy Headmaster and ran the modeling club. I had been War gaming and video gaming with the kids. I was extremely happy. We had the baby. We had everything.

So in 1991, I planned my battlefield tour. I persuaded Pauline that we would take Harriet and we would just enjoy being in the diners and that this was Daddy's holiday. This was theme parks, but the theme was cannons and grass. I planned the trip meticulously. We booked the flight with Jerry Wardley one of the school's parents who worked for Thomas Cook. We were flying to Baltimore in Maryland. We touched down; we were in America again! Next morning we had breakfast in the hotel restaurant. Another guest in the restaurant was a travelling salesman, who was from New Jersey. I said, 'New Jersey is the Garden State, isn't it?' He was amazed that I knew that is was the Garden State. I knew it was the Garden State, because I had read the New Jersey license plates. New Jersey figured largely in Baillie's life because Princeton University was in New Jersey, but I didn't know that at the time, yet I always mention New Jersey given half a chance. Perhaps that is why I enjoyed my four summer holidays in Jersey so much with my father. It was a familiar sounding name?

After breakfast we headed out. We got in the car and we drove up to Gettysburg, my dream had come true. It all seemed so familiar and emotional. We covered 1300 miles, countless historical sites and battlefields and toured all the way to Appomattox Court House and then back along the Blue Ridge to Baltimore. For me it was a journey of a lifetime. I was just a breath away in time and on sacred soil.

So, I watched my miracle grow up. Now she is twelve, beautiful, blonde and looks like my wife. I now have two blonde-haired girls to look after and I am a very lucky man. This now leads us into the next chapter, which is where my quest to discover how the Universe works really took off!

Chapter Thirteen
Photograph

It was a cold March day with just the first glimmers of spring. My daughter had passed her 11+ examination to the local grammar school and we had just returned from the school ski trip to the French Alps, which had been marvelous. I was feeling on top of the world, but not quite sure of which direction to go in. It was March 25 and it was *World Book Day*. The school had issued the children with book vouchers, which could be exchanged at any participating bookshop. Harriet had developed a taste for murder mysteries and was determined to buy an Agatha Christie novel with her voucher. I remember the day perfectly, because it was the day that transformed my life, a day like no other.

After school we went down to Waterstones in Folkestone. I parked the car, walked through the town and into the shop. Harriet zoomed off to have a look at the crime section. Not wishing to engage my mind with thoughts of crime and thrillers, but being more factually orientated, I had headed towards the history section. I have always had an absolute passion for American Civil War photographs. I even imagined that one-day I might find myself in a photograph, that I might walk in somewhere and see a photograph with me in it dressed in American Civil War costume. I had spent thirty-five years looking for my name - Baillie, spelt the Scottish way - in the American Civil War. To just even find my name mentioned in the Civil War would have been an amazing feat.

I walked over to the history section and spied a book, *Private Soldiers; Public Heroes* published by the Civil War Times Illustrated, a collection of articles and photographs on the American Civil War. I pulled the book from the shelf, being instantly attracted by the photographs on the cover. This was definitely my sort of book. I opened the volume and could not believe my eyes, for very quickly I spied on the left-hand page my name - *Baillie* - written in large letters.

I then looked at the photograph on the other page, but I was so elated at finding my name that the image did not register on my consciousness. I then read on the other page, *Alexander Baillie Kell.* It was the middle name, but my name was there. After thirty-five years of trying to find a link with the American Civil War I had struck the mother lode.

This for me was like winning the lottery. In fact it was more important than winning the lottery, because a number of years ago I had seriously started to wonder. Especially with my obsession with playing War games in the American Civil War period, re-enacting it and shooting black powder, whether I was really going plain crazy with this so called hobby. It certainly was beyond obsession. It was a very emotive subject. I had already coined the phrase *Emotion is the language of the soul* in 1997. I started to feel a tingle and goose bumps. I read the text, Darien, Georgia. 'Where the heck is Darien, Georgia?' I thought. All my re-enactment had been in Virginia. I had been in the 43rd Virginia Cavalry with John Singleton Mosby, riding those horses and shooting those Yankees, up in Virginia. I had been to Gettysburg; everything was based in the Blue Ridge Mountains of Virginia for me, yet there was the word *Georgia*.

I couldn't believe it. I shut the book up and put it back on the shelf. Time to go, Harriet was calling me. I made a conscious decision not to buy the book. I can remember thinking, its £20. That's a lot of money. My wife doesn't like me buying too many books as I have hundreds of books and we have the old adage, 'Why have you bought another book? You already have a book, why buy another one? In fact you have loads of books.' I had been well trained by my wife not to buy any books on impulse purchase, so I closed the book and thought, I'm not paying £20 for one picture and one phrase with the word Baillie in, I put the book back. We paid for Harriet's purchase and we duly went home.

But that evening as I watched television the picture and the book nagged my consciousness. I kept thinking, what are the chances of that happening? What is the probability of walking into a shop, selecting a book from the shelf and opening it at the very page that your name is on? I was aware from my physics and math studies that I had begun to successfully deduce how the Matrix works. The Matrix works on coincidence. In fact, coincidence is not the unusual freak occurrence; it is actually the norm. It is, how the Universe works. *Coincidence is the norm!* So the coincidence of finding my name was beyond a coincidence. I was in a quandary. Four days later I finally cracked. I just had to have that book!

After school I drove down to the shop. I couldn't even remember the actual name of the book. I hoped they hadn't sold it. Oh my God, what happens if they've sold it? I would lose it. I would never find it again. I drove the car hurriedly and parked it. I ran along to the shop, rushed in, went to the same shelf and phew; the book was still there in the same place! I opened the pages and flicked through it. As with everything else, when you are trying to find something you can never find it. It took me quite a while to find the page I wanted. It was then that I looked at the picture with my conscious mind engaged. Obviously my subconscious had registered the image, but my conscious memory had just recorded the fact that it was a figure in a military uniform. I looked at the face and then I started to shake. I trembled with excitement. I couldn't believe it. For me it was like looking into a mirror, in fact doubly so because the actual photograph is a mirror image. The buttons are on the wrong side. This is a common occurrence with Civil War plate camera technology; the positive image was often printed in reverse. Many belt buckles show the words US the wrong way round. So for me as I stared into the eyes I could see myself. It was myself. It was a mirror image and instantly a phrase came into my head, *gazing into the mirror of time I spied a familiar reflection*. I had come face to face, not only with my name in the Civil War, but with my own reflection in the Civil War! What were the chances of finding someone with the same name, the same spelling and the same face? This was far beyond coincidence.

The import of the discovery then hit me. I realized I had won the lottery four times over. A tear sprang to my eye as I trembled with emotion. It really was a defining moment. It was like finding the Holy Grail after a lifetime of search.

I took the book and paid for it, put it in a brown paper bag and drove home. I thought sooner or later I'm going to have to own up to my wife, because she is going to realize I've got the book. So I sat there on the lounge settee, opened the book and started to read. When my wife came in I just said quite simply, 'By the way, have you seen this?' One of my classic understatements, she looked at the picture and replied, 'That's you!'. Now this is so unusual for my wife, because she is the ultimate skeptic. To her physical reality is everything, but even she could see the likeness in the picture, so I was not self-delusional. The image was there it looked like me. She said, 'Do you think that's you?' I didn't like to jump up and say, 'YES! That's me, I'm a Civil War soldier!' because quite frankly it's a bit hard to believe for a skeptic. So I cautiously said, 'I don't know?'

I then started to read the description on the page, this photograph had been found by a gentleman called Dr Norman C Delaney. He had found the photograph in an attic amongst a load of papers, whilst he was researching and had pieced together the story of his own particular naval hero's younger brother. John McIntosh Kell, who was a Confederate Naval Commander, and was Chief Executive Officer on the CSS Alabama with Raphael Semmes, had a younger brother. During his research Dr Delaney had unearthed this piece of evidence, a long forgotten photograph. He had pieced together from the family letters a description of the gentleman in the photograph; a gentleman with a rather haunted look.

He thought it a shame to have lost the photograph and that the public had a right to see it. So, he put it into the Civil War Times Illustrated, a monthly magazine, with an article based on Alexander Baillie Kell, the younger brother. This had been published in 1988. The book that I was holding was a recent compilation of magazine articles from Civil War Times Illustrated and luckily the editors had selected the article and the picture for inclusion in the book.

I shall thank them, Dr Delaney especially, and the editors and the publishers, to my dying day for without that one image my whole story would not have come to light. For now the Matrix had turned up the vital piece of evidence I needed. This was the crucial piece of evidence. I had been searching for this in order to make sense of my life. Up to now the Intelligent Universe which was the title of my thesis and my researches and investigations, had all been very third person. But now it had become personal. It had become very personal and I was absolutely ecstatic, thrilled. This for me was vindication.

I never quite realized how this photograph would change my life. At the time it was just the icing on the cake. Since then it has had profound ramifications in changing my life totally, especially the way I look at things, and especially my career and my belief systems and my fortunes. For this was the absolute turning point. With the discovery of the photograph I had regained my lost confidence. From being uncertain throughout most of my life, I was now 100% sure. This to me was worth more than gold.

I could hardly believe it. I was in possession of the Holy Grail. I read and re-read the description. After reading the description three or four times I realized that every facet, every single facet, line and detail of the description was me.

Alexander Baillie Kell was born on a plantation in Darien, Georgia. I knew where Georgia was, but where the heck was Darien? I looked at the map. I looked instinctively at Atlanta and found Darien wasn't there. I then looked at the index and discovered that Darien was actually on the coast. I hadn't even realized Georgia had a coast. Most people are not aware that Georgia has a 100-mile coastline between Florida and South Carolina. There it was, smack bang in the middle, Darien.

I then read through the description. He was born on a plantation. He had sisters. He had gone to the Kentucky Military Institute - straightaway I thought of my War games. He had gone to Princeton, the university. I had gone to university. He was a high-toned Georgia gentleman. I had always fancied myself as a high-toned English gentleman, despite being born to a working class family - although my father was somewhat exceptional, we were none the less working class. I had always aspired to being a country gentleman. The description fitted perfectly, like a glove. He had tried to run the plantation. I had gone to Newcastle University and I had studied agriculture. Agricultural Zoology, a similar sort of calling. He had fought in the Civil War as a Confederate cavalryman for the 5th Georgia Volunteer Cavalry. I had re-enacted the Civil War as a cavalryman for the 43rd Virginia Cavalry. I could no more stick a Yankee jacket on than die! I had always had to be cavalry and I had always had to be Confederate, always gray and yellow. There was no way I was going to be a Yankee conscript.

He had survived the war. That was nice to know. I had always thought that perhaps if I did have a past-life memory, I might have been killed and that was perhaps the reason I remembered it, because it was all so emotional. I was right about the emotional bit, but I hadn't been killed, I had survived the war. His fiancée dumped him. Oh dear, that didn't sound too good. He became lonely and unsettled. Oh dear!

And didn't get married. He worked on the railway. I had worked on the railway. I had a model of an American Baldwin steam locomotive over my board for the last ten years without knowing why? I had always been attracted to steam engines. I had always liked steam engines, especially American 440 locomotives. Wow! Beyond coincidence!

He never got married. That's a bit worrying. I had definitely got married and I had made sure I got married. That's stuck in the throat. He had paralyzed feet and applied for a pension when he was penniless. Oh dear, my left foot has had numb toes since I was about forty. Not badly though, it started off with just a tingle in the toes caused by my spinal troubles from rugby, but gradually the toes on my left foot, the three small ones, had become numb, so I empathized straightaway with the condition, paralyzed feet and rheumatism. He died aged eighty-four. Mmm, that's quite good I thought. Eighty-four, is a respectable age. My mother had died at sixty-one and my father had died at sixty-four. Baillie was obviously a survivor, thank goodness. Perhaps that bodes well for me for the future. I often worried about dying young, but obviously if Baillie can make it to eighty-four, so can I. Unfortunately he had died in terrible circumstances being looked after by his deceased brother's wife. This would definitely need some looking into, but there I had it in my hands the next phase of my research.

Pouring over the maps I realized, nobody wanted to go on holiday at Easter, because we had just been on the ski trip, so we had enough money go for a holiday to America again. Then I realized that Darien, Georgia is just up the road from Florida. Straightaway I looked at the teletext and I booked an Airtours holiday to Florida, two weeks in Orlando flying to Sanford Airfield. Obviously we would end up in Orlando, but we could drive up to Georgia and have a look at Darien, maybe spend a week there, even go into South Carolina. My mind was starting to run away with me. I had always wanted to go to Fort Sumter.

This is when I decided, once I had booked the holiday, to hit the net. I was physically going in July; come what may we would go to Georgia. We would stand where Baillie stood and we would see what Baillie saw. I was starting to get my scientific research dander up! This is a solvable puzzle. All we need is some hard work.

So, I hit the Internet. Darien came up trumps. The good old Americans have some wonderful web sites. McIntosh County had a web site! They had the Confederate soldiers listed, and there, sure enough, was AB Kell. Baillie was listed as a veteran. He was obviously one of the sons of McIntosh. McIntosh County were Scots. Straightaway I knew exactly who I was. I had always felt Scottish and never English and I had always felt American. Now we had the whole thing in one go! We had Scots and Americans living side by side. The Scots had become Americans. They had gone to McIntosh County to get away from the English. Hurrah! Suddenly everything made sense. This was starting to be the roller coaster ride of a lifetime and I was on the biggest downhill slope ever. This was so thrilling!

I then hit gold. My Internet trawling came up with the 5th Georgia Cavalry home page. This was run by a guy called Ashley Pollette, whose great grandfather had been in the 5th Georgia Cavalry and was dedicated to the men of the 5th Georgia Cavalry. All I had done was type in 5th Georgia Cavalry and up it came, like a magic lantern. The Internet is really an oracle. It is like a crystal ball. You consult it at every opportunity. A lot of the time the search turns up nothing, but suddenly boom! There is the piece of information you've been searching for. The 5th Georgia Cavalry web site was it! This was Mecca. This was the spiritual home of Baillie. I decided then and there that I would try to repay some of this debt by trying to help build the web site. Ashley had appealed for all people with any connection to the 5th Georgia Cavalry to try to contribute to the building of a web site with any information whatsoever. I didn't know whether Ashley would be ready for me, but I was certainly ready for anything just like a Confederate trooper.

Ashley was indebted to a gentleman called Tommy Houston. I thought Tommy Hooston, but actually it was Tommy Houston, the way you pronounce it in Georgia not Texas, and I was determined to help Tommy and Ashley with their building of the cavalry web site. I contacted them and so started our partnership, a partnership, which has proved very fruitful in both directions. I hope that I have been able to contribute a little to make up for how much they have helped me. We were off to Georgia, bags packed, ready to go. I couldn't wait for school to end. I even had my hair cut short, because I knew it was going to be hot in the Georgia swamps with the mosquitoes and the alligators. I had no illusions of what I was up against, but even I wasn't really prepared for what happened. The whole experience was totally amazing. We were to get a dose of reality big time, and the answer to a lot of questions.

Chapter Fourteen
Some Answers

I was excited. Gosh, I was really, really excited! The weeks were ticking by fairly rapidly and the end of term was approaching. I had assembled the information I needed in one of my black folders, which is what I always do when I have a research project on and it was building up nicely. I had identified Baillie. I had found the old photographs of myself showing that the likeness was an incredible match. I even had fished out my old Civil War re-enactment photographs, especially that classic photograph taken by John Cullis when I was thirteen charging with the Confederate flag, dressed as a Confederate cavalryman.

Thanks to Ashley and Tommy I had a complete profile of the 5th Georgia Cavalry: their engagements, their campaigns, where Baillie had been on his horse and all the actions he had taken part in, how the war had progressed and how ultimately they had been defeated. I discovered on the map where Darien was. And this is where the map started to become quite spooky for I had noticed that down below Darien, there was a place called Folkston. It wasn't spelt the same as our Folkestone, but there it was nevertheless, spelt phonetically - Folkston - well, that was amazing! Our Folkestone in England is spelt that way because Lord Radnor, who owned most of Folkestone in the 1890's, got fed up with the rest of Kent making fun of the people who lived in Folkstone. For they cruelly lampooned the town by making the anagram *Kent Fools* from the word Folkstone, so he declared that in order to stop this happening he would put an extra *e* in the name.

That was quite bizarre, seeing the word Folkston. I had been born in Folkestone and there it was on the map of Georgia, just down the road from Darien where Baillie was born. As I looked to the right on the map I was ever more amazed. There were the words *St Mary's.* St Mary's is a town on the coast of Georgia and the river St Mary's flows through Folkston towards the town St Mary's on the coast, linking the two. I now worked at St Mary's and St Mary's is a coastal village just down on Romney Marsh towards Dungeness, coincidentally Romerly Marsh (sic) and Dungeness are also both on the map in Georgia. But perhaps it wasn't pronounced Folkestone, I thought. When I go there the first thing I must ask is, 'How do you pronounce this?' It was all too amazing, too good to be true.

Upon further investigation I looked down from Folkston and there to my astonishment, were the words *St George.* Now I had gone to St George's School and to St George's Church as a boy. My school magazine had even been called *The Georgian.* It was almost as if the Matrix was having a laugh at my expense. The Matrix has a somewhat delicious sense of humor, one could say. But, that's not all. I was later to find that St George had a very profound significance for my other half. For Baillie also had an intimate connection with St George's Church in Griffin, Georgia.

At the time I just knew St George, Folkston and St Mary's stuck out like a sore thumb. Upon reflection it really was the Folkston, St Mary's that hit my consciousness so obviously, so powerfully. The sledgehammer of irony was at work and it still bites every time I see the map, even now. The Matrix was playing games. This had become very X-Files! Even my hardened colleagues, who were most skeptical about the possibility of me being a Civil War soldier come back again, certainly whistled or raised their eyebrows when they saw Folkston, St Mary's on the map. This geographical link with Baillie was beyond coincidence, far, far beyond coincidence. Yet as we were beginning to realize with this story, coincidence is the norm. In fact I was becoming a little bit immune to coincidence. Even feeling confident enough to make predictions on up coming lines of research, good science indeed!

We set off and with a sense of intrepedation I boarded the airplane ready for Georgia. Life was about to become very interesting. This time I was going to America with a purpose. I wasn't just having a wishful holiday, I wasn't just wishing that I had been American, or that I had been born in America, because I felt American. This time I knew I was American. I knew at last who I was. I had a sense of identity of what I was, of who I was and where I came from. It was a feeling like no other in my life. *I now knew for certain that I had been born an Englishman, but that I had the heart of a Scot and the soul of an American.*

I sat on the airplane on our seventh trip to the States, and drank my duty free drink with a sense of sure knowledge that I was going home.

Pauline and Harriet were just pleased to be going, because Harriet certainly likes Florida and so does Pauline. Pauline hates the cold and the English climate, especially in the winter and Harriet really likes Disney, Florida. In fact all sorts of things about America, especially the fast food outlets, Dunkin' Donuts and the sort of tourist shops one finds near Daytona Beach.

As we landed that usual Florida heat hit us, the warm subtropical air on our skin. I remember looking at the coastline as we came into Florida and seeing all the sand and the rivers snaking across South Carolina and Georgia. We passed through US Customs and Immigration. We were home! I really felt like I was home this time. But passing through immigration had been a near thing. I had my NASA hat on with my American eagle pin; the Immigration lady looked at me a bit strangely, asking 'Have you got any family in the States?' I almost said, 'Yes.' But I thought I wouldn't jump the gun. It would be a bit hard explaining that you are the image of a dead Confederate cavalryman to an officious US Immigration Officer! In my flustered panic I managed to call her Sir. 'Yes Sir, Madam, Sir!' Marine Corp style, which didn't go down too well and I nearly didn't get my entry visa stamped. *I must remember to be much cooler next time!* In my overjoyed sense of being back home I had nearly blown it.

We took delivery of the car it was a Dodge Intrepid; the car is always a major part of the holiday. And we were off, cruising out of Sanford Airfield on the freeway to the coast. We hit Daytona forty minutes later and turned left. That night we stayed at the Days Inn on the I95 coastal route. I was going home. The sense of expectation was unbearable. Just a few more miles up the road and all would be revealed. I could hardly wait. To cool off we jumped into the pool. Then refreshed we had a look around down town Daytona, dined at a restaurant and then went back to the motel. Next day we woke up very early still feeling jet lagged. Straightaway I packed the car I was anxious to get going; despite being early morning it was already 100 Fahrenheit! Jumping in the car we set off on the way picking up doughnuts for breakfast. We always liked doughnuts for breakfast. It just didn't get any better than this.

Driving up the freeway along the I95 through Jacksonville, we drove on into Georgia across the state line and the tension mounted. The places I had looked at on the map started to appear. *Brunswick,* there was Brunswick, so just up the road would be Darien. We turned off the I95 to the left, past the Darien shopping mall. We pulled into the motel I had booked online. This was when the holiday took a turn for the worst as reality kicked in. On the Internet the Motel had looked fantastic, but in reality it was an old motel from the 70's, in the process of renovation. The girls were not too keen. Anyway, I wasn't put off. It was full steam ahead, I had reached Georgia; I had reached home. It was starting to rain a bit, well actually a lot, excessively so in fact. *Rain, on holiday, oh no!* Yes, rain. Harriet was starting to get a little bit fraught, it was gray, rainy and hot not her favorite combination. *We were on holiday, how dare it rain!* I felt like I was in a National Lampoon film. I was the ever optimistic and annoyingly cheery dad, dragging my disgruntled wife and irate daughter on some bizarre expedition born of a mid-life crisis. I began to smile, which only exacerbated the situation. Of course it should always be sunny on vacation, but Georgia being slightly north of Florida, was very hot, very humid and rainy at this time of the year.

There were huge great puddles everywhere, as far as the eye could see. I had never seen such puddles. 'Oh my God!' I thought, 'Did it rain like this all the time, this time of year?' Well, we would find out soon enough. Eventually after the worst of the rain subsided we were able to get out of the car and I strode purposely into the reception area of the motel. The rather nice lady looked at me and in a deep Southern accent said, 'How y'all doing?'

'Excuse me can you tell me how this is pronounced on the map?' I said straightaway without pausing for breath.

She looked at the map and said without hesitation, 'Well honey that's called **Folkston.**'

'Eureka!' I thought. 'Hurrah! It's not just me hallucinating. It is actually called Folkston.'

'Thank you very much, for we come from Folkestone in England.'

'Well, isn't that just a coincidence!' she replied.

'*Yes, exactly!' I thought, 'Absolutely! The Matrix loves coincidences.'*

We booked our rooms and were told to drive around to the back by the pool and choose a room. My wife straightaway did not like the look of the rooms. Harriet did not like the look of the swimming pool either. There was an armadillo wandering around; Harriet not used to seeing armadillos and realizing that the pool was a perfect mosquito paradise became somewhat despondent. Pauline took one look at the room and said, 'I'm not staying here. I'm not coming all this way on my holiday and staying in a room like this.' We returned to the reception where the nice lady said we could have a room upstairs close to where we had parked the car. We went back and had a look, *Nope!* That wouldn't do either. She then said we could have a room on the other side of the block. This third room my wife decided was acceptable. We finally settled into our room and made for the mall to get something to eat; we were all starving. We were relieved to find a Kentucky Fried Chicken, Taco Bell and McDonalds three-in-one place, which was apparently the *in place* to go. We soon discovered Darien to be devoid of the usual tourist activities. According to the sketchy history books that I had read, since the Yankees burnt it in 1863 nothing much had happened apart from shrimp fishing and some timber felling.

Please excuse my ignorance folks - This was before I had purchased a copy of Buddy Sullivan's tour de force, *Early Days on the Georgia Tidewater,* I am now much wiser and realize just how magical the whole place is! This was before I had discovered about Sarah Sallie Spalding and the Sapelo connection. I now know that this is one of the most hauntingly beautiful places on Earth. Made more so by the extremes of heat and conditions. My own subconscious memories prove this to be so. It is Sapelo Island and Sallie that has haunted me not Mary Sullivan, Rocky Knoll and Griffin.

Now to explore Darien; I didn't know what to expect. The Cafe Risqué looked intriguing with its rather risqué drawings on the outside and with the odd big Mack truck pulled up, it was obviously a truckers' paradise! Eventually we came across the Visitors Center and pulled in. This was the Visitors Center I had seen on the Internet and I had talked to Ann Davis, who works there. I had told Ann I would come and see her as soon as I arrived. It really was just like coming home. There were lots of little books. I avidly asked Ann several questions about where the Kells lived and what sort of maps and books I would need. Fully arming myself with the necessary literature, and having introduced myself, I was off on my quest. There was time to have a little drive around before dinner.

Knowing we couldn't do everything in one day we limited ourselves to a small area. First stop on the itinerary had to be Kell Avenue. The plantation, Laurel Grove, had long ceased to exist, not having been burnt down in 1863, as I had thought with the Yankees burning Darien, but having been partially burnt down in 1867 after the war, when it was derelict. I knew from the guidebook that nothing remained, but there was Kell Avenue. As I had seen it on the Internet.

We drove along Route 99 and suddenly there it was, Kell Avenue! We almost drove past it. I stopped the car and jumped out triumphantly. Immediately I was attacked by several hundred mosquitoes and assorted *sand flies, ninja gnats* and *no see'ems.* I hadn't really bargained on this. I knew the mosquitoes came out at night, but I didn't realize that they bit the hell out of you during the day as well, I had forgotten all that. Anyway, I was so excited I grabbed the still camera and asked Pauline take a picture of me standing by the plaque. It indicated that John McIntosh Kell, Alexander Baillie Kell's brother, had been born at Laurel Grove Plantation just down at the end of this avenue. Pauline obligingly took the trophy photograph. Like some triumphant explorer I stood there, video camera in hand, Pauline all the time dancing around trying not to get bitten by mosquitoes. For our mosquito repellent wasn't working, it was obviously only designed for the *whimpish* English variety of pest. It just wasn't strong enough for these redneck macho mosquitoes.

Kell Avenue 1999: Baillie has made it home, the feeling was incredible. I at last knew where I belonged.

Next I drove down Kell Avenue and jumped out at the end where Laurel Grove used to be, Mystic Oaks Drive - that's a nice little touch. Mystic Oaks Drive meets Kell Avenue. This is where the plantation was. Over the road was a large Seven-Day Adventist Church made of brick. Everything in Darien was made of wood including many shacks. This was a large, very fine brick building. A spiritual center indeed.

Driving back, video camera in one hand, Harriet began to look distraught. 'Why are you videoing this Daddy?' The strain was taking its toll. The girls were not happy.

'I don't think people are going to believe it when I get home, this is totally amazing.' I explained. The live oaks with the Spanish moss hanging funereally were like something out of *Gone with the Wind.* The trailer homes added a sense of transience to the place.' Obviously Darien had moved forwards since the days of the Civil War, yet the invisible presence of emotional history hung in the air. The ghosts of the past were there all around. I could see them, hear them and feel their presence.

'Where to next?' I thought out aloud. 'Let's drive to St Andrew's Cemetery.' St Andrew's Cemetery is where Baillie's parents were buried, so I drove along the road and turned off to find the marker. Parking the car, there was a little low rusty gate. The whole thing now looked like a scene from a Clint Eastwood movie. The live oaks with the Spanish moss, the mausoleum-shaped monuments, the sense of death in the air and the mosquito-infested marsh beyond. Destroying the spell in an instant, Pauline said, 'Surely you're not going to video the cemetery?' I had intended to video the cemetery, but I thought I wouldn't argue. As I put the camera away I reverently replied, 'I might be sometime, I'm just going to try and identify the monument to Marjorie Kell, Baillie's mother and John Kell his father.' Thinking it was going to be an easy job.

I jumped out of the car into the heat and the sun. Thinking the mosquitoes would only come out at night just as the vampires of legend, I assumed that if I stayed in the sunshine they wouldn't bite me, if I went into the shade they'd be hanging around the trees, so I kept to the main avenue. The gate creaked open. I walked in expectantly making my dignified entrance. It was like a scene from *The Good, The Bad and The Ugly.* I felt my heart pound. I looked at all the monuments. Surely it would be easy to find an answer. But no, it wasn't! There were just too many monuments. Oh no, I started getting bitten. I started to run. I ran to the left, the mosquitoes kept hitting me, kept biting me. I ran even more, looking this way, that way, to the right, to the left, just like the scene from the film. When I had got as far as the corner of the cemetery, a point as far away from the car as possible, I realized that this was a bad idea and I decided to run, most unceremoniously, back to the car as fast as I could go. Like a bat out of hell I zoomed out of the graveyard, threw myself at the car, undid the door, jumped in and slammed the door. The mosquitoes banged against the door trying to get in, their little *beaks* hitting the glass. Two or three had managed to get in and I had to swat them, much to the derision of Pauline and Harriet.

Harriet was still not very happy. This was not her idea of a holiday. 'Well,' I said, trying to be jolly, 'that's not too bad. Let's go back to the hotel and freshen up. Tonight I'm going to take you to Archie's Seafood Restaurant.' I had read about Archie's in the tourist guide it was *the place to go* in Darien. Well, it seemed like a good idea. We washed up and suddenly, after tea things didn't seem so bad so we drove back into town. It was still damp, still wet. It was now evening and the sun had come out, thank goodness. We had lost the gray clouds. It started to feel a bit more like a holiday. I parked the car, as if I knew what I was doing, outside Archie's Restaurant, which is a brilliant sort of retro 50's style restaurant. It was a real piece of genuine Americana. Even the waitresses look as if they came straight out of Twin Peaks, and cherry pie was on the menu. I loved it! I thought, 'This is most excellent.' Unfortunately Pauline and Harriet have a morbid fear of any food that vaguely looks like an animal. 'Nice touch!' I thought. Harriet could not take her eyes off the alligator's head - it worried her, well she was only ten. Up on the wall was a large sail finned marlin that had been stuffed - obviously somebody's prized trophy. Pauline and Harriet immediately winced again. That's my girls! They've just been brought up too soft in England, now this is what I call real education.

The following day as I was shaving I realized I would have to come back another day. I really wanted to stay, but this wasn't a holiday for the girls; it was a guy thing.

Back into the Taco Bell things brightened up. We had breakfast; the girls liked that. I had tried my best to educate them, but to no avail. So, off we all set, off to Ludowici. Tommy and Margaret Houston live there and we decided that as it was Sunday morning we would go to pay our respects, then head back to Darien and drive on into Florida.

Tommy said, 'You can't miss Ludowici, because it's a one-stoplight town. That's all there is in Ludowici!'

We drove the twenty-eight miles from Darien, through the backwoods. I just couldn't believe my eyes. In fact at one point I even had to stop the car. The countryside looked exactly like Blean Woods near Canterbury, where I had made my Civil War film as a lad, all those years ago. I just couldn't believe what I was seeing. No wonder I had made my Civil War films in those woods. The woods reminded me of this, it even looked English with the present weather, although it was somewhat hotter. It had the exact same feeling leaving the coast to travel inland, except the scale was five times bigger and it was Ludowici, not Canterbury, at the end of the trail.

Eventually we hit town and sure enough we hit the stoplights. Driving over the crossroads, we shot past the gas station and on down the Elim road. Yet I still couldn't find where Tommy Houston lived. Thinking we had gone too far, I decided to turn round, go back and ask for directions at the gas station. Surely we had gone down the wrong road? As we drove into the gas station Pauline was decidedly nervous, for this was backwoods Georgia, like something out of the X-Files. A few folks were in the gas station, blacks and whites. I don't know whether it was my after shave, but everybody certainly looked at me. I thought it best to be honest. So I went up to the counter and said in a very posh English accent, 'Excuse me, could you tell me where Tommy Hooston lives?'

The guy behind the counter just looked at me and said, 'You don't come from round here do you boy?'

'No actually I am from England.'

Then, another local guy buying a sunday paper said, 'Hooston, Hooston, say you're in the wrong county boy. There's a Hooston lives over in Long County, but that's eighty miles away.'

'Well I'm sure Tommy said he lived down the Elim Road in Ludowici, so I think I must be in the right place.'

Then realization dawned, 'Ah, *Houston*, you mean Tommy Houston,' accentuating the *house* part, I had assumed it was pronounced *Hooston* as in Texas, but it was Houston, 'he lives right down the road on the right, about three miles.'

Armed with that piece of information, I said good day to the gentlemen in the shop and went back to the car. Sure enough we had the right road, we just hadn't gone far enough down the road.

Drivng down the road a little bit further I shot past Tommy's drive, to see Tommy coming from his house waving. Tommy lives on Ordnance Sergeant Parkhurst's old farm, twenty-eight acres with a single-story building set back in the trees. Again, the similarity to Blean Woods around Canterbury was most noticeable. I was really excited. I jumped out of the car, shook Tommy's hand. Straightaway we hit it off. A big ol' dog came round to us and Tommy shouted, 'Down Dixie.' Well, what else do you call a dog? 'Dixie Dawg, you're stinky ol' dog. Now don't you jump up at these here nice folks from England.'

He then proceeded to tell us the tale of how Dixie Dawg, a rather attractive Rottweiler, found his way into the family. 'We stopped the truck,' because everybody drives pick-up trucks, big old 4x4 pick-up trucks, 'in the middle of nowhere and the dawg jumped into the truck. We looked around and said, 'Anyone own this dawg?' And nobody owned the dog, so that's how we come to get Dixie Dawg!' We all like animals so straightaway we got on with the dog. Dixie was very, very friendly, although somewhat intimidating if you were not a friend of Tommy's!

Tommy breeds quarter horses and his wife Margaret shows them. American quarter horses are a bit like our dressage horses except more Wild West in origin. We entered the back of the ranch house through the bug screen having made friends with the horses - and a little black colt that Tommy had just bred. Conversation flowed about horses, the Civil War and the 5th Georgia Cavalry. Inviting us in we entered into the lounge where it was nice and cool. The air conditioning was on and the ceiling fan was rotating. Tommy introduced us properly to his son, Roger, and straightaway got down to business. The girls amused themselves while I looked through the family records. Tommy showed me the original photographs of his great grandfathers, Richard Benjamin Middleton and Thomas Weyman Houston, and showed me his gun. At this point Roger's eyes lit up and he said, 'Yep that's my great great granddaddy's gun. It's got four notches on the handle, right there, four notches.' Evidently Thomas had been rather useful with a pistol. Unfortunately he had died of dysentery in the fighting around Atlanta in June 1864. Later on I was to paint a picture of his last journey for Tommy entitled *The Long Walk.*

Tommy showed me his family records and we talked about all sorts of things, from guns to the Church and Freemasonry. They are all very strong Freemasons around that area and Masonry plays a large part in

American life, because Masons founded America. All the original signatories to the Declaration of Independence where Freemasons except only one, Benjamin Franklin. Indeed Masonry played a large part in the life of the regiment during the Civil War. Tommy showed me the saddle that Margaret uses for the quarter horse events, which was a very elaborate affair, a western style saddle with a lot of silver trim. I definitely thought that I must come back some other time, this was all too interesting. I needed to have a longer conversation with Tommy. We write almost every evening with e-mail, but it's still much better to actually meet and greet somebody in the flesh for real.

Roger, Tommy's youngest son was a real Southern gentleman and made me feel most welcome. I felt right at home, all the time everything felt right. Every thing I had ever dreamed about was here. These were my folks, my way of doing things. This was where I belonged. I knew at last who I was and where I fitted in. It was such an emotional experience for me. Several times I was moved almost to tears. After about an hour I presented Tommy with a box of Confederate soldiers, which I had made especially to commemorate the trip and gave him another set for Ashley should Tommy see him. He said he would post them off to him as Ashley lived in Florida. At the time I thought Ashley lived in Georgia. Tommy's other son not at home was Tommy Houston III, an Ex-Lt. Colonel US Infantry. They all worked and lived on Fort Stewart Reservation just up the road, near Savannah and Tommy's son had retired recently from the army and gone out to Colorado to work for a big corporation.

Tommy was a delight to talk to. He explained about his army career. How he used to blow stuff up with explosives and how now he was more into farming, woodcutting and environmental services, especially cleaning up army waste by acting as a consultant. He seemed to have about three jobs even though he was retired. Not wishing to tax Tommy too much with our presence, we left after an hour and a half and said our good-byes. I affirmed that I would definitely return one day soon. We headed on back into Ludowici up the road and then back through what looked like Blean and Thornden Woods, Canterbury. We stopped the car again just to look, take it all in and headed on back to Darien. By then it was about 3:00p.m. in the afternoon.

Before we went back to Florida, we had a last chance to go on into Darien and have a look at Fort King George. Fort King George is a marvelous affair. It is the second oldest fort in the United States. The

British, who invited a company of loyal Scots over in order to make this part of Georgia secure, founded it. The Spanish were in Florida, the French in Mississippi/Louisiana and the English in South Carolina. The English really wanted a buffer zone to protect their settlements, but being the English, they didn't want to live in a swampy marsh which was infested periodically with yellow fever and malaria, so they invited some loyal Scotsmen to do it for them! The Scots were mainly Lowlanders, some from the Lanarkshire area and in fact two Baillie's had come over with the original settlers. The original garrison had to fight with the Guale Indians. They ate mainly shellfish and had big shellfish mounds, which were used for roads and making local building material called *tabby*, a form of cement used to make prefabricated cast buildings. Unfortunately the tabby ruins are all that are left today of many old buildings, as all wood decays and is attacked periodically by termites. Buddy Sullivan the Director of the Sapelo Island National Estuarine Research Reserve, a most knowledgeable and excellent historian has documented the local buildings thoroughly and the full story may be read in some of his many books listed in the bibliography.

The sheer ephemeral nature of the building materials was quite striking. Most had rotted away a long time ago. There were very few original buildings as the Yankees burned Darien in June 1863. The whole locality really is *Gone with the Wind.* It has that splendid sense of haunted desolation, the sheer fact that physically there isn't much left to look at, yet from the historical descriptions of the people at the time we know that so much happened here. The present local Georgian's have done a tremendous job, though, of rebuilding Fort King George so that modern-day Americans and International tourists can have an impression of what the actual fort looks like. This was started twelve years ago and the main blockhouse is now the center attraction. This year the outer walls have been finished and the long barracks. An excellent replica boat complete with bow cannon was nearing completion in February when I visited. I really must congratulate all those volunteers and enthusiasts involved, it is so heartening to see history rising from the ashes of the past, to be enjoyed by tomorrow's generation.

As we parked the car the heat was stifling. Mosquitoes were still biting and we were all generally rather itchy. Expectantly we strolled in to the welcome center and made acquaintance with the Ranger. Everybody was very friendly there. We went into the orientation room and watched a short film about how McIntosh County was settled by the Scottish ancestors of the present *Darienites.* Behind the desk was a gentleman that had been a re-enactor and I had spotted him in the film. He told me how he had been recruited for making the film *Glory*, which they had made down on Jekyll Island near Brunswick. They had built a two third size scale fort from sand. Being mostly descendent from Confederate soldiers they wanted really to enlist in the Confederate Army, but unfortunately the movie people had too many Confederates. They desperately needed some Yankees. Nobody was very keen on being a Yankee, but when the Film Company offered $110 a day plus free meals, they all volunteered very quickly. So you can actually see them as genuine extras in the movie *Glory*.

The film was based on the story of Robert Gould Shaw. He became Colonel of the 54th Massachusetts Regiment, an all Negro regiment led by white officers. Shaw wanted to demonstrate that the black soldiers could fight as well as the white soldiers and on equal terms. In a desperate frontal attack on Battery Wagner in Charleston Harbor, Shaw died leading the assault, along with approximately 50% of the regiment, but although futile it did prove the point. The black soldiers were as good as the white soldiers given the opportunity. *Glory* reflects a true account of Robert Gould Shaw and the 54th Massachusetts. Unfortunately two months previous to the assault, they were caught up in the burning of Darien, much to Colonel Shaw's disgust. Later on his mother was to pay for the restoration of the church in Darien. Both North and South considered the burning of Darien a barbarous act. Many accounts exist of this unfortunate episode and *Darien; The Death and Rebirth of a Southern Town* by Spencer B King Jr. is perhaps one of the best.

Back home we would remember the large sign saying *Beware of the Alligators* because there are the occasional resident alligators, especially in the pond just in front of the blockhouse. Harriet *enjoyed* seeing that and asked me again if they were still there this year. From the blockhouse you can look out over the marsh towards Blackbeard Island. You can also look south towards Jekyll Island in the distance. A branch of the Darien River flows lazily past. The Fort used to be on the main river, but it is no longer due to the forces of nature. In the distance, however, still flows the mighty Altamaha, the major artery of the region.

We left the Fort at 4:30p.m. and reluctantly made our way back to the main road. I thought, 'For the girls' sake we have to go back to Florida.' But in my heart I didn't want to go. Wishing for one last look at home, intuitively I turned right instead of left. I had the idea that I would eventually meet up with the freeway by going north towards Eulonia, which is where Baillie had his plantation called *Rushlands*. I thought I might catch a glimpse of it as we drove past onto the Interstate. It was a last, desperate chance to do something with my quest, for at the time I didn't know whether I would ever make it back again? We drove along the road for about eight or nine miles and then suddenly, instinctively, I just turned right, off the road towards the sea. Emerging through a clearing of trees we came across a rather large and impressive building. It was the Sapelo Island Welcome Center. 'Oh my Goodness,' I thought, 'that is the Sapelo Island ferry! This must therefore be Meridian Dock.' Somehow I just knew all of this; it all seemed so familiar. Sure enough, we went into the air-conditioned building and there was the Museum, Rangers Office, and Welcome Center with all the details of what can be seen on Sapelo Island; only a thirty minute boat ride from the dock.

It was 5:00p.m. on a Sunday afternoon and there was no way we were going to be able to go over in a boat at that time of night, especially when we still had to drive back to Florida. Looking out the window I unexpectedly spied the famous lighthouse, glinting with its pristine new coat of paint in the early evening sunlight. I knew of the Sapelo lighthouse, but I didn't consciously realize the significance of its isolated form at the time. 'Oh look, there's the lighthouse,' I said, 'with its red and white stripes, shining in the sun.' One can clearly see it in the distance through the telescope at the window. It is was just a thirty minute boat ride away across Doboy Sound, so near yet so far, exactly as I had seen on the Internet. The moment past and I turned away. In the end I knew we had to head back to Florida if we were going to make it to a hotel before dark. We hadn't planned to stay anywhere so we knew that we would have to check in and it was a good three hour drive away.

As we were leaving Pauline said, 'I think I'll just take a picture.' Again, I was miles away thinking absentmindedly, just determined to come back some other day. I wasn't really concentrating on taking pictures. But I'm glad she took the picture, because there we have the momentous picture of Harriet and myself standing by the signboard saying '*Sapelo Island Welcome Center*,' which eventually proved to be a vital clue in the uncovering of the story. I was only to realize the significance of this a year later, upon further, much further research and the complete unlocking of my subconscious emotional memory.

Harriet and Daddy, July 1999: Taken at Seaworld, Orlando the following week. The imagery of the lighthouse and Sallie clearly depicted and we did not have a clue that we were re-enacting the story until I discovered the link in May 2000. I have included this picture as it is much clearer than the one mentioned above.

Reluctantly we packed up, got into the car and headed back to the open road. Off we went, back to Florida. Down through Jacksonville, exactly as we had come two days previous. Ormond Beach was the first resort we hit off the Interstate 95 just north of Daytona. We pulled into our favorite hotel, a *Days Inn* and marched up to the desk with a coupon. We checked in, and informed the desk clerk that we would probably stop the week, so they gave us a good deal. Straightaway Harriet's eyes lit up, we had a swimming pool and the beach. This was more like a resort hotel. It was exactly what the girls wanted just to *chill out* after our adventure in the Georgia backwoods and swamps.

Harriet's expression had now totally changed. She was a vision of happiness, smiling away as she unpacked her bag. The first thing she wanted to do was to hit the pool. So, swimming costumes on, we rushed down and jumped in the pool. We swam around until about 11:00p.m. at night, the sky darkened and the crescent moon came out and it was just like a scene from a movie.

A few nights later after two attempts we saw the shuttle lift off from Cape Kennedy as we stood on the beach at Ormond tracking the flight path for a good four minutes. I contemplated my own journey of discovery, from a little boy playing at being a Confederate cavalryman to now a grown middle-aged man, knowing of the photograph and Baillie. I realized that I had come so far on my journey, but even though that journey was not over, I was in possession of evidence of what to me has to be one of the greatest discoveries of all time. Tears welled up in my eyes as I smiled to myself in the dark, then the vibrating wall of low frequency engine sound hit us and I thought,

'YES! BAILLIE'S BACK AND I'VE BEATEN THE MATRIX!'

Chapter Fifteen
Puzzle Solved

By now it was autumn 1999. We had returned from visiting Georgia and our Florida summer holiday. During the summer back at Herne Bay I had sat and analyzed all the events. Certainly Darien was the right place, everything felt right. That was really a defining moment. The people over there, the attitude, everything fitted. It was where I really belonged and I was really happy with my discovery. I knew I was on the right track.

Baillie was the answer. Everything that I had done, ever since I was a small child had been driven by his character. Somehow I had either accessed his memories through my DNA, as he had the same face and name as me, or in fact I really did have his soul memory. As a physicist I was quite happy with the idea that there is no Time in higher dimensions and in fact Time is really just an artifact of our 3-D reality. Therefore I had no problem in accepting the idea that the soul memory is capable of being in more than one physical being. In fact, I was rather pleased with my discovery.

Horses, gunpowder and the Confederate Cavalry had driven my life. But it was at this stage that I was about to be confronted with the ultimate puzzle. At a lot of my lectures many people had asked, 'Why you? Why do you remember?' I had asked myself the same question, 'Why me?' Then again, why not, I suppose. Somebody has to remember. Perhaps my life last time around was in turmoil and such an awful shambles that I was bound to remember? Certainly it was highly turbulent and emotional. But I still hadn't cracked the main piece of the puzzle. Up until this point I was merely playing with boys' toys; the black powder weapons, War gaming, soldiers, the memory of the flag and of the excitement. But I really hadn't cracked the main puzzle.

October 6, 1999 I was awarded an Honorary Doctorate for my work, which had now reached a conclusion of sorts with the finding of

Baillie's photograph and subsequent demonstration of the continuity of consciousness. My work and achievements in the field of Physics had been recognized and I really felt that it had put the seal of approval on my *Intelligent Universe* thesis. I celebrated Guy Fawkes Night on November 5, by lighting the school fireworks display for my twelfth time.

This Firework Night was going to be a special celebration for I really felt that I had come of age. I had returned to my native land of America, I had become American again and I had been recognized as such. Firework Night drew near and preparations were underway. I checked all the fireworks, but on the day in question the weather was absolutely awful. I can quite honestly say that it was the most windy and wet fireworks party I had ever tried to put on. By 4:00p.m. I was checking the fireworks and carefully looking out the window. People were beginning to panic as to whether to cancel the event or not. Twice the PTA asked whether we should call it off. However, I held my nerve, and knowing that the English weather and luck would probably be on our side, kept to our original plan. I was justified in this because by 5:00p.m. the weather was clearing. As I laid out the firework positions, the rocket tubes, the mortar tubes and the static displays, the weather had cleared. By 6:00p.m. people were starting to wonder why we were trying to call it off, such are the vagaries of the English climate!

I then had to try and light the bonfire. Bonfires are always very tricky and normally one has to be very careful. This one was particularly wet and I had to have two attempts at lighting it using kerosene. The bonfire lit, finally, with a satisfying whoosh and, despite the wet and damp, managed to get going. Having lit the bonfire it was much easier to see how to set the fireworks off. As the fireworks went up, I put my rebel kepi on with the yellow cavalry stripe. It really felt quite an honor to be using gunpowder again and remembering Baillie, *who liked throwing fireballs.* When I read that piece of evidence I really started to realize that Baillie must be me! There it was, a little scrap of paper in his Princeton paper collection, *Baillie suspended for throwing fireballs in the entry of North College, October 22, 1849.*

I was trying to sort out exactly why I had remembered. It was still niggling me. I was still hot on the trail and pursuing every piece of information. The one fact that really, really worried me was the description in Norman's original article that, *his fiancée had dumped him when he was forty years of age, seeing in him no promise.* I couldn't really accept that, it really upset me. I thought Baillie to be a better person than that. I knew he was a bit of a romantic fool and he obviously liked women. He had lost his opportunity to marry, but I was sure that it wasn't all, his own fault. It really played on my mind. I considered once again using hypnotic regression and started looking in the telephone directory to find a suitable person to go and see. At one point previously, I had even got to the front door of a hypnotic regression therapist in Herne Bay, only to shy away at the last minute. Because, I thought it would invalidate my results. I really wanted to avoid using one at all costs, if possible, but I was now getting increasingly desperate.

I really felt that I had achieved something. I had answered my own particular question and I had done it within the last year of the 20th Century. I was all set to face the new millennium, the 21st Century, being a new person. Knowing who and what I was and where I came from. As I returned to school I was very happy, but I still had that element of doubt in the back of my mind as to exactly who Baillie's fiancée was? This proved to be the point where the Matrix was to step in big time, because I had found coincidence to be the norm in the Universe. In fact coincidences now were occurring all the time and this was to be another colossal coincidence of unbelievable magnitude.

Quite by chance, on the first friday, as I was walking into chapel I happened to talk to Rosemary Lagrue, Head of RE. I had always admired Rosie from a distance, but I was a little bit nervous of her, as she was a Catholic. I had this absolute vision of her as being the perfect Catholic mother and, as Head of Religious Studies, obviously extremely fervent in her beliefs. What would she make of Baillie the rebel Physicist, with his Intelligent Universe theory? I was to learn very soon that to the contrary, she was the most perfectly open-minded enlightened person that I have ever had the good fortune to meet. Quite by chance on the way out of the assembly I had started talking about the photograph. I don't know what made me talk about it. It just came up in casual conversation. We talked in the Staff room for some time and later in the day as I showed Rosie the photograph, I became strangely quite emotional. I really wanted to solve the puzzle. Why had Baillie's fiancée dumped him? Why had he never got married? Why had he had such an unhappy last part of his life? No man is an island and certainly when one delights in the company of women it seems very strange not to have ended up married.

This was obviously the basis of a lot of my insecurity and lack of confidence as a small boy. Spilling over into my teenage adolescent years and my insistence upon getting engaged extremely quickly to my wife. Also the reason behind my nightly phone calls to Pauline while I was away at university in Newcastle. I was desperately insecure. I needed a permanent relationship and the sense of relief when we finally got married in 1977, had been palpable to all concerned, especially to me. I really felt that I had achieved my goal, it was a big worry off my mind.

Rosie saw the emotional impact of the photograph on me and started to become intrigued. This was the beginning of an amazing six months of revelation and discovery. A roller coaster of X-Files investigation - for Rosie was to become Scully in our partnership, *or rather, Sully, as quite by chance her maiden name is Sullivan and her nickname at college was Sully.* I now began increasingly to envisage my role as Fox Mulder. I had pursued my quest completely alone for twenty years. I had had nobody to share the information with, apart from the lectures I gave and the audiences I entertained, but all the research I had done on my own. There comes a point however, when you cannot research anymore on your own. You need help. You must also have a witness to the grand experiment you are going to perform. For an experiment in front of your self is no proof at all. One has to demonstrate an experiment in the open public forum for such a demonstration one needs a credible witness.

Rosie was to become the credible witness. She was a perfect partner. She was totally opposite to me in every way, she was obviously a woman, she utilized her intuition and her mode of operation was completely based on faith. I am the scientist I have to adhere to the rigors of the scientific method. For a scientist all things have to be demonstrated, have cause and effect, theory and then experiment. Without the experimental proof the theory is of no value. We had developed many fine mathematical theories about the interaction of consciousness with matter and the quantum mechanical view of the universe, but in the end an experiment must take place. Unknowingly at the time we were about to embark on one of the greatest experiments I ever undertaken. In fact it still makes me shake with excitement when I think about it.

The experiment was to be interactive, intuitive and evolve rapidly into remote viewing, using a subconscious emotional painting technique. We became better and better at executing the technique. Eventually being able to predict data before receiving the evidence to substantiate it. It all started off when I produced my annual Christmas card. I envisaged Baillie on his horse approaching Laurel Grove in the winter of 1864/65. It would have been December 1864 to be exact. Baillie returning from the trials of war, was staring bleakly at the once beautiful Laurel Grove, now desolate in the winter mist, in the background was Fort King George. The sketch was based on his sister, Hettie Kell's, original drawing of their home, Laurel Grove. I was very happy with the effect, so happy that I actually scanned in the Christmas card and sent it to Ashley Pollette and Tommy Houston. They liked it so much they placed it on the 5th Georgia Cavalry website, thinking it a fine addition. This was a proud achievement.

The real import of this was only to hit me when I sat down to read Dr Norman Delaney's book *John McIntosh Kell of the Raider Alabama.* Norman was the person who had found the photograph and Norman had written the definitive book of the life and times of John McIntosh Kell, the older brother of Alexander Baillie Kell. I had saved the book especially for the Christmas holiday. Due to the unfortunate English weather conditions the Christmas break is often spent indoors. That Christmas we played our fair share of board games, Cluedo and Monopoly, and it was time to retreat to my own company and my Christmas present to myself, Norman's book.

I was so enthralled that I couldn't put it down. It described in every detail John's life. Baillie made several appearances in the story, which I related to immediately. In every instance he behaved exactly as I would have done in the situation described. With my exact same character and behavior, in fact I related totally to all his actions.

January 2000 came round and at the beginning of term things got very hectic at school. In order to relax a little in the evenings when I got home I started painting pictures of the 5th Georgia Cavalry. This was basically just to say a thank you to Ashley Pollette for creating the web site. The first picture was a rendition of the 5th Georgia Cavalry charging down Aiken High Street in South Carolina. This incident took place in February 1865, when Company I were cornered and decided to break out in the only way they knew how. With a spirited charge down the main street the Company pushed all the opposition out of the way. I certainly wouldn't have liked to be a Yankee on that day!

This picture was well received and I followed it with two of my favorite pictures from the Civil War cards that I drew and painted with watercolors. Both pictures showed the Confederate Cavalry attacking the Union Infantry and in the first case a Confederate cavalry officer cutting down a Yankee private. The second picture was a similar picture with a Yankee being cut down by a Confederate Cavalry Officer. A third was very similar, but I chose not to draw it; it was too overtly bloodthirsty. At this time I had no idea why these cards in particular should be my favorites out of the eighty-eight, but I was soon to discover the answer.

More pictures followed. The next was of Brigadier General Anderson leading the 5th Georgia Cavalry forward. But now the pictures were starting to come from within my head, and I found myself homing in on Baillie. I was able to see the scenes and depict them graphically on paper with the technique I was developing. I was quite pleased with the effect. *All Quiet on the Picket Line* was a picture of Alexander Baillie Kell in 1864, on picket duty. My style was changing, becoming more personalized. In *Boots and Saddles, Sergeant John Smith* and *To the Last Round*, Baillie was in amongst the action. Importantly, I started to identify myself within the pictures and the pictures started to become windows into another time.

I suppose you could call it a form of remote viewing or psychic intuition. I prefer my own term *subconscious emotional painting.* I identified myself in the middle of the picture *To the Last Round,* with my shirt sleeves rolled up firing away at the Yankee Infantry attacking the position, a sort of desperate last stand. Other pictures were *Color Bearer,* which I was quite pleased with, *Watering the Horses* and the scenes of camp life. Then I was inspired by the tale of a young soldier who charged with the colors, the Adjutant of the 9th Michigan Cavalry, W H Henderson was his name. I could see the scene in my head and I set about painting the picture, taking figures from various other paintings and putting them together. Again I was quite pleased with the effect.

It was about this time that we started to understand and get some feedback on the pictures. Just recently - September 2000, we had confirmation of W H Henderson's appearance from his immediate family descendants and incredibly he does look like the person I portrayed in the picture. Even the details of his uniform and his age all tally. This was becoming very real. The people in Georgia were checking the details of the pictures I was painting from my head and coming back saying, 'Yes that really did happen!'

My painting of the cavalry passing a church with the congregation outside was the first to receive definite confirmation. I had seen the picture in my mind's eye, and started to paint it as best I could. I then sent it off to Georgia to Tommy and Ashley. The reply filled me with amazement:

Date: Tuesday, March 21, 2000:
To: Dr Ian C Baillie
From: Tommy Houston
Re: Defenders of the Faith

I was greatly impressed with the Painting 'Defenders of the Faith', and as I studied the work, it brought to mind a very important milestone in the life of the 5th Cavalry. When the unit was stood up in February 1863, they were bivouacked at different places along the coast. Company K, was at Camp Gignillatt in McIntosh County. Company H had moved up to Liberty County. Company G and Company D, Liberty County Units were at Palmyra on Colonel's Island on the Liberty County Coast. The units were ordered to report to Camp Davant near Thunderbolt in Chatham County, and it was there where the regiment first began to train as a regimental size unit. On their way to Chatham County the four companies of the 2nd Battalion, D, G, H, & K stopped at Midway, and worshipped together with the Midway Congregation; the sermon was preached by Reverend D. L. Buttolph. I believe that your painting would be much more pertinent if it portrayed this sermon at the Midway Church.
The church in your painting does not look like the Midway Church. I hope that you will possibly do a painting portraying this event. The Midway Church has great significance not only to Liberty Countians but also McIntosh Countians, because so many men in K & H companies were related to people who belonged to Midway... Jones, McIntosh, Winn, King, Varnedoe, Middleton, McGowen, Mallard, Baker, Norman, Fleming, Way and Devarger, to mention a few. I am sending you a photo of the church for you to use if you see fit to doing the painting. I am proud that I am a Selectman in the Midway Church, and we have church there once a year, the last Sunday in April.
Must run for now
Tommy

Tommy then sent me a photograph of Midway Church. From the photograph I was able to re-draw the picture and produce it with an even more accurate depiction. This picture was so well received that Tommy insisted on issuing it to members of the congregation of Midway Church. I was just happy that people were benefiting from my talent.

Say a Prayer for Daddy: This depicts Pvt. Thomas Weyman Houston 5th Georgia Cavalry CSA, just before he leaves for the fighting around Atlanta.

I then started to home in on the steam train aspect of Baillie's life, painting pictures of the steam trains, wood burners. The two renditions *Last Train to Olustee* and *Iron Horse, Iron Men* were very well received. It was at this point that even Tommy started to sit up and take notice saying, 'I guess you must have been there, because I can't see how you can paint these things so accurately, with the atmosphere and the feel, without having actually been there.' The people in Georgia were starting to become more interested in my work and beginning to realize that my interest in the web site was rather unique.

At this time Tommy told me about his great-grandfather, Thomas Weyman Houston, and of the last day he spent with his family. At the time Tommy's father was aged five. Together they walked all the way from their little farmstead, six miles to the nearest railhead. Two months later he died during the siege of Atlanta. So I painted a little picture entitled *The Long Walk* for Tommy to commemorate the event, just a way of saying thank-you to the folks. I was quite happy with the effect, but wanting to do a better one my next painting was *Say a Prayer for Daddy* in which I tried to capture the religious aspect of the cause.

I was becoming more and more immersed in painting using the *subconscious emotional painting* technique. But the decision to show Rosie the pictures was to take things on to an even higher dimension, quite literally. It was a meeting of minds just the right combination to create an interaction. Rosie is very intuitive. By using her emotion and intuition, I was able to add further details to my pictures and recollections. She was starting to draw my soul memory out and put it under the microscope so that we could analyze it. This was very much a two-way process and for the first time in my entire quest of twenty years I had a partner, and a very valuable partner at that.

The next picture I painted was *Duty Calls.* It was based on Baillie saying goodbye to his mother. I was very pleased with the painting. This was very atmospheric and described the scene perfectly. I depicted one of the black slaves holding Baillie's horse. Sure enough this checked out. I was told by e-mail that Baillie did indeed have a groom called Jim. So Jim would have been holding his horse and looking after it. The two girls in the picture were meant to depict Hettie and Mary Kell. Evelyn being married to Charles had long since left the plantation. So Baillie was saying goodbye to his mother, Mary and Hettie standing close by. The picnic hamper on the floor showed that they had packed provisions. All of the details were later confirmed. It was almost a premonition of the letters I was to receive three or four months later from Dr Delaney. Each detail that I had painted appears in the e-mails so I was actually drawing from my subconscious and depicting real events. These were Baillie's memes.

Duty calls: Baillie takes leave of his Mother and two sisters in late 1862. The blonde sister, in the foreground to the left, played on my mind and it was then that I discovered that she was not a sister, but Sallie. The picture therefore more accurately shows Hettie and Sallie with Margery saying farewell.

One of the ladies in the picture started to take my attention. The blonde lady was supposed to be Baillie's sister Mary. She was wearing an electric blue dress. There was something familiar about the blonde hair and the pose that started me thinking about Baillie's fiancée. This feeling nagged me, it was still part of the unsolved puzzle. Why had his fiancée dumped him? And who had his fiancée been? Surely he must have known her? This was a very tight community and everybody knew everybody else. This is the point where Rosie was able to give me the vital focus point for cracking the puzzle. I will let her explain in her own words the crucial moments leading up to the ultimate discovery:

Date: Friday, June 9, 2000:
To: Dr Ian C Baillie
From: Rosie Lagrue
Re: Finding Sallie

Hi Ian,
Looking back on it now I realize finding the identity of the love of Baillie's life took months and more. I think the evidence shows the Matrix at work behind all of this. The Matrix was at work with you and Norman to bring about the find of the photo. Yet Norman selected to do his research on John McKintosh Kell twenty years ago. In 1994 you predicted:

'The end of this millenium will see Science and Religion coming closer together to form a new spiritual world movement.'
ICB C'94

In 1997, our two schools merged to form St. Mary's Folkestone. You became the new Head of Science. I became the new Head of Religious Studies. The alliance formed a partnership at the beginning of the new millenium, just as you predicted! We soon nicknamed ourselves Baillie and Sully after the famous working partnership Mulder and Scully.
The puzzle that haunted you lay deep within your subconscious. 'Who was Baillie's fiancée?' and 'Why had she dumped him?' This meme was buried so deep you were not going to be able to uncover it without the help of your partner Sully. That is why the Matrix put us together. Together we needed to solve the puzzle as to why Baillie hadn't married. I was struck with the feeling that you felt undermined. At the time women folk did not appear in your paintings. There was nothing coming through from your subconscious to give us the bigger picture. In the staff room I probed and questioned you. I raised the subject of the Irish philosopher and socialist William Thompson not marrying despite his love for Anna. Then came about the first picture with the women folk *Defenders of the faith*. I was driving you on to releasing the memes of the women in Baillie's world.
But it was at the end of spring term, the dinner dance at Wards, when the setting was set for the memes to be released. The music and dancing created a moment we were reaching with your paintings. Through these 'Windows of Time' we entered Baillie's world. For a brief moment in time I witnessed you between dimensions. I was instantly standing with Baillie and aware of his memories. Memories of the love of his life settled with me, to be deciphered later. I had

> focused my mind on this one single problem. I was determined to find out about the lost love. And it happened.
> On May 7, 2000 I emailed through the answer to why Baillie had not married. The love of his life had been a lady of status and wealth. After the war Baillie could no longer offer her the life style. Now your memes started to flow stirring memories of the dances, and the tune Turkey in the Straw. You realized Baillie was always honorable. If he could no longer offer his pre-war wealth and status it was *Gone with the Wind* time.
> Days later you had a remote viewing experience. Your memes released the name Spalding. From then on it all started to unlock soon followed by the connections in this life.
> Finding Sallie was as significant as finding the photo. They both had equal impact. Finding Sallie was the final missing clue that made sense of your entire life and its parallel connection with Alexander Baillie Kell. All of your questions were answered.
> This is cosmic, Ian. It is the work of the Matrix. It is a colossal honor to have been part of it all and to have brought about the find of the great lady Sallie.
> Mary Sullivan is humbled in her presence.

Arise humble Mary for you are more than a match for Sarah Elizabeth Sallie Spading, I owe everything to you and you have my undying gratitude and affection.

Prompted by these astounding events my subconscious was primed to surface in a moment of relaxation and contemplation. It was then that we had the big breakthrough. I was sitting in the bath one night, quite tired after a long day at school. It was a thursday and I let my mind go, as you do when you relax, and I started thinking about the problem. Baillie would have known his fiancée. His fiancée would have known the family. Who could it have been? Suddenly in a flash of inspiration I thought it must have been one of his cousins. Now his eldest sister, Evelyn, had been married to Charles Spalding so I immediately thought of the Spaldings as being a possibility. Baillie would have wanted to marry into a family with money and to marry a most attractive, educated, articulate and intelligent woman. There were not too many of these.

Putting my dressing gown on after getting dry I rushed into the study bedroom and took out *Early Days on the Georgia Tidewater* and looked up the Spaldings. Charles had a brother called Randolph and as I turned to the page I was immediately attracted by the drawing of

South End House, this had been exactly like the house that I had been seeing in my subconscious mind since I was young. I could remember dancing. I could remember the tune Turkey in the Straw, Southern reels, a ball in the grand fashion and the long white columns. Low and behold the long white columns were there in the picture! Then I looked underneath and I found to my delight, that the picture had been painted by Sarah Sallie Spalding aged fourteen at the time. She was obviously a gifted artist.

Then I suddenly made the magic connection. Sarah Sallie Spalding would have come over to Laurel Grove as a regular visitor. Laurel Grove was only five miles from Sapelo Island and accessible by boat. The family connections were strong. Baillie's sister Hettie, Sallie's aunt-in-law, was a teacher. Her uncle Charles was married to another of Baillie's sisters, Evelyn. Sallie would have come over and spent time with Baille's sisters. Hettie had also produced a picture of Laurel Grove, probably with Sallie, or one had inspired the other. Either way Sallie was the proper artist. Sallie had real artistic talent. And then it came to me. Here was the link! Baillie was always interested in art, painting and music. The common link had been forged: Sallie was the lost fiancée.

But this was not strictly true as we later found out that Mary Sullivan, 1870 was Baillie's real fiancée. Baillie's love for Sallie had been a most intense exquisite and passionate love affair. Baillie worshipped her, but being only five years younger than her mother, Mary Bass Spalding, he had kept it all such a dark secret. May be a pact to marry was agreed. Photographs were definitely exchanged; a girls first true love is always the strongest no matter what happens after! He would have to have made a superhuman effort though to convince Sallie's protective mother of his real intentions of marriage. In the end this was the dark and fearful secret Baillie took to his grave and this was the real reason why none of this was ever mentioned in correspondence between the family - How utterly romantic!

I then imagined what Sallie looked like and suddenly everything came into view. Sallie would have been blonde, just like the figure in my picture. She would have been seventeen in 1861. She would have been beautiful, articulate and intelligent. Baillie would have watched her growing up. Her father, Randolph, who liked a good time and was a little bit fond of the drink, had thrown very expensive parties ever since his father had died in 1851. Baillie had attended those parties. This would have been very much part of his social life and calendar.

These would have been the most wonderful times he ever had and all the time the young Sarah Sallie Spalding was growing up. As a young girl Sallie would have attended the balls and the parties. But by 1860 she had grown into a beautiful young woman and now Baillie had fallen utterly and hopelessly in love with the devastatingly beautiful Sarah *Sallie* Spalding.

I confided my intuition and insight to Rosie. Showing her the picture she confirmed that everything about this felt right. Baillie was in love with Sarah *Sallie* Spalding. I then started to realize that I had known this story all my life. Now came the challenge of trying to unlock my subconscious by painting what Sarah *Sallie* Spalding looked like.

I thought back to Summer 1999, when we went to Georgia and then to Florida and to one night in Old Town where my own daughter, Harriet, Pauline and I decided to have a photograph taken dressed in Civil War, Southern style. I had always wanted to try and capture those times again in photographs. In 1997, we had tried to get the image right at Chessington World of Adventures. We were pleased with the photograph. It looked quite authentic. This time entering the Old Town photographic studio in Kissimmee on US 192, I was determined that I should break the mould and be a Yankee. The girls of course would be Southern belles in their crinoline dresses. It was late, 10:30 at night. The girls went off to get changed. The photographer then asked me what I would like to be. Suddenly without pause for thought I found myself saying, 'a Confederate Cavalry Officer'. I had had my mind fixed on being a Yankee, but instead I said 'a Confederate Cavalry Officer'. My subconscious was in control!

I set about putting the uniform on. I wasn't very happy with it. It wasn't a particularly accurate one apart from the boots. I was busy putting them on and examining them when a vision caught my eye; a vision that is forever fixed in my memory. Harriet walked in from the right. The light was dim. She was wearing an electric blue, *Southern belle dress* with a parasol and large hat. Around her neck she wore a small pearl necklace with a red heart. I literally lost my breath. My wife had followed on, but my eyes were on the electric blue dress, the color that I had always liked my wife in. Now Harriet was wearing it and looking so grown up.

We had the photographs developed to take home with us. I kept the best one framed on my desk. The image of Harriet had such an impact on me, but why? As I turned everything over in my mind the answer leapt out at me. Of course, dressed as a Southern belle, my own daughter Harriet was the image of Sarah *Sallie* Spalding. Harriet actually looked exactly like Sarah *Sallie* Spalding! Remember this was all in my subconscious, bleeding through into my conscious all the time. I set about putting it down on paper. I used Sallie's own picture of South End as the background and I drew Harriet in the electric blue dress in the foreground. On the floor I put a Confederate Cavalry jacket, signifying that Baillie was somewhere around in the picture. I painted the picture most obsessively, with attention to detail. I really was homing in on the real *Sallie*. The effect was quite magical and as I showed the picture to Rosie the next day tears welled up in my eyes. I really had captured Sarah *Sallie* Spalding on paper. At this time I had no idea what Sarah *Sallie* Spalding looked like, apart from in my own mind, but I was pretty sure this was accurate. I then started analyzing my own relationship with my wife and started to realize that this was exactly why I had fallen for her - it was the blonde hair. Looking back at my life I realized that the obsession with young ladies with blonde hair had run as a constant theme.

It was Pauline's blonde hair that had attracted me to her and the blonde hair motif came into view. Next I then realized, with Rosie's help, that the photograph was very important. We realized why the photograph had been taken. It was a very special photograph and obviously cost a lot of money. It was a proper portrait. This picture had been taken specifically for Sallie Spalding. Baillie had wanted desperately to marry Sallie and he was afraid that she would forget him while he was away, so as a keepsake he had had the photograph produced for her.

Excited, I painted two more pictures. *The Proposal,* which was Baillie leaving Sallie, asking her to marry him after the war was over, as she went away to Milledgeville and safety, from South End, and he went off to ride with the 5th Cavalry. The second picture showed the significance of *The Photograph,* showing Sallie Spalding holding the photograph that Baillie has just sent to her. We realized further and further, as Rosie became more involved in helping me solve the puzzle, that the photograph had been taken with Sallie present and that this was the reason why Baillie was so *shot away* in the picture. He was absolutely head over heels in love with Sallie. Sallie was everything to him. She was behind the camera and he was looking at her while he had the photograph taken.

The Proposal: Baillie and Sallie make a secret vow to get married after the war is over. She will soon head to safety and he will ride with his regiment to defend the honor of his true love and State.

I then realized that there would also have been a picture of Sallie. I had been desperately trying to find a picture of Sallie, subconsciously knowing that there must be an image of her somewhere. I myself had carried a picture of my wife Pauline in my wallet for twenty-three years. It came to me why the photograph of Sallie didn't exist, the photos would have been taken at the same time. Sallie would have had her portrait taken. Baillie would have taken that portrait to the battlefield and he would have kept it in his jacket pocket. Under such arduous conditions the portrait was doomed not to survive. I hope I am proved wrong one day and that we do actually find the portrait, but that was the scenario. Sallie has the portrait of Baillie and because she stayed safe the portrait stayed safe. The photograph was the keepsake.

I soon after realized the lighthouse was very important in the images and started painting pictures of Sallie running down to the shore by the lighthouse. Sapelo Island Lighthouse was right by South End House and Baillie could have seen Sapelo Island Lighthouse from his own room at Laurel Grove. At night it's light would have reminded him of where his own true love lived, just five miles across the marsh. He may even have sneaked away in the middle of the night and rowed over Doboy Sound to land on the beach to see Sallie in a secret liaison. The excitement and the romance were starting to take hold and suddenly we were in a roller coaster love story. The times with Sallie would have been wonderful and Baillie would have remembered them forever. *Emotion is the language of the soul* and this was some thing, which surely was so emotive that it would have survived death.

I painted a picture of Sallie and Baillie by Laurel Grove, down on the marsh, with the lighthouse in the background and one of Sallie running down the beach. I then realized that the little white house next to the lighthouse was the reason why I kept making little white houses. The little white fronted houses were a feature of all my War game buildings. I had always been very interested in those little white houses, even so far as painstakingly copying General Mead's HQ at Gettysburg, which was a little white house. I realized that when I went up at the top of Stone Street (The Roman Road to Canterbury) that the little white cricket pavilion house took my attention, as did the Dunker Church on Antietam Battlefield. The little white house was very important, because that was where they met! As Baillie landed in his boat and ran up the beach to meet Sallie the little white house was in the background next to the lighthouse.

The lighthouse began to play on my mind. Then one saturday a thought came to me, I started to remember that my artwork had a recurring theme running through it. I went up into the loft to find my art, for the lighthouse reminded me of the lonely tower, the picture that I had painted over and over again in my art at university. This was my first piece of spray can art and I was so pleased with the effect that I kept repeating it. On that saturday afternoon of May 2000, I had not seen my artwork for twenty years. I found the artwork in an old trunk in the attic over the garage. Feverishly I brought it down and opened it up, trying to find the picture of the lighthouse and the lonely tower. What I was not prepared for was the fact that my artwork showed the whole story. The story we had uncovered had been put down in paint twenty years previously. I had had no knowledge of this story until now.

I was absolutely amazed. The whole love story, every subliminal image was put down in graphic detail. Every picture told part of the story. By now I had found out a little bit more about Sallie. Sallie had indeed been married off after the Civil War, but poor old Baillie, who hoped to marry Sallie when he came back, was very disappointed when her family, especially her mother, announced that she would marry Archibald C McKinley 1842 - 1917, a lawyer from Milledgeville. He was much more Sallie's age, being only a couple of years older. He was a lawyer and he was comfortably well off. He had managed to survive the Civil War with his fortune intact, whereas poor old Baillie had lost everything, being on the coast. McKinley was his rival.

As I showed the artwork to Rosie and Rosy Norley the art teacher we stood in disbelief. For there in front of us on the lab bench lay the whole story. I hurriedly showed both Rosies all my paintings and we had the whole story. It was an absolute magical moment, conclusive proof that the subconscious mind is capable of translating messages into reality and that this story had been kept for 140 years and now we knew the answer again. This was a pivotal moment. I was just so emotional, trembling, weak, so excited. This was X-Files time, big time.

I then realized why I didn't like the infantry. My pathological hatred of the infantry was nothing to do with the infantry per se, as they were generally jolly good chaps. It was to do with McKinley. McKinley had been my archrival. McKinley had stolen my girl. Baillie never forgave him. I was later to find that perhaps he did forgive him a little, but I don't think he ever got over it. I then realized why after the War, Baillie was so busy getting oxen and ploughing Rushlands. He was trying to get it back into service. Never mind the Yankee soldiers, they were not a problem. They were soldiers just like Baillie. He still had a chance of marrying Sallie. It didn't much matter about the war as long as he married Sallie. Sallie was everything and when he lost Sallie, he lost everything. He was distraught, emotionally drained by the hardships of war and much more importantly losing his one true love to McKinley.

McKinley was a Second Lieutenant in the Georgia Infantry. He had been wounded in both shoulders at Vicksburg. This discovery jogged my memory. I suddenly remembered my favorite figure, a figure that I had created myself. It was of a Confederate officer on a stretcher, wounded in both shoulders! I fished him out. I had painted him ten years earlier. There was no way I could have known why I liked it. I showed it to Rosie and she just couldn't believe it. This was McKinley on a stretcher, bleeding from both shoulders! I was lucky, because the *Early days on the Georgia Tidewater Book* had McKinley's diary. I started to read McKinley's diary and realized that he wasn't such a bad guy. He, too, had re-enlisted and had fought to the end of the Civil War. He had married Sallie, but life had been very hard. Sallie had lost their baby on the night it was born so their life wasn't very happy either. It hadn't all been easy.

Reading McKinley's diary I was amazed to discover a photo. Of course Mrs. A C McKinley was Sallie. Here were two photos of her, both of when she was sixty-eight years of age. There was Sallie, the image of Sallie captured in a black and white photograph. She was a little old, hunched up lady, but in the portrait of A C McKinley and Sallie by the motorcar Sallie's smile and hair were unmistakable. One can see that if she straightened up, put a ball gown on, and went back fifty odd years, she would have been my beautiful Sallie, the one that I had painted in the picture, exactly detail for detail. There she was my Sallie.

Sallie and McKinley: Sapelo Island 1912, Sallie is sixty-eight, but still beautiful. One can imagine her in her electric blue ball gown aged sixteen in 1860, when Baillie first fell in love with her.

All of these discoveries were unlocking feelings of jealousy and heartache. Talking through it with Rosie we began to realize the significance of these life stories replaying to find a happy ending. We realized that one of the things one should try to do is to repair the damage of passed emotional experiences, especially negative ones. So I set about painting a picture of reconciliation with McKinley. In the picture Baillie was giving McKinley a hard tack biscuit. I called the picture *A Hard Tack to Swallow*, being a pun on the biscuit. Baillie offers the biscuit of friendship to his rival, A C McKinley at the end of the war after the Battle of Bentonville. It was then that McKinley married Sallie. The biscuit symbolizes Baillie handing Sallie over to McKinley, though Baillie is still holding the biscuit in the picture. It was probably one of the hardest pictures I have painted. I really found myself having to force myself to do it. Deep down I still hated McKinley and I still hated the infantry; I still hated losing Sallie. All that hurt welled up. Rosie could see the tears in my eyes. This was real. This wasn't fake; the emotion was extremely intense, far too intense to be hoaxed.

In the photocopier room at school Rosie put her arm around me. That was one of those moments. We really had cracked the puzzle. We then knew. I realized that this one story had driven my whole life in every detail. Every decision that I had made since I was born in 1954, was driven by this story, but to a positive outcome this time. This was the reason I had needed to get married, why I had asked Pauline to marry me and got engaged before I went to university. Why I was so insecure in that I had to ring her every night from university. This was the very reason why, when I married her in 1977, I had achieved my aim. I then realized that Pauline was Sallie from the lighthouse. When I had seen Pauline in the fish and chip shop with the two lighthouses on either end, this was the Matrix at work, synchronicity in the Matrix coming together. Pauline was the blonde lady from the lighthouse. I had married the Spaldings who were business people. Pauline's family were also business people. They lived near Minster marshes, Darien is right on the marsh. The synchronicity over and over and over. The Matrix playing games. The fractal map, Folkston, St Mary's.

But all this time I was still painting pictures of life in the cavalry, but Rosie was becoming more and more involved in the story. We then realized that perhaps Celtic people, Scots, Irish with Celtic DNA, are in tune with emotion much more than the practical business type people. Using the emotional sections of our brains we are better at remembering.

The Baillie's 1997: Taken at Chessington World of Adventures near London, this picture shows graphically the happy ending that should have been. Baillie is the Cavalry officer, he has married Sallie and Sallie has had her child. This is what should have happened and yet we had no knowledge of the story at the time, my subconscious memory was on overdrive.

The puzzle was still not fully solved even nearing the end of term it was no nearer being resolved. The emotional intensity had gone into full gear. I realized my art had depicted all this emotion subconsciously. I had pictures of McKinley, pictures of Sallie, I had the whole story. It was all there in minute detail, the images of the lighthouse, everything. I then realized that I had a picture of myself in Ibiza surrounded by blondes of all ages including my wife, on the beach. In the middle of the scene I am making a sandcastle which is the exact image of the lighthouse, with the little building next to it! This was surely shades of *Close Encounters.* Not only was I painting this object from my subconscious, I was making models of it as well, on the beach, out of sand.

We were still not sure of Rosie's part in the story. Rosie was obviously involved in the story - St Mary's is on the map. Then suddenly a breakthrough happened just in the last dying weeks of term. Dr Norman Delaney started sending copies of the actual letters from his original research, that he was only now taking out of his attic after all of the years he had had them. The synchronicity was beyond coincidence. In one letter Evie mentioned that she thought Baillie's fiancée, CMS, was not truly in love with Baillie. *I doubt if his ladye love is in earnest,* it says, underlined. But the fiancée was CMS; it wasn't Sarah Sallie Spalding. The date of the letter was 1871. Baillie was no longer living in Darien; he was living in Griffin, Georgia, near Atlanta. It seems he could no longer stay in Darien. Laurel Grove had burnt down in 1867. In fact, one is likely to conjecture that maybe that had something to do with Baillie having to move away. Obviously Baillie couldn't take it anymore, seeing Sarah Sallie Spalding over by the lighthouse, married to somebody else; it was just too much for him.

Baillie had moved to Griffin, Georgia, he was working on a farm on a place called the *Sully Place.* Suddenly that name started to mean something: Sully is short for Sullivan, which is an Irish name. As Norman sent me the e-mail the name Catherine Mary Sully came to mind. That was the name that came into my head as I saw the e-mail. As soon as I read it I bounced the message back to Norman. Norman researched the archives and the Georgia census for 1860 and 1870 and, sure enough, there were the Sullivans. He homed in on Mary Sullivan aged eighteen in 1870 and her sister Catherine Sullivan had been one in 1860. Surely Catherine would have been twelve in 1870, but she was not listed on the census so she may have died. The father, Patrick, had remarried and Mary was now eighteen. Patrick Sullivan, a farmer, had moved from Ireland... the Irish connection.

Then we knew exactly where Rosie Lagrue fitted into the puzzle. Our Rosie was none other than Mary Sullivan, Baillie's second love, and fiancée. Baillie had had two attempts at getting married, not one, and he had met Mary at Rocky Knoll in Griffin, 1868. He was determined to marry her, but again it all went horribly wrong. The family disliked Mary for some reason probably, because she was beneath their station in life. The Sullivans were of farming stock; not from the higher social setting of the plantation owner's cultured and refined lifestyle. Baillie ended up with no money and the father discouraged the marriage. At least Mary didn't dump him. Mary had loved him very much. Mary had been cast out as she did not get on with her new stepmother, also called Mary. Her real mother Easter had died in childbirth and Patrick Sullivan had remarried. She had worked as a housekeeper for the aged Varner's at Rocky Knoll. Baillie had tried to move in with John and Blanche despite there being little room. He had met Mary and they fell in love. He tried desperately to make a go of farming, but to no avail probably managing the Varner's land for aunty after her husband Hendley had died in late 1868. Upon the death of poor desolate childless old aunty some thirteen months later, Blanche inherited everything. Even her sister Hattie contested the will. This was so serious it caused an estrangement between them. Baillie and Mary were casualties of the fallout. Mary lost a home and Baillie did not inherit a penny despite managing the property. So, the possibility of their relationship being successful was completely thrown on the rocks again.

Now we had the answer to both questions, 'Who was Baillie's fiancée and why had she dumped him?' Lack of money was the very road to ruin with regard to both Baillie's relationships. If he had concentrated more on money he would have had the wherewithal to have had a successful relationship. But then again, perhaps I wouldn't have remembered a thing and this story would never have been written. One can philosophize that in the great scheme of things it was all part of the Matrix. If we think of our individual physical lives going back throughout history and that our souls are immortal, then we are re-living stories at different sections of history. So this probably goes back to the English Civil War, even back to the Scottish glens. We could see the relationships going back to Scotland, same characters, same faces, and same stories! One of my favorite films is *Highlander*, which has a very memorable Scottish sequence going back to the Middle Ages. I could see Baillie romping down the sides of the glen, claymore in hand, wielding it with both hands. This was the Japanese Kendo I had practiced. I had started Kendo at school as a club. I had wielded the shinai two-handed.

We then knew Rosie, born Rosemary O'Sullivan, was indeed Mary Sullivan. In 1870 Mary Sullivan had received a gold ring on her eighteenth birthday, an engagement ring from Baillie. Just as Rosie had received a gold pen on her eighteenth birthday. But all the plans had come to naught. This was why Rosie had been so involved in the story. In October 2000, we had the final evidence that Rosie was Mary

Sullivan. One morning Rosie told me of the tragic story of the parting of Baillie and Mary at Griffin train station one bright morning in December 1871. I could immediately visualize the scene, see the big black engine waiting, feel the damp steam, smell the wood smoke and feel the brightness of the sun. I started to plan the picture. The next morning I walked into my registration room and there on the desk quite coincidentally was the perfect image of Rosie in an 1870's dress. The book was called *What Katy did next* and it had the Eiffel Tower in the background. 'That's it!' I thought and borrowed the book to make a sketch for the painting. Later in the day I asked Rosie what color the dress should be and she replied that it should be blue, 'perfect' I thought. That night I produced the drawing and showed it to Rosie the next day. Without hesitation she said, 'Oh my God that's my wedding dress!'

The day after she brought her wedding photographs in and sure enough the dress was identical with the exception that the dress was cut with less material and in white. In 1982, Rosie had designed the dress and accessories from memory, an image from her mind, but at the time she had no idea why it had to be that design. She then realized that she had been the architect of the wedding fulfilling the subconscious desires of 100 years previous. For me it was the perfect proof of the validity of her identity. She had acted the same way as I had; she needed to get married as I had, to correct the past. The experiment had been repeated. Subconscious emotional memory had been re-enacted.

This was what we had come together to unlock. This was the mission. We were both involved. Folkston and St Mary's on the map, the merger of the two schools, the coming together, the process by which we unlocked the puzzle. We lived through it. The emotion was incredible as we decoded the story, piece by piece. I told Pauline about the pictures and explained it to Harriet. They were very flattered, but not totally convinced of my story. But then again, Baillie is a Celt and Celtic people are much more emotional. You have to have emotion to translate the story into reality. The story has a life of its own.

As term ended I donned my Confederate uniform that I had had made for my prospective book. It seemed only fitting that I asked Rosie to take the photographs, because Sallie had been there when Baillie had his photograph taken. Now Mary Sullivan would be there, taking the photographs of Baillie on the horse. We had completed the circle.

In an almost mystical ceremony we came together to take the

photographs. First of all shots in the Science Lab, Baillie in uniform. Then we moved out to the countryside to Claudia, my favorite horse, who just happens to be blonde and I rode to Denge Woods. The pictures were amazing. It was as though Don Troiani's paintings had come to life. The accuracy of the uniform, the weapons and the horse were all there. This was just so real, a breath away in time. It was an appointment with destiny. We had come together and solved the puzzle, despite all the odds. Nothing would be the same again. I realized then that we had a tremendous story; *the Matrix meets Gone with the Wind crossed the X-Files!*

But the horses and the gunpowder had merely been one aspect of the story, the real deep-seated meaning of why me? Why did I remember? Why this terrible unfulfilled love story that happened twice - in the words of Dr Delaney, 'How many put-downs can a poor guy take?' Not only did his family put him down and his brother put him down, but he lost both his fiancées as well. And he lost the war. No wonder I remembered it. Who wouldn't! It all had been solved.

The Lone horseman: Baillie with Claudia on picket duty, Denge Woods near Canterbury, Kent, July 2000.

Shoot: The Confederate negotiation position! Baillie rides again, July 2000.

Claudia: A beautiful blonde haired filly! The mystic bond between rider and horse is quite something special, July 2000.

Chapter Sixteen
Squaring the Matrix

On Wednesday January 24, 2001 at 10:00p.m. local time I walked across the tarmac of Corpus Christi jetport, Texas. It was a clear night and the lights of the oil refineries had sparkled magically like fairy Christmas trees as we descended to land through the dark sky not fifteen minutes previous. I was carrying a cereal box and the care that I took with it had amused the airhostess during the journey from Atlanta. Her curiosity piqued, so I paused to explain that I was carrying a very special scratch built model of the CSS Alabama to a very special man. For I was on a cosmic voyage of profound importance. She was so enthralled by the perfect little model that she insisted I show it to the Captain and co-pilot, gladly I agreed, yet I was just steps away from fulfilling my mission and the tension in my chest was palpable. Consequently I was the last to walk down the aircraft steps, but the combination of these events made the next few moments timeless.

In the distance, at the terminal building door, was a lone figure illuminated by the electric light streaming from within, somehow I instinctively knew that it was Dr Norman C Delaney. I had planned this meeting for almost a year and I had traveled an ocean and a continent, the 6,000 miles just to shake his hand and embrace him. That moment was now. Overjoyed I paused, stood to attention, saluted and said, 'The cavalry's arrived Sir!' All of my fine rehearsed speeches went out of the window as the emotion poured forth. We had made physical contact in the Matrix; the circle was now complete. Feeling somewhat like a nervous schoolboy meeting an august academic professor for the first time, I made hurried conversation. He was every inch the gentleman I had expected and known from our correspondence, so kind and eloquent, I was quickly at ease in his presence. It was as if we had always known each other. Calm, yet wanting to say so many things in such a short space of physical time, we strode purposefully toward the baggage reclaim. The tension was so great that I seized the opportunity caused by the wait for the bags to quickly spill the contents of my valise on to the floor. Placing a bright yellow cavalry Captain's kepi onto my head I saluted and explained in one giant outpouring of data, that we had cracked the puzzle.

All Baillie had wanted to be was a Captain, an officer, to win Sallie and be like his brother. Emotionally I presented Norman with the model that I had lovingly fashioned whilst on the beach at our house in Herne Bay, the previous summer and the reproduction Confederate Naval Officer's belt buckle and tunic buttons that I had carefully selected as a fitting gift for the *professor.* The other passengers were totally unaware of the significance of what had just come to pass, after a gap of over 100 years Baillie had been reunited with his brother in the physical Matrix!

After claiming our baggage we walked slowly across to Norman's car in the parking lot. The warm sea air was noticeably different to English cold sea air. I always love the salt taste and smell of the sea, but this had the added dimension of being balmy, a delicious experience for the senses. I felt immediately at home. I was deliberately calm, yet exploding with information that I wanted to share now that we had finally met. Norman was also under his calm exterior dying to hear Baillie's tale, so I related the story from the beginning as we drove to the Sea Ranch Motel on Ocean Boulevard. After checking in to room 138 and despite the late hour, I gathered my sacred possessions onto the bed to show Norman. I had intended to wait until the morning, but enthusiasm got the better of me. The need to sleep vanished. I showed Norman the artifacts that I had lovingly kept all these years. I proudly displayed the historic flag that I had made aged thirteen, the original Civil War cards, original photographs and my re-enactment uniform. It was all very emotional. At one point I jokingly said whilst handing Norman a thousand dollar Confederate bill, 'Here's the money I owe you!'

'It's only money,' Norman replied, 'not important.'

'Yes, it's only worthless paper now,' I replied and I realized that we had learnt our lessons well. Love, friendship, emotion and family, are the true currency of the Universe. *He is John!* I thought quietly to myself.

Our initial enthusiasm sated Roger Lewis and I prepared to wave adieu from the motel steps. Unexpectedly Norman returned from the car, his eyes alight with impish fire, no doubt at the contemplation of the coming week's events. He lovingly produced as if by magic, a box of breakfast things, bran muffins, oranges, orange juice, tea bags and coffee, packed carefully by his wife Linda. The blue and white checkered napkins, cups and utensils showed a woman's touch. Such a kind gift, which we readily accepted most humbly. And with that we descended the stairs and finally said our good nights. The clear air and bright stars of a late Texas evening, acting as a star spangled back drop to the scene; it was absolutely perfect. I eventually got to sleep some hours later, after reliving the events of this momentous day in my mind. For I wanted to consciously remember every detail forever.

Thursday, January 25, 2001

I awoke at 5:00a.m. my mind still contemplating events. Yes, Norman looked a lot like John, even without the familiar beard; he had that same kind, gentle tone of voice. I realized then that I had been directly accessing past memories, whilst in a relaxed state and that I was indeed here to square the Matrix. I could help to complete the Delaney's life pattern. For years Norman and Linda had regarded Baillie as a lost soul and dubbed him *poor Baillie*. They had lived with the haunting image of the photograph, but now I could say that Baillie was neither, *poor* nor lost and that everything was all right. An emotional wave came over me as I lay in the dark - tears welled up in my eyes. They were tears of joy at knowing the cosmic purpose of my mission here and that my efforts would be so worthwhile. I had to do this; they needed me to do this. The synchronicity of the Matrix meant that Norman was John, Linda was Blanche and Steve his youngest son Johnnie. All waiting for Baillie to show up on his horse, out of the blue, just as on that fateful November day in 1864! Well, the horse had been replaced with an airplane and I had traveled over 6,000 miles, but I had made it. 'Yes!', I thought in the pre-dawn stillness, Baillie will make things right, Baillie will make amends and square the Matrix, Baillie will see it through.

A leisurely morning ensued; Norman arrived after lectures at 12:30p.m. He immediately handed me a beautiful e-mail sent by my daughter Harriet, it said simply in poetry, *follow your dream Daddy*. I marveled at the speed of modern communication and that my twelve year-old daughter had been able to send such a wonderful message to me all those miles away. We drove south along the shoreline to the Corpus Christi Naval Airbase, near Pardre Island. We then went back to the Seashore Grill for lunch. Mid way through the meal and completely out of the blue, Norman asked, 'Do you think Baillie really liked Blanche?'

'Yes,' I replied instantly, ' it might have caused a few problems!' I smiled. This had obviously been on Norman's mind for a long time! Baillie had always written to Blanche and shared her tears whilst John was at sea, consoling her at the loss of her young children. John had not forgotten. After lunch we visited the Bay View cemetery and stood by the grave of Colonel Tom Parker, founder of the famous Texas Rangers. Norman delighted in the role of historical tour guide and we savored the local sites together. After the guided tour we went home to meet Linda and told her the whole story. Quite what she made of it all I am not sure. But she was most interested in the family snaps of Harriet, Pauline and our life in England. She was a perfect lady and radiated serenity. Norman is indeed a very lucky man to have found such a gentle and loving partner, much as John had with Blanche.

Just before 5:30p.m. we accompanied Norman to Del Mar College for his evening class. I was eager to see the campus, having only seen it on the Internet. We waited in the library and were amazed to see so many excellent oil paintings of President Abraham Lincoln hanging in every conceivable niche. Over one hundred in fact and our amazement was compounded when we discovered the artist to be Japanese! Obviously a lost American soul compelled to emotionally paint reiterative images of the past. It all sounded and looked fascinatingly familiar. After class we returned home to view Norman's Civil War collection and to meet Steve. I was intrigued to discover that Norman had begun his career aged sixteen, inspired by no less a character than Brevet Major General George Armstrong Custer, the famous Yankee cavalryman. Definitely shades of Baillie I thought! In quick succession Norman produced an *1861 Springfield* musket belonging to his Great Grandfather, Lowell Mason, a Burnside breech loading cavalry carbine and a saber, complete with *wrist breaker* strap made by Norman! I had expected to see just naval artifacts, but here was the cavalry! I was pleased to see an entire Civil War reference library displayed, showing that Norman was very definitely rooted in the period. But the cavalry artifacts, including a standard issue US Cavalry felt hat with yellow cords was, most telling. Then Norman led us to his study and the whole period came to life. The passageway and the study were a veritable museum of artifacts, we all felt so at home. Norman had definitely *gathered his familiar* throughout his life. And all triggered off by an absorbing emotional interest in a flamboyant cavalryman!

Dr Norman C Delaney aged sixteen: It was an emotional and passionate interest in the life of General George Armstrong Custer that had made Norman determined to become a History teacher.

When visiting the Alamo I bought a bargain hardback on *Custer* in San Antonio. Through this book I discovered that Custer had experienced similar problems to Baillie. His true love, Elizabeth Clift Bacon, the only child of a respected judge, was considered to be of too higher social class for him to marry. But when *General* Custer came to call, the relationship was approved and her hand in marriage given. Promotion had won him the toughest battle of his life, that of the hand of his lady d'amour.

Custer was wounded whilst charging Stuart's Horse Artillery in the fight at Culpepper Court House, Virginia, September 13, 1863. An exploding shell killed his white stallion outright and a shell fragment tore across the top of his boot and nicked his leg. General Pleasonton was so pleased with the *Boy General's* performance that he gave him a twenty day leave of absence, which *Old curly* put to good use! The description runs thus and exactly parallels Baillie's dilemma:

> 'If any of Custer's friends assumed he would take it easy those next 20 days, they were dead wrong. As soon as he got to Monroe, he launched the most important campaign of his life. Since November 1862 he had been in love with Elizabeth Clift Bacon, the loveliest belle in a town that boasted of its pretty girls. Her father, Judge Daniel Bacon, was one of Monroe's leading citizens, and while Custer remained a junior officer he had been deemed socially unsuitable and eminently unworthy to marry the judge's only child. But when General Custer sought young Elizabeth's hand, the girl's heart could no longer respect her father's scruples, and melted at the energetic pleadings of her gallant cavalier. Before Custer returned to the army, he and his *Libbie* had secretly pledged themselves to each other. Over the next few weeks Custer pressed his suit through the mail with Libbie's father, and by the end of November Judge Bacon had surrendered. The Boy General had finally been caught - and by a girl in petticoats - he was now engaged to be married.'

In fact Custer had diametrically mirrored Baillie in fortunes, he being the positive, rising star and poor Baillie being the frustrated negative, the lucky and the unlucky. Even the dates of this event are synchronous, for Baillie had his promotion refused by Richmond

September 9, 1863. The exact wording of the above description fits 100% Baillie's situation. It was all to do with that promotion again!

Norman's Massachusetts's Yankee roots had given him a Union bias, but this was not a surprise as John had been a loyal Lieutenant Commander in the United States Navy for some twenty years. Ironically, Norman confided in me that he actually suffers vertigo from an inner ear condition and gets easily sea sick, the Matrix definitely has a sense of humor, one could say?

The weekend loomed and we set off on friday afternoon for San Antonio, a straight drive of 143 miles. That morning whilst waiting for Norman to arrive I walked along to the Railway Hotel just next to ours to take pictures of a large-scale model replica of the *General*, a 440 locomotive; it seemed that the Matrix was at work again. It was a shame that we had passed this engine in the dark, but I looked forward to seeing the real *General* at Big Shanty, Kennesaw, upon our return to Georgia. Upon reaching San Antonio we checked into out motel and then headed out to Bonanza's for a steak. Judging by the high Police presence the restaurant was obviously the hang out for the local law enforcement officers, which provided an entertaining slice of Americana for us to observe. After dinner we browsed around a well-known half price bargain bookshop, and because Roger, Norman, Steve and I, are all teachers, we had absolutely no problem with our evening entertainment! For me it was an Aladdin's cave of Civil War books, I picked up copies of Norman's latest naval book, *Raider's and Blockader's*, a book on Jeb Stuart, one on my favorite childhood heroes, John Singleton Mosby and of course the obligatory book on Custer. It was in every sense a perfect evening.

Saturday, January 27, 2001

This was to be the highlight of the holiday. It was the day that we visited the sacred soil of the Alamo. Norman and I had both played Davy Crockett as small boys and now united once again, we were to stand together on the very site where this historic event had taken place. It was definitely goosebumps time, but strangely I felt very little emotion. Deep profound interest and awe, yes, but as I analyzed the experience later in the motel, I noted that it was the singular lack of emotion that was noticeable. This was in absolute contrast to Civil War battlefield sites, which generate a massive emotional chain reaction in my body. To me it clearly demonstrated my inseparable link to the Civil War. Interestingly, the Kells would have had further cause to remember 1836, for apart from the Alamo, it was the birth year of Julia *Blanche* Kell, John's wife, on January 31, another neat coincidence. Perhaps this had further fixed that important event in the combined memories of the two brothers?

Reunited in the Matrix: Dr Norman C Delaney and Dr Ian C Baillie at the Alamo, San Antonio, Texas: January 27, 2001.

Sunday, January 28, 2001

The day came all too quickly and after breakfast we visited the *Witte* Museum, another of Norman's favorite places. It combined natural history with geography and anthropology, a truly fascinating insight into Texas. Coming from England we found Texas civilization all so incredibly new! We then paid a visit to the cemetery and military museum at Fort Sam Houston, which again proved most interesting, spanning as it does from very early days to present times. I was drawn as ever to the large collection of Civil War memorabilia, which elicited its usual emotional hold on me. We then drove back across the vast expanse of openness to Corpus Christi, at one point I was amazed to

see what I thought to be a female ostrich, but I soon remembered that it was a roadrunner, just as in the cartoons I had seen. The sheer vastness of the landscape was such a stark contrast to England's green and pleasant land; it was quite fascinating by comparison. Norman announced that Linda had a surprise meal prepared for us, as it was *Superbowl Sunday*. The local High School kids have a BBQ bakeoff, where they cook chicken and such for all the football fans that would be glued to the television. After checking in at the Bayside Motel we returned to Norman's house. The meal was a great success and we adjourned to the study to examine artifacts and talk Civil War. Not wishing to fatigue Linda, we headed back for an early night at 21:00 hours. Coincidentally it was Civil War Sunday on a rival channel, so we settled down to watch bits of *Gone with the Wind*, whilst I completed my journal and reflected on the weekend's events.
Monday was occupied by a visit to the mighty World War II flat top, USS Lexington and the adjacent Texas State Aquarium. Norman was rightly proud of the enormous carrier in the harbor. And demonstrated his pride at the links shared by the US Navy and Corpus Christi, with tales of Zachary Taylor's 1845 expedition to Mexico and the explosion and sinking of the USS Drayton in the harbor.

Monday, January 29, 2001

Time was now pressing and I had agreed to give a short lecture on *Cromwell: Our Chief of Men* to Norman's history class. I delivered my own perspective on our much-vilified *Roundhead* and the events that precipitated our disastrous English Civil War 1642 to 1651. Coincidentally many parallels can be drawn between the two events, our Civil War gave rise to the very successful British Army and Empire, just as *the* Civil War has given rise to the present technological super power that is America, with its associate military machine of excellence. I had often invoked the image of the Southern Cavaliers and the Northern Roundheads in my mind. I kept very much on track with the lecture, but deviated in the last dying minutes to my story of *Baillie* and the strange parallels in my life. This unleashed an immediate response from the audience, two of whom were so interested, that I talked with them for another hour on the topic after class. I find that the discovery of my past-life and the emotion it provokes, has this profoundly dramatic effect on audiences, because of this I had sought to avoid side tracking during my lecture. It was immediately after this sharing of information that I returned to Norman's college office to get back on track. As I entered Norman's office I let the video camera run, something I am now pleased I did, for I immediately spied that Norman had strategically placed a personalized *Lighthouse* motif mouse mat, directly opposite his desk propped up against the wall. *Eureka!,* This was the proof that I sought! Norman had subconsciously given pride of place to the lighthouse image, just as I given pride of place in my study to the picture of *Sallie*, together with my flag, belt buckle and kepi. I had previously discovered that the subconscious *gathers the familiar* as Rosie would say and places these objects in direct view of the conscious. Here was a perfect example. I have had many presents from students and most, if not all, have eventually been tidied away. Only the Civil War imagery remains on display, surviving the ravages of time. Norman had been given the mat as a present from an appreciative student. He hadn't tidied the mat away, but had placed it in the most prominent position available! As far as I was concerned it was case proven. ***Norman, like me, held the subconscious imagery of Sapelo.***

Pleased with my discovery we picked Roger up and headed for a farewell lunchtime meal at Landry's Seafood Restaurant in Corpus Christi harbor. Afterwards, we strolled along the quayside absorbing the majestic vista of ships, fishing boats and pelicans in the sun. All too soon Norman had to leave to go back to college. A wave of sadness came over me as I saw him cross the road. He had promised to return to the hotel in the evening to say goodbye, but for me this was the emotional point of departure. That afternoon I completed laundry duty and read the documents on Baillie that Norman had given me. These photocopied priceless treasures had lain in his attic for some twenty years before being retrieved. Now I could see the *Commission letter* for myself, marvel at the *muster card* war records of Baillie, see the handwriting and read the pension application citing *paralyzed feet.* All the while I could feel my own numb toes on my left foot reminding me that, in truth I was reading about myself. A tingle went down my spine.

That evening we said our farewells and the discussion turned to the Georgia Governor's decision to strip the Confederate battle flag from the state colors in the next few days. By poetic justice Roger and I would be flying back to Georgia in the early hours of the next morning. Baillie would be there to lay the ghost to rest. We concluded that love it or hate it, we were now in a new millennium and change was inevitable. I had been previously drawn on the stop over at Atlanta Airport, to a framed collage of the Confederate battle flag cleverly using balls of cotton for the stars and chains for the stripes. It was a very powerful piece of art and it had caused me to think, as good art should, about the Black perspective of the past. With the completing of my mission, I too felt that it was a time for change. *The world is my country and to do good is my religion,* the immortal words of *Thomas Paine* echoed in my head. It was the philosophy that I ascribed to and now reiterated wholeheartedly.

We had squared the Matrix! Baillie had told his brother that he had never meant to argue and fall out all those years ago. That he regretted not being able to apologize before his brother's death in 1900. He told him how much he loved him and respected his sense of duty and ideals. All was put on an even footing as we righted the unfinished business of a century ago and so it was back to Georgia to continue the squaring.

The flight back was tinged with sadness as we flew into the early morning dawn. I knew that I could keep in daily contact with Norman, but that physical touch would be missing. I now fully understood the complexities of this marvelous man and I had touched physical base. As we entered a holding pattern over La Grange, Georgia, I could see the bayous and bright red clay of *home*. I was profoundly aware that I was returning in triumph to my native state. I wanted to immerse myself in the clay, to kiss it, to touch it - so dramatic, so evocative. The dense green foliage contrasting with the bright red soil, it was just as I had depicted it in my pictures. We touched down 09:00 hours January 31, 2001. In no time we had rented a car and headed north to Kennesaw Mountain. This was the site of Baillie's most vivid memory of hauling the cannons up to the top of the mountain and shooting down on the Yanks. I tingled all over in anticipation. After checking in to the Days Inn, Kennesaw, we headed north again to Big Shanty to view the famous locomotive, the *General.* The beauty of the engine had not diminished with time and I was well and truly immersed into the Civil War experience. Later we drove to the Battlefield Park and reached the top of the mountain as the sun was setting. I had that same feeling of being, *just a breath away in time* as I strolled amongst the cannons lining the crest. I had experienced the exact same feeling at Gettysburg, on *Little Round Top*, as I strode between the guns in 1991, the setting sun and twilight combining to induce a mystical connecting experience. I was reliving the past. I walked forward to the edge, held my imaginary musket and took several shots at the Yankee ghosts. It was exactly as I had remembered; the emotional feeling of security was overwhelming. The Yanks hadn't stood a chance.

We decided to drive to another part of the Battlefield, Cheatham Hill. Here the infantry had fought for a week to a bloody stalemate in late June 1864; the trenches not 50 yards apart at a place called appropriately, the *dead angle*. The quiet, the twilight and the energy of the place combined to echo in the soul. This was hallowed ground, consecrated by those that fought and died here in that terrible struggle. The folly of humanity, such beauty marred by violence, now still. In a twinkling it was back to present-day reality as we drove through Marietta's early evening commuter traffic to the Big Chicken! So named for it's colossal 50 foot steel statue of a chicken, which being so large is used by the airline pilots to navigate their way to Atlanta's Hartsfield International Airport. It is now a very different world. I felt just like a *Wellsian* time traveler, thrust from the 19th into the 21st Century. The next few days were punctuated by visits to Point Park, over looking Chattanooga, Missionary Ridge and Chickamauga Battlefield - for Roger and I as Civil War buffs, it just couldn't get any better. We smiled at the knowledge that our respective spouses were probably well contented not to be there! On the final day just prior to our journey to Griffin, we entered a model shop next to the restaurant we had frequented the night previous. I had barely uttered the words, 'It's a shame they haven't got a model of the CSS Alabama,' when lo and behold, I spied a large box on the top shelf. By sheer coincidence there was the Revell model that I had sought for half a lifetime. The Matrix was definitely with me. Now Norman and I, both had the coveted model. With that we drove the ninety odd miles through the backwoods skirting Atlanta to Griffin and another date with destiny.

Friday, February 2, 2001

This was it, the big one. I was in effect going to visit my own grave. The previous evening I had telephoned Alice Blake to synchronize our arrival in Griffin. She had mentioned in our conversation that she was related to Sam Watkin's of *Company 'Aytch'* fame. Coincidentally not a couple of hours previous I had been reading the same book in the museum shop at Kennesaw Mountain - another coincidence in the Matrix. We arrived just after 2:00p.m. and immediately jumped into their people mover mini van to head for Rocky Knoll, where Baillie spent his twilight years. Andrew and Alice Blake both have a tremendously keen sense of history and love of research. A fellow office colleague had fortuitously passed Alice my message some months previous. The colleague had in turn received it from the Reverend Spurgeon Hays of St George's Episcopal Church, Griffin. This was where Baillie had had his memorial service October 1, 1912. It was my initial contact by e-mail with the Reverend that had led to this chain of coincidence. Now I was in the delightful presence of this aristocratic lady and her gallant husband. Events gathered pace as I related the story during the five mile drive north to Rocky Knoll. The tape of Confederate music playing accompanied my tale perfectly, everything was happening completely live and spontaneously. We arrived at the place. Alice had kindly laser copied two pictures of Rocky Knoll and Blanche for me from originals held by a local friend of the d'Antignac family. Munroe, John's grandson can be seen in the photograph with his grandmother. She had further given me a photocopy of a newspaper clipping, showing the house immediately prior to its demolition in the late 70's. It all felt right, the trees, the position on the knoll and the railroad - all frozen in space, only at a different point in time. I enjoyed the crunch of the autumnal leaves from the previous fall. Such a beautiful place.

Blanche in 1861: With the little ones Johnnie, Boysie and Dot Tragically only Johnnie would survive the war with his mother.

Blanche in 1900: Here we see the exact same pose as in 1861, but with the grandchildren. Munroe d'Antignac is on the right. The photograph of Baillie was found when Norman visited him in 1965.

Opposite:
Rocky Knoll 1900: Baillie spent his twighlight years here. John and Blanche can be seen to the left of the picture in the foreground. They are looking towards the Atlanta - Griffin railroad track.

After exploring and discovering the site of the old well and making a short video presentation, we headed back to Griffin. Passing St George's Church on 10th Street, we crossed the center of town and came to Oak Hill Cemetery. Andrew and Alice had found the grave, but they did not let on as to its location. We took a right into the cemetery. I was stunned at the size of the area it covered. As we wove through the maze of monuments I held my breath. Then we stopped. Leaving the van we took a few steps on to the Kell plot. There was John's tomb, emblazoned boldly with the inscription, *Kell - Patriot, Hero, Christian.* A medium sized bleached Confederate battle flag caught my eye and made me tingle with emotion. It stood beside the veteran's headstone that stood proudly erect at one end of the tomb. The stone held the details of John's rank and career along with the awesome name, CSS Alabama. Then Alice said softly, 'And here's Baillie.' Her gentle voice barely impinged on my concentration. I moved quietly towards her, to the next plot over, stripped as it were to the basic grave necessities, this was in stark contrast to John's grandiose family plot. Yet, I was right Baillie had been buried alongside his brother, but not in the same plot! Blanche had taken care of this, 'God bless her.' I stood in silent contemplation. I was not emotional. I was a scientist examining *cause and effect,* I was just so pleased that I had actually made it to this point. The moment passed. I then realized that they had inscribed the wrong date on the flattened headstone, it read 1913 instead of 1912. Poor Baillie, they couldn't even get that right and not the slightest mention of his war record. I felt right then and there that I was here to right this wrong, it was without doubt part of my *squaring the Matrix* mission. But my mood softened immediately, as my eyes were drawn to the left, there was Hettie. Instantly an emotional wave passed over me. 'We are all together,' I thought. The tremble of the lip, the tears and the taste of salt in the throat passed after a minute or so. Then I spied Mary, Baillie's older sister, next to Hettie. This time there was no reaction. Interestingly, it was Hettie that had triggered the emotional reaction not, Mary. Hettie was Baillie's favorite sister and mentor to Sallie. I had discovered that subconscious memories trigger emotions and that emotions cannot lie - for *emotion is the language of the soul.* To deny your emotion is to deny your soul. This was good evidence for that process.

Baillie's grave: Oak Hill Cemetery Griffin, Georgia 2001. My childhood memorabilia is brought full circle.

After several minutes we embarked for the Veterans' *Stonewall Cemetery* across the way. The site is crowned by the Confederate war memorial that used to stand at the crossroads, in the center of town. We then moved to the cemetery office and by coincidence our route was blocked by a big 4x4 jeep. As the conversation started with Andrew I guessed the identity of the lady in question, 'You must be Sherry Husak, I wrote to you some months back!' Before she could answer I was out of the van and talking to her excitedly, much to everybody's amazement. I was on a roll, I knew that it must be her, it was the Matrix at work. She was just about to close up and leave for the weekend. I said that I would like to place some sort of memorial to Baillie, she indicated that I should come back monday morning to discuss the proposal, with that I bade her farewell and a pleasant weekend. It was all working out magnificently.

That evening we drove to Barnesville some 19 miles south of Griffin to stay at Tarleton Oaks, a beautiful *Bed and Breakfast* in the style of the Deep South and home of Fred and Terry Crane. Fred had starred as Brent Tarleton, one of the Tarleton twins in the epic film, *Gone with the Wind,* based on Margaret Mitchell's famous classic of the same name. We were here to experience the ambience of the Civil War period and this was exactly the right place to be. Roger and I both felt slightly out of place in this most romantic of settings without our respective partners, but we were here to attend a cannon shoot the next day given by Bill Lindsey, Alice's brother. That evening we attended a gathering of the Barnesville social elite! We felt so privileged to be invited into Bill and Susan's home and to be welcomed so generously as family. The superb Southern cuisine was complimented perfectly by the conversation, which centered naturally on the Presidential Inauguration of George W Bush. I related my story and we examined the artifacts that I had brought in connection with my childhood. After dinner we moved to Bill's Civil War gun collection and discussed the following day's cannon shoot that was to be held in my honor. It all felt so special.

Andrew Blake capped it all off by presenting me with a print of the CSS Alabama. I had mentioned the coincidence earlier in the day of finding the model and of John and Baillie, when admiring the print on the wall of the oak paneled hall of his beautiful home. By coincidence he happened to have a spare copy, needless to say I was completely overwhelmed by such generosity, what an evening it had been. With that we retired for the night to Tarleton Oaks. Finding Terry still up, I related my story to her. The romance of Baillie, Sallie and Mary Sullivan caught her imagination and time slipped rapidly past. Fred concerned at my remark that Terry had more than a passing resemblance to Mary, came to check on the proceedings! So sweet, in fact they reminded me very much of how Baillie and Mary would have been, had they married. The coincidence and imagery kept on coming - it was the Matrix on overdrive.

Next morning I donned my Confederate Cavalry Captain's uniform and descended the stairs to breakfast. It really felt like, *Gone with the Wind*, everything was perfect, Fred and Terry entered into the spirit of things and after an outstanding breakfast we set off for Bill's. Whilst Bill donned his uniform, I watched as the 3/4 scale Napoleon field piece together with 12pdr. Mortar, were loaded onto the pick up truck. We then drove to the shooting ground on Maggie and Rodney Page's farmland. A host of spectators gathered for the proceedings including a troop of local Boy scouts. I enquired as to what target we would be shooting at. Andrew's son informed me with a smile, 'Why that's a real live Yankee mini van!'

'Splendid, one likes to know at whom one is shooting', I replied in my best English accent.

'Yep, it's even got a Yankee license tag. We plan to take some pictures and send them up North just to scare the folks!'

These are my sort of people I thought and smiled. They can beat us in a war, but they can't kill the Southern spirit of independence, even after 140 years. The cannon shoot using tomato paste tins filled with concrete was a great success, hitting the mini van several times and the mortar even more so. The graceful curving arc of the shot being particularly pleasing to the crowd as it sped towards the target. Bill even allowed me to fire a shot from the cannon. Baillie and cannons perfect, the infantry, cavalry and the artillery working together in unison, as they did at Kennesaw described in Baillie's letter. Our hosts Maggie and Rodney Page, in their beautiful home gave *apré shoot* drinks and generously presented me with the 3rd National Confederate colors, *the stainless banner* as a memento of the occasion.

Captain I C Baillie, CSA: At the cannon shoot, returning home in style, Barnesville, Georgia, February 2001. Roger Lewis captured this jaunty pose for posterity.

What a day to remember. That evening we headed into Griffin for a Southern pit BBQ with Andrew and Alice, which we voted the best meal of the entire trip. Returning to Tarleton Oaks we arrived halfway through the *character evening soirée* organized by our hosts Fred and Terry. Being terribly English we did not wish to disturb the proceedings, which were in full swing with two couples romantically spending their twenty-fifth and fortieth wedding anniversaries at the Oaks and so we went to bed. Next morning I could have kicked myself for missing such a wonderful experience, for I had no idea that they had character look-a-likes from the movie and I could easily have put my uniform on and joined in the action! My embarrassment was complete, but Fred forgave me and I promised to return one day to make amends.

Sunday, February 4, 2001

Brigadier Truman Boyle of the Georgia State Patrol made a surprise visit. Truman had attended the cannon shoot and wished to give us some commemoration patches together with a key ring, which was very much appreciated - such, is the generous spirit of Southern folk. He also showed us his patrol car, a beautiful metallic blue and white cruiser - extremely impressive. After chatting with the other guests in the sunshine we took our leave. Immediately behind Tarleton Oaks was a Confederate cemetery. The Oaks had been a Confederate hospital after the Battle of Jonesboro and a train wreck earlier in the war had necessitated the use of the land as a cemetery. We stopped to pay our respects to the war dead, then went on to visit Alice and Andrew, before checking in at the Days Inn, Griffin for a quiet evening.

Monday, February 5, 2001

The pre-arranged visit with Sherry at Oak Hill cemetery proved a success. As I was able to prove Baillie's war record Sherry confirmed a veteran marker would be placed and paid for by the United States Government. Coincidentally, Norman had provided me with the exact relevant documents. Back at the motel we gathered the documents and returned for Sherry and Carol her assistant to make copies. I could hardly believe my luck, Baillie would finally gain his recognition and the Matrix would be truly squared. After some time in the library, we spent the afternoon in Atlanta, visiting the famous Cyclorama painting, Commissioned by General Logan to commemorate the siege and fall of Atlanta in 1864. I was reminded of my trip to Gettysburg ten years previous with its famous cyclorama painting. It was an inspiring end to the middle phase of our trip, courtesy of Alice and Andrew Blake.

Tuesday, February 6, 2001

Griffin train station was the scene of the emotional parting between Baillie and his fiancée Mary Sullivan. We traveled there to re-visit the scene. I remembered the parting of Baillie and Mary Sullivan on that bright December morning in 1871, as I scooped up a handful of red soil to take back to England. It some how seemed appropriate to take three railroad spikes as a souvenir, there were plenty of loose ones lying around on the ground. Baillie had suffered emotional crucifixion on this site and the three railroad spikes bore symbolic witness to this act of parting. Following this we paid our last respects at St George's Church and then Baillie one last time. We took some pictures in the bright sunshine and then departed for the coast. It was time to try to get to that lighthouse!

On the way we stopped at the notorious prison camp *Andersonville*. A silent chill still fills the air. It was my least favorite place of the trip. After a quick cursory look I was glad to be moving on. As dusk gathered we turned left and headed for the coast via Waycross, but we planned to stay in Brunswick, as it was somewhat larger than Darien. After supper we continued our journey arriving just after 10:00p.m. Checking in to the Days Inn we settled down for the night, the next day I would get to that lighthouse, I was determined.

Wednesday, Feb 7, 2001

We visited Tommy on his farm, I was raring to go to Sapelo, but I soon discovered that we would have to book the ferry, I had forgotten that. After lunch with Tommy and his wife Margaret in Jessup, we drove back into Darien to visit Fort King George. Tommy had arranged to meet Everette Moriarty, his good friend and local historian. Somewhat thwarted, I contented myself with the visit to the fort and was pleased for Roger who had not visited it before. I was further impressed by the amount of reconstruction work that had taken place since my last visit in 1999, the barrack long building was now complete and a jolly boat too, with brass working cannons.

Tommy Houston's Ranch: Ludowici, Georgia, February 7, 2001.

Everette handed me a copy of Buddy Sullivan's latest book, *Images of America, Darien and McIntosh County* in the shop. On page 50 to 51 was a historic portrait of the members of John McIntosh Kell Camp #1032 taken in 1901 - and there was Baillie! I immediately recognized him, Everette was intrigued as to how I could do this and I replied, 'It's easy to recognize yourself! I even have the same planter's hat in my wardrobe at home.' The moustache, the watch chain, the umbrella, the bow tie, the hankie in the top pocket, the pose, it was just like me- no doubt about it. I also immediately recognized Archibald C McKinley to his left and Alexander Campbell Wylly with brother William to his right. Everette was quite amazed as to how I knew their names and I was later able to confirm this as the picture had been arranged in rank order. Both McKinley and Wylly were Lieutenants. McKinley married Sallie and Wylly, although a friend, blocked Baillie's promotion. And there they all were on the same photograph, united by the common bond of having fought in a terrible Civil War. What a spectacular find! This had been worth it. The day was not a total loss. With that I cheered up and we went for a coastal tour along the Ridge to Meridian dock. We stopped at Ashantilly, home of Thomas Spalding, Sallie's grandfather and arrived at the dock. It was there that I learnt that the ferry was fully booked for the next week; the earliest we could gain passage would be on the day we were due to fly back! My frustration was complete, the Matrix was denying me access to the one thing that I desired to complete my quest - to get to Sapelo lighthouse. It was exactly as depicted in my pictures of the lonely tower in the 70's - so near yet so far, just beyond reach. All I could do was to hopelessly gaze through the telescope again, as I had done on my previous visit a year and a half ago.

Baillie 1901: A marvelous find courtesy of Buddy Sullivan and Everette Moriarty. The eyes say it all; Baillie has seen a lifetime of disappointment.

It was now 5:30p.m. and the Ranger was closing the station, feeling somewhat at a loss I decided that we should visit St Andrew's Cemetery to find Sallie and Baillie's folks before heading to Archie's Seafood Restaurant for dinner. We drove quietly back to Darien and turned left to the cemetery gates. I wasn't going to be beaten, I kept thinking of how to get to the lighthouse? The gathering dusk added to the atmosphere of the live oaks and the funereal hanging Spanish moss swaying gently in the breeze. The sense of *Gone with the Wind* haunts this place. The familiar names of all those characters that I had read about in Buddy's book were there, all actors on the stage of life just 100 to 200 years previous. With a shout disturbing my thoughts Roger called out that he had found the Spalding - Kell plot. There they all where gathered around the chieftain, Thomas Splading of Sapelo; the Brailsford's, the Kell's, Evelyn and Charles Spalding, but where was Sallie? Even William Wylly managed to get there! But no Sallie! It was another strange puzzle. Perplexed I left as darkness fell.

Roger and I headed towards Archie's in the car. I was pleased that the alligator head was still there and smiled, remembering Harriet's reaction to it. The seafood was terrific as ever and Archie's well and truly lived up to its reputation.

Thursday, February 8, 2001

We decided to visit the Okefeenokee swamp, the entrance reminded me of *Jurassic Park*. I often say to my students that we can *build* our own dinosaurs, as all you have to do is cross an alligator with an ostrich and you get something that runs at forty miles per hour and bites your head off! Now that has to be worth going to see! The boat journey through the swamp was incredible, especially the mirror effect of the sky in the dark peat water. This combines to give the illusion of floating through space, no water no sky, it just all merges into one. A great bit of physics in action! We saw Oscar the big ol' gator and enjoyed being tourists for the day. On the way back we decided to travel via *Folkston* just to say, we had been there. As we are both from the genuine *Folkestone,* we thought this most appropriate. Roger also wished to cross over into Florida, as he had never been to that State. I was gratified to find the little town of *Boulogne* on the opposite bank to *Folkston* across the St Mary's river. This confirmed that Folkston was indeed named after my hometown - now there's a coincidence. Returning to Brunswick, we had a pleasant evening perusing the local antique shops.

A town called Folkston: The Matrix equivalent of my hometown in England; a coincidence?

Friday, February 9, 2001

We were due to attend the wedding of Tommy and Margaret's youngest son, Roger Houston to Erin on the saturday in Savannah. It seemed that Baillie would get the chance to relive the wedding of Sallie to McKinley in 1866; a further squaring of the Matrix. But this time I could enjoy it and not suffer the distraught emotion of the jilted partner. On the way I called in at the Darien visitor's center and picked up a boat flyer for *Happy Rebel Inc. - Boat trips.* Now there's a name I could relate to! Perhaps, I would be able to get to that lighthouse after all? I called over to pay my respects to Ann Davis in her cottage on the bluff. We had a wonderfully spiritual conversation and exchanged stories about family, life, death, the Universe and everything. Coincidentally she had just had printed the new *McIntosh County Family Cemetery* book. I was able to ascertain that Sallie was indeed buried in the Spalding plot, but that there was no marker. How sad, how ironic, as elusive in death as she was in life, poor Sallie. I was at a loss to know how McKinley could have let this happen, for I would have built a veritable *Taj Mahal* of a mausoleum, in honor of her beauty. I remembered the loving inscription she had placed on her father Randolph's marker stone, how could anybody not have given to her what she gave in life to those she loved. This spoke volumes of McKinley's marriage, it was a marriage of convenience - practical, perfunctory and cold. Poor, poor Sallie, I will have to return to right this wrong at some future date in order to complete the story. Yes, upon reflection, this was probably why the Matrix was preventing me reaching the lighthouse? It is obvious to me now as I write this that I must indeed at some future date place a proper marker for Sallie. Then and only then, will the Matrix let me reach the lighthouse and my journey will be complete. My Sapelo Princess deserves no less!

Leaving Darien with a heavy heart I drove with Roger north towards *Rushlands* in modern day *Eulonia.* Sure enough there were the rushes still to be seen, alongside the old stage road. Heading up Interstate 95, we turned off right to visit *Fort McAllister*, site of another of Baillie's memories. The CSS Nashville was sunk opposite the fort and is clearly mentioned in one of Baillie's letters as awaiting its chance to escape. I enjoyed the large 32 pdr. cannons and the atmosphere was so retro, so perfect, re-enactors had even left the tools of the gun as a photo opportunity.

Fort McAllister: Baillie is back with the cannons, where the historic letter was written dated August 14, 1862.

From there we moved on to Fort Pulaski and Tybee Island, with yes you've guessed it - its wonderful lighthouse. Fort Pulaski was awesome, the pock marks of its rapid reduction by the Union forces in 1862, still clearly visible. This had heralded the end of brick built fortifications. Easily repaired mounds of earth were the order of the day from then on. That evening I phoned *Happy Rebel - Taz* and arranged with him to visit Sapelo by boat upon our return from Charleston, South Carolina, the following tuesday. There was still an outside chance that I could squeeze the trip in before heading back to England on the wednesday. Then we drove to the Crab Shack, Tybee Island and sat outside on the dock around the bright, if somewhat smoky burning wood braziers. The day's events replayed in my head and with the smell of the wood smoke I drifted back to those nights spent sleeping under the stars with the cavalry. But, I also kept thinking of Sallie, tomorrow I would again witness *Sallie* going up the aisle to be married. How would I feel? Perhaps I needed to relive this- part of my squaring the Matrix.

Saturday, February 10, 2001

We arrived on time and took up our places in the Church sitting on the side of the Groom's family. The service was beautiful, we were privileged to be allowed to attend and again I felt very much like a *Wellsian* time traveler. Erin was stunning, her fairy tale dress perfect, she was every inch a princess. Roger the very definition of a Southern cavalier waited at the altar. The service profound and sincere was soon over. The emotion of the occasion so poignant to our quest added that extra dimension. Savannah's elite had gathered to watch a beautiful princess be married to her prince. If the costumes had been changed for crinolines and frock coats we would have been transported back 135 years in an instant. The reception at the Savannah Country Club, Wilmington Island was a grand affair. One could observe the dynastic families nodding their approval at this love match. It was all perfect - well that is until Bridegroom Roger's car keys and wallet got locked in the Men's room and nobody on the staff had a spare key!

After the wedding we headed back for a walk on the beach and some fresh air to clear the head. We were now on the final leg of the journey. We would end appropriately where it all began at 4:30a.m. on

April 12, 1861 in Charleston Harbor, South Carolina. We were off to Fort Sumter.

Sunday, February 11, 2001

The following morning was a bright, windy, sunny, but cold day as we called into Old Fort Jackson on the way into Savannah. The cannon re-enactment was fun and well done. After visiting the shop we headed for the Savannah River front, then on to the Mighty 8th Airforce museum. The exhibits brought back my nostalgic days at the USAF air shows, RAF Mildenhall in the 80's. The museum was excellent and if I wasn't on a horse with my Confederate uniform on I could easily see myself as a *Glen Miller* style US Army Captain with a jeep, not forgetting the evocative music of course! As the afternoon turned cloudy we headed north. The journey there was pleasant and uneventful, but the weather was taking a turn for the worst. We relaxed and took the back roads up US 17, heading for the Charleston peninsula and the Patriot's point, Days Inn.

Monday, February 12, 2001

We headed out into Charleston Harbor to visit Fort Sumter. The weather had turned cold and rainy, the majestic flat top USS Yorktown, moored by the jetty mirrored her sister the *Lady Lex*, but the weather was not a match for Corpus Christi. I thought back to Norman and our happy times there. The tour was still on though and we gingerly made our way across the middle of the harbor, to Fort Sumter. Upon arrival we disembarked. We were glad to get into the warmth of the museum, with its bunker like casement. The Rangers were very knowledgeable and I thanked them for their perseverance under these awful conditions, they responded cheerfully that they were glad that we had bothered to come out and see the monument. I then decided to walk over to the far side nearest the shoal on the southeast corner of the fort and was delighted to see a dolphin splashing in the water. The beautiful creature was just playing at beaching itself and rolling in the waves as they crashed over it, in total harmony with its own environment. The whole display lasted some five minutes, before the dolphin swam off. I was mesmerized, it was a cosmic moment of perfect reflection, as I connected with the conscious Universe and lifted myself above the mechanistic violence of another bygone age. The spell broken, I retired wet and chilled to the boat and thence onward with Roger to the shore.

We then took a ride into town. I wanted to find the address of the reproduction cap makers label in my re-enactment Captain's kepi. It seemed a nice idea and well, we needed to eat somewhere. We found the shop, which is now, an affluent looking jewelers and went to the pizza restaurant next door. Packing up that night, I reluctantly phoned Taz the *Happy Rebel* and cancelled the boat trip for the morrow. I knew, I was beaten - the weather was just too awful and the sensible thing would be to head back to Atlanta.

Tuesday, February 13, 2001

We spent the day on a long drive across the rolling hills of South Carolina and on into Georgia. We stopped for lunch on route in modern day *Aiken*, the site of the historic charge by Company I, 5th Georgia Cavalry, down the high street. This was one of the first pictures that I had painted, which set the ball in motion just a year ago. We entered Atlanta in the rush hour and found the downtown Days Inn. We had skirted Stone Mountain on the way in, due to misty weather and the late hour of the day, declining to visit the monument due to prevailing conditions. Packing up we had a quiet evening, we then decided to visit the *Atlanta Historical Center* in the morning, before heading for the airport.

Wednesday February 14, 2001, coincidentally Rosie's birthday

We visited the museum and the *Turning point* exhibit on the Civil War. I had left a message at the desk for Myers Brown, to say thank you for the information on the 5th Georgia Cavalry flag that he had so readily sent to me in England the year previous. Then as Roger had wandered off, I was standing alone contemplating the static Civil War camp exhibit. When all of a sudden I recognized the haunting lilt of *my tune*, the one I often found myself whistling, *Turkey in the Straw.* The melody was drifting through the air from the speakers above my head. A tingling sensation of emotion came over me as the violin notes resonated in the room. How perfect, it was the Matrix calling to me. Then as I drifted along to the music, I rounded a corner and there before me was the flag of the 5th Georgia! Not stored away, but on display in the Cavalry exhibit cabinet. I stood transfixed gazing at the flag and listening to the music's familiar cadence, my feet started tapping and I smiled a big smile. **The Matrix was signifying the end of my quest, it was saying, welcome home, well done - this is for you Baillie....**

Update: June 10, 2001

Today three o'clock local time at Oak Hill Cemetery, The United Daughters of the Confederacy and the Sons of Confederate Veterans will unveil and honor the newly inscribed head stone marker for Alexander Baillie Kell 1828 - 1912. Alice Pounds, the Chapter President, has kindly sent me the order of service:

Date: Saturday, June 9, 2001:
To: Dr Ian C Baillie
From: Alice Pounds
Re: Tomorrow's Ceremony

Ian,
Enjoyed talking with you Saturday. The weather is clearing, should be sunny and hot Sunday. I am sending you the order of service, so you will know what is going on at 3:00p.m. I will send you a copy of the printed programs when I send the pictures.
Welcome and Introductions:
Mrs. Alice Pounds Chapter President
Invocation: Mrs. Dorothy Galloway
Greetings: Letter from Dr. Ian Baillie:
Dear assembled friends of the United Daughters of the Confederacy & the Sons of Confederate Veterans,
I would like to express my deep felt, sincere and humble gratitude to you all for being here today to honor Baillie at this historic dedication ceremony. Although I am unable to be with you physically, I shall be present in spirit, for my prayers will be with you all at this precise time. Private Alexander Baillie Kell of Company H, 5th Georgia Cavalry, CSA, known affectionately as Baillie was an unsung hero of the Great struggle for Southern Independence. Like so many brave sons and daughters of this land, he unhesitatingly sacrificed everything for his Native State when the time came to call. He was in that respect a true American, independent, tough, self reliant and resourceful.
For the Kell family, honor and duty came above all else. *The enemy may destroy our homes, our lives and our lands, but they can never, never break our Southern spirit.* And so at the end of the day it is enough for us to know that Alexander Baillie Kell throughout his long life served

ever nobly, executed his duty faithfully and acted honorably, at all times.
May God bless each and every one of you for remembering this day.
Ian Charles Baillie

Unveiling of Headstone: Joel Hewitt, Great Grandson of 2nd Lt. George W. Newbern, 4th Georgia Cavalry (Clinch) Co. I
Dedication of Headstone: Mrs. Alice Pounds
Placing of Flag
Tribute to Alexander Baillie Kell: Ronnie Pounds, Commander John McIntosh Kell Camp #107 SCV
Introduces James Fowler Placing of Floral Tribute: James S. Boynton Chapter Members
Benediction: Mrs. Alice Pounds

Date: Saturday, June 9, 2001:
To: Alice Pounds
From: Dr Ian C Baillie
Re: Tomorrow

How lovely! I shall imagine it all happening at the correct time. You are all righting a terrible wrong and giving much needed recognition to a man that gave everything. For had he stayed at home looking after his own interests as his Brother in Law Charles Spalding did, he would have been personally much happier. With wealth intact he could have married and had a fulfilling relationship. He chose to do his duty as his brother did, but it cost him everything. Today we remember his sacrifice for his beloved State as we do all others that selflessly gave their all in the Great War for Southern Independence 1861 - 1865.
I look forward to meeting you all personally on my next visit.
God bless
Ian
'We fought to the end and surrendered in good order as Southern Gentlemen should...Hillsboro, NC April 26th 1865'

And so with this solemn act of recognition the Matrix has finally been squared...ICB 2001

Baillie's new headstone: June 10, 2001. The squaring of the Matrix, Baillie has finally got his recognition. I predict that the picture of Sallie will be in the inside coat pocket next to his heart.

Alice and Andrew Blake at the ceremony: It was only with their kind help that I managed to locate Baillie's final resting place.

Alice and Ronnie Pounds, with James Fowler and Joel Hewitt, Great Grandson of 2nd Lt. George W. Newbern, 4th Georgia Cavalry (Clinch) Co. I.

By coincidence Joel and James depict exactly what Baillie aspired to become and what Baillie was! On the left, Joel is correctly dressed as a 2nd Lt. of Confederate Cavalry and James, on the right, is dressed as a Private.

Afterword

I hope that you have found this story interesting? It is a true case study, which will open up much discussion and debate in this field of research. It is not a belief system and I have merely presented the evidence as I have found it. I do not intend it to be the definitive answer to the age-old problem of: 'What happens when we die?' That question is for each and every one of us to answer in our own time. Many wiser people have tried to answer this and to persuade others of the righteousness of their case; we have even gone to war about this all pervading question in the name of religion. But usually in past history people have lacked the evidence for their fine hypotheses, choosing to rely on faith alone. The difference with my story is that I have the evidence to show that, subconscious emotional memory survives physical mortality. I have formulated my own extensive conclusions and ideas surrounding the evidence and I am happy with my answer to the question. But it is for the reader to decided for himself or herself what they chose to take, if anything from this case history.

Is it all good science? Well I have rigorously tried to avoid the use of such techniques as hypnotherapy in order to avoid criticism from my fellow scientists. I have tried to ensure an open test by using a witness and performing the experiment in public. I have also developed a scientific technique, gathered data, analyzed and drawn a conclusion. It is repeatable and I hope that other readers will be persuaded to participate in unlocking their own *memes* from the closet of their own subconscious. For I am not unique, my personal history may be a little extreme in its emotional nature and color, but I am just an ordinary person trying to make sense of my feelings. I am sure that there are many other such cases out there, which will reveal similar haunting tales by emulating my techniques. It is also my aim that this work will bring encouragement to those people who have bottled up their emotions, for fear of being labeled as outsiders or heretics by the mass population. I have always been a very strong individual and have often argued against mindless ignorance and established dogma. It is the true rebel in me; I need to be different and not to follow the herd. For we can only make progress if we look under the stones of our perceived wisdom into the dark cracks of the abyss of ignorance. We must be true seekers of knowledge and look beyond the illusion of our everyday physical reality in this astounding Matrix that we inhabit, with out burying our heads in the sand of familiarity.

The story continues, for I do not think that it will end for me personally until I physically leave the Matrix again, indeed *the story has a life of its own.* I shall end by quoting the introduction to my history project written in 1970 for my Certificate of Secondary Education. I think that this historical document just about says it all:

> There are so many different things to write about on the American Civil War. I have chosen what I consider to be the most interesting and colorful side of the conflict. I present a profile of the uniforms of all services in the American Civil War. I have cheated slightly, as the American Civil War is my pet subject and number one hobby and has been for the last 5 years. My interest is so deep that I have built up a vast collection all to do with the Civil War, including books, weapons, map (sic), posters, charts, soldiers uniforms, money and flags.
>
> I have become very good at sowing (sic) as I make flags and uniforms. My backing is for the South and I am strictly Confederate in my ways. I am also an ardent war-gamer and specialize in the civil war period I have built up a vast army of hand painted model soldiers and re-fight famous Civil War battles frequently with my six form friend David Pilcher who is also interested in the Civil War. My greatest feat was the completion of my 'Confederate Battle Flag' 3 foot by 5 foot with poles made at woodwork. Also a full size cannon that sits on my back lawn.
>
> I belong to two national societies one is the: Confederate High Command and two is the: Southern Skirmish Association
>
> There (sic) aim is to relive the past with mock battles and dressing up as Confederate soldiers, going to Confederate Army camps and the annual Southern Ball in full officers dress. I myself am a Lieutenant (sic) in the 43rd Virginia Cavalry.

Commanded in the Civil War By (sic) Major John Singleton Mosby a branch of Jeb Stuarts(sic) Virginia Brigade. I could ramble on for hours I am entering my personal collection as models for my project and I hope you will enjoy this trip into the past. I did most of this from memory, and welcome any questions or queries you may have about the American Civil War.

Note. We hold no political aims and views. Signed.

Lt. I. C. Baillie
43rd Virginia Cavalry. P.A.C.S C.S.A. C.H.C.

Well the from memory bit was right!!!

Dr Ian C Baillie June 4, 2001

e-mail: ian@docbaillie.demon.co.uk

Global presence: http://www.docbaillie.demon.co.uk

Appendices

Full text versions of the four main letters written by Baillie follow. I am indebted to Ian Lekus of Duke University, Durham NC, for his help and kindness in supplying copies of these and other original letters from the library there.

Letter I:

Rushland Aug 14th 1862
My dear Sister
Will you forgive me for not answering your letter & thanking you for those nice & usefull(sic) presents you sent me, as camp life has given me such an aversion to writing that it has become quite a task for me to write a letter, except to yourself & other dear friends. Our camp is situated on a river, in a beautifull(sic) oak & hickory grove, formerly, the residence of Mr Morris, an hour & a half's ride from home. I have fine fish for dinner every day and all the other good things that are to be had out of salt water and of all things, that could not have suited me better, we have a quartette(sic) club of singers, in which I take part and I flatter myself that our singing is hard to surpass. Our Savannah members of the company are nearly all of them men of great musical talent.

Mother & Hettie have gone up to Walthourville on a visit to Sister Mary & only hope that they may be persuaded to make a long stay, for it is quite lonely now at Rushland & at Walthourville with the McIntoshes and Bryan's, they will no doubt have a merry time, very much to the astonishment of the Liberty people, who never leave their houses, not even call upon strangers. What favourable news we have from East Tennessee & Virginia, from which, I cannot but think, will arise a divission (sic) and strife amongst the people of the North. I don't suppose you've heard any more from brother since leaving Nassau. May his cruize (sic) on this new steamer be as successfull(sic) as that of the Sumpter's, of which I have no doubt it will be, if she is as fast a steamer as the Sumpter. The Nashville is still lying under our battery at the mouth of the Ogeechee, awaiting her opportunity to escape, and I hope that she may be soon favoured, and once she is out, she can out sail any of the Yankee Steamers on the Southern waters. What an extremely hot summer we are having & most fearful are its effects upon the soldiers about Savannah, though I believe that they are now being removed from the city to more healthy situations along the coast.

My dear Sister I should like very much to see you and the children, but should no opportunity offer itself, I must resort more to letter writing. Confound those orders I say, that took brother back to England, for I flatter myself, that I should have lead you on a visit to Rushland again, had he been allowed to return home.

There is a man of the name of Bagsby that is putting up extensive salt works, which will cost him not less than $20,000 before he commences operations, he is three miles from our camp & I believe he is a citizen of Macon. I expect shortly to go down to Sapelo with the Capt. & twenty men to bring back some of the negroes on the island that have gone from us, & I do hope that I may come across some of ours. I never should allow any of mine, if we should be fortunate enough to get them back to remain three days on the place, but take them right away & sell them. We are to go down at night with muffled oars in three boats; then to reconnoitre the island to find out the strength & position of the enemy if there are any there, before any attempt is made to rescue the negroes.

My dear Sister, with the hope that you will excuse this short & miserable scrawl of a letter, I now end it and with much love & kisses for the children.

I remain Your Affectionate brother
Baillie

Notes:

This is very important, I always spell 'Hettie' with an *ie* as in the Scottish fashion, not Hettie as the rest of the family spelt it. I also did this with Johnny the eldest son of my brother John McIntosh Kell. As can clearly be seen in letter III below; I wrote 'Johnny' (I confidently predict therefore, that if letters of Baillie are found mentioning his brother's nickname, 'Donny' then they will be spelt *Donnie*)

Another point is that I always put the date as month, day number with suffix and year e.g. Aug 14th 1862. I have found it extremely irritating to remove the suffixes in order to edit this book into a consistent modern format. Again I always used to put the suffixes as shown in these letters I to IV. The proof is in the detail, because I

always do the same thing. Therefore Baillie has to be me; it is beyond reasonable doubt!
Reproduced by kind permission of the Rare Book, Manuscript, & Special Collections Library, Duke University, Durham NC.

Letter II:

Camp Davant August 12th 1863
My dear Sister
I received your answer to my note today & thank you kindly for giving me the detailed information about the strings so promptly. Please get me three treble E & one B which is the next largest and the violin strings you may get two of the first and one of the last, which is A on the violin. I do not know what the price of them all separately so I enclose you ten dollars.
There is another Col. Anderson, a Carolinian I think that is in the army at Charleston, but no part of our regiment has been sent there. Should I get into an engagement I shall immediately drop you a line, though I do not anticipate my chances of it at present, though there is no knowing.
Gen. Evans of South Carolina has arrived with his brigade from Mississippi & they are now encamped on the island, but the General's headquarters are in Sav. And as he outranks Gen. Mercer, he will be in command of this department & Gen. M. will take the field. I attended Christ church two Sundays ago and by invitation I dined with the Bishop and he kindly gave me a standing invitation to dine with him when ever I came to church, so I think I shall attend frequently; and as often unless I am taken sick. I must come into town & let him know that he may have me properly visited & cared for. There has been a great deal of sickness from typhoid fever & a number of deaths but I have never been in better health. Our tents are moved out now entirely clear of the stables, which I think will cause an improvement in the health of the regiment.
In going to Cos. Charles' you get off at Quitman about half past six in the evening, where you take supper but Valdosta, ten miles this side is the regular supper house; at Quitman you get in a four horse coach after supper & you arrive at Retreat about eleven O'clock, right upon the road, 11 miles from Quitman. Tell Munroe that Roanoke is at Rushland & he is so old that I have given him his freedom. Tell Johnnie that I will have a pony for him when I get back home. I must now close as I will have to go on picket to Sav. in a very short time.

With much regards to your father & love & kisses to the children, I am

Your affectionate Brother
Baillie

P.S. Do let me know what the violin strings come to.

Reproduced by kind permission of the Rare Book, Manuscript, & Special Collections Library, Duke University, Durham NC.

Notes:
Baillie played the guitar and violin! I play the guitar and I was always breaking the D string (modern nylon wound strings). Interestingly with old wire strings it is always the top two that break, I noticed this in a photograph of an original Civil War guitar. The tune 'Turkey in the straw' keeps going around in my head and I believe that Baillie played this on the fiddle for his comrades around the campfire. Certainly I took up the guitar to do the very same thing whilst camping in my younger days.

The detailed travel information is very much in character with me and certainly the references to supper stops and dining is definitely me. It just goes to show that I don't change my tune!

Letter III:

To the front 6 miles from Marietta june 18th 1864
My dear Sister
I received your pleasant & affectionate letter a few days ago, but postponed answering it untill(sic) rejoined Wheeler's Corps. I am quite well, excepting a cold which is very disagreable(sic), making me feel almost useless to myself & to any body else. I have not been yet to find out where Nath is, as we are on the extreme right of the Army & there is nothing but cavalry here: I was told that the 47th regt. Of which Jimmie Holme is Ordinance Serg. is a mile & a half on our left, but no ones allowed to leave camp out of hearing of the bugle; I am very anxious to see all of my friends in the army, but as we are expecting every moment to hear boots & saddles sounded, we cannot go off anywhere.
Day before yesterday, we had some skirmishing in our front: but our squadron of our regt. was engaged in it, but lost no men our squadron & the remainning(sic) two, held a very strong position upon the side

of a high hill & behind a fence, against which we piled up the rocks formming(sic) as perfect a battery as we could wish & with the Enfield rifle, the best that is in use anywhere, we were spoiling for a fight; upon the top of the hill in our rear there were two batteries of cannon & a line of sharp shooters, but the Yanks were of course repulsed before they reached us.

We left Augusta a week ago last Saturday arriving in Atlanta the following morning; in the afternoon I walked out to hunt up Mr Pinkerton, but did not go far before I met him in the street and my presence there was so unexpected & my uniform such a complete disguise that he did not recognise me for some moments, he took me immediately to his house. Keeping me untill(sic) next morning. I had received a few letters from Mother since my arrival here & mentions not having heard from you, but concluded that you had not returned yet from Griffin. I am very glad to hear that your health is much improved & also that Johnnie is looking so well, but I beg my dear sister that you will not allow the loss of those dear little treasures to affect you too seriously. Tell Johnnie that I will certainly bring him a Yankee pony if I can catch one. I am very much obliged to you for your kindness & will certainly avail myself of your offer if I have the opportunity of being sent to the Macon hospital. I really do not know when the great battle is to come off, but it is thought as soon as the roads become passable, after the excessive rains that we have had. I can hear the booming of the cannon & firing of small arms, but that is nothing at all unusual. Col Anderson has been given command of a brigade & he intends using our regt. for charging only. taking(sic) the rifle from us & issuing us with sabres(sic) and revolvers.

Letter ends abruptly no second sheet available from records:

Reproduced by kind permission of the Rare Book, Manuscript, & Special Collections Library, Duke University, Durham NC.

Notes:
Baillie was involved in the Battle of Kennesaw Mountain of which this letter is the prelude.

Interestingly enough, his brother John McIntosh Kell, Executive Officer of the CSS Alabama was about to fight the famous duel off of Cherbourg France on the next day; June 19th 1864.

I have a complete subconscious memory of the battle described in the second paragraph. This prompted me to build the musket and the full sized cannon when I was 15 years of age! The picture 'Battle for the Saltworks 1864' that I painted from images in my subconscious may be the memory of this action described so graphically in the letter?

Battle for the Saltworks 1864: A direct memory captured in paint six months before the letter was received from Duke University.

Blanche (Julia Blanche *Munroe* Kell) John's wife affectionately called Sister by Baillie, has just lost her two youngest children Boysie and Dot to diphtheria. She was in a state of great distress, hence Baillie's comforting words. She then volunteered to be a nurse in the Macon hospital, in order to keep busy and to overcome her grief. Hence her kind offer to nurse Baillie if he is wounded in the coming action.

Johnnie her eldest son survived the illness and became a Medical Doctor after the war, but tragically died of TB just after qualification in his early twenties.

Letter IV:

June the 21st
I write you a few lines more to inform you that our cavalry had a severe fight with the enemy two days ago, about two thousand strong on each

side, but our squadron was not engaged in it, the loss in the two squadrons engaged was 4 killed & 25 wounded; in the other cavalry there was only two killed & I don't know how many wounded, the Yanks were finally driven back with great slaughter. I enclose you a few dollars with which please get me a pencil for letter writing: you can cut it in half if it is too long to enclose the full length & please send it as soon as you are able to get it. I suppose Nath's regt. is on the left as all the forces are being concentrated there & towards the centre as Johnston is doing his best to bring on a general engagement.

Ever Your Affectionate brother
Baillie

On the reverse side:

Gen. Lee has telegraphed Gen. Johnson(sic) that he has given Grant the most complete whipping of any Gen. That has been in command of that army & our army here has all confidence in Johnston & the opinion is that he will serve Gen. Sherman as he did McClellan before Richmond having retreated over a hundred miles & had it not been for Magruder and Huger, the whole Yankee army would have been compelled to surrender. Do let me know when you hear anything more of brother and send it to H Troop, 5th Ga. Cav. Wheeler's Corps. Army of East Tennessee - Atlanta - Ga.
With my best regards to your father, I remain

Your Affectionate brother
Baillie

P.S. Please excuse the condition that my paper is in which became so after writing the letter & had to keep it in my pocket not being able to get it to Marietta.

Notes:
This letter is clearly written just before the Battle of Kennesaw Mountain, June 27th 1864. The regiment was engaged at Kennesaw Mountain on the 19th and at Big Shanty on the 20th.

The detail about the pocket is interesting because this is where Baillie would have kept his portrait of Sarah 'Sallie' Spalding.

Bibliography

There are so many books that have helped me in this quest, that it would be extremely long and tedious to list all of them. I shall therefore only list those that are directly relevant to this actual book.

Bagby, Milton (Edited by), 1996
Private Soldiers & Public Heroes
An American Album of the Common Man's Civil War
Rutledge Hill Press, Nashville, Tennessee
ISBN 1-55853-688-4

Coggin, Jack, 1962
Arms and Equipment of the Civil War
Doubleday and Company Inc.

Daiss, Timothy, 1999
In the Saddle
Exploits of the 5th Georgia cavalry During the Civil War
Schiffer Military History, Atglen, PA
ISBN 0-7643-0972-2

Davis, William C, 1989
The Fighting men of the Civil War
Salamander Books.
ISBN 0-86101-395-6

The Commanders of the Civil War
Salamander Books. 1990
ISBN 0-86101-510-X

The Battlefields of the Civil War
Salamander Books. 1991
ISBN 0-86101-571-1

Delaney, Norman C, 1973
John McIntosh Kell of the Raider Alabama:
The University of Alabama Press
ISBN 0-8173-5106-X

King Jr., Spencer B, 1981
Darien
The Death and Rebirth of a Southern Town
Mercer University Press, Macon, Georgia
ISBN 0-86554-003-9

Kunstler, Mort, 1993
Gettysburg
Turner Publishing Inc
ISBN 1-878685-79-1

Jackson and Lee; Legends in Gray
Rutledge Hill Press, Nashville, Tennessee 1995
ISBN 1-55853-333-8

Lane, Barbara, 1996
Echoes of the Battlefield
A.R.E. Press:
ISBN 0-87604-355-4

Lloyd, Mark, 1990
Combat Uniforms of the Civil War
Brian Trodd Publishing House Limited
ISBN 1-85361-088-7

MacDonald, John, 1988
Great Battles of the American Civil War
Guild Publishing, London.

McFeely, William S, 1994
Sapelo's People
W.W. Norton & Company
ISBN 0-393-31377-8

Myers, Robert Manson, 1972
The Children of Pride
A true story of Georgia and the Civil War
New Haven and London
Yale University Press.

Schaitberger, Lillian B,
Scots of McIntosh
The Darien News, Darien Georgia.

Sullivan, Buddy, 1990
Early Days on the Georgia Tidewater
McIntosh County Board of Commissioners
ISBN 0-9625808-0-5

Memories of McIntosh
Darien News Inc. 1990

Images of America, Darien and McIntosh County
Arcadia Publishing
ISBN 0-7385-0596-X

Troiani, Don, 1995
Don Troiani's Civil War
Stackpole Books
ISBN 0-8117-0341-X

Urwin, Gregory J W, 1983
Custer Victorious
Associated University Presses, Inc. New Edition
THE BLUE & GREY PRESS
ISBN 0-7858-0748-9

Van Doren Stern, Philip, 1962
Republished as a paperback 1992
The Confederate Navy A Pictorial History
Da Capo Press
ISBN 0-306-80488-3

Wells, Herbert George. 1913
Little Wars
Frank Palmer, London.

Williams, Major George F, 1894
The Memorial War Book
Lovell Brothers Company, New York: Reprinted 1979
Arno Press Inc
ISBN 0-405-12293-4

Winn, Les R, 1995
Ghost Trains and Depots of Georgia 1833-1933
Big Shanty Publishing Company
ISBN 0-9645265-06

Printed in the United Kingdom
by Lightning Source UK Ltd.
100375UKS00001B/358-375

9 781843 750000